LETTERS OF
Catharine Cottam Romney, Plural Wife

Letters of Catharine Cottam Romney, Plural Wife

EDITED BY

Jennifer Moulton Hansen

UNIVERSITY OF ILLINOIS PRESS

Urbana and Chicago

This book is printed on acid-free paper.

Library of Congress Cataloging-in-Publication Data

Romney, Catharine Cottam, 1855–1918.
    Letters of Catharine Cottam Romney, plural wife / edited by
Jennifer Moulton Hansen.
        p.   cm.
    Includes bibliographical references (p.   ) and index.
    ISBN 0-252-01868-0 (cl.)
    1. Romney, Catharine Cottam, 1855–1918—Correspondence.
2. Mormons—West (U.S.)—Correspondence. 3. Women pioneers—West
(U.S.)—Correspondence. 4. Polygamy.   I. Hansen, Jennifer M.
(Jennifer Moulton), 1949–   .   II. Title.
BX8695.R62A4   1992
289.3'092—dc20   91-20686
    [B]   CIP

CONTENTS

ACKNOWLEDGMENTS

It has been a privilege and a pleasure to prepare this volume for publication. I have enjoyed the association and kindness of many people who have helped, and I thank them for what they have done. I would like to make particular mention of a few of them.

This collection would not be possible without those who saved the letters, passed them on to others, and were willing to share them for this volume. Letters and photos were provided by Edyth Romney, Genevieve Moulton, Lula Romney Clayson, Maurine Boyd, Ella Bentley, Annie Call, and Howard Thompson.

Others who willingly shared pertinent information include Marsha Stratton, Ronald Riding, Beverly Cutler, Jasmine Edmunds, Pauline Thomander, Edward Kimball, Maria Ellsworth, and Melvin Oveson.

One of the high points of working on this project was the association with some of my cousins. Ruth Naylor and Beverly Cutler helped proofread the transcript of the letters. Donna Bench researched genealogy, and Beverly Cutler helped get the project on track to a scholarly press.

My sister Jolane Moulton very graciously devoted many hours to drawing the maps of the areas in which Catharine lived.

My sister Michele Meservy responded willingly to long-distance requests for information from Brigham Young University Library and located one of the photos of Catharine. Her children Melodie Meservy and David Meservy also helped.

I appreciate the assistance of personnel at the various archives and libraries. Among these, Toni Haws, who serves at the St. Johns Stake Family History Center, located important photos beyond those requested; Nancy Schroeder was able to obtain copies of the

Orion Era from the University of Arizona; and Patricia Lea did research at the Arizona Historical Society.

Among the scholars who took time to consider and comment on the letters were Charles S. Peterson of Utah State University; David Whittaker, Thomas Alexander, and Jessie Embry of Brigham Young University; and Linda Newell and Peggy Lee of the University of Utah Press. Dean Jessee directed me to the *Guide to Documentary Editing*. Maureen Beecher's early enthusiasm for the letters helped me over several rough spots.

Suzanne Cavanaugh edited an early version. Virlie Westwood, Brad Westwood, and Catherine McCabe provided helpful suggestions.

My parents, Heber and Genevieve Moulton, have been extremely helpful in ensuring successful completion of the project. My mother provided letters and photos; my father made many helpful comments on the manuscript; and they both did research for it. They were willing to help in any way, including offering to publish it themselves if need be.

I appreciate very much the helpfulness and professionalism of the staff of the University of Illinois Press. Of particular note is Jane Mohraz, who edited the manuscript, carefully checking for accuracy and consistency, and making many incisive and helpful suggestions. It has been a pleasure to work with such a sensitive and patient editor. I also thank Elizabeth Dulany, who asked for submission of a final manuscript, and other staff of the press who helped prepare the manuscript for publication.

Finally, I would like to thank my husband Eric Hansen for his support and intellectual companionship thoughout this project. He has provided technical assistance, including three generations of computers, software, and a printer. From the beginning he deemed this to be a project worthy of our best efforts.

INTRODUCTION

Catharine Jane Cottam Romney (1855-1918) is the subject of this volume and the author of the bulk of its pages. Born in Salt Lake City only a few years after the arrival there of the Mormon pioneers, she spent most of her childhood in St. George, Utah. Motivated by faith in God and love of her family, she pioneered in St. Johns, Arizona, and the Mormon colonies in Mexico, returning to Utah at the end of her life. A plural wife of Miles P. Romney for over thirty years, she was the mother of ten children.

Though not a public person, Catharine was considered by those who knew her to be a great woman. When, in response to a teacher's question, her youngest daughter stated that she knew she could never be as wonderful as her mother, her teacher replied, "You don't need to be. She had so many good qualities that if she could divide them up among her five daughters they would all be wonderful women. She was a *great* woman."[1]

Besides telling Catharine's story, the letters are rich in details of the settlement of the American West and Mexico. This volume is designed to place the letters in the context of her life and the times and places in which she lived. The letters are arranged in chronological order, and brief narrative segments fill in information not in the letters themselves. Supplemental information is presented in brackets or notes. A genealogy in Appendix 1 further identifies people mentioned in the letters.

The more than 170 letters date from 1873 through 1917. The earliest letters were written from St. George in 1873 to Catharine's parents and brother, who were visiting relatives in Salt Lake City. She reports on daily life in St. George. In one private letter addressed only to her parents, Catharine talks of her struggle to decide whether to become a plural wife of Miles P. Romney. In September 1873, following her parents' return to St. George, Catharine and Miles married.

In 1881, the Miles P. Romney family was called by church leaders to pioneer in St. Johns, Arizona. From Arizona, Catharine recounts the curiosities of Mexican festivities, law and lawlessness, the struggle between Mormons and non-Mormons over politics and polygamy, their flight to avoid the federal marshals, the births of babies, news of people from home, domestic and church activities, and family interactions.

Following the convictions handed down in the polygamy trials in Prescott, Arizona, in November 1884, church leaders advised polygamous members to seek a place of refuge outside the United States. Miles and his wife Annie were among the first to arrive in the Mormon colonies in Mexico. Hannah, Miles's first wife, remained in Arizona with her children for a little more than a year before going to Mexico, and Catharine and her children spent two years in St. George with her parents. In January 1887, Catharine and her children joined the rest of the family in Mexico, where approximately half the letters were written. In the early years in Mexico, the people struggled to survive. Gradually, however, they prospered, establishing farms, industries, and stores and building beautiful homes. In these letters, the Romney children, twenty-nine of them, grow up, marry, and serve missions. Catharine's parents grow old and die. One of the last letters written from Mexico describes family life after the death of Miles.

Following Miles's death, Hannah, Catharine, and Annie continued to run their farm and store. In 1907, they sold the farm to Hannah's son, Gaskell, and divided the proceeds among themselves. Catharine and Annie each had a home built near one of their children, where they remained until the Mexican Revolution in 1912, when Mormon colonists were forced to leave Mexico. By then Hannah had already returned to the United States. The few remaining letters were written to Catharine's children from Arizona and Utah, where she lived until she died in January 1918.

The letters provide a picture of the daily lives of people a hundred years ago. We learn that they sewed on sewing machines and played the organ. They cooked on stoves fueled by wood they cut themselves. When they traveled, they carried water with them, slept in bedrolls, and cooked their bread by campfire. They walked or else rode on horses or in wagons or buggies. There were no antibiotics, but they vaccinated against smallpox. Women died in childbirth. People built their own houses or perhaps hired Miles P. Romney to do it. They read the Bible, performed Shakespeare and romantic dramas, and published newspapers. They elected officials and erected public buildings. They made their own soap and starched and ironed their clothes. The children went to school, taking turns when their help was needed on the farm.

The Miles P. Romney Family

On September 15, 1873, at age eighteen, Catharine became a plural wife of Miles P. Romney. At that time, polygamy was practiced as a tenet of the Church of Jesus Christ of Latter-day Saints, commonly called Mormons. Miles married five women: Hannah Hood Hill on May 10, 1862; Caroline ("Carrie") Lambourne on March 23, 1867; Catharine Jane Cottam on September 15, 1873; Annie Maria Woodbury on August 1, 1877; and Emily ("Millie") Eyring Snow in February 1897. Hannah, Catharine, and Annie each married in their youth and remained with Miles throughout his life. The other two wives were with the family for only a few years: Carrie divorced Miles before Catharine married him, and Millie married him only a few years before he died. It is thus Hannah, Catharine, and Annie who figure prominently in the letters. The letters portray a warm and loving relationship among these three. This view is generally substantiated by recollections of the children of Miles, although there was apparently sufficient family discord to have given Catharine the opportunity to earn the title of "peacemaker."

Miles P. Romney

Miles was a builder by trade, having learned from his father, a talented architect and builder who had worked on the Nauvoo Temple and had served as the master mechanic in the construction of the St. George Temple. A Romney-built house was noted for its pleasing design and fine workmanship. Miles also served in such diverse capacities as ward architect, attorney-at-law, newspaper editor, superintendent of education, and chief of police. He preached in church and actively promoted education and recreation. He took the lead in many plays, designed and built the sets, and coached the other actors, thus helping to provide a culture in the wilderness that lifted people above the desolate environment that might otherwise have defined their existence.

Hannah Hood Hill Romney

Hannah was the wife of Miles's youth. Living in polygamy was a sore trial for Hannah. She did it because she believed it to be a commandment of God. Sustained by her faith in God and knowledge of the gospel, she stated, "I have had many manifestations of the truthfulness of it [the gospel]."[2]

Hannah was remembered by her son Gaskell as being calm and compassionate, a perfect complement to her husband, who was often excitable. Annie referred to her as "kind and good." Catharine said she was "faithful, true and good." Hannah served as president of the Primary (the church's auxiliary for children) in both Arizona and Mexico, suggesting that she was a woman of patience and creativity. She would tell the children stories and have them make things and recite.

Hannah was very resourceful in dealing with the demands of pioneer life. Miles once told her that he didn't know how the family could have survived without all her hard work. But she desired more than survival. She wanted her children to be educated and enjoy good culture and society, and she worked hard to ensure they would.

In the course of her life, Hannah traveled by team from Toronto, Canada, her birthplace, to the Mormon colonies in Mexico. When she was a young girl, her family moved to Nauvoo, Illinois, where she remembered seeing the Prophet Joseph Smith. She crossed the plains to Utah with the pioneers and then moved south to St. George, Utah, and St. Johns, Arizona. Her courageous journey from Arizona to Mexico with her children is a further testament to her faith and fortitude.

After Miles died, Hannah became so disconsolate that finally her son Leo remarked that she did not seem to care about her children any more. She decided she must try her best to carry on. She went to Salt Lake City for a year, where she visited her sister, and then returned to Mexico. When Leo took a job in Arizona, she went with him. During her remaining years, she traveled, visiting her children. At the age of eighty, while staying with her son George, who was the president of Ricks College in Idaho, she dictated her life story. Several years later, while visiting some of her children in Mexico, she died at the age of eighty-six.

Annie Maria Woodbury Romney

Annie was eighteen when she married Miles in August 1877 in the St. George Temple. Annie and Catharine shared a common background, both having grown up in St. George from their early childhood, although Annie was three years younger than Catharine. Annie's older sister, Eleanor Jarvis, was Catharine's good friend and the recipient of some of the letters in this volume. The few extant letters written by Annie evidence a style and tone similar to Catharine's.

Annie was revered as an outstanding schoolteacher. As a teenager, she had studied in Salt Lake City at the University of Deseret. She was the first teacher hired by the Mormon community both in St. Johns, Arizona, and in the Mormon colonies in Mexico. In Mexico, she and her students carried their books and chairs to a rough stockade, where they held class. She drilled them in spelling and arithmetic and taught them geography and ethics. They read their lessons aloud. Franklin S. Harris, president of Brigham Young University, praised her as "the finest fundamental teacher of my life."[3]

Annie also did her share of domestic chores. It was "hard work to get [her] chores done now in the morning before nine o'clock," and she would work until midnight trying to keep up with her sewing and mending.[4] In Colonia Juarez, Mexico, she operated the post office, opening it early in the morning and working into the night keeping the books. On the farm, Annie made candy to sell in the store. She also worked in the auxiliaries of the church.

After leaving Mexico at the time of the Revolution, Annie; her unmarried children, Erma, Frank, and Ann (whose husband had died while on his mission); and Ann's daughter, Lucile, settled in Provo, Utah. Annie kept house while Ann taught and Erma, Frank, and Lucile attended school.

In 1918, Annie moved to St. George to help her sister, Eleanor Jarvis, care for their mother in her final days. Later she returned to Provo for several years. Her granddaughter Ella lived with her while attending Brigham Young University. "I remember many times," Ella recalled, "when President Franklin Harris, President of B.Y.U., came up to us to tell her what a wonderful teacher she was and how much she had influenced his life. She loved good music and good literature. She loved the gospel and certainly lived its teachings in a beautiful way. She was a wonderful cook and could season even simple food to make it taste delicious."[5]

During the summer of 1929, she moved to Salt Lake with her daughter Erma (whose husband had died) and her children. There she contracted pneumonia and died at the age of seventy-one on January 14, 1930.[6]

The Children

Miles P. Romney was the father of thirty children, twenty-nine of whom reached maturity. All remained true to the faith of their parents. They followed such occupations as educator, banker, home-maker, seamstress, clerk, carpenter, farmer, entrepreneur, book-keeper, printer, and lawyer, and they participated in such activities as music, drama, writing, needlework, politics, and church work.[7]

The Letters

Many of the letters are written to Catharine's parents, Thomas and Caroline Cottam, and her siblings. The Cottams were a close family, enjoying dinners and holiday celebrations together. Of Thomas and Caroline's five children to reach maturity, Catharine was the only one to move far from home for a long time. Her letters were a cherished means of maintaining the link between Catharine and her family.

Catharine's daughter Lula recalled that every Sunday morning she found her mother at the kitchen table writing letters. Catharine once wrote, "I feel very thankful that we can all read, and write, so that we can hear from each other."[8] Yet she questioned the value of her letters: "I do not know whether my letters are interesting enough to compensate for the time I spend in it."[9] She deemed it a "fine accomplishment" to be a "really good correspondent."[10]

The letters written to Catharine's parents and brothers were pre-served by her brother, Charles Cottam, until 1950 when they were given to Catharine's son, Thomas Cottam Romney. Thomas quoted briefly from a few of them in his autobiography, A Divinity Shapes Our Ends as Seen in My Life's Story. In 1985, Thomas's widow, Edyth J. Romney, donated them to the Church of Jesus Christ of Latter-day Saints. Catharine's granddaughter, Genevieve Romney Moulton, obtained a copy of this collection from the church archives.

Letters written to Catharine's friend Eleanor Jarvis were given to Ella Farnsworth Bentley by her mother, Eleanor Romney Farns-worth, who obtained them from Eleanor Jarvis's daughter Rose. Copies of two other letters to Eleanor Jarvis were provided by Mau-reen Eyring Boyd.

Beverly Romney Cutler, Catharine's granddaughter, told me about the Vernon Romney collection located at the Brigham Young University Archives. This collection contains letters written to Catharine's sons, Vernon and Junius, between 1913 and 1917. Catharine's daughter Lula Romney Clayson, the only living child of Miles P. Romney at the time these letters were prepared for publication, and Howard Thompson, a grandson of Catharine's sister Emma, provided several letters. Letters to Thomas C. and Lydia Romney were provided by their daughter Genevieve Moulton.

Editorial Methods

The purpose of a documentary edition is to publish letters, diaries, and so forth, conveying to the reader, in printed form, as much as possible about what could be learned by reading the original. Mary Jo Kline, who authored a treatise on documentary editing, maintains that documentary editing is one of the more important forms of scholarship of the twentieth century, though doubtless those with a more analytic bent would disagree. In Mormon history, Juanita Brooks led the way with her documentary editions of the writings of John D. Lee, Hosea Stout, and Martha Spence Heywood. Andrew Karl Larson and Katherine Miles Larson published the diaries of Charles Walker. Kenneth Godfrey, Audrey Godfrey, and Jill Mulvay Derr selected and edited an interesting collection of shorter pieces of Mormon pioneer women. *Dear Ellen,* edited by George Ellsworth, is a brief collection of the letters of two pioneer women, both named Ellen. Dean Jessee is editing a multivolume series of the writings of Joseph Smith. There are others.

The methods used to edit these letters are based on principles discussed in Mary Jo Kline's *Guide to Documentary Editing.* Kline urges the documentary editor to select rules of editing in line with the purpose for producing the document and then apply the rules consistently. In keeping with her suggestions, the following rules were used in preparing these letters.

Spelling: Although the modern reader not attuned to this genre might have preferred to have the spelling standardized, the original spellings have been retained. Occasionally, however, I have inserted missing letters in a word to clarify its meaning. These insertions are indicated in square brackets. Sometimes a slip of the pen was ignored. A few times she wrote a word twice, but I only included it once.

Capitalization: Capitalization appears as it did in the original. She often began sentences with lower-case letters and sometimes wrote *i* instead of *I.*

Stray pen marks and hyphenation: Some documentary editions take great care to indicate where every mark of the pen was placed on the page. For example, if a word is divided between two lines with a hyphen in the original, this fact is noted, even though the word comes in the middle of the line in the transcription. I did not think that this information was helpful for understanding these letters. If two words are run together but their meaning is clear, I did not note the fact that they were run together in the original, considering this to be a slip of the pen.

Punctuation: Punctuation was problemmatic, in that the letters were full of periods in the middle of sentences. I interpreted some of these as commas and deleted some. Where a period at the end of a sentence was missing, an extra space, but no period, was added to mark the break between sentences.

Placement of words on the page: The headings and closings to the letters were not uniform. For example, sometimes the heading appeared on the left side of the page, sometimes on the right; sometimes the date appeared before the inside address, sometimes afterward; sometimes the inside address was written on separate lines, other times on one; sometimes Catharine's signature was part of the last line of the letter, while other times it was on a separate line. For simplicity's sake, the placement of the headings and closings has been standardized. Often Catharine wrote a postscript. These postscripts are added at the end of the letter without explanation. Passages in italics between the letters and in square brackets within the letters are mine.

Background Information

Supplemental sources were many and varied. Family information was readily available, including accounts written by those who knew Catharine and her generation and even writings of her father and brother. Catharine's only surviving daughter was happy to share her memories as well as stories her mother had told her. The archives of the Church of Jesus Christ of Latter-day Saints, Brigham Young University, the University of Utah, and the Utah State Historical Society were searched with productive results. A researcher at the Arizona Historical Society checked some files. Copies of the *Orion Era,* the newspaper Miles P. Romney edited for a while in St. Johns, Arizona, were found at the University of Arizona, and microfilms of the *Apache Chief,* the anti-Mormon newspaper in St. Johns, were acquired from public offices in Phoenix.

I hope that Catharine would be pleased with this volume and trust that, if she were not, she would look on it with compassion and kindness, as was her nature.

NOTES

1. Lula Romney Clayson, untitled autobiographical sketch, photocopy of typescript in author's possession, 1.

2. Hannah H. Romney, "Autobiography of Hannah Hood Hill Romney," photocopy of typescript in author's possession, 5, 6, 28. Two of the granddaughters of Miles P. Romney who knew Hannah, Pauline Romney Thomander and Jasmine Romney Edmunds, said that she expressed to them a positive attitude toward polygamy and her husband's other wives. Conversations with Pauline Romney Thomander, April 1986, and Jasmine Romney Edmunds, July 1990. She said to Catharine's daughter Ethel, "Honey, for me, heaven wouldn't be heaven without your mother." Ethel Romney Lillywhite Peterson, an untitled sketch of the life of Catharine Jane Cottam Romney stapled to Eleanor R. Farnsworth, "Miles Park Romney," typescripts in Miles P. Romney file, Nelle S. Hatch Collection, BYU Archives.

3. Ella Farnsworth Bentley, "A Glimpse into the Life of Annie Maria Woodbury Romney," photocopy of typescript in author's possession, 25, citing a telegram sent by President Harris when Annie died.

4. A.M.R. to Mrs. E. C. Jarvis, December 30, 1888, Juarez, Mexico, typescript in Miles P. Romney file, Nelle S. Hatch Collection, BYU Archives.

5. Bentley, "A Glimpse into the Life of Annie Maria Woodbury Romney," 25.

6. Ibid.

7. Thomas C. Romney, Life Story of Miles Park Romney (Independence, Mo.: Zion's Printing and Publishing, 1948), 313-25, 327-30, 334-46, 350-61.

8. Catharine to her parents, April 16, 1882.

9. Catharine to her parents and brother, May 25, 1873.

10. Catharine to her son Thomas, April 17, 1896.

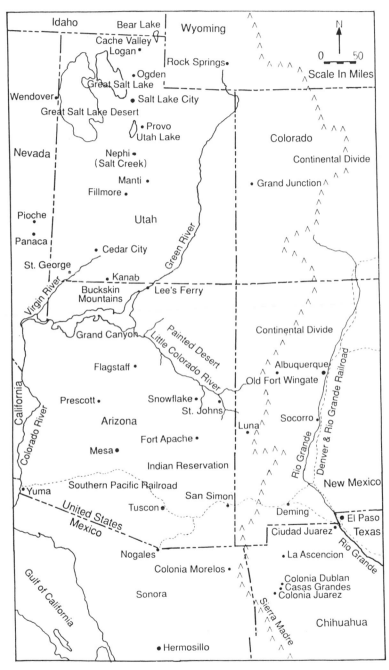

Overview of the area in which Catharine lived. (Map drawn by
Jolane Moulton)

Catharine Jane Cottam, age sixteen, "the prettiest girl in St. George." (Courtesy of Genevieve Moulton)

Thomas and Caroline Cottam and family members in front of their home in St. George, 1873. From the left are George T. Cottam and Thomas P. Cottam (seated in wagon), Emma Cottam Thompson and her daughter Emma Cottam Thompson, Thomas Cottam, Caroline Smith Cottam, and Charles S. Cottam. (Courtesy of Howard Thompson)

The St. George Temple under construction. Miles P. Romney's father, seated second from right, supervised construction of the temple. (Courtesy of Utah State Historical Society)

The St. George Temple around 1985.
(Courtesy of Heber Moulton)

Annie Maria Woodbury married Miles P. Romney on August 1, 1877, in the newly completed St. George Temple. (Courtesy of Ella F. Bentley)

PART ONE

St. George, Utah Territory

Catharine Cottam's older brother, George, said that she was the prettiest girl in St. George. Tall and refined, she had twenty-eight black curls that almost reached the floor when she sat down. She was such good company that there was no one he would rather take to a dance. She returned a sisterly affection. There was the time she returned home late at night after a visit to her grandparents in Salt Lake City. Not wanting to wait until morning to greet him, she climbed the hayloft where he was sleeping, threw her arms around him, and kissed him. It was not George but his friend, Brig. Later Brig asked her to marry him, contending he had fallen in love with her that evening. That marriage was not to be. Catharine's future lay with Miles P. Romney.[1]

Catharine Jane Cottam was born January 7, 1855, in Salt Lake City, seven years after the first Mormon pioneers arrived there. Seven years later, in the October 1862 General Conference of the Church of Jesus Christ of Latter-day Saints, her father's name, Thomas Cottam, was read as one of those called by President Brigham Young to help build the Kingdom of God in Utah's Dixie.[2] They would raise the means and move three hundred miles south to St. George, a small but growing settlement in the southwest corner of what is now Utah.

Thomas Cottam had been advised previously by Apostle Ezra T. Benson to settle in northern Utah's Cache Valley. Thomas had made a trip to that area, but the family had not yet moved when the call to Dixie came. Thomas's wife, Caroline, was relieved that they were to go south, because the family did not have sufficient warm clothing to weather the bitter cold winters of northern Utah.[3] Settling in southern Utah entailed no fewer hardships, however. The alkaline land was barren and desolate. Once, the Santa Clara River dried up for twenty miles upstream,[4] although, fortunately, town lots were watered by springs that were not affected by the drought.[5]

President Young selected devoted members to settle this desolate region. Apostle Joseph F. Smith once remarked that upon his return from a mission to the Pacific Islands he noticed that some of the most faithful members were no longer living in the Salt Lake Valley. Later, when he visited St. George, he found them there.[6]

Apostle Erastus Snow was designated president of this southern mission. He instructed those called to colonize there that they should bring, along with their farming tools, other implements of civilization, such as school books, a rocking chair, and other items that would help them feel a little more at home. President Snow also saw the need for skilled craftsmen: "I want to know if we have a good turner attached to this mission; if . . . not, I want the privilege of selecting one."[7]

Catharine's father, Thomas Cottam, was a turner. Skilled in fashioning exquisite furniture, knobs, and decorative posts, he had learned his trade as a boy in England from his father, John.[8] During Thomas's early years, his family was fairly well-to-do. He had enjoyed the privilege of attending school and had studied with a private tutor, gaining a love for the great literary masters. When he was about sixteen, his family met with financial reverses and their estate, Low Moor, was sold at an auction. The Cottams moved to a nearby village and continued to make and sell furniture.[9]

When he was twenty-one, Thomas Cottam married Ann Haworth, a "kind, noble, good girl" who worked in a factory.[10] Within two months of their marriage, they were both baptized into the Church of Jesus Christ of Latter-day Saints, a decision they each had considered for several years. The year following their marriage and baptism, they sailed on the ship Hope to New Orleans and traveled up the Mississippi River, arriving penniless in Nauvoo, Illinois, the gathering place of the Saints, in April 1842. In July, their son John Alma was born.

In June of 1844, their beloved prophet and leader, Joseph Smith, and his brother, Hyrum, were shot and killed by a mob in nearby Carthage, Illinois. Thomas's first thought was to return to England, but he soon realized that the church would continue. Its troubles were not over, however. Malaria spread throughout the city. Thomas and Ann both became very ill, and Ann died on October 11, 1844.

In February of 1846, residents of Nauvoo began to flee the city. Their enemies had already burned some of their buildings and threatened more trouble. Thomas Cottam helped steer the boats across the icy Mississippi River. He later wrote, "It would require a far better historian than I to depict the sufferings of the Saints individually or collectively."[11]

Thomas left his child with relatives and found work building settlements on the prairie. In a letter dated June 18, 1846, he wrote to his parents in England, "Miles on miles, all over the prairie, wherever you cast your eyes there were white covered wagons and tents. I met numbers of people that I knew." Upon returning to Nauvoo he had found many of the once beautiful homes and gardens abandoned and overgrown with weeds. "As for my house etc., lot and land," he wrote, "I shall have to leave them, very likely unsold, people know we must go, so they can get them when we are gone. I do not care a fig about them it is a day of sacrifice."[12]

Thomas went to St. Louis, Missouri, where he met friends from Nauvoo, George and Caroline Charman, whom he had welcomed into his home in Nauvoo when they had first arrived from England. Their one-year-old daughter Caroline, born in Nauvoo, had died in St. Louis in November 1846. George became very sick and asked Thomas to care for Caroline if he should die. On October 9, 1847, not long after George died, Thomas and Caroline were married. Their daughter Mary Ann, born a year later, lived only one day.[13]

In St. Louis, Thomas made furniture, worked at a press, and delivered newspapers. By 1852, Thomas and Caroline had raised the means to travel to Utah, along with their two-year-old daughter, Emma, and Thomas's son, John Alma.[14] They arrived in the Salt Lake Valley on September 13, 1852. Their son George Thomas was born six weeks later on October 29, 1852. Then followed Catharine, born January 7, 1855; Thomas Punter, September 28, 1857; and Charles Smith, September 16, 1861.[15] Thomas's and Caroline's parents and a number of their brothers and sisters from England joined them in Utah. The Thomas Cottams lived in the Salt Lake Valley for ten years, until their call to Utah's Dixie in 1862.

The Cottams traveled the three hundred miles from Salt Lake City to St. George in thirty-three days. They left behind the beautiful farmland and fertile fields of northern and central Utah and journeyed to the dry and alkaline desert to which they had been assigned. When wagons bogged down in sand, they doubled up the teams and drove the wagons in shifts. As they neared St. George, they crossed the rim of the Great Basin. To make the descent, they tied logs on the backs of the wagons to act as brakes.

During the trip, some of the family got whooping cough, and settlers who otherwise might have been hospitable were afraid of them. One family invited them in though. The father of that family, Robert Parker, cut out paper birds and flowers, to the delight of the children.[16]

Ten days before Christmas 1862, the Cottams arrived in St. George. On Christmas Day, the children were treated to pieces of an apple, a few pieces of molasses candy, and some raisins that Caroline had carried from Salt Lake City.[17] Caroline was expecting a baby that Christmas. Sarah Ellen was born the following April, but she lived only a few months.[18]

Thomas built a one-room house with a willow and mud ceiling and dirt floor, where the family lived for four years until he was able to build an adobe house. About three months after their arrival, he opened his own turning shop. He hired a man to turn the lathe for large jobs, but the boys were strong enough to turn it for the smaller jobs.[19] In June 1863, construction began on the magnificent St. George Tabernacle. Thomas worked on the building itself and produced beautiful furniture for its interior.[20]

Catharine and her childhood friends often gathered in her father's shop, where he taught them spelling and arithmetic and told them stories of his conversion to the church and his travels across the plains. Thomas Cottam taught his daughter to braid straw hats and weave chair bottoms from rushes, skills she later used to help provide for her family. He passed along to her his kind and temperate disposition and a love of reading and literature, which also served her well in later years.

Catharine also learned from her mother, Caroline, an efficient homemaker who, besides helping her husband in the shop, worked quickly and skillfully to care for her family and to beautify their surroundings. Caroline talked about her conversion to the church in England, the loss of her job as a domestic servant when she returned to her employers' house with wet hair after her baptism, her marriage to George Charman, her voyage to the United States to join the main body of the church, the death of her husband and baby, her marriage to Thomas Cottam, and their trek across the plains to the Valley of the Great Salt Lake.[21]

The Cottams, along with many other Dixie settlers, maintained contact with their family and friends in the Salt Lake Valley. In 1870, Thomas traveled to Salt Lake City to help build a house for his parents.[22] In 1873, Thomas and Caroline both went to Salt Lake City, taking with them their sixteen-year-old son, Thomas. Their other children stayed in St. George. Catharine's sister, Emma, had her own family to care for. She had married William Thompson, a widower with two young daughters, Matilda and Amelia. George and Charles, Catharine's brothers, stayed in St. George to drive the cattle, gather firewood, and care for the crops.

Catharine had previously visited her grandparents and cousins in Salt Lake City.[23] This time she stayed in St. George. True, she was needed at home, but a stronger motivation for remaining behind may have been that she did not want to be separated from the man she loved. About six feet tall with sandy hair, Miles P. Romney was a dynamic and enterprising leader in the church and community, a master carpenter, actor, and orator.[24] Twenty-nine years old, he was twice married (in those days, polygamy was entered into as a commandment from God), but he was recently divorced from his second wife, Carrie.[25]

Now eighteen years old, Catharine Cottam remained in St. George while her parents went to "the city." She kept house in her mother's absence, substituted for her father in his duties as assistant sexton, did her milking job, worked in the garden, and quilted. By evening she felt tired. She sat down to write.

9" May 1873
Father and Mother

Dear parents   I sat down last night to write but was too sleepy and had to give it up. I do not feel very well to day and therefore will not write much this time. We have got along pretty well since you went. Geo[rge]. [Catharine's brother] [went] to diamond valley the next day;[26] and since then he has been to the field watering. he found Br[27] [William] Squires cow but she has'nt yet calved. Ben Paddoc has not sent for his cow yet. Charles [Catharine's brother] has been hoeing in the garden, and I trimmed the grape vines yesterday. I find quite a number of them are killed down to the ground but are sprouting out from the root. Emma [Catharine's sister] sends her love. They are pretty well, she will try to write next time. Sister [Elizabeth Reeves] Liston was here yesterday and spent the afternoon with me. We had a good meeting Monday night but not a good representation from some of the wards [congregations], no special business done. Br [Jesse] Crosby lectured Wednesday evening, subject, the earth, it was very interesting and instructive. lectures are discontinued for a time on account of the shortness of the evenings. I believe I am lonesome already, and I want to see you real bad. please give my love to Thomas [her brother] and accept a large portion yourselves from your affectionate daughter.

C. J. Cottam

15" May 1873

Dear Father Mother and Brother   It is nearly nine oclock and time to go to bed, but as I feel very lonesome tonight, I thought I would try to take a little comfort in writing to you, as I cannot see you; it seems such a long time since I saw you last. George started to the Meadows yesterday and thought to be back tomorrow (Friday) but he met Henry Platt (who came in yesterday) and told him to tell me not to be alarmed if he were not home so soon. Ute Perkins brought George's bay mare, (that he got off John R. Young [nephew of Brigham Young],) today, I think, Geo. sent it from the Meadows. Br [William] Squire does not feel very well today. he has so much work to do in the shop,[28] beside his wathering [watering], and it seems to be too much for him. I do not feel very well today, and with you and Geo., all having gone, and with one thing and another, I am afraid I have got the blues, so I had better go to bed and try to sleep them off.

Friday morning,   we had a nice shower of rain last night which has cooled the air some, but I dont expect there was enough to soak the ground much. Dear Parents I am just beginning to realise my importance as your business agent, assistant sexton etc., in the absense of George, it is to be hoped that I shall not become proud through it. This morning Joseph Carpenter came to see about having a grave dug for his brother, 2 months old. (he thinks he had the epizootic[29] and lung fever.) I sent him to William [Thompson, Catharine's brother-in-law], but he did not know any thing about it, so I went and got Br [Isaac] Hunt to do it, they are going to bury this afternoon. I have just recorded it. I also recorded Br Robbins since you went. Last Sunday there was a telegram read from sailor Jack, or John Lloyd, from Panaca, stating that Judge Mccullough died the day before of Pneumonia. Since you left, George let Br. [Archibald] Mcneil have some chairs that you promised him, also Jim Dean, two common chairs for office pay. and Ephriam Wilson a large rocking chair for $3.00 in money and the rest on the office.[30] Charlotte Richie was married at Washington, last Sunday, to a very rich gentleman Mr. [William Hubbell] Sherwood, from Pioche, and I think she has gone there to live.[31] she had her wedding party on monday. I suppose she was dressed handsomly, her wedding ring cost something like $180.00 and her engagement ring $25.00, so I heard. I feel very thankful that God gave me Parents who have taught me to look for something better and more lasting than riches. I do not envy her, her beautiful home in Pioche, nor even her costly cloths. William [Catharine's brother-in-law,] Emma [Catharine's sister] and children are tolerable well. the little ones are considerable, and are very attentive to me, especially when I have some cakes on hand. Wednesday afternoon I went to a quilting to Sister [Mary Standiforth] Nelsons, which is the only day I have been visiting since you left, and have not had any company except Sister [Elizabeth] Liston part of one day last week. I still have my job of milking. Dan has not calved yet. we are keeping her out of the herd now as George thinks she ought not to be run now. Our five little chickens are all alive and doing well, but one of them had a narrow escape of being drowned in the swill bucket last Saturday. I saw it just in time to save its life. I have not heard how Br. Joseph [W. Young] is for a day or two but think he is some better.[32] Peter Granger is getting along very well considering the injuries he recieved. Please give my love to all our folks, and accept a large portion for yourselves. From your affectionate daughter and Sister

C. J. Cottam

Thomas would probably like to know what kind of a mare this one of Georges is. I am not a very good judge of horses, but for his benefit I will say it seems to be very gentle, is a dark bay, and is quite slim built.

I think they have lowered the vane on the tabernacle since I wrote because it was too slim and bent with the wind

25" May 1873

Dear Parents and Brother   As William Lund is talking of starting to the city [Salt Lake City] tomorrow I thought I would try to write a few lines to you   we received a letter from you for which we have been looking the two last mails. I assure you we were very glad to hear from you, and to hear that you, and all the folks are well, and enjoying yourselves. I trust it will continue the same as long as you remain there and in fact all the time. This makes six times I have written to you, and I often feel that I could write to you when I do not. I do not know whether my letters are interesting enough to compensate for the time I spend in it. Danny had a fine heifer Calf last night though I think it is rather small. We are now milking a cow of Joseph Judd's, (which John sold to him,) and shall probabally keep her some time. We are still milking Paddoc's cow. We are all tolerable well, and I think we are trying to do as well as we can, or at least wishing to. Br Joseph [W. Young] is a little better, but still very weak and low. Sister [Ann Cannon] Woodbury does not get along as well as I should like to see her   she has had a chill or two but is some better now. Eleanor [Cannon Woodbury Jarvis][33] and I have not yet found time to visit each other yet. Br. [William] Squire had a letter from his folks last Friday. I have not seen Sister [Elizabeth] Liston lately. I fancy she is at the Clara [Santa Clara]. I have been to Sunday school every sunday since you left but it has been late. Br [Samuel L.] Adams got home Friday night. he preached in meeting today. Monday, George has gone to hunt Brother Squires cow, who ran away last week. Br. [William] Lang and family send their kind respects. he wishes me to tell you he is better but weak yet. he had to pay 20 dollars for his mules. Br. Adams started to bring them but they ran away and Br. Lang has sold them to Jim Judd.

C. J. Cottam

25 May 1873

Dear Parents   I feel impressed to write a few lines to you in private, on a subject I have no doubt you feel anxious about. I feel rather delicate about mentioning it, but will endeavor to talk about it a little. It is about Miles and I that I wish to speak. Dear Father and Mother/ I know what it is to love, and be loved, and I think I should be very happy if you all felt well about it, but as it is, I feel very unhappy at times, for it grieves me to know that I feel as you would not have me feel. You may think that if I had a disposition to do as you would like, I should have given him up. I have tried many times to bring my mind and feelings to it but have failed, even since you started I thought I had better give him up, and he told me although it would cost him many a pang to give me up, he would release me from my promise if I wished him to and would say the word, and oh Mother! I know I am weak and foolish, but I love him so much that I could not say we would part forever. I know he loves me, and I believe sincerely that he is trying to, and in fact has reformed considerable, and he says he feels better and stronger, and more determined to do right, and he firmly believes that with my love, influence and assistance, he will become a better man.[34] I do not think you would be as prejudiced if you were better acquainted with him. I cannot help respecting him for his good moral and religious principles, which I do believe are genuine. I am not blind to his faults, and we have talked about them considerable. he wishes and is striving to overcome them, and I trust he may, and think he will if he continues to try in the propper manner. I ought not and do not expect him to become perfect all at once. I have talked with George about it. you probabally understand his feelings on the subject. still he said to me, if I loved him and could love no one else, I had better marry him. Miles wishes very much to have the good will and confidence of my family and friends, and he says he will try to conduct himself so as to win it. I sincere trust he will succeed in his desires in asmuch as they are right and consistent. Dear Mother I have often thought when practice has kept in late, that you fancied I had been with Miles, but such was not the case, as he has never yet taken me home from practice. I have been down to his house twice since you left, one evening when I happened to meet him on the street, and he asked me to go down, (as he very often does,) and one sunday afternoon when he was at Toquer with Br [Alexander F.] Macdonald, then George Jarvis and Eleanor, (with whom I was walking down the street,) went in with me. Sister [Hannah] Romney is very kind and sociable, always asks me to come and see her, and said she would like me to come and use her sewing machine as often as I liked   she expressed a wish to get acquainted with Mother. Miles has been here but once or twice, since you left, that was one day to borrow the cemetery keys (to put up a fence around a grave) and to bring them back, he has wanted nobs two or three times but has sent instead of coming, as he said he did not want to cause more talk than necessary while you were away. But I must plead guilty of walking out with him several times. Dear Parents I pray God that this matter may turn out right, and just as it will be best for all concerned. do not let it trouble you nor mar your happiness and enjoyment, for I shall try to take care of myself, and do the best I can while you are away.

He has told me sometimes that he made it a matter of prayer continually, and wished me to do the same, and also to pray for him that he might be able to over come his faults and over come temptation. we have prayed that if it would not be right for us to marry that our feelings for each other might change, and if it was right that your feelings toward him might change, and you understand him as he is.

8" June 1873

Dear Parents, This is Sunday morning and as there is not any school I will write a few lines. We got a letter from you last Friday from Ogden. I was sorry to hear Father was not well but hope he is better now. Geo. and Chas. have been to the field for a load of lucern [alfalfa][35] but have returned. They will not be able to write this time. Geo. says the water is nearly dried up in the Clara [Santa Clara River]. I have now to tell you some very painful news, but you will perhaps hear it before you get this. On Friday last the brethren started to take Joseph W. [Young] to Long Valley. yesterday he died at Harrisburg. I think he is to be buried this afternoon. Br [Isaac] Hunt is out diging the grave now. Please excuse my short note and bad writing as I am in a hurry, it is nearly meeting time so I must conclude with kind love to all. From your loving daughter, in haste.

C. J. Cottam.

John R. Young came in last week and was going back with his brother. They have sent for his second wife Julia.

The death of Br. Joseph seems to have cast a gloom over the whole community.[36] Last Friday we got a telegram from Br. [William Hiram] Carpenter from Pine Valley to have a grave dug for his little girl who had just died. I got Br. Hunt to dig it yesterday morning and they buried in the afternoon. Br. [Aaron] Nelson sends his kind regards. noon meeting out. Choir meet at 2 oclock to practise. Br.

Josephs body is to be taken to the tabernacle at 3 oclock when the funeral service will take place. Julia has not yet arrived.

C.J.C.

June 20" 1873
Br. and Sister Pyper[37]

Dear Friends   After this long silence I will answer your very kind and welcome, though short letter   I have written to Father and Mother so often that I have not had time to write to any one else. I will inclose a few lines in this to them. If I cut my letter short I hope you will please to excuse me as it is getting late and I want to go and see a sick friend. I should like to see you, all very much but dont know when I shall come that way. Please remember me kindly to Grandma [Cottam], Br. [Robert] Gardner, and all of your family. I am pleased to hear that Alic. [Alexander Pyper, son of Brother and Sister Pyper] has got a good girl for a wife, for I think he deserves one, and I wish them much happiness, and hope they will apreciate each other as they ought, but as some do not. I suppose I shall soon hear of Mary, and Catharine getting married, and also William [other children of the Pypers]. We are having a very hot time here at present. no rain and the water in the field is drying up. I expect you have heard of the death of Br Joseph W. Young, after a lingering illness   his loss is deeply regretted and seems to have cast a gloom over the whole community. The work on the temple is progressing pretty well from what I hear, also the tabernacle, though there is much to do inside the outside begins to look nice.

Catharine J. Cottam

Most likely, the Cottam and Romney families had been ac-quainted for many years. Miles P. Romney was born in 1843 in Nau-voo, Illinois, the city in which Catharine's parents had met. Both Miles Romney (the father of Miles P. Romney) and Thomas Cottam had worked on the Nauvoo Temple,[38] and both families had lived in Salt Lake City prior to moving to southern Utah. The elder Miles Romney, a master architect, was in charge of construction of the temple and tabernacle in St. George. Thomas Cottam and Miles P. worked under his direction.[39]

In 1862, at the age of eighteen, Miles married nineteen-year-old Hannah H. Hill, a convert from Toronto, Canada, and a next-door neighbor of his brother's family in Salt Lake City. Three weeks later, he left for England, where he served as a missionary for three years. Hannah stayed in Salt Lake City, where she bore their daughter, Is-

abell, and worked to support herself and her daughter. When Miles returned, he built them a comfortable home.[40]

Then Heber C. Kimball and, later, Brigham Young counseled him to take a second wife. He married a beautiful young convert from Scotland, Caroline Lambourne. She relocated with Miles and Hannah to St. George in 1867, bore two children, and decided she had had enough. They divorced, and she and her children returned to Salt Lake City where she remarried.[41]

Miles P. Romney enjoyed living life to the fullest. For April Fool's Day one year, Miles and a couple of friends conspired to move the Captain Milne Artillery Company's cannon from the court house premises to a walled corral, to which only the sheriff held a key. A boy noticed them and reported them to the authorities. Prosecution of the case was avoided when the victims agreed to drop the charges in exchange for a case of the best Dixie wine. Both culprits and victims sat down together to celebrate.[42] Miles's weakness for wine was something that he did not try to justify.[43] Even though he was trying to overcome it, this problem, along with his divorce, would have worried Catharine's parents.

Miles often channeled his energy into theater productions. When Miles P. Romney took the lead in a dramatic presentation, his audience forgot they were pioneering a desolate wilderness. In one play, Miles's sister Mary portrayed the wayward heroine. She implored the villain, Miles, to let her see her children again. "Never! Never! A thousand times, never!" he thundered. A miner from Silver Reef sitting in the audience became so unnerved that he rose to his feet and, brandishing his gun, yelled, "You let her see them again, or else!!!" And he fired three bullets into the ceiling.[44]

Miles was every bit as dynamic in real life as he was on stage. He worked as a carpenter on the tabernacle and temple, spoke in church, and served on planning committees.[45] He wrote letters to the editor of the Deseret News under the biblical pen name "Amram."[46] He and his associates bought a steam sawmill and a planing machine and did "a good business in furniture, sash and blinds in St. George."[47]

Thomas and Caroline Cottam returned to St. George to find that Catharine's feelings for Miles had not lessened. On September 15, 1873, Catharine and Miles were married at the Endowment House in Salt Lake City.

Hannah remained in St. George and worked on fixing up the house. She carried warp and rags for a new carpet to the weavers and hauled the finished product home after dark to tack down in Catharine's room. "I had a room finished for Catherine with new carpet and furniture all ready for her," Hannah wrote. "I cannot explain how I suffered in my feelings while I was doing all this hard work, but I felt I would do my duty if my heart did ache. I had such a hard time with his other wife that I feared I would have the same kind of trial again, but when I came to live with Sister Catherine it was quite different. She was very considerate of my feelings and good to the children. She helped in the house and did not expect all of my husband's attention. When he came home he appreciated what I had done. He admired the home arrangements and was surprised that I had accomplished so much in such a short time. His appreciation of my work partly took away the heart ache."[48]

Catharine's first child, Caroline Cottam Romney, was born on June 21, 1874. In October 1875, Miles was called to serve another mission. The following April, their son Thomas Cottam Romney was born.

Miles's missionary labors took him to the backwoods of Michigan, Indiana, and Wisconsin, where he walked between five and twenty miles each day. He preached until his lungs were sore "but never . . . more than an hour or hour and a half."[49] On August 10, 1876, Miles wrote to Catharine that he had preached his final sermon in Viola, Wisconsin:

> The house was crowded, some coming 3 or 4 miles to hear, and I assume I told them plain facts, and at the close received 5 invitations to stay over night. Will preach in other places a farewell sermon, and then if George [Romney, Miles's brother] sends me money Hurrah! Hurrah! for home, before the Last of Sept. I could stand on my head now. Pres Young says to us "You are Honorably released Brethren, you have done well" Thats better than whining out of a mission, isnt it. Tell all the children that when you get this, if all is well Pa, will be on the road home, and then he'll try to get them Shoes and Stockings. Bless you all. You have all done well, and God will bless you all. rejoice, and be exceeding glad for I'm coming home, "Coming home, Coming home, dont you hear the drums" Yes, we are a coming home hurrah! hurrah!

Miles did return home to his family and to his building and business activities, dramatics, military unit, and public service and church work. He became bishop of the First Ward, stake superintendent of the Sunday school, stake president of the Young Men's Mutual Improvement Association, general superintendent of the St. George Builders Union, and a local missionary. He coached the St. George Dramatic Association, supported the St. George Library, and promoted education. As superintendent of Washington County schools, he wrote to the Deseret News advocating the establishment of an academy in St. George, pledging "in proportion to his means, [to] pay as much as any other man towards it."[50]

Hannah also participated in a business venture. In 1875, a group of St. George women, who wanted to save money by buying goods wholesale, organized the Ladies' Co-op, and Hannah was elected to the board of directors. The store flourished while it was located in Mary Ann Gardner's home, where the women could work and shop informally. At the suggestion of the Relief Society, women scrimped and saved to buy stock in the store. After a few years, Apostle Erastus Snow suggested that they move the store downtown, across the street from the St. George Co-op Store, and the women complied. Soon discord developed. A new president was appointed who was paid for her services, and some of the women felt guilty for competing with their husbands' interests. In 1880 the women sold out.[51]

As a counselor in the stake presidency of the Relief Society, Hannah accompanied Miles to the surrounding communities and as far away as Nevada to fulfill their church assignments.[52]

Catharine enjoyed being part of the Romney family, and although Miles and Hannah left her at home from time to time, they were not unconcerned about her and her needs. Sometime between 1873 (when Catharine and Miles were married) and 1877 (when Brigham Young died), Brigham Young hosted a party at his winter home in St. George, to which the Romneys were invited. Miles and Hannah planned to attend a school board meeting in the early evening and to meet Catharine later at the party. After their meeting, Miles and Hannah stopped at home to check on things and found Catharine there, upset. She had gone to the party, only to be informed by one of Brigham Young's daughters that they were expecting only Miles's first wife to accompany him. Since other plural wives were there, Catharine felt she had been singled out for this humiliation because of her previous status as a servant in the Young home. Miles sent word to the party that the Romneys would not be coming. Brigham Young went to the Romney home to inquire and apologized on behalf of his daughter, but Miles refused to go.[53]

Catharine was also concerned about Hannah's feelings. The entire Miles P. Romney family was welcomed for dinners at the home of Catharine's parents. Catharine, however, felt that sometimes her mother spoke too sternly to Hannah's children. When Catharine mentioned this to her mother, Caroline Cottam defended herself, *claiming that she would tell anyone's children how to behave in her house. Catharine knew better than to talk back,*[54] *but at least she had tried to intervene in Hannah's behalf.*

Perhaps Hannah's experience with Catharine would have helped ease her mind when Miles married again. On August 1, 1877, Miles married Annie Maria Woodbury in the recently completed St. George Temple. Annie was an active participant in many community activities. She served as assistant librarian for the newly founded St. George Library and acted in plays put on by the Dramatic Association.[55] *Destined to become one of the great teachers of the Mormon frontier, Annie had been privileged to study at the University of Deseret in Salt Lake City when she was sixteen years old. The next year she taught school at Harrisburg in southern Utah and then at the First Ward schoolhouse in St. George. After she and Miles were married, she taught in a small building next to the Romney home.*[56]

Like Catharine, Annie had grown up in a family devoted to the gospel and willing to work hard and endure hardship in responding to the call of their leaders. The Woodburys had arrived in St. George the first year of its settlement.[57] *At age three, Annie probably would have been too young to remember the first Christmas in St. George. It rained all day, but between showers the people danced. A young boy was able to play for the children's dance after one of the women fashioned strings for his fiddle from a spool of silk thread.*[58] *The Woodbury orchard was one of many washed away during one of those early years when the Virgin River went on the rampage. Determined to stay in St. George, the Woodburys replanted.*[59]

On April 6, 1877, the Saints had met in the St. George Temple and dedicated it to God.[60] *Completion of the temple marked the beginning of a new era in that it symbolized the success of the Dixie pioneers in sinking roots in that alkaline desert. Many people, such as the Cottams and Woodburys, who had gone to Dixie as young parents, had watched their children grow up and begin their own families. Among this second generation would be those who would push forward into new areas of settlement. Utah's Dixie would no longer be the last outpost on the Mormon frontier.*

NOTES

1. Lula Romney Clayson, "Catherine Jane Cottam Romney—A," photocopy in author's possession, 3; Lula Romney Clayson, "The Life of Catherine Jane Cottam Romney," photocopy in author's possession, 11-12.

2. "Journal History of the Church of Jesus Christ of Latter-day Saints," October 19, 1862, LDS Church Archives.

3. Charles S. Cottam, "Brief History of Thomas Cottam," photocopy of undated typescript, Cottam Family Collection, BYU Archives.

4. Andrew Karl Larson, *Erastus Snow: The Life of a Missionary and Pioneer for the Early Mormon Church* (Salt Lake City: University of Utah Press, 1971), 355, citing Erastus Snow to Brigham Young, September 28, 1863.

5. Ibid., 378.

6. Albert E. Miller and Mary Ann Cottam Miller, *The Immortal Pioneers, Founders of the City of St. George, Utah* (St. George, Utah: N.p., 1946), 16.

7. Quoted in Larson, *Erastus Snow,* 321-22.

8. Details regarding the early lives of Thomas and Caroline Cottam are taken from Thomas Cottam, "A Short Family History of Thomas Cottam, His Wives and Children, Wrote Chiefly from Memory, St. George, Washington County, Utah Territory USA, March 30, 1893," typescript, Juanita Brooks Collection, Utah State Historical Society; the same manuscript under the title, "A Cottam Family Record," Cottam Family Collection, BYU Archives; the same manuscript under the title, "Sketch of the Life of Thomas Cottam," in Wilma Petty and Frank J. Petty, comps., *A History of George Thomas Cottam and Rachel Holt Cottam, Their Children and Their Ancestors* (Cedar City, Utah: Published by Authors, 1977), 111-15; Thomas Cottam, Thomas Cottam's Record Book, June 18, 1877, St. George, photocopy from William Howard Thompson, St. George, Utah, in author's possession; Thomas Cottam's Record Book, St. George, January 1, 1881, photocopy from William Howard Thompson, St. George, Utah, in author's possession; Charles S. Cottam, "Brief History"; Clayson, "Life," "Life History of Catherine Jane Cottam Romney," "Catherine Jane Cottam Romney—A," and "Catherine Jane Cottam Romney—B" (two accounts bearing the same title which I label "A" and "B"), photocopies of typescripts in author's possession.

9. Thomas Cottam, "Short Family History"; Charles S. Cottam, "Brief History."

10. Thomas Cottam, "Short Family History."

11. Ibid.

12. The entire letter, dated June 18, 1846, was published in the *Millennial Star,* September 1, 1846.

13. Thomas Cottam, Thomas Cottam's Record Book, 1881, 8, 26, 27.

14. John Alma died in a wagon accident in Salt Lake City when he was eleven years old. William Howard Thompson, ed., *Thomas Cottam 1820 and His Wives, Ann Howarth 1820, Caroline Smith 1820* (St. George, Utah: Thomas Cottam Family Organization, 1987), 2:1.

15. Thomas Cottam, Thomas Cottam's Record Book, 1881, 26, 27. Catharine's grave marker lists 1854 as the year of her birth. Wasatch Lawn Cemetery, Salt Lake City, Utah.

16. Lucile C. Fish, "I Remember Papa: Charles Smith Cottam," in Thompson, *Thomas Cottam*, 2:737.

17. Clayson, "Life History," 2. Catharine recalled that her favorite Christmas was the year her father carved thirteen dolls with jointed limbs. After receiving their own, she and her siblings took the remainder to other children. Many years later, her daughter Lula visited a woman who had been a recipient of one of these dolls. It was still in perfect condition, and the woman still recalled the incident with delight. Clayson, "Life History," 3.

18. Thomas Cottam, Thomas Cottam's Record Book, 1881, 26.

19. Charles S. Cottam, "Brief History."

20. Chairs made by Thomas Cottam are on display at the Daughters of the Pioneers building in St. George and the museum at the entrance to Zion Canyon. Thompson, *Thomas Cottam*, 1:52.

21. Clayson, "Life History," 1, 2, 8.

22. Thomas Cottam to his wife and children, October 12, 1870, Catharine Cottam Romney Collection, LDS Church Archives.

23. Clayson, "Catherine Jane Cottam Romney—A," 3; Clayson, "Catherine Jane Cottam Romney—B," 2.

24. Thomas C. Romney, *Life Story of Miles Park Romney* (Independence, Mo.: Zion's Printing and Publishing, 1948), 70.

25. Hannah H. Romney, "Autobiography of Hannah Hood Hill Romney," photocopy of typescript in author's possession, 7.

26. George Cottam recorded in his diary that he went to Diamond Valley to drive cattle and to gather wood.

27. Br. and Sr. are abbreviations for *Brother* and *Sister.*

28. William Squire, blacksmith, shared a shop with Thomas Cottam on the corner of the Cottam lot. Agnes Pickett, "A Brief Story of the Life of Emma Cottam," in Thompson, *Thomas Cottam*, 2:5.

29. An epidemic fever normally infecting animals.

30. Barter was the common means of doing business because cash was in short supply.

31. The Mormons were cautioned by their leaders to avoid the evils of the Gentile mining towns, such as Pioche and Panaca, Nevada. Andrew Karl Larson, *I Was Called to Dixie, the Virgin River Basin: Unique Experiences in Mormon Pioneering* (Salt Lake City: Deseret News Press, 1961), 57.

32. Joseph W. Young, president of the St. George Stake and former mayor of St. George. (A stake is composed of several wards or congregations.) The course of his illness and death is followed through the next few letters.

33. Eleanor was the daughter of Orin Nelson Woodbury and Ann Cannon Woodbury, who was mentioned in the previous sentence of the letter. A number of the letters in this collection were written to her. She married George Jarvis on October 21, 1872. Her younger sister, Annie Maria Woodbury, married Miles P. Romney on August 1, 1877. For more information on the Woodbury and Jarvis families, see Appendix 1.

34. She was probably referring to his weakness for wine. Andrew Karl Larson and Katherine Miles Larson, eds., *The Diary of Charles L. Walker* (Logan, Utah: Utah State University Press, 1980), 550. Although the church's Word of Wisdom prohibits consumption of alcoholic beverages, wine was initially produced in Utah's Dixie with the expectation that it would be a cash crop, but its production caused numerous social problems and was eventually discontinued. Bringham Young strongly condemned drinking liquor as early as 1869, though it was not until later that observance of the Word of Wisdom became a requirement for holding positions in the church. Larson, *I Was Called to Dixie*, 345-50; Leonard J. Arrington and Davis Bitton, *The Mormon Experience: A History of the Latter-day Saints* (New York: Random House, 1980), 299. Miles's son Junius said that he did not know until he was an adult that his father had "some pronounced weaknesses which he was able to entirely overcome as a result of his strong desire to do so, and sustained as he was by the love and devotion of three of the noblest women, I think, that the world has ever known." Junius Romney, "Impressions of My Father and Mother," in Thomas C. Romney, *Life Story of Miles Park Romney*, 298.

35. Lucern (alfalfa) proved a great boon for agriculture. It grew where other plants would not, required very little water, provided food for livestock, and helped prepare the soil for other crops. Larson, *I Was Called to Dixie*, 320.

36. Regarding Joseph W. Young, Charles L. Walker noted in his diary, "He died as he had ever lived, true to God and his Brethren, and his name will never be forgotten by the Saints of southern Utah. I watched over him with my brethren many a weary night, fondly hoping he would recover but he is gone." Larson and Larson, *The Diary of Charles L. Walker*, 370. Robert Gardner stated, "His loss was lamented for he was a poor man's friend." Robert Gardner, Jr., "History of Robert Gardner, Jr.: Written by Himself at St. George, Utah, 1884 Jan. 7," typescript, photocopy, BYU Library, 35.

37. John and Madaline Gardner Pyper were converts to the church from Scotland. Contemporaries of Catharine's parents, they married in Nauvoo and had spent some time in St. Louis before immigrating to Utah. They settled in Salt Creek (Nephi), Utah.

38. Caroline Eyring Miner, *Miles Romney and Elizabeth Gaskell Romney and Family* (Salt Lake City: Publishers Press, 1978), 16; Thompson, *Thomas Cottam*, 2:35.

39. Albert E. Miller and Mary Ann Cottam Miller, "A Historical Story of the Building of Washington County, the Part Accomplished by the Tradesmen and the Buildings Erected," in Hazel Bradshaw, ed., *Under Dixie Sun: A History of Washington County by Those Who Loved Their Forebears*, comp. Daughters of the Utah Pioneers, Washington County Chapter (Panguitch, Utah: Garfield County News, 1950), 317-43.

40. Hannah H. Romney, "Autobiography," 3-4; Thomas C. Romney, *Life Story of Miles Park Romney*, 27, 61; U.S. Federal Census, 1860, Salt Lake County, 14th Ward.

41. Hannah H. Romney, "Autobiography," 5-7; Thomas C. Romney, *Life Story of Miles Park Romney,* 61, 74-75.

42. Miller and Miller, *The Immortal Pioneers,* 197-98.

43. Larson and Larson, *The Diary of Charles L. Walker,* 550.

44. Romney family story.

45. Larson and Larson, *The Diary of Charles L. Walker,* 304, 306, 312; Miller and Miller, "A Historical Story," 323; Thomas C. Romney, *Life Story of Miles Park Romney,* 71, 97.

46. Thomas C. Romney, *Life Story of Miles Park Romney,* 147, 227.

47. Ibid., 112-13, citing *Deseret News,* October 1, 1873.

48. Hannah H. Romney, "Autobiography," 7.

49. Miles P. Romney to Catherine J. Romney, Viola, Wisconsin, August 10, 1876, Catharine Cottam Romney Collection, LDS Church Archives.

50. Thomas C. Romney, *Life Story of Miles Park Romney,* 226-27, citing *Deseret News,* June 26, 1880; ibid., 70-74, 97-107; "To the Board of Directors of the St. George Library Association," Andrew Karl Larson Collection, Utah State Historical Society.

51. Larson, *I Was Called to Dixie,* 257-58; Zaidee Walker Miles, "The Ladies' Co-op," Andrew Karl Larson Collection, Utah State Historical Society; Bradshaw, *Under Dixie Sun,* 309-10.

52. Hannah H. Romney, "Autobiography," 9.

53. Catharine told this story on a couple of occasions. Once was when Brigham Young's daughter, who was a visiting speaker at a conference in Mexico, saw Catharine and rushed over and threw her arms around her. Catharine's daughter Lula wondered why Catharine seemed somewhat cool toward her. Another time, Catharine's son Thomas was talking about going to a party put on by some of his students who had told him not to bring his wife. "If you go," Catharine said, "you're not the man your father was." Clayson, "Catherine Jane Cottam Romney—B," 3; Clayson, "Stories by Aunt Lula," audiocassette recorded by Heber and Genevieve Moulton, Bountiful, Utah; Clayson, correspondence with author.

54. Clayson, "Life," 15.

55. "To the Board of the Directors of the St. George Library Association," Andrew Karl Larson Collection, Utah State Historical Society; Bradshaw, *Under Dixie Sun,* 323.

56. Thomas C. Romney, *Life Story of Miles Park Romney,* 349; Ella Farnsworth Bentley, "A Glimpse into the Life of Annie Maria Woodbury Romney," photocopy of typescript in author's possession, 3, 4, 7.

57. Ann Cannon Woodbury, "Reminiscences of Ann Cannon Woodbury," Angus M. Cannon, ed., in Beatrice Cannon Evans and Janath Russell, eds., *Cannon Family Historical Treasury* (Salt Lake City: George Cannon Family Association, 1967), 175.

58. Zaidee Walker Miles, "The First Christmas in St. George—1861," Andrew Karl Larson Collection, Utah State Historical Society.

59. Thomas C. Romney, *Life Story of Miles Park Romney,* 348-49.

60. *Deseret News,* April 11, 1877.

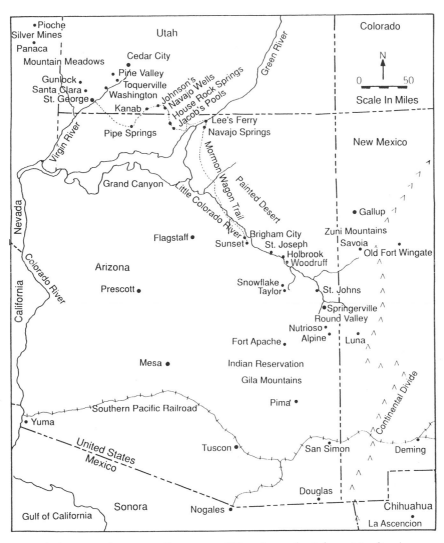

Arizona and surrounding areas. (Map drawn by Jolane Moulton)

Mormon settlers traveling to the Little Colorado area crossed the Colorado River at Lee's Ferry, Arizona. Catharine described this journey in her letter of May 13, 1881. (Courtesy of the Utah State Historical Society)

Mail wagons. Miles P. Romney and David K. Udall subcontracted with Solomon Barth to carry the mail from Ft. Wingate, New Mexico, to Ft. Apache, Arizona. (Courtesy of the St. Johns Stake Family History Center)

The Arizona Cooperative Mercantile Institution or A.C.M.I. in Snowflake, Arizona. The Mormons hoped to be more economically independent by owning and operating their own stores. (Courtesy of the Church Archives, Church of Jesus Christ of Latter-day Saints)

Snowflake, Arizona, 1884, about fifty miles from St. Johns. Catharine and
Annie Romney, Eliza Udall Tenney, and Ida Hunt Udall went to Snowflake
in 1884 to avoid being subpoenaed to appear as witnesses against their husbands in the polygamy trials. Catharine describes their flight in her letter of
July 20, 1884. (Courtesy of the Utah State Historical Society)

PART TWO

St. Johns, Arizona Territory

Today, St. Johns, Arizona, is a peaceful little town tucked away in the mountains of eastern Arizona. Mostly Mormon now, not much evidence remains of the confrontation between Mormon and non-Mormon that flared up during the first few years of its existence and sent a major portion of the Mormon population fleeing for safety in the dead of winter.[1]

The first attempts by Mormons to colonize the Little Colorado area in 1873 failed.[2] To those trying to settle there, the land appeared uninhabitable. One wrote that there was "no rock for building; no pine or timber within 50-75 miles of here." He said it was not a "plase fit for a human being to dwell upon." It was "the moste desert lukking plase that I ever saw, Amen."[3]

Brigham Young, however, declared that if he had been there, they would have found enough water,[4] and early in 1876, he asked for about two hundred volunteers to settle in the Little Colorado area. Settlement of this area would help the church expand throughout the continent. President Young realized it would be a difficult place to settle, but he expected that those responding would be resourceful.[5] Indeed, within a few months, there was a string of small Mormon settlements along the Little Colorado River: Sunset, Brigham City, Obid, and St. Joseph.[6]

Situated among low rolling hills in the upper reaches of the Little Colorado River, the St. Johns area, considered large enough to support two hundred families, was not so forbidding. Due to several unusually rainy seasons, crop and range land appeared to be fertile. Pure water surfaced in the McIntosh Springs four miles to the east, and fuel could be obtained from cedar groves on the bench areas to the west and south. Thirty miles south, ponderosa pine covered the lower slopes of the White Mountains.[7]

During the 1870s, the St. Johns area had come into use by New Mexican ranchers. It became a crossing in the Little Colorado and a stop on a mail route. A few Spanish-speaking people settled in the area. In 1873, Solomon Barth and his brothers, Nathan and Morris, bought twelve hundred acres and settled there with some Mexican workers.[8]

When Joseph Fish, a Mormon pioneer, visited St. Johns in December 1879, he found a Mexican town with about seventy-five families. The dirt-covered, flat-roofed houses had dirt floors and lacked windows. In town were "two stores, two billiard halls, one saloon, and one monte bank, where most of the male population spent the greater part of their time and money." The few Americans did all the business, keeping the Mexicans "in a state of peonage."[9]

Hoping to establish a Mormon community there,[10] church leaders decided to buy out the Barth brothers, the major land holder in St. Johns.[11] In November 1879, Apostle Wilford Woodruff instructed Ammon Tenney to consummate the purchase of twelve hundred acres of land, which he had been negotiating with Solomon Barth and his brothers.[12] The purchase price was 750 cows. The church would hold the land until it could be purchased by individual settlers.

Bad feelings between Mormons and non-Mormons existed before the Mormons had even laid out their townsite. Many of the white settlers in St. Johns were already "bitterly anti-Mormon," some of them having been among those who drove the Mormons from their homes in Missouri in 1838.[13] In particular, Mormons and non-Mormons clashed over the subject of polygamy, Mormons practicing it as a commandment of God, non-Mormons condemning it as a relic of barbarism and vowing its extinction. Early on, disputes over land titles and misunderstandings in the political process stirred up feelings on both sides. Spotting trouble, church leaders concluded that if their colonies in eastern Arizona were to survive, they must have control in St. Johns. They called more people to settle the area, which, in turn, fueled the distrust of the local residents.

The Mormon community in St. Johns grew quickly. Mormons initially settled in Salem, a mile and a half from St. Johns proper.[14] By March 1880, there would have been well over two hundred members in the St. Johns area, as 190 of them traveled to a stake conference in Snowflake, some fifty miles away.[15]

Conflict surfaced when it became evident that there were problems with the contract for the purchase of land from the Barth brothers. The agreement was loosely worded, the water rights were not properly recorded, and the Barths had only squatter's rights, some of which were contested by other residents. Further, the Barths had failed to include an important water right. To Mormon leaders, it appeared that the Barths intended to take advantage of them.[16]

During the summer of 1880, there was trouble over a nominating convention. The "St. Johns Ring," composed of a group of non-Mormon merchants headed by Solomon Barth and the Hubbell family, aspired to locate the county seat in St. Johns. Having been frustrated in the 1878 election, a representative of the Ring approached Tenney suggesting that the St. Johns Ring and the Mormons unite forces. Tenney presented the plan to Jesse N. Smith, stake president, who left it to Tenney to invite Barth to a special nominating convention in Springerville in preparation for the 1880 election. Tenney, however, failed to notify Barth of the convention. He belatedly met with Ring leader, J. L. Hubbell and promised him the Mormon vote on a ticket that the two of them worked out. When the members of the Ring learned that the Mormons were already committed to the candidates selected at the Springerville caucus, they refused to listen to an explanation and turned angrily against the Mormons.[17] At the fall election, the Ring resorted to fraud, stuffing ballot boxes and rigging ballot counting. All the candidates supported by Mormons lost.[18]

David K. Udall, who had been called to preside as Bishop in St. Johns, arrived there with his family in October 1880.[19] About that time, Erastus Snow visited St. Johns and recommended the Mormons relocate to a portion of their purchase that was on higher ground adjacent to the town of St. Johns.[20] Alarmed at the proximity of the surveying, about thirty of the town residents sent a letter to Bishop Udall. They had concluded the Mormons intended to surround and oppress them, and they warned they would do what they could to impede this settlement. Udall responded by letter, offering to call a public meeting when Tenney was back in town.[21] He sympathized with those whose squatters rights had been ignored by Barth. Nevertheless, the Mormons put the question to a vote among themselves and decided to relocate to the upper part of their purchase.[22]

Because of the fraudulent dealings of the St. Johns Ring in the 1880 election, as well as land and water disputes, church leaders concluded that for their own safety and security in the region, they must build up enough population to protect their interests and claim the land and water rights by actual use. They directed that all members arriving in Arizona settle in St. Johns.[23]

The Romneys were among those called to settle in St. Johns. It was thought wise to move only part of the family at first. Miles would return for the rest in a few months. Travel conditions would be difficult. They would carry water in barrels attached to the sides of the wagons. At night, they would roll out their bedding and sleep under the stars, while wild animals howled in the distance. The parents would stay up late cooking bread over the campfire. Among the first group to go from the Miles P. Romney family were Miles, Catharine and her four children (Caroline, 6; Thomas, 5; Junius, 3; and Claude, 1), Carrie's son (Will, 13),[24] and two of Hannah's children (Minnie, 13; and Miles A., 11). With four children under age seven, the three older children would be helpful. Miles would come back for the rest of the family in a few months.

Friends of the Romneys preceded them. Sam Jarvis, brother-in-law of Catharine's friend Eleanor Jarvis, and his young wife, Fanny DeFriez Jarvis, who had recently come from England, went to the Little Colorado area in 1879. Many other Dixie folks would also be there, including Joe and Maude Crosby, Brother and Sister Andrew Gibbons, the Sam Adairs, the Henry Platts, Will and Annie Lund, and other members of the Jarvis and DeFriez families. Some went by call, others in search of better opportunity.[25]

On Monday, April 11, 1881, George Cottam noted in his daybook, "We all go to see Miles & Catharine over the river."[26] Later that day, when the Romneys reached Hurricane Hill, their horse refused to climb. They sent for help, and Catharine's brother, Thomas, rode into camp that night. The next morning, he sent them on their way with a fresh horse, Old Charlie.[27]

May 13" 1881
St. John   Apache Co.   Arizona

Dear Father, Mother, Brothers and Sister,   I must write to you all at once for the present, and I suppose it will be just as satisfactory as you are all so close together. We had not heard a word from any one till two days ago when I got a letter from Isabell [Hannah's daughter, age 18], dated Apr. 26, and last night Miles got one from Hannah of the same date. the mail here seems to be very irregular in coming in but goes out once a week. I will give you a short account of our trip from the time Thomas [Catharine's brother] left us. I will say here I never felt more thankful in my life than I did the first morning out when we found Thomas camped with us. We shall never cease to remember with gratitude, the kindness of all of you, both then and before we started. anything that I could say would fail to express my feelings.

We reached Kanab all right except that Claude [age 1] had a large sun blister on his nose, which got better in the course of a week or two. he cut one tooth and stood the journey well, driving the team where it was good road, and fighting when he couldn't, throwing the whip and other things out, and requiring most of my time to look after him. Junius [age 3] was a very good boy all the way.

Miles telegraphed to Thomas from kanab and I sent a Postal card to Father. I went to Eleanor Mcallister's and baked bread. they were very kind. they are doing well, have a nice place and like there. I saw Kate Judd (as used to be), all well. We stayed half a day and started out with Br. [James] and Sr. [Emily] Lewis (we found them very nice *quiet* people, traveled with them all the way which was a great advantage as they knew the watering places. The day after we left Kanab we had a rain storm which was rather disagreeable and made it hard on the mules necks, which had begun to be sore. It proved to be a blessing however as it packed the sand farther on the road. that day (Saturday) we nooned at Navajo wells, deep holes in the rocks full of rain water with steps to go down to it. we camped part way up the Buckskin mountain. Our first Sunday we spent in travelling across it. it is said to be ten or twelve miles across, and such a mountain!, up hill and down, but very pretty withal with it's forests of cedar and pine, plants and flowers. I found wild wall flowers almost exactly like the tame ones except lighter colord. also sweet-williams. we camped this side of the mountain, the wind blowing a hurricane almost. the next morning we drove to house rock spring. splendid water right out of the mountain, one old cabin with a man from Orderville to whom the place belongs. camped at Jacobs Pools. also good water. found a man and boy camped there holding the spring while a party of Government Surveyors should pass. we met a Brinkerhoof boy and another man there from Long Valley going to the Ferry with grain. next morning our mules were gone. Miles and Willie had to walk back eight miles through heavy sand they were nearly choked, and Miles had large blisters on each heel, so that he had to wear his slippers all the rest of the way. started in the afternoon. next day we passed Soap creek. saw some deep gullies or washes running down to the Colorado, which looked to be cut down through a rocky bed, about one or two hundred feet deep. we also passed Badger creek the same day where there was a camp of government surveyors, locating a railroad line. we passed a man from the Ferry and Miles sent you a Postal card had some very sandy road, and much turning and twisting to avoid the deep washes, travelling almost in evry direction. We reached the Ferry (after crossing a very bad piece of rocky road in approaching it where the wagon jumped off rocks a foot or two at a time) about 11 o'clock in the morning of Thursday 21", it was very calm and we decided to cross immediately. a young man of the Surveying party was there who kindly offered to row us women and the children over in the small boat we thankfully accepted his offer, and enjoyed a most delightful ride, without the least fear as there wasn't a ruffle on the water. we made the trip in about five minutes I could have had another ride if I had chose to accept. the children did and enjoyed it. The large boat was an hour or more in making the two trips. they can only take two wagons at once. the price is $2.00 per wagon with single team. Charlie [the horse] was somewhat frightened and executed a double shuffle on coming, but did very well. It is a curious looking river from where I viewed it in the afternoon from the top of what is known as Lees Backbone, over which we passed the same day. here you can see the river hundreds of feet below you winding its way between perpendicular banks of solid rock without a tree to be seen and devoid of vegetation. But of this mountain over which we had to pass. It is called three miles across, and of all roads I should judge that to be the worst. there is one place where if a person went two feet out of the road they would go down a precipice hundreds of feet. Thomas [age 5] had a narrow escape of stepping over as we were walking across. after this we had splendid roads most of the way, driving through perfect flower beds for miles at a streatch, slippery elm, poison segoes, etc. until we struck the little Colorado [River], on Tuesday 26" Where we met Laura Starr, and husband, with pack animals. I did not know who she was until she had passed, not expecting to see her there, and mounted on a Jack. Miles sent a Postal card by him to Hannah. After this we travelled near the river coming near enough to water once or twice a day; there is cottonwood timber most of the way up this river, quite large groves in some places which looked as if they had stood there for generations. We had considerable heavy sand once in a while. saw what is known as the Black Falls. we all went in bathing even to Claude. found splendid feed for the teams. On Saturday 30" we passed Brigham City and a mile farther on came to Sunset. the former is composed of several rows of low log and rock houses joined together in a sort of Fort and is being deserted as the land is said to be poor. From Sunset I sent a Postal card to Father. at this place they are all living together in the Order[28] in a fort   evrything around looks thrifty and they seem to be doing well. Prst. [President] Lot Smith [founder of Sunset] tried to get Miles to stay over Sunday to meeting, offering us their hospitality and every accommodation, but we were anxious to go on. We now began to pass the grading of the R.R. and many men and teams tents etc.   on Monday May 2" we passed through St. Joseph. log houses in the shape of a fort with beautiful level fields. we also passed a small place called Holbrook a railroad camp. Next day we came to Woodruff, similar in appearance to the rest of the towns I have described. Saw the first Mexican houses this side of Holbrook. they are made of dark brown adobies the color of the dirt with flat roofs usually having one door and one small window. as homely looking houses as I ever saw.

Wednesday we passed through the most beautiful valley I ever saw and a ranch belonging to a man named grear. said to own 2,000 head of stock. Splendid roads and feed. We reached St. John about noon on Thursday, when I posted a card to you. We were fortunate enough to get a house to go right into next to Br. [James] Lewises. it is a log house without a floor but we are quite comfortable. There is a beautiful townsite here and splendid prospect for farming. I fear I have wearied you so will tell you about the town another time. Miles and the boys have been to the mill this week 30 miles and brought two loads of lumber for [a] house. good roads and grass knee high. were gone part of three days. they are plowing a little today to put in some corn. Dear George, Miles says to tell you he has sold the mules and wagon and paid for his land (83 acres and a city lot,) and will bring Charlie back. he is looking very well but not quite as fat as when we started, though he thinks he is quite as strong as he has grained him all the time, his kind regards to all.

We like our Bishop [David K. Udall] very much. he is a real nice man. We were there to supper on Sunday. I have just weaned the baby and shingled him [cut his hair], so he is quite a man. will send Mother a lock of his hair. I wish you would all send me a lock of yours as you have opportunity with the name of each—children and all. kiss them all for me.

Dear Brother Thomas   I was very sorry to hear from Isabell that you had been sick, but at the same time gratified to learn you were better. I feel much concern about the diptheria, but hope all the rest have escaped, and that its ravages are stayed.

Dear Charles   I couldn't forget you if I would as long as this hook lasts. I dont know what I should have done without it, we have spoken of it many times around the camp fire, for we have sat up till very late some nights baking bread to fill so many mouths. Miles is the handiest man I most ever saw camping out.

Emma   I shall expect a letter from you soon as well as from all the boys.

I hope Thomas and Charles will tell me all about George [Woodbury] and Roz [Romney Woodbury]'s[29] wedding presents etc. and all the news of the town.

Dear Father and [*page missing*]

26" June 1881
St. Johns   Apache Co.

Dear Father and Mother   It is a week since We received your very welcome favor of May 29" and you must please to excuse my tardiness in answering as I have been so very busy. I had a letter partly written when I got yours, which I will send to the boys, and will send this to the City as I expect you are on the way there now. I am pleased to know you are going, and Emma, and Thomas, with you   I hope you will arrive there safely, find all well, and enjoy yourselves very much; it almost makes me feel that I should like to be with you for a week or two, if duty did not call me elsewhere, not that I am discontented here at all, for Miles does all that he can for my comfort. but I should so like to see dear Grandma and all the folks. please give my love to her and them and keep a large portion for yourselves. give my love to Emma and Thomas   tell them to visit, and see sights, for me too, and I shall expect a long account of evrything from each. We are all [well] except Miles' lungs (which have been bad ever since we came,)[30] and the baby [Claude]   he doesn't feel well, for a day or two. he has two double teeth and is getting more. Miles said to tell you he would try and write next time. he has gone to the Stake Conference 50 miles away [Snowflake] with the Bishop. went on thursday and will be back tuesday I hope   We have been living in our own house nearly a week. it is a lumber room 16 by 18 feet, has a board floor, and is quite high and very comfortable; since we moved he has built me a small kitchen, which makes me very comfortable. I have got a new stove No. 7 improved Charter Oak. I am very well pleased with it, only they have forgotten to put up any baking pans or kettle covers, so that I have to borrow, but I have very kind, good neighbors, who let me use their stoves before I got one.

This is Sunday night, and as I have been at home all day and am all alone with the wind whistling around the house and the children all asleep I feel rather lonesome, so I think I shall go to bed.

I hope you will go to Ogden while you are up and see old friends I made a discovery the other day, quite by accident and much to my surprise. one of my nearest neighbors, Sister [Mary Ann Ellis] Watkin is the daughter of Sr. [Mary Ann Emmit] Ellis and niece of Thomas Emmit. A nephew of his is also here, son of another sister, Sam Browning. I was quite pleased to meet someone of whom I had heard even though I was not personally acquainted. We talked of Grandma and wondered if she was with the Old Folks Excursion, as that was the day 22". Sister [Mary Ann Ellis and Mary Ann Doxey] Watkins are both very nice women, in fact I never met a more sociable, good hearted, set of people than I have met in St. John, take them as a whole. they have all treated me with the greatest kindness.

Dear Father you say you are a poor hand to make an interesting letter, but Miles said when he read it, it contained more news than all the letters we had got put together and I assure you we both enjoyed it very much. I am pleased to hear that Quin is out of his misery at last. I[n] regard to water it is not near so scarce as at home, I think they do not water at night nor on sunday. there is a water master but I think he has no particular time for letting water out only as his judgment directs. But I suppose as more people come and more land cultivated, they will have to be more particular. of course there are no gardens in town to water yet, (except 2 or 3). but when there are the same stream will be used. the little Colorado). I think they will work at the city ditch next winter.

I suppose we are to have quite a celebration here on the 4 [Fourth of July]. I hear that Miles name is down for Orator but I don't know for certain. the Public square is laid off right next to our lot. I see they have got the Liberty pole there, about 75 feet long, and are going to build a bowery. Our people have had two suits in the Justice Court against some Mexicans and White men for taking the water out up the river for irrigating, to the injury of our crops, when they had no right to it. The Bishop and Water Master I think were the Plaintiffs. Miles had to conduct the first suit entirely alone against two lawyers on the other side as O Brian, the Lawyer whom our brethren wanted Miles to assist was not here.[31] one case has been decided for—and the other against us, but I think it will be appealed to the County court, which will sit here in the early part of July. Miles said he never saw the Devil striking out so plain in his life, as it did in the court room. the Lawyers went with their revolvers in plain sight. I think all will come out right in the end, as we have the Lord on our side.

C. J. Romney

Miles has been very busy with one thing and another. he hoped to see Br. [Erastus] Snow at conference. I wish I had plenty of time as I can think of much to say. Give my love to Uncles, Aunts, Cousins, and Friends.

Dear Mother, I have made a nice rug while Miles has been gone. a basket of flowers. had to work very hard to get it done.

5" July
St. John

Dear Father & Mother   It is just 2 months today since we arrived in St. John, and nearly three months since we bade you goodbye. We had a very good time on the 4". They built a very nice bowery, put up a liberty pole about 75 feet high: and the sisters made a beautiful flag. between 20 and 30 feet in length. (this I helped to make, it was a big job)   there was a procession formed, which marched to the bowery (which is quite near our house) where meeting was held. many Mexicans, and outsiders were present, and the County Officials were invited to seats on the stand. The Oration was delivered by Miles. the Declaration of Independence read by Willard Farr. a brother lately from Ogden.[32] these were followed by Songs, etc. and a speech from Mr. O.Brian a gentile Lawyer who seems to feel very favorable to our people. his remarks were excellent showing that all American citizens were entitled to the same rights and priveliges independant of all prejudice. and no matter to what sect they belonged: others were invited to speak but declined doing so. all passed off quiet and plesantly, and many expressed themselves as being well pleased with the exercises. The Bishop [David K. Udall], wife [Ella Udall], and Br. [Andrew] & Sr. [Rizpah Knight] Gibbons ate dinner with us, and in the afternoon we went out on the square to see the foot races and other amusements. As music could not be procured for dancing, about 15 of the neighbors came and spent the evening with us: we had a very enjoyable time. The time was spent in reading, reciting, singing, and social chat, so you see we made something by having a large room.

On July 1, 1881, Miles P. Romney and David K. Udall subcontracted with Solomon Barth to carry the U.S. mail from Ft. Wingate, New Mexico, to Ft. Apache, Arizona, by way of the Zuni Village, St. Johns, the Romney Ranch, and the Mineral and Cooley's Ranch. Heavy rain and snow made travel difficult or sometimes impossible, and unfair fines recommended by government postmasters combined to create a loss of $1,000 each for Romney and Udall.[33] Catharine refers to this business in the following letter.

15 July 1881

Mr. Charles S. Cottam   I received your welcome favor of the 23″ June, on the 9 ult.   I started to write this letter to Father & Mother, some time since, intending to send it to the city. (I have written one there too them) but I hear they are to be at home about the 24″ and if this be the case it would be useless to direct to the city. When they come home please ask them all to write and tell me all the news. I feel very anxious to hear, and know how they have all enjoyed themselves. Tell George I should very much like to have some word from him to show that he has not quite forgotten his far away Sister. please to bear in mind that anything which transpires, at, or about St. George is interesting to me. anything which comes from St. George, even old Charlie seems like a dear old friend, he is up at the mill now with the rest of the horses recruiting a little. Willie [Carrie's son, age 13] has started to ride the mail between here and round valley 80 miles from here, makes two trips a week, goes one day and comes back the next, when he is there he stays at Bp.[34] [Peter J.] Christofferson's: (he is brother to Rena Keat;) he gets two dollars a trip.

I was quite amused at your description of your housekeeping. I should like to look in unseen and see you making bread and preparing a meal and then the two of you sitting down alone in your glory.

I am sorry to hear of your having a felon.[35] I also regret very much to hear of Aunt Jenney [Cottam Punter] being so bad again. Miles is working at the Co-op Store putting in new counters, shelves, floor, etc. We now get our water from a well which has lately been dug about a block from us, it is nearly 40 feet deep and has a plentiful supply of excellent water which springs up through fissures in the solid rock. From your loving sister

C.J.C.

Please give my love to all. Rachel [George's wife] and children if they are at home. Emma's folks would like to hear from the girls. I see by the papers Aunt Rate Church is dead.

At the end of July, Miles and two of Hannah's children, Miles A. and Minnie, returned to St. George to bring the rest of the family to St. Johns. Unable to sell their property in St. George for even one-fourth its cost, Miles boarded it up and left it in the care of Catharine's family.[36]

8 Aug 1881

Dear Father and Mother   I must write to you again, although I have not had a letter from you for a very long time. we have had three letters from you two written in May and one in the early part of June. so you cant wonder if I am nearly homesick. though I still have faith that there are letters on the road for me. There have not been any through mails lately, on account of the recent rain storms washing the R.R. track away. I wrote to the city to you once, and have written two or three times since to St. George.

I am so anxious to hear all the particulars about your trip and how you found all the folks. I dont even know if you have got back yet or not, but suppose you have.

Miles started home a week ago last Saturday   has been 9 days on the road. he was very sick for about a week before he left which made me feel very bad about his starting, but the Bishop went to Holbrook soon after, and brought me word he was better. I think he must be near the Ferry [Lee's Ferry] by this time. Minnie [Hannah's daughter, age 13] and Miles [Hannah's son, age 11] are with him.

We have been having a great deal of rain for some time past, which has caused the grass to spring up until all around is beautiful and green. calves pasture all around our house. there is scarcely a day passes but we have a shower, and it has rained very hard since Miles left.

The Farmers are all very busy harvesting. Br. Holgate told me yesterday he had corn 7 or 8 feet high. green corn is just coming on. also summer squash. green beans are very abundant. peas didn't do well this year. It seems to be especially adapted to the raising of corn, beans, and squash. I believe the wheat has also done pretty well where the stock hasnt been on it. I fear our crops are going to turn out rather slim this year. we may have a squash or two. hope for better luck next year. if the field fence is completed.

I suppose you have plenty of fruit ripe by this time. Mother: I should like one of your nice large pears, and a bunch or two of grapes. I expect you will notice quite a difference in your fruit crop this year as I am not there to eat so much of it.

I have not been able to find a pig yet that I could get as they are very scarce, but I have got one old hen. how is that for a beginning? We have no cow yet, but have some very kind neighbors who send me a little milk nearly evry day lately. cows are gaining, since the grass sprung up. Bp. [David K.] Udall expects to start to St. Louis in a few days, to select goods for the joint Co op stores. will likely be gone a month.

Junius [age 3] and Claude [age 1] have been quite sick for about a week, but are much better, so that I begin to get my propper rest again and feel much better myself.

Judge Franklin, our Probate Judge has been very sick, and though it is said he has two or three wives (in different places) he has had no one to wait on him but an old Mexican woman. it seems hard but serves him right.

There is an old Mexican woman living here who is a hundred years old tho 4 generation of her posterity are said to be living here. she has almost lost her sight and hearing and is bedfast. With love to all, I remain your loving daughter

C.J.R.

"On September 1," Joseph Fish reported, "we received news of an outbreak of the Indians at Fort Apache. They had burned the outbuildings at the Post."[37] *At a town meeting in September 1881, the men of St. Johns organized the "United Forces of St. Johns" to act as "Minute Men" if needed for protection against the Apache Indians.*[38] *The following fragment was written to Miles while he was in St. George gathering the rest of the family.*[39]

to organise into companies, and prepare to defend themselves if it should be necessary. Our brethren are by themselves. and the Mexicans and outsiders by themselves, with one of our men, Bate Williams, as captain over all.

The Bp. [David K. Udall] was pleased to hear of you. he has written. I told you in my last of some of our folks having their horses stolen they got them back all right and did'nt see any of the theives.

Evrybody has left the mill, and ranches near by. still I dont aprehend any danger to this place if we do right, for we know the Lord is able to overrule all things for the good of his people, and he will also "help those who help themselves'.

Dear Husband may Our Heavenly Father bless and protect you and all with you on your journey hither, that we may soon, all meet again. is the prayer of your loving wife

C. J. Romney

I am very much pleased that you are going to have company down, so are Br. and Sr. Udall.

I will direct so that Father will get this if it is too late for you. and save returning.

Sept. 18" 1881
St. John

Dear Father & Mother   I suppose Miles and the folks have started by this time, at least I hope so   I have had but one letter from him, that was written a month ago today. I expect there are more on the road, but the mail has not come from Apache for two or three weeks on account of Indian troubles. I think the excitement is dying out as I dont hear anything of it lately. I have had only one letter from you since your return from the city, and none from Emma or the boys.

Dear Parents. I feel that we shall have need to live faithful to the Lord in this place, in order that we may claim his blessings and protection, for I believe there are some as wicked people here as can be found anywhere on the footstool of God. and without the Lord on our side we would stand a poor show, but as far as our people are concerned, we have I believe some good, faithful, Saints here, and I feel perfectly safe here.

I must give you an account of a most horrible crime which was commited here last wednesday night. Two young men, one only 19 years of age were arrested and brought here to jail, for the murder of two other men a storekeeper and his clerk, somewhere in this county. Their trial or examination was going on and would likely have terminated in the course of a day or two, one of them had cleared the other by confessing that he killed both men, but claimed that he did it in self defense. he also remarked the same evening that he didnt fear the law, but that he did fear violence. they were both, the same night murdered in their cell. there were supposed to have been 30 or 40 men there to do the cruel deed. I suppose they were afraid the law could not get sufficient hold on them and they are so full of a murderous, bloodthirsty spirit, that they had to take the law into their own hands.

so far as I know there has been nothing done to discover the perpetrators, except to offer $2,000 reward for the discovery of the criminals, and this is looked upon as a perfect burlesque, for there is little doubt, but the officers themselves are the most guilty, and my opinion is that there is no crime too bad for them to commit.

The boys are said by those who saw, and talked to them, to have the appearance of being quite nice young men, and one of them was well known to some of our people here, and was well thought of. word has come since their murder, that they were justified in killing the two men as they threatened to kill them, but I havent heard the particulars. The details of this horrible affair are almost too barbarous to mention, and I dont know that I should have said anything about it, only you would be likely to hear rumors, and I thought you would feel less uneasiness if I told you about it. so dont feel uneasy about us having such neighbors. for the Lord has said "Thus far, and no farther, shalt thou go" and we know he is able and willing to protect his people, if they will do right.

It doesnt do to think too loud here, but it is suspicioned by some that the boys were given poison in their supper, and were dead two hours before the hanging took place as their appearance did not indicate death by strangulation. They were buried in rough coffins, with the ropes still around their necks, and without even having their faces washed, or boots pulled off, and such things were said to be very common in St. John before our people came here, and since they came only a year ago last spring, a mexican was killed in jail. But enough of this. I am thankful that we live out on our lot, away from this sinful place a little. Please give my love to all my Brothers, Emma, and all the children. also to Aunt Mariette [Calkin]   I shall answer her letter before long. the reason I haven't done so before is because she said she could hear of me through you and didnt care to write very often, as she did'nt have much to write about.

Next saturday our Conference convenes at Snow Flake. I hav'nt heard any news of Br. [Apostle Erastus] Snow but it is likely he will be there. I wish it were near enough for me to go.

I wish I had asked you in time before the folks came to send me a spoonful of plaster paris as my lamp has come loose, but it will be too late now.

Dear Father & Mother I feel very anxious to hear from you. it is such a treat to get letters especially since I have been alone. I can't say that I feel afraid, or lonesome, except once in a while a little bit. evrybody is kind and sociable and you know the time passes away so much quicker when a person has plenty to do to keep busy, and it is easy to find plenty for such a slow person as me.

I must tell you Mother that Caroline [age 7] has knit herself a pair of stockings and done them pretty good. she has also peiced 60 small blocks of patchwork which I have set together and am going to quilt this week. she would go on with this kind of work if I had the pieces. The children are all well, and often talk about you. Goodbye, from your loving daughter.

C.J.R.

2" Oct 1881

Dear Father & Mother   Br & Sr Andrew Gibbons[40] start tomorrow for Utah, and expect to visit St. George   they are going to take this note and a small parcel to you. They were my near neighbors when I first came here, and were very kind

There is no mail running from Apache on account of Indians, so I have not had a letter for several weeks, and feel very anxious. I dont know when to expect the folks nor any thing about it.

I have never had a line from Emma, George, nor Thomas. We are all well. I felt quite miserable for a month or more, but am feeling much better.[41] more at present   I havent time to write so good bye. Give my kind love to all. I remain your loving daughter.

C. J. Romney

This bit of lace is for Sr [Mariette] Calkin   please give it to her.

Oct 19" 1881
St. John   Apache Co.   Arizona
Mr. and Mrs. George T. Cottam,

Dear Brother and Sister   I received your very welcome letter, written on the 21" Aug. about two weeks ago, but have been very busy, and not had time to answer sooner. I am pleased to hear that Rachel [Cottam, George's wife] and the children have been to the Meadows all summer, as they have likely, by so doing, escaped sickness.[42] I should have liked to have seen you and Charles keeping batch this summer. did you have much company to cook for, or was you inhospitable enough to let them to go home hungry?

It seems hardly possible that young George [George and Rachel's son, age 1] can walk. does he talk too. Claude [age 1] does not talk much but he is forward enough in other things. and as hard a case as ever. he thinks he is the "biggest toad in the puddle" as the saying is.

Old Charlie [the horse] did well coming down again and looked pretty well when he got here. he is a faithful old fellow and makes friends of all who have anything to do with him. I was glad to hear you was not vexed because Thomas let us take him. he was always treated well. I hope we wont have to sell him, but horses are very slippery things to have in this country. there have been a good many taken right out of the field. so you see a person might be well off one day, and poor the next. consequently we may deem it wisdom to sell as many of the animals as possible for cows, or something that we need. but there isnt much sale for either teams or wagons just now, as evrything has been stopped on account of indian troubles. flour has gone up to $8.00 per cwt [hundredweight]. I think considerable wheat would have been raised had circumstances been favorable. but the field was not all fenced and sunflowers very bad and these together with the heavy rains which came just at harvest time, caused considerable loss. I think farmers will begin to find out that fall wheat will be the most profitable: corn has done well, as also have beans and squash, in fact the country seems particularly adapted to the raising of these articles. also onions and red peppers are grown in large quantities. the latter is one of the principle articles of food with the Mexicans and they seem to take great pains to cultivate them. it is said that a wolf wont eat a mexican, on account of their being so strong of pepper.

Potatoes have not been raised here to amount to much as yet as they have mostly been eaten up by bugs of some kind. though there was a swiss man and his wife who came here last spring after we did and they turned in and made a business of fencing, plowing, planting, and tending their city lot. and in two months from the time they came into St. John, they had beautiful potatoes to sell besides, peas, beans, corn, melons, and other things. she has gone around selling vegetables, most all summer. and it is really wonderful the amount they have raised on that small piece of land. I guess we raised 50 or 60 squash, though not very large. this was more than we expected as ours was one of the outside peices in the field and handy to stock.

Dear Rachel I thank you for sending Ratie's [Rachel Cottam, George and Rachel's daughter, age 4] picture. I hope you will send me all of your likenesses as soon as it is convenient. there is no artist here though this town can boast of 4 stores. one belongs to our people, one to an American, one to a Jew, and the other to a Mexican. But I must close for the present. I remain as ever your loving sister.

Catharine J. Romney.

I almost get tired of writing letters, because I have to write the same thing over, and over, and I fear I bore you almost to death. If I were in St. George, and you away I think I could write something interesting because I could tell you of people you are acquainted with.

Nov. 6" 1881
St. John   Apache Co.

Dear Father & Mother   I received your very welcome card of Oct. 22", this morning. We were very thankful to hear that you were all well, and somewhat amused to hear of the rumor which had reached you of the folks being killed by indians   we also got papers today, two of which alluded to the same thing. Miles says he can in no way account for such a rumor getting started as they expressed no fear, although they kept a sharp lookout, and they saw only three indians on the whole route, though there was great excitement, and many alarming rumors. we feel, very thankful to our heavenly father that this rumor has no foundation in fact. we heard that Grandma Romney was quite unwell and felt very anxious about her, but I suppose she is no worse, as you would be likely to have heard.

We are all well. Joe Crosby and Maud [Crosby] got here all right yesterday morning. they are staying with us at present. they came with Br [Albert E.] Riggs (the Bishops brother-in law) from Kanab.

Annie wants to know if you would please to mention how her folks are, when you write, if you happen to hear, in case she does not get letters at the [two words illegible]. Miles built two small lumber rooms on to this, last week, for bedrooms for Hannah, and Annie and I use the room we live in, as I did, before, we have moved the stove in and are quite comfortable, considering all things. Dear Mother I feel very grateful for all you sent me. you must have taken great pains in putting up so many seeds. I must be breif, as I wish to post this to go early in the morning.

Will Platt lives with us and drives the mail. Please give my love to all, not forgetting Aunt Mariette [Calkin] I dont think of any news, Indians all quiet. the soldiers gone back to Wingate.

C.J.R.

Accept of our love and gratitude from your affectionate son and daughter M. P. and C. J. Romney. Miles wanted me to write and let you know we are still alive. Please give my love to Grandma, and all our folks in the city [Salt Lake City] when you write.

20" Nov 1881
St John   Apache Co.   Arizona

Dear Father and Mother   I feel as if I must write to you once a week if it is only a few lines because I know you will be anxious to hear how we are. I have not had any word for two weeks when I got a postal card from you. I have written one card and one letter since. Will Platt got a postal card from his Father [Henry Platt] last mail. The mails come quite regular now.

We are all well and as comfortably situated as we could possibly expect in the time. Miles has built two small lumber bedrooms on one end of the house for Hannah and Annie. While I use the large room. the girls the tent, (Miles bought one since he came back) the boys the wagon box. and the little children have a bed fixed up in the kitchen, so you see Mother we dont have to make beds down on the floor. and though our bedsteads are not so nice as the ones we had at home, they answer the purpose, and we sleep just as soundly.

Miles has succeeded in selling two of his wagons, one span of mules, and old Kit and has got some lumber, and wheat, for winter. a very necessary article in our family, especially now as we all have wonderful good appetites. a hundred lbs. of flour wont begin to last us a week. Miles says he is going to pay me the cash for the mare as soon as possible. we were afraid to keep her for fear of losing her altogether, as there are so many horses stolen. the man who got her has turned her out in the field   he says he is going to keep her to raise colts. old "Charlie" is looking pretty well. he has'nt anything to do but pick his own living. he comes up to see us nearly evry day, and get his bit of grain. Miles has built a lumber shop, here on the lot, and Joe Crosby is working with him. he and Maud have rented a mexican house, and are living over in the Mexican town.

10 wagons of immigrants have come in, in the past week or two, and more expected, so there is a prospect of a population after awhile.

The children are all well. Thomas [age 5] and Junius [age 3] & Ernest [Hannah's son, age 4], spend most of their time in building barnes, hunting lone horses and making mud ones. I dont know but Thomas is destined to become a sculptor some day, judging from the skill he manifests in the moulding of mud. he makes his horses so long and slender, that his Auntie [Hannah][43] tells him, they ought to have six legs, instead of four. you would laugh to see them, some look more like a rhinoceros than anything else. but they serve to amuse them for hours at a time, when it is warm enough for them to be out. and we are very glad to have them amused sometimes, for the sake of a little quiet.

I forget whether or not I told you in my last, that Katie Pymn called to see us a few weeks ago. she lives at "Nuteroso" [Nutrioso] about 75 miles from here, the same place that the "Brown" brothers and Will Lund live. we sent his parcel by her. they are all well and like the place. Ed. Brown called on us last week. Miles saw Richard Bleak passing through here a few days ago, and invited him to breakfast, but he didn't come.

22" Nov. 1881

Dear Father & Mother   I received your most welcome letter, (began on the 19" and finished on the 30" of last month) last night, they came by the eastern route, via S.L. City and Denver, the first mail matter we have got that way. I regret very much to hear of you both being sick, and I could not run in to see you, (but you have my faith and prayers that you are enjoying health and strength again.) I ought not to complain when you were both seperated from your parents, by thousands of miles, without scarcely a hope of seeing them again in this life. Dear Father do not imagine for a moment, that you could send so many letters or cards that they would not be appreciated, for all hands wait eagerly to hear the news. at the same time I do not wish to be selfish and trespass too much on your time. We were very thankful that you told us of Grandma, as we have so few chances of hearing of her. I am very sorry to hear of her still having the chills. it must go very hard with her, at her age.

Miles says to ask you if you wont please to take the wheel barrow and make use of it, if it will be any good to you. he forgot to speak about it before he left. we feel very grateful for your attention to the place. but dont water at nights, nor over do yourself. I did not know that Dan Kemp lived in this country? what is his business at St George. it seems to me I heard of his being married a year or two ago, but Annie has understood that he was going to marry Isabell Kemp. how is it?

I am glad you had such a plesant time on Georges birthday. please give my love to Grandma and all the folks when you write. also give my love to Aunt Mariette [Calkin], Sr. [Eliza Ann Brace] Lund, and all friends, and especially to my brothers and Sisters.

My only quiet time for writing is after the rest have gone to bed, and then I am like you say you are, "too sleepy to collect my thoughts," in addition to this I have very poor pen and ink at present, and there is no better in just now, so I dont know whether you can decipher this or not. Your letters are very newsy and interesting, not only to me, but the rest of the folks as well. Annie got a letter from her mother last night.

Last night we were invited over to Br. Ammon Tenney's to spend the evening. we had a very pleasnt time, and the best violin music which I ever heard, by an old gentleman by the name of Br. [August] Myhneer, who used to live in S.L. City. he is certainly a master of the instrument, and can almost make it talk. he is a Swede. and to look at him you wouldn't think he could handle a fiddle.[44]

The folks join me in love. I remain your loving daughter

Catharine J. Romney

We heard that Miles's brother was going to St. George but did not learn whether he did or not. Prest. [John] Taylors [president of the church] visit will be quite a treat to you all.

4" Dec. 1881
St. Johns   Apache Co.   Arizona

Dear Father & Mother   I must write my weekly letter, to let you know that I am still alive, and well as are all of us [illegible] weeks tomorrow [illegible] letter from you but Isabell [illegible] last night from Miss Farnsworth [illegible] you were all well and Thomas had not yet returned home, he must [illegible] with a cold time of it in the North country. Miles received a letter from Rob. Lund [husband of Miles's sister Mary] [illegible] that Grandma was quite weak [illegible] having the chills, we feel quite concerned about her, poor Grandma: it seems too bad for her to be afflicted with that miserable disease at her time of life, and in her otherwise feeble state of health; if I have time I may write to her and enclose with this, if you will please to send it to her. We have seen in the papers an account of the sudden death of Br [Benjamin Franklin, Sr.] Pendleton[45] I feel to deeply sympathise with his bereaved family. for though he was quite aged and could not be expected to live a great many years longer, still the blow seems as if it must be harder, because so sudden and unexpected.

We have heard of the death (at Salt River) of Jesse Johnson. sad news.[46] Poor Maude [Crosby]. she is staying with her cousin Sr [Eliza Udall] Tenney, while Joe [Crosby] has gone to Nuteroso for two or three weeks to set up a saw mill for the Brown Brothers.

There are quite a number of new comers lately around. this place presents a very different appearance from what it did six months ago. there were about three or four houses to be seen on the present town site, and there are now in the neighborhood of twenty, such as they are, besides others going up, to say nothing of tents, wagon boxes, etc. We have been having very plesant weather for three, or four weeks past, once in a while a windy day but not very bad. the nights are quite cold.

Some of the brethren still haying. Br. [Nathan] Tenney and son have just got in from Apache, where they have been for several weeks, cutting, hauling, and selling hay to the soldiers. I suppose they have done well at the hay business this season. they have I believe been getting $20 per ton out there, and they got $60 or $65 for a ton when the Soldiers passed through here about two months ago. Most of the brethren are busily engaged in preparing for cold weather.

Miles has built a small shop here on the lot and is quite busy, has plenty of work at present, he has made several pairs of bedsteads, and such things.

Dear Father & Mother. I dreamed of being home to see you last night, which has made me think about you more than usual today. Give my love to the Boys, Rachel, Emma, William and the children, each and all. I think some of them might write me occasionally so that I could at least hear from home once a week if only a few lines. If I only wrote once a month I dont know that I could write a letter that would be interesting, except what pertains to our own family. as there is no news to tell, that you would be likely to care about hearing. tell Aunt Mariette [Calkin] I dont forget her, but send her ever so much love. Remember me to all old friends and neighbors.

I think I shall write to Grandmother and Aunt Sarah [Smith Burns] at my first opportunity.

Br [David K.] and Sister [Ella] Udall have had a very sick child but it is better now.

Christmas will soon be here, but I fear "Santa Claus" will forget to come this year. Goodbye, from your loving daughter

C. J. Romney

Caroline keeps teasing me to teach her to write, so she can write to you. her Grandpa told her, her first letter was to be written to him, and she has not forgotten it.

A merry Christmas, and happy New Year to all.

Jan. 1, 1882
St. John

Dear Father & Mother   "A Happy new [year] to you"   This is the beginning of another year, and I cant help but wonder what changes another year will make, but I pray God that it may bring happiness, peace, and prosperity to all of us.

We are having lovely weather for this time of year. We spent a very quiet but pleasant, and happy Christmas. it was a beautiful day. we had a real old fashioned english dinner, roast hen, and plum pudding, and potatoes, the second mess[47] that we have cooked in Arizona, and you may be sure we enjoyed them. Br Anderson came to dinner and spent the evening. we nearly made ourselves sick with laughing at him repeating the words of "Old Grimes" and other songs, and Miles trying to sing them after him. it was really amusing. Christmas is a great time with the Mexicans   they kept up an almost incessant firing, for several days and nights before.

And on Christmas eve the town was illuminated with candles on the out-side. some of the buildings, especially the Church. and with numerous bonfires, in the streets. they also held mass and rang the church bell at intervals, until midnight. when they went through a preformance of seeing Christ born. the Priest holding a small box on his knee with a doll in it which he kissed, then the people walk on their knees and kiss it and drop in their offerings, which is I suppose in accordance with their means, ranging from 25 cts. to $20.00 so you see it is a rich harvest time for the old Priest. and he no doubt enjoys such times. We did'nt any of us go to see it but some of the neighbors did.

I understand there are to be 8 weddings on the 12 of this month. it is against their faith to marry in December. I hear that he has from $5 to $25 for each ceremony which he preforms according to the wealth of the parties united.

President [Jesse N.] Smith was here last week on business, and held meeting last thursday night, in our new school house. it is not quite finished yet, but is quite a credit to the community. it is made of hewn logs, is 40 by 25 feet. and quite respectable looking.[48]

the next conference is to be held here, in march.

Joe Crosby had a horse die about a week ago. it ate some poison weed.

I hav'nt had a letter from you for seven or eight weeks. I can't account for it.

Miles and I each have a very bad cold. I have been very hoarse for over a week, though this seems to be quite a healthy place. there have been but three deaths here among our people since I came. one was a child that was choaked to death. one Br Grear who lived 20 miles from here. and then a child of Br [Ammon] Tenneys, who was burned 2 weeks ago, and was getting better, when it was taken with croup, and died last thursday night.

Caroline [age 7] says give her love to you, and tell you she would like to see you all.

2". Miles A [Hannah's son, age 12] and Gaskell [Hannah's son, age 10] have been after wood again today. they go quite often. they can get quite a load of dry cedar in less than half a day. and though there is no sale for it, it is a great help to get plenty for our own use.

There are four stores in town, the Coop, one Jew, one gentile, and one mexican, so you see we have quite a variety.

Please give my love to all, not forgetting Aunt Mariette, Sr. [Eliza] Lund, and all old friends. I remain your ever loving daughter,

Catharine J. Romney

The folks join me in love to you.

The schoolhouse built, bids were taken for a schoolteacher. The job was awarded to the low bidder, Annie Romney.[49]

March 3" 1882
St. John's   Apache Co   Arizona

Dear Father & Mother   The mail came in yesterday but did'nt bring any of us any thing, so I must write and send this off with Thomas's.

We have been having some lovely days lately, just like spring, but it is very windy and disagreeable today.

This is Isabell's birthday   19 years old. she sends her love to you, and kind regards to the boys. she wants to know if you will please ask Matilda [Thompson, Emma's stepdaughter] why she dos'nt write. she will write to her soon, but is very busy in school just now   she says she would like to write to Mother some time, if she would like to hear from her.

There has been quite an excitement here today. the school house came near being burned down. school was in cession and a hundred and thirty or forty children there. just after ten oclock one of the girls happened to look out of the window and saw the woodpile on fire and it being quite large and very near to the house. the flames almost reached the windows. she told Annie, who immediately opened the doors, and let the children out. she also had the bell rung, to attract attention. (it has only been put up a few days)   I was outside our house at the time, (which is less than half a block from the school house) and hearing the bell, I looked around to see what was the matter, and seeing the flames I ran to the shop and told Miles. he and another man went to the fire, and another ran up town to give the alarm. and soon nearly all of our people, both men and women, were on the ground, with buckets, tubs, and barrels, of water, all doing their utmost, to render assistance. and their labors were crowned with success, though it seemed almost a miracle, as a very strong wind was blowing the fire right against the house, the logs caught fire, and one window was burned out. the children were badly frightened. but none of them hurt thank fortune. just think what a narrow escape for them. and what a loss if the school house had been burned up. They have got three nice new chandalier's. two with three lamps each, and the other with one lamp. and though the bell is rather small, and not a nice toned one. still it answers the purpose for the time being. I feel very much frightened of fire. for our house is all lumber. and our tent and wagon box would all be burned down in short order, without the least chance of saving anything. but I pray God that no such accident may happen to us.

Miles' thumb is getting better all the time. he has been trying to work this week. he has made five or six chairs. We are all well.

Miles had a letter from Br [Alexander F.] Mcdonald a few weeks ago. his family were all well.

The people here seem to have quite a spirit of going to meeting, so far. yesterday was fast day. and I believe there were as many as fifty grown people out to meeting, besides children. and then we had about 40 of the sisters at our monthly meeting of the Releif Society in the afternoon.[50]

There is an old blind Mexican here, who belongs to the church, and our Society have been making him some warm woolen quilts, and the Bp. [David K. Udall] has got him a wool bed, and bedstead, to make him comfortable. they took them to him today. I must now say goodbye for the present. I remain as ever your loving daughter

C.J.R.

Kind love to all.

Apr 13" 1882
St John's

Dear Father & Mother Your most welcome letter of March 26" came to hand yesterday, together with one from George & Thomas, of the same date, also one from Aunt Mariette, so that I had a real feast. Miles came in from the office, and gave Minnie [Hannah's daughter, age 14] a letter, that came for her. I asked if that was all the mail. he said there were a lot of papers. I felt very much disappointed as I had'nt had a letter from you for a long time, and did'nt think he was trying to tease me. but in a few minutes my disappointment was turned to rejoicing. when he pulled my three letters out of his pocket.

Dear Parents your letters were full of interest to me, and the folks all seemed to enjoy hearing them read, and send their love to you. I am very sorry to hear of Fathers health being so poor. I do hope you are better. do both try and take care of yourselves for I know you work too hard.

I was pleased to hear of the good conference. I feel as if it would be a great treat to hear Br [Erastus] Snow preach once more, if the benches did use to get hard sometimes before he got through. It seems to me there have been a great many deaths in St George since I left. Strange Br [Nathaniel] Ashby should be brought so far to bury.[51] his family have certainly been sorely afflicted in the past year, in one way and another. Br [James William, Sr.] Nixon has left a large helpless family. I wonder if they will be able to do any thing with the Trumbull mill, to help themselves.[52]

Br [Robert] Parker's family have had their share of sickness, I think. I trust their health is all improved ere this. You mention Sr. Richards calling to see Grandma, and she being so poorly. I am very sorry to hear that she is not any better. please let us know how she is whenever you hear, and are writing as we dont hear from her very often.

How is Sr [Eliza] Lund? We are all well. I dont think the children ever looked so rugged and healthy in their lives.

Miles says to tell you he is still a cripple with his thumb and he dont know that it will ever be quite right again. though he manages to handle his tools a little with his fingers, it is uphill business. We are expecting to get three cows in a day or two. Willie [Carrie's son, age 14] has gone after them now.

5 oclock p.m.   I had to stop writing. we had some visitors call in. five Mexican women, and some children. I dont know how they happened to call. but I suppose they were out for a walk and came in out of curiosity. they were the first who have ever been here. they sat and talked quite awhile but we could'nt understand much. they looked at the Organ and asked if it was a Piano.[53] so Annie played and we sang two or three songs for them, which seemed to please them very much.

they wanted to know if I was a Mexican, and insisted that I was. they paid me a compliment saying I was. (Moe Boneta,) [muy bonita] which means (very pretty,) when they went they invited us to come and see them.

It was just a year last tuesday since I left home, for Arizona. I wonder if you thought of it. I did and almost got the blues. I believe I felt worse homesick than I have any day since I left. but it wont do to feel homesick, because this is my home now, and I know that you have both passed through the same trial of leaving your parents, as have many others. at any rate I feel very thankful that we can all read, and write, so that we can hear from each other.

The children send their love. Caroline [age 7], and Thomas [age 6], are both going to school. Caroline reads in the First Reader and Thomas in the Primer. Junius [age 4] is anxious to get old enough so that he can go. Claude [age 2][is] a great—sturdy fellow. he has been to Sunday school today with the children. The children all go to Primary. Hannah says they average about 60 members at their meetings.[54]

Baby [Park] was three weeks old yesterday.[55] (I wrote to you while I was in bed)   I fear he is going to be a cross little chap, and I dont know how I am going to get along with a cross baby.

I am sorry to hear that Grandmother and Uncle John & Aunt Sarah [Smith Burns] are all in such poor health.

It is lucky that you didnt suffer any greater loss from the fire.

When you write to cousin William, or see him again, please give my love to him. also to all inquiring friends. and especially to my Brothers and Sisters, one and all.

I expect I shall have to quit, as I cant do much at writing with the baby. I used to pride myself on my writing, but it is a long time since

I have taken much pains with it. I think I am doing pretty well if I write so that it can be read at all.

Is there any truth in the report that Matilda is married to Br Bleak?[56]

It hardly seems possible that some of these young people are old enough to marry.

How do you like my babies name (Park)? I will answer the Boys, and Aunt Mariette letters at the earliest opportunity. From your loving daughter.

C.J.R.

Apr 23" 1882
St. Johns
Mr. & Mrs. George T. Cottam

Dear Brother and Sister   Your welcome letter of March 20" came duly to hand, and as baby has gone to bed I will commence to answer it. We are having a curious kind of a spring, at least it seems so to me. we have more wind than I ever saw in my life. if it was dusty like St. George I dont know what we would do. the day before yesterday 21" it was very stormy all day, it had blown very hard all night, and in the morning it snowed an inch or two, but soon melted, it also rained hard and blew, during the day and at night it cleared up fine and moonlight; yesterday morning was lovely. the sun came out nice and warm, and remained very plesant all day, just like the good old fashioned spring weather at home. this morning, for two or three hours we thought as we were going to have another nice day. but it turned out quite windy. I think we shant notice it so much when we get fences, and trees to break it. I have been to meeting today, and since, Annie and I have been for a walk, to see Sr. [Rizpah] Gibbons. they wish to be remembered to all.

Miles was appointed at conference to preside over the home missionaries of this place, and went yesterday to Round Valley to fill an appointment for preaching today.[57] he wont be back before wednesday. They are talking of building a grist mill this season here, and Miles is appointed to suprintend the construction of it. but there wont be much pay on it at present, as it is to be built by the people, and it is desired that most of the labor be turned in as capital stock, but it is much needed, and will doubtless pay well, in what it saves the people from having to import flour, and pay $8.00 per hundred for it. I was surprised to hear of Emma Nixon being married to John Mathews. how are the family getting along? (do the women live together?) I am sorry to hear of Clara's colt dying.

I am very sorry to hear that Rachels health, and the children's is so poor. we are all well, and the children all the very picture of health. I never saw a hardier looking lot of children in my life. I hope yours all look and feel as well. I suppose you are having very warm weather by this time. the spring is quite backward here.

We have two cows now and expect to have another soon, but they dont seem to be very good ones. I cant think of anything to write, so will say goodbye for the present. with kind love to all I remain your sister in love.

Catharine J. Romney

April 30" 1882
St. Johns

Dear Father & Mother   I have got a bad headache but I guess I had better try and write a little as sunday is my only chance.

Miles took us for a ride today, and I do wish you could see the country that we did; it seems wonderful to me, who scarcely ever saw anything but the red rocks, and sand plains of Dixie. the natural facilities of this country are certainly ahead of the southern part of Utah, though of course there are a great many drawbacks here, as in evry other new country. We passed today over so many beautiful, rolling, hills, covered with grass, and lovely level benches, reaching for miles, with stock grazing here, and there, in every direction. the terrible "locks [?]" which has made such sad havoc among the horses here this winter, looks as beautiful as if it were entirely harmless. it grows in bunches and is in full bloom now. the flower is between a red, and purple and something the shape of wild, sweet peas.

Miles was at Round Valley last sunday, to fill a missionary appointment, and went up to Nutrioso so that he did'nt get back till wednesday. he says he never saw such a splendid country for stock raising. he has got contracts for building two, or three, houses there, for which I feel very thankful, as there dont seem to be any work here to do at present. he expects to go up there the end of this week, and will take Hannah and Isabell, [Hannah's daughter, age 19] and part of the children up there for the summer, as he expects to get a number of cows to milk.[58] he will hire some men, and will have to go back, and forth, between here, and there, to see to business here, in regards to a grist mill which is going to be built here. Will Lund is doing well.

Will Platt, came over from Apache last week. he brought news that the indians have broken out again, below Apache, and had killed 32 men, mostly ranchers, 40 or 50 miles below. I hope there will be no particular trouble in this part of the country.

Br [Joseph Hyrum] and Sr. [Mary Ann Doxey] Watkins, the husband of Mary Ann Ellis [Watkins], will start this week on a visit to Ogden. they will come by way of St. George. likely you will see them. they will stay at Br. Clarks.

If our Bishop should happen to wander that way, in the company of my friend Miss Ida Hunt, of Snow Flake, dont be surprised, but please dont mention it till they come. I hope you will see them.[59]

But I must say goodbye for the present: from your loving daughter.

Catharine J. Romney

[Page missing] Taylors. brave, manly, unflinching, spirit, and his firm faith in God, together with that of the rest of our leaders, seems equal to any emergency. We had heard rumors that our brethren had been counseled to put away their Plural Wives for the time being, but I did not believe it came from headquarters, for I have more faith than to think that the Lord would require anything of his people, without opening the way for them to carry it out, and if one principle of our religion proves a failure, how can any of them stand?[60]

I took the baby and had him blessed last fast day.[61] "Park Romney." he is considered by his mother to be a fine looking fellow, and just as cunning as anybodys baby.

We shall miss Dixie very much for awhile for some things, more especially for its fruit, and factory [cloth], though I hope in time we shall be able to have both here, but it will likely be years first. we used to think yarn and cloth was poor, but I think some of the imported is much poorer. but shoes are the worst   they seem to bring a very poor quality here. they dont begin to compare with the Salt Lake or even our Dixie made shoes for wearing. that is what we have had.

But I must close with kind love to all. I remain your loving daughter

Catharine J. Romney

Please excuse my poor writing. I have to write with the baby on my lap, or any way to get it done.

30 May 1882
St Johns
Mrs. Emma Thompson

Dear Sister   I was very much gratified at getting a letter from you once more (for it is along time since I had one before.) and especially your likeness. thank you for it. I think it an excellent one. I did'nt know but you had almost forgotten me. I am so glad to hear from any of you, and I have never got a letter without answering it, though I am sometimes not very punctual. I have just answered Eleanors [Catharine's friend and Annie's sister, Eleanor Woodbury Jarvis], and it is over two months since I got it. for I have but little time in daylight, and I am too sleepy to write much of an evening

I hardly know what to write about as there is very little of interest going on here. if I were in St George and you somewhere else I think I could interest you more.

The Young Ladies Association had an entertainment here about a week ago, consisting of Dialogues, recitations, singing etc.   it went off splendidly. all preformed their parts very creditably, and won considerable applause. some of the Young Mens Association helped them. Minnie [Hannah's daughter, age 14] took part, and Isabell [Hannah's daughter, age 19] was to, but went away too soon.[62]

There was a free show of some kind up in Mexican town night before last, by a troupe of Mexicans who were traveling through. we did'nt care to go to such a place, but Miles went. it was a farce, and some "slight of hand" tricks, but the talking was all done in spanish. it is the first thing of the kind I have heard of among them since we came.

I often see people here who remind me of some one I have known before. one young man here Jim Ramsey looks very much like Thomas. a brother named Straddling, looks almost the image of Br [Isaac] Hunt and an old gentleman by the name of Love looks and talks like Br [Asa] Calkin used to. there are others who remind me at times of different persons. Br [Willard] Farr reminds me sometimes of Dub Woolley and sometimes Oscar Bently, and his wife of Sr. [Emma Jackson] Adams, and Lizzie [Adams Macfarlane]. Goodbye, from your loving sister,

C.J.R.

Please excuse this short letter this time as I have some salt rising bread to mix and it must be done soon. Tell Mother and the boys I will write soon. C. J. Romney

June 3" 1882
St Johns
Mr. and Mrs. Thomas Cottam

Dear Father & Mother, I received your most welcome letter with Emmas and her likeness. but I answered hers first as I had just written to you. the mail goes out this morning, and I think you will be anxious to hear so will write if only a short note. It is saturday morning and I ought to be very busy. I got a letter from Thomas last night, which I will answer as soon as I can I have answered evry letter that I have got since I came to St Johns, except the last ones from the boys, and those I will do soon. I hope my letters all go safe. We are all well. baby [Park] growing nicely. Sr. [Rizpah] Gibbons waited on me when he was born. Sr. Ramsey is often out of town. goes to Woodruf and all over the country, so I did'nt engage her.

We are having quite warm weather, but considerable wind I think it wont be so bad when we get fences and trees, but when we will have the trees it is hard to tell. yesterday was a very windy day. Caroline said "she wished she had never seen this old windy town." The children are learning pretty well at school. Caroline has gone in the 2 reader, and Thomas is just through his primer, and going in the first reader. he seems to take a great interest in learning. he hasnt been one term yet.

6". Dear Parents I didnt finish this when I expected so will write a little more.

Miles was down [from Nutrioso] two weeks ago. but got word that Hannah was very sick, so had to start right back. but thank the Lord she got better, and is up and around again. we got a letter from her the other day. she said she didnt think she could, live for awhile, has spasms [contractions] I believe.[63] We expect Miles down sometime this week. the folks are milking eight cows, so they have all the milk and butter they want. Hannah sent us some butter, as good as any I ever ate. she says she likes that place much better than this and would rather live there.

I was quite sick the night before last and yesterday. but am better again. I think it was billiousness. Annie is still teaching school. has quite a number of mexicans.

We have got another cow today, so I hope we shall have a nice mess of milk.

Our chickens are doing pretty well, just now, and we are trying to raise some little ones. we have seven a few days old and have another hen setting. I think chickens will do well in this country. There is some excitement in regard to indians again.

A letter was read in meeting on sunday, from Prest. [President] Jesse N. Smith, advising the people to be cautious, and not expose themselves needlessly, as one of our brethren has been killed about ten miles from Snow Flake, a Brother Nathan Robinson, and a Brother Plumb had been shot at about seven miles from there.[64] the soldiers were in persuit of the hostiles. Will Platt, came in from Apache yesterday. he thinks there is'nt any danger this way, as the indians have gone west. but the brethren are getting up a millitary organization, in case of emergency. I dont anticipate any danger, but the excitement may cause a stagnation of business, as it did last summer, if lumber making and hauling, and loging, etc. is stopped.

I cant think of anything that will interest you so will close for the present, with kind love to you. do take care of your selves, and dont work hard. Good bye. From your loving daughter

Catharine J Romney

1 July 1882
Nutrioso

Dear Parents   I will add a little more to my letter, though I dont suppose there will be any chance to post it till I go home, which will be in two or three days   it is several weeks since I have heard from any of you. I feel quite uneasy about it.

Willie [Carrie's son, age 14] and Gaskell [Hannah's son, age 10] went down to St John last week, and Miles A. [Hannah's son, age 12] and Thomas [age 6], came up last tuesday the 27" and brought bad news from there. Br [Nathan] Tenney one of our nearest neighbors was shot and killed last saturday, the 24" of June, the greatest day in the year with the Mexicans. they call it "St Johns day". I will give you the particulars as near as I can, from the reports we have heard.

The Mexicans were up in town in the central part to see a circus, and a great many of our people were there too, when the Mexicans began firing at some young fellows who were there, three brothers by the name of Grear who live about 20 miles from there. the oldest brother dos'nt belong to the Church, though most of the family do.

his Father died about a year ago. they are great stock owners; a few months ago this oldest son (who is a very hard case) cut a Mexicans ear off for stealing one of his horses; this was the cause of the outbreak. the Grear boys, (the youngest only 14 or 16 years old, and has been going to Annies school all winter) with one or two others, got into an unfinished house of Br. Kemps, which is right close to the Mexican town, and returned the fire, and shot three Mexicans, two of whom were not expected to live at last accounts. The Mexicans killed one young man in the house by the name of Jim Vaughn, an outsider.

[part missing]

I have got this letter rather jumbled up so that I dont know if you can hardly make it out. Please excuse errors.

20″ July 1882
St Johns

Dear Father & Mother   I am getting sadly behind with my writing. have been busy shortening the baby [dressing the baby in short clothes], etc. I received your very welcome letters, Fathers of May 22″, and Mothers, June 21″. I wrote a letter from Nutrioso and a Postal card soon after I came home, but the mail did'nt go out for some time.

Miles came down a week ago last tuesday morning, and went back on Friday. While he was here we had Prest Jesse N. Smith, Br. [Ira] Hatch, and John Hulet here to dinner with us. they were considerable for a day or two as we had just got the late papers. The boys will remember J. Hulet. he used to go to school with us, to Br. [Richard] Horne, he lives at SnowFlake. We had a plesant visit. Dear Mother I got the things you sent me and thank you very much, was very much pleased with all, the shoes are real nice. they look like good ones. I am sure Caroline [age 8] will be pleased with her dress. I am trying to get it made before she gets home. I [sent] her, and Thomas [age 6] with their Aunty [Hannah], dont know just when they will be home, but am anxious to see them. Mattie [Carrie's daughter, age 12] is with me. Will Platt is boarding here, and clerking in the store for a short time till Br [Willard] Farr has a rest.

Mother you did'nt say whether you liked your Motto or not.

Please tell Charles I will try and answer his soon, and will write to you again before long. I am pleased to hear through you of Grandma's Cottam and Romney, but sorry they are both so poorly. with love

C.J.R.

2″ Aug 1882
St. Johns   Apache Co.   Arizona
Mr. George T. Cottam

Dear Brother   The mail has'nt been running for two or three weeks, but I have found a chance of sending letters in the morning, by a perso[n] who is going to Woodruff, and can post them there, so I must write, if only a few lines, in answer to yours of July 4″. I was pleased to hear you were all well   hope you continue so. I am thankful you have good crops, and had got your harvesting done. I fear you boys are working too hard and will make old men of yourselves before you should be. be careful of your health. you ought to have been born lazy like your sister. but I dont find time to indulge my natural propensity now [even] if I have got a good baby. Caroline and Thomas are still at Nutrioso. I want to see them very much.

I saw Will Lund and George Peck when I was up there. they are both looking very well. George lives with Will and Annie [Lund]. he is a happy looking old bachelor. Will inquired after you. they have splendid prospects, each of them 40 acres of grain in. Will says he never saw crops grow so easy in his life. they have three children. they milk a good many cows and make butter and cheese.

Crops here are some of them looking pretty well, though rather short of water. feed is not so good as last year as there is not near so much rain. it began earlier and then quit, and has been very dry and warm for over a month. some people have got a few potatoes in but the bugs have almost devoured them. harvesting has begun. good-bye from your loving sister.

                                        C. J. Romney.
I have got a boy who bids fair to soon be as big, pretty, and smart, as yours, so dont get to feeling too important in your old age.

George I enclosed a note to Grandma Romney   would you please to put it in an envelope seal, and send it to her.

13″ Aug 1882
St Johns   Apache Co   Arizona

Dear Father & Mother   I have just heard of a chance of sending a letter to Woodruff, though I have but little notice, so can not write much   will drop a few lines to let you know how we are. A week ago last saturday Miles brought Annie home with her children and Caroline. they came in one day as they had one of the buckboards or buggies, which they had left from the mail business, and which he had not been able to sell. On sunday he took me for a nice ride, and on monday morning, Miles, Mattie [Carrie's daughter, age 12], and Junius [age 4] started for Nutrioso, about 10 oclock. When about 9 or 10 miles out, Miles was either knocked, or thrown, from the buckboard, and lay unconscious for about four hours in the scorching hot sun.[65] we cannot tell how it occurred, as Mattie did not see any one, though she says she was looking the other way. her attention was atracted by hearing her Pa say, "O my head," and looking around she saw him just falling out of the buggy, and it having a top on, he of course must have gone far enough forward to strike on the wheel with his stomach, which he evidently did, sustaining severe internal, injuries, though no bones were broken. Miles feels confident that he was struck with a loaded black whip or something of the sort, across the temples and head, and he had considerable pain there, and a scar on his temple. he saw two Mexicans on horseback riding along by the river most all the way, and the fact of his going through some cedars at the time he was hurt makes it look quite probable, also the fact that after Br. [John W.] Berry found him, and while trying to bring him to, a mexican, rode up within 50 yds. turned out from the road, and galloped past. Mattie and Junius were very much frightened. they got out and spoke to their Pa several times, but receiving no answer they thought he was dead. they started to run home and came about 8 miles when they saw one of the Berry boys, and a man by the name of Tro[paper torn] the latter took Junius on his horse [illegible] came in with the children and Br Berry went back to Miles, about whom he could see no sign of life, but he fanned him and moved his arms, until he revived, and finally succeeded in getting him into the buckboard, though he fainted 4 or 5 times before we met him, in a team which Joe Crosby and some more of the brethren started in with us, when the children came home. they put him in the wagon and brought him home, where he lay in a very precarious condition for two or three days, and I doubt if he would ever have recovered if it had not been for the power of the Priesthood, through the administration of the elders, and the untiring efforts and skill of Sr Ramsey. everybody was very kind, sitting up at night etc. Hannah heard of it and got here thursday night with the team.

Miles was very anxious to get back to Nutrioso to see after his work, and [paper torn] [as] he felt very much better, we fixed him a bed in the wagon, saturday morning, got a young man to drive, and he and Hannah started. Br. Taylor met them about 18 miles from here and Miles was doing as well as he could.

It seems like a miracle that the team had stood perfectly still for so long, (it must have been 4 hours) as they were very spirited horses. We certainly must acknowlege the hand of God in it. Some people think it was a sunstroke, but we cannot tell.

Mattie and Junius got very thirsty while coming home, and nearly gave out, though she carried Junius a little way. The childrens story is very touching. they prayed for their Pa, and that they would see someone to go and help him, and after a long time Junius said, "Mattie! why dont the Lord come down?" I asked him next day what he did. he said, "nothing only I told the Lord Pa was dead, and asked him to save him." They feel confident that the Lord sent Br Berry, as he was hunting horses. I have given you the details as near as I can. If rumors of it reach St. George, I wish you would please to read this to Grandma Romney that she may not feel uneasy, and think it is worse than it is.

Dear Parents I fear you will be out of patience with me for writing such a scribble, when I can write better but I am so hurried. there has'nt been any mail for a long time, but I live in hopes there will be again sometime.

I am in a quandary to know whether or not I have answered Thomas's last letter, but I think I did. Please give my love to all the dear ones, and believe me, your loving daughter .

C. J. Romney

Junius has gone back with his Pa and Aunty [Hannah], and Thomas [age 6] is still there   he likes to chase calves.

Mother, I do believe I have got one of the sweetest babies that ever was. he is as white as can be, and is such a big, fat, boy.

12"   have just got a note from Isabell [Hannah's daughter, age 19]. Miles is feeling much better. got there all right.

I am sending you the first paper issued in St. John.[66]

29" Aug 1882

Dear Father & Mother   I received your kind and welcome letter dated Aug 6" yesterday, and was very pleased to get it, though it caused me feelings of sorrow and sadness, to know that you were both sick, and also of George's sickness. poor boy! he [has] the same failing that both his Father & Mother are troubled with. too much ambition for his strength; he must take better care of himself or he will be an old man, broken down, and worn out, before he should, and Thomas too. as for Charles he is more like myself. I think we both have the happy faculty of taking care of ourselves, and not working too hard. we are so near alike in this that he cant take any exceptions to my saying this. however I think we all ought to take as much care as we can of the health and strength which God has given us. I wish I could convert you all to this fact, so that you would not work too hard. it worries me a great deal. I have written quite often. I dont think you get all my letters. I sent you a paper about two weeks ago, one of the first printed in St John. I hope you got it.

Please give my love to Aunt Mariette. I got her letter a week ago. shall write as soon as I can.

Remember me kindly to Br [William] and Sr [Maria Morrel] Squire. (has'nt she been to the city this summer?) also Sr [Eliza] Lund. Br [William] Trost, and all old friends.

We have been having very warm weather and not much rain.

We hav'nt heard from Nutrioso for two weeks. I feel anxious to hear, and to see Thomas and Junius. chasing calves is just the kind of work that suits Thomas.

Br [George] & Sister [Ann] Jarvis and Josephine [Jarvis][67] and Sr [Margaret] Peck called to see me over a week ago. they were all well. had been to Nutrioso on a visit. Br. and Sr. Jarvis talked of starting home in a month.

We are all well, and I hope and trust this will find you all the same.

Annie began school yesterday, with 15 scholars. I think she will soon have more.

I see Br Jensen is just hitching up to start to Woodruff so must send this over or shall miss the opportunity of sending this.

I think the crops here are pretty good. that is some of them beans, squash etc. are doing well. but the worms are very bad in the corn, and bugs have almost destroyed the potato crop.

I havent tasted but a few messes since I came to Arizona, but get other vegetables occasionally. I miss the fruit very much. my mouth fairly waters for a good bunch of grapes a peach or pear, but more than all I want to see Father and Mother, especially when I know they are sick, but then you have both had the same trial to pass through, so I must not murmur. may God bless and preserve you and give you health and strength is the prayer of your loving daughter

C.J.R.

I feel anxious to hear how Br [Robert] and Sr [Anna] Parker are.

Sept 24" 1882
St Johns   Apache Co   Arizona

Dear Father & Mother   I have not had a line from any of you for three or four weeks. the last was dated Aug 6 and I beleive I have written twice since I got yours, and have been very anxious to hear again, as you were both poorly at last accounts. I do hope you are enjoying better health now.

We are all well who are here. Miles was here over a week and went back last monday. he is feeling better, but is much thinner than he was two or three months ago. he expects to be done at Nu-trioso in a few weeks. the folks there were all well when he came down. Isabell [Hannah's daughter, age 19] is teaching school there, and has about 30 scholars. she is to get $100.00 for the term. Annie is teaching school here and has 35 scholars, but will likely increase as winter approaches.

I have all my children with me again. Caroline [age 8] and Thomas [age 6] are both going to school. Thomas was gone from me over two months, and Junius [age 4] five weeks; their Pa said they had been very good boys, and Thomas had got to be quite a worker. he has kept wood chopped very well for the last week.

I took Caroline and had her Baptised and Confirmed, last Fast day. It seems strange, that I have a daughter 8 years old.[68]

Park has made some progress in his little life. he can now sit alone. he will be six months old tomorrow. he is a beautiful big, baby. his Pa says he is the prettiest boy and got the ugliest name of any he has ever had, but I dont agree with him in that for I like his name. I think too that Ernest [Hannah's son, age 4] was just as pretty a baby. but of course I let him have it his own way. I wish I could get babys likeness taken to send you.

Dear Parents if it is ever so that you can, I wish you could each have your likeness taken for me so that I could have it framed. if I ever can get the money to spare I shall send you some for that pur-pose for I know that you have not the means to spend for it.

I do hope George is well again and that all those who are dear to me are well and happy.

I see by the papers that the lines are being drawn pretty tight. I was pleased to read the Address of the First Presidency to the Latter Day Saints.[69] I hope will all hold out faithful to the end.

I am often reminded of the early days of Dixie, though people havent began to pass through what they did there, yet many have become discouraged, and returned to Utah, or gone to other settlements, some with the pretense of only staying a year. but I think it doubtful if they return.

It is almost meeting time so I must close. last Sunday old Br Wilkins who used to live at Washington, was speaking. (he lives 15 miles up the creek) we also had a good discourse from Br M. P. Romney.[70]

Sr [Ella] Udall had a wee daughter born a little more than a week ago. they are both doing well. Ida [Hunt Udall] has been with her for more than a month. God bless you is the ernest prayer of your loving daughter.

C.J.R.

Conference will convene at Snow Flake next saturday. There is to be a Convention held here next tuesday to nominate County Officers Our people were defrauded of their right at the last election. I dont know how they will come out this time. If Br [Henry] Platt should inquire about Will [Platt] he is working at carpenter work with Miles at Nutrioso

25" Sept 1882
St. Johns
Mrs. Mariette S. Calkin

Dear Friend   Your welcome letter of July came duly to hand. I have been tardy, but will now try and answer.

You had not been very well. I hope you are quite well again by this time.

We had some hard rainstorms the week before last, which were followed by some heavy frosts,—making it quite like winter for a few days, and killing the corn crops, melon and cucumber vines etc. and causing quite a loss to farmers. they are very busy now hauling up the fodder etc.

There has'nt been near so much rain this season, the spring was more backward, and the frost has come earlier. still some few have made quite a success of their gardens. (the water can be good on the lower lots, but not so high as ours till the city ditch is made.)

Old Uncle Sam Adair, (who used to live at washington) and wife live here with their granddaughter and husband.[71]

The old gentleman is quite feeble, but he has devoted his time to tending their garden, and has raised a great abundance of vegetables, for themselves and to sell. I hear they have put down 80 gallons of cucumber pickles, beside selling large quantities. they have also made about 100 gallons of preserves off their garden, substituting melons for the fruit generally used for this purpose. they answer very well. I have been busy all day making a few preserves of green musk, and watermelons, and scalding, and cutting off the cob, a little corn to dry.

There is a little molasses being made this season, but I hav'nt learned how much. we got some skimmings the other day, and made the children some molasses candy, the first in Arizona. it did'nt seem any trouble for them to get to liking it again.

I think there are some very good people here, though some have grown faint-hearted and returned to their leeks and onions.[72] of course there are many trials, incident to the settleing of a new country, and I suppose this place has been harder than some other parts of Arizona, but I am satisfied that the Latterday Saints, who honorably fill their missions, will be better off in the end, than those who disobey counsel. Miles has bought a place at Nutrioso, and I think it likely that Hannah will live there most of the time. in this I think he has made a wise move as he must have some employment for the boys, and lay a better foundation for a living for so large a family as ours is. We dislike being separated so far but it seems unavoidable at present. Some have said that they thought because Miles has moved part of his family, that he will eventually leave here. but I think he is made of the rong kind of stuff for that, for he has never yet backed out of a mission, and I hope he never will.

Dear Friend I have sent you a fan that I have made from the feathers of a wild turkey. it is in a parcel directed to Father. would go direct to Kanab, and have to wait there till there is a chance for it to go on. so it may be some time before you get it. I would like to be remembered to all inquiring friends, if I have any.

Maybe Father & Mother would like to look this over if you like. I remain as ever your loving friend.

C. J. Romney

Sr. [Mary Ellen Farley] Freeman sends kind regards. I think she, and husband are going to conference at SnowFlake this week.

Miss Emma Thompson

Dear Neice [Emma Cottam Thompson's daughter, age 13] I was much suprised to get a letter from you. I think your big sisters might do the same tell them.

I hope the childrens eyes are well again.

Tell your Ma, if she has forgotten my address, she can ask Grandpa for it, but I expect she keeps busy all the time. give my love to her and all the folks. kiss that little Joseph [Emma and William's son, age about 22 months] for me.

Thomas [age 6] is the only one of the children up yet   he says to tell you he is getting bigger, and chops wood for his Ma. that is what he has got up so early for. he and Caroline [age 8] are going to school to Aunt Annie. [He] is in the first reader and Caroline in the second. she was much pleased with the ribon you sent her. she wishes she had something to send you.

Thomas, Junius [age 4] and Claude [age 2] felt quite [disappointed]   they said no one every sends them anything.

Claude is a funny fellow   he asked me yesterday if he should get up on the house and break his neck, and the other day he wanted to know if I wanted him to go out doors and let the wind blow him away. he is always saying something funny. I know you would like to see Park [age about 6 months]. he is sitting alone the last two weeks.

Do all you can for Grandma. I am glad you live with her. tell Nelly [Thompson, age 11] to write. Your loving Aunt

C. J. Romney

Mattie [Carrie's daughter, age 12] would like to get a letter from you. I haven't seen her lately.

8" Nov 1882
St Johns

Dear Parents,   Another mail has come in, and no news from you. My anxiety is better imagined, than described. Why cant I hear how you are?

Miles will start to Nutrioso in the morning, he says tell you he would like to have you pay us a visit, and come and see the country.

Miles came down quite unexpectedly this time. he had been registered and was going to vote at Nutrioso, (the law is different from what it was in Utah, and they can vote anywhere in the county, not obliged to be in the town precinct I believe, as there is a great register which is kept at evry voting place, which contains the names of all the voters in the county.) but he saw the Great Register and discovered that his name was not on, scratched off through spite, so he came right down I expect to see about it. The Bp. [David K. Udall] wished him to stay, and be here on election day (yesterday) whether he could vote or not. accordingly he was the first one to present himself at the polls. he explained matters, and they concluded to let him vote on the strength of his certificate. but just then a mexican who speaks english got up and said he had good reasons to believe that Mr Romney was breaking the laws of the U.S. by being a polygamist. Miles very calmly said "that is none of your business sir, and something that you have nothing to do with. I am prepared to take the oath." so when they found they could'nt catch him on that, they concluded not to let him vote, on the ground that his name is not on the register. so he did'nt get to cast it after all. They then challanged the Bp. on the same grounds. but Miles told them to please to adminster the oath. this he took. so they let all the rest of our people vote without questioning. The Bp. kept Miles at the polls with him all day, and till 12 or 1 oclock last night counting the votes, and as we did'nt see him from early morning, we were nearly frightened out of our wits, as there were dozens of shots fired, and quite a hurrangh, right in the dead of night. we were very thankful when he got home all right. he says he never saw such a pantomine in his life. I think it a good job he was here [even] if he did'nt get to vote.

Some fears are entertained that the Democrats with our people will lose the day. but I hope not. that is I hope it will be overruled for the best. The Republican ticket got a few the most votes in this precinct. The Republican Nominee for Delegate was here. "Judge Porter." he was quite gentlemanly all day. but when he found that none of our people voted for him he became quite abusive to the Bp. (who wisely treated him with silent contempt) laying it to his influence, and the influence of G. Q. Cannon, and our leaders, he acted in a disgraseful manner, using some threats, telling what he would have done, had he got our support, and what he should do now when elected to Congress. he challanged Bishop Udall to a fight this morning. The Bp. is a cool headed man, or there might have been a scene.

This will give you a faint idea of the spirit of some of the people with whom we are surrounded. and also of the character of a man who is running for office. But the most we have to fear is ourselves, if we are wise and do right. God will protect us and defend our cause. I must close as it is getting late. Yours in love.

C. J. Romney

9" Thursday night   St. Johns, Ariz.   Beloved Parents,   As I hav'nt posted my letter yet I will add a few lines. I was much pleased this afternoon at receiving a letter from you, but sorry to hear you are still so poorly. Dont you think Father that you could get some medecine that would help you. I was afraid you were having those bad spells again. Do take care of yourself Dear Father, Mother worries I know to see you work so hard. Poor Grandma. I am sorry she is so feeble, but I suppose we cant expect anything else at her advanced age. And Grandma Romney is still having the chills is she. Poor soul she must be nearly used up.

I am pleased that Br [George] and Sr. [Ann Pryor] Jarvis have arrived safe, and Sr. [Maria Morrel] Squire. please give my kind regards to them all.

I am astonished to hear of Sarah Elizabeth [Smith Noall, Catharine's cousin] having a baby. I had'nt even heard of her being married. if you have sent me word I never got the letter. when you write again please tell me when, and to whom. did she marry Sr Squires nephew, young Noals.[73]

I am glad the things got there all right. but I am afraid it is too late for the fans to be useful. I did write and tell you I got the things you sent by Ida Hunt [Udall]. but perhaps you never got my letter. I was very grateful for them. The boys were delighted with the cards Emma sent them. I will answer her letter soon.

Miles started early this morning. Kind love to Aunt Mariette. Sr. [Eliza] Lund and all our folks. and keep a large portion for yourselves. Praying God to Bless you I remain in love

C.J.R.

The first issue of the Orion Era, *edited by Miles P. Romney, appeared on January 6, 1883. Its tone was one of general good humor, and it promoted local business.*[74]

15" Feb. 1883
St John

Dear Father & Mother I have been answering Charles letter and will enclose a few lines to you, though if it is brief, you must please excuse me, as I hardly know how to find time to write lately. so many little ones to make, mend, and care for, keep my time pretty well occupied; but as Miles sends you the paper [*Orion Era*], of course you will keep posted in St John matters, if I dont get to write often. but I assure you—if my letters are less frequent, I dont think of you any the less often.

Miles is working on the house today, but it is very little time that he gets to work for himself. in consequence of his not getting time to propperly brace our new house, it came near blowing over, last week, in the terrific wind storm, which we had, it moved 3 or 4 inches off the foundation, but he persevered until he secured it. Annies bed room, which is made of lumber, came near blowing over the same day, while Miles was away at the office, and we had to get some of the brethren to fix it. at the same time, a fire had started in our woodpile, but we got it put out without doing any damage.

Miles health is better, though, his cough troubles him sometimes, and he had one bad spell with his heart about a week ago. the first for a long time. The children are all well except Claude [age 3]. he has a cold and fever today. I feel very thankful for the health we all enjoy.

Hannah has not been very well for a few days, though she keeps around and is better again.

Park [11 months] has got three teeth.

Caroline [age 8] has been trying to write you a letter and is very anxious for me to send it, as she says "Grandpa" told her to write her first letter to him.

I dont think you can read it, so I will interpret it on the other side of this.

I must conclude with kind love to all relations and friends, and a large portion for yourselves. I remain your loving daughter.

Catharine J. Romney

Love to Aunt Mariette, Sr. Lund, etc.

Dear Grandpa and Grandma

When I left St George you told me to write, so I am trying to learn to write as best I can.

I am going to school to Aunt Annies.

Thank you for the nice new dress you sent me. I think it is very pretty.

We are all well. Good bye from Caroline.

Caroline would have learned to write better, but they have not had desks for them to write at school.

Apr. 2" 1883
St. Johns   Apache Co   Arizona

Dear Father & Mother   I wrote to you a week ago but neglected to post it so you will doubtless think me very careless. But I have been very busy lately and have had a bad cold and cough. and all the children have had colds. also Alice [Annie's daughter, age 23 months] has been sick for three or four weeks. I think she must have the rheumatism in her legs as one of them has been quite swolen, and she screams whenever they are moved or touched   we fancy they have been a little less painful the last day or two. I hope the poor little soul will soon be well again. she has a good appetite, and seems to feel tolerable well, as long as she lies perfectly still. she is a sweet, lovable, child and such a talker. School will be out this week.

Conference is just over. It has been well attended. there was not room for all. It was a splendid conference. Apostles [Brigham] Young and [Heber J.] Grant were with us. We had considerable company, as also did most of the people, as there were a great many people here from other settlements. yesterday we had. Brs. Young, Grant, Smith, and several others to dinner. and then company all night and a breakfast this morning. but they are all gone now. They are holding meeting at the Meadows today 8 miles below   quite a number went from here. Miles & Hannah went. The people of this out of the way land seem to rejoice to have some of the Apostles to see them.

Dear Parents I must acknowledge the receipt of some dried fruit but I cant tell who has sent them. but whoever it is, I hope they will accept of my thanks and gratitude. we can certainly appreciate them, both the apples and grapes. they are very nice. I can't tell who directed it unless it was Rachel [Cottam, George's wife]. I am not certain that I know her handwriting.

Baby [Park, age 1] is doing nicely. though he has a very bad cold just now. he has seven teeth. he dosnt show much signs of walking very soon.

Caroline [age 8] and Thomas [age 6] seem to be learning pretty well at school. Caroline is in the third reader, and Thomas will likely go in when another term starts.

How are Sr. [Eliza] Lund and Aunt Mariette [Calkin]? please tell the latter I hope to answer her letter before long.

Mother, How is your Relief society getting along now. Is Sr. [Anna] Ivins still President? please give my kind regards to her and Sr. [Minerva] Snow when you see them and to all old friends. Do Father and you still go to the Temple?

I often think how I should love to come home on a visit, but then I think how I should hate to part again and then I have so many little children I should'nt know how to either leave or bring them, so I know not when we shall meet again, but I have faith that we shall sometime, if God will.

I trust that you may both be spared many years yet.

Sr. Ramsey called in today   she is always on the go. full of business. I must now conclude. With kind love I remain your affection daughter

Catharine J. Romney

26" Apr. 1883
St. Johns

Dear Father & Mother   I was so very much pleased to receive your welcome letters of Apr. 7" and 9". It seems a treat to get letters from Emma, and the boys, but after all there is nothing that can quite fill the place of one from Father or Mother. Oh if I could only hear of you all being well and hearty again. I feel so sorry to hear of the Scarlet Fever being in St. George. poor Rachel [George Cottam's wife] she seems to have a hard time of it, with her little family. but I trust their lives will all be spared. I got a letter from George over two weeks ago, and havent answered it yet. as I have been quite miserable for nearly two weeks. I have had a bad time with my face and gumbs. my face has been swelled for about two months. Sr Ramsey took two teeth out for me last week, and Miles has got Sr. [Rizpah] Gibbons to steam me and give me an emetic two days this week and I think it has done me good. she has also been putting Alice [Annie's daughter, age 2] in a pack with wild sage tea, and giving her emetics the last five days, and we feel quite encouraged as she seems to be improving. if you see Sr [Ann Cannon] Woodbury you might tell her please. Annie wishes me to give her love to you. also Hannah. she has been washing, and I havent seen her today. but she had a bad headache yesterday.

Miles is shingling the home now what time he gets. he has got 8,000 of the shingles and expects the rest in a few days. he has just been telling me. I must hurry and get well so he can move us up soon.

I weaned the baby about ago for fear he would nurse my sickness and not be so well. he has done pretty well. he is a good baby. He has seven teeth only.

Caroline [age 8] and Thomas [age 7] can carry nearly all the water we use now as the well has been fixed handier. this is quite a help. and Thomas cuts all the wood we burn, almost. he has been carrying shingles today, his Pa says he is a brick to work   he and George [Hannah's son, age 8] have carried 3,000, up on the house today.

Junius [age 5] and Claude [age 3] spend all the time they can up at Annie's, especially when their Pa is at work there.

Dear Father. I am glad you are pleased with, and interested in the "Orion Era." Miles labors hard to make it interesting and useful. He says, tell you he should certainly stop sending you the paper if you sent subscription for it especially after your kindness in sending so many things as you have. I[t] seems to me that you will feel as if we are nearer together since you can read the local news of our town so often. Do you get them regularly. Miles says he has never missed sending it. Sends his kind regards.

I feel very sorry to hear of Grandma being still sick. Please give my love to Sr Seegmiller and all old friends, and neighbors.

Br [Joseph Hyrum] and Sr [Mary Ann Doxey] Watkins have not come back, and I hardly think they will.

So Charles has gone to Salt Lake for the summer? I expect you miss his help. Br Platt and family got here all right a[s] well as usual. I nearly tired Angie and Isabell out, with asking questions the first two or three days.[75] they have bought a place. Will [Platt] has rented one, he and our boys, Miles [Hannah's son, age 13] and Gaskell [Hannah's son, age 11], are up at the ranch, fencing. Good bye. From your loving daughter.

C.J.R.

It seemed so good to see Br [Henry] Platt and the rest of the family.

The following was on a folded piece of paper with "Mr. Thomas Cottam, Senr." written on the outside.

Dear Father & Mother   I wrote to you a little over a week ago. have been quite sick since, (very unusual for me) am much better again. If I dont write soon dont worry as it will likely be lack of time. I am so behind with my work. I hope to get well and strong right away. I have had a carbuncle on my breast but it is getting better since Sr Ramsey lanced it. (please dont say anything about it.)

Alice [Annie's daughter, age 2] is getting some better. Poor Annie has had her hands full with the two of us. though Hannah does all she can. she and, Miles have staid all the time at nights, while I was so bad. The children have colds, but not bad. Hear of much damage by wind, in the States, and Utah. we have had considerable wind, but not hard enough to do damage, so feel thankful.

I think those who have been sick are mostly getting [better]. it has been a kind cold and distemper going around in St Johns. No deaths. Most always healthy before.

Beloved Parents I do hope you are well. You are not forgotten in my prayers I assure you. Do you manage to get what you need to make you comfortable? I dont feel able to write more now so will enclose this with Eleanors. With kindest love. Please give my love to all. Expect to get letters from some of the boys.

C.J.R.

June 3" 1883
St Johns

Dear Father & Mother,   I received your welcome letter of May 20", yesterday, and am very thankful to hear of your both being as well as you are.

It is such a blessing to be able to write, so that we may hear from each other once in a while. but of course you dont feel uneasy at all if I dont write quite so often, since you get the paper, as you get what general news there is here. Doesnt it make you feel.as if we are not so far away?

Miles went to Round Valley yesterday so as to fill a missionary appointment today. he will return tomorrow. I am afraid he wont get rich at Editing a paper in this country. but as long as that is what he was requested to do, I suppose, it is all right. but I am thankful to be able to say that we have the necessaries of life, and are very comfortable for a new country. though we should have been much farther ahead, if it had not been for that unfortunate mail business, and Miles being laid up so long with his thumb, but we must not complain if we can only have health; and I do feel to thank the Lord that we are all better.

We have had this spring, (what is unusual for us) a very sickly time in our family. Miles has had one very bad spell with his lungs.

Hannah was very sick for more than two weeks but is much better, and around again; Alice is much better than she was though her legs are still bad. Annie packs her in cold water nearly very day, and it seems to help her. Annie has a gathered finger, poor girl she has had too much to do with so many of us being sick. but I am glad that I got well before her finger got bad. I was sick, or rather not well, for about two months. thought I was going to have a gatherd breast and tried to lacken it for two or three weeks, when it proved to be a carbuncle. and I did'nt stop till I had four, but they are well now. I dont think I should have had so many if I had known what it was and drawn it to a head, in the first place.

Br [James] Keat was down last week. he ate supper and breakfast with us. seems to like this country very well. Br Platts folks are about as usual. he and Henry have been up with Will to Kitchen to put in some seeds, fence the land etc. Sr [Almeda Jane] Platt dosnt feel contented here, but I dont know whether she would feel so anywhere else or not. I havnt seen Angie [Platt] lately, but when I did she wished to be remembered to you all. when any of you write you might mention how her folks are, and then I can tell her.

We moved up in our new house while I was sick. it is not near finished, but does very well for summer and Miles expects to get it nearly finished by winter, if all is well. I must give you a brief description of it. it is a frame building, clapboarded on the outside and lined with adobies. faces the east, with one door and two windows in front, has two large rooms downstairs, and two upstars, and he intends building a dining room and two small rooms on the back of it. we cook in the little room, that Hannah lived in all winter. Our house is right on a hill and we have a lovely view of the town and surrounding country. Good bye. God bless you. From your loving daughter

C. J. Romney

I will try to answer Georges letter soon. Please give my love to all the folks. also to the folks in the city when you write.

July 5, 1883

Dear Father and Mother   received your very welcome letter of June 10", yesterday. Oh how pleased I was to hear from you once again though sorry to hear that Mother had been sick again. I often wish that I could know just how you are, when I am going to bed at night, but perhaps it is better that I cant as I should only worry the more when you are sick.

I hope Emma is safely through her sickness and well again. please give my love to her as well as to all the rest of the folks.

I find by your letter that you work as hard as ever. I do wish you could both take it a little easier.

You said in your letter you would enclose a letter from Charles to me. but I guess [*illegible*] though I fancy I am yankee enough to do some pretty good guessing. he speaks of some Mrs Johnson, whom I suppose is his future Mother-in-law, and of a certain young lady whom he calls Beata. this I believe to be the future Mrs. Charles Cottam; am I right?[76] What has been the matter with his knee? If you come across my letter please forward it when you write again.

I had been wondering for a long time why he did'nt write to me, and had come to the conclusion that he had found some pleasanter way of spending his leisure time. I am at a loss to know when and how he got acquainted but may be it is'nt for me to know.

Park [age 1] doesnt walk alone yet. but Thomas [age 7] and Junius [age 5] have hold of his arms, walking him away down the hill, and I am sitting by the window, and can scarcely write for thinking and looking out at them. he is a sweet pretty boy, and looks cute in his little green gingham dress and panties. but then I am his mother you know so must be excused for thinking so, though I am not the only one.

Br Platt and Henry [Platt] have been received as members of this ward so I suppose they intend staying. I suppose the women folks are not very well, and never go out. I have only seen Angie [Platt, Henry's wife] once since a few days after they came.

Monday 9" July. Dear Parents. it is over a week since I commenced this letter.

When I was writing before Miles and Annie were away at conference. Annie was so worn out with waiting on her children so long that we thought as they were so much better, she ought to have an out. They were gone four days: and enjoyed themselves very much. they saw many old acquaintances. Heber Jarvis[,] El. [Ellis] & Annie Wiltbank, Br [James] & Sr [Verbena ("Rena") Christofferson] Keat, both of whom were sick. she doesnt like this country. Wants to go back. thinks there is no place like St. George.

Annie saw Christiana Riding that used to be, that lost her husband a few weeks ago. she has had a baby born since he died. Poor woman. she is to be pitied with such a helpless family of little ones on her hands. five I believe. I hear Sr [Louisa Wilden] Burt is dead. what family of little motherless children he must have. I feel to sympathize very much with him.

You will see an account of the celebration of the 4" here if you get the paper all right. Judge French and a good many strangers were present. We had a splendid time. I dont know when I ever enjoyed myself better. the singing and speeches were excellent.

I fancy the old Judge looks very much like Br Jackson used to. he reminds me of him very much, just about as stout etc. The Grear boys who were indicted for the murder of a mexican at the time Father [Nathan] Tenney was shot last summer, were acquitted yesterday. The court has not got through yet.

The programme for the 24" was read last sunday. I see my name is down for a speech in behalf of the Relief Society. Miles advises me to write and read an address, but I scarcely feel equal to the task and dont know what I shall do yet. for I was never up before the public in my life, except to represent the society in the ladies conference, or something like that, and then was nearly frightened to death.

Hannah's health keeps very poor. last monday was her birthday and Annie and I got a very nice supper for her in honor of the occasion, for a surprise, just our own family and Will & Isabell. we invited the Bishop [David K. Udall] and Ida [Hunt Udall] and her sister. (Sr [Ella] Udall has gone to stay with her sister at the ranch, for a few weeks.) but they had company come themselves.

We spent a very plesant evening at Br [Willard] Farres last Thursday evening. his birthday. they are very nice people.

I saw Sr [Rizpah] Gibbons today, she is pretty well.

Miles has built a large room on the back of our house for a kitchen and though it is all unfinished we are quite comfortable now.

Miles and all of us are tolerable well at present. I trust you are the same. Love to all. I must say good night as it is getting late.

Yours in love.

C. J. Romney

St. Johns   Apache Co.   Arizona
Mr. Charles S. Cottam

Dear Brother,   Your welcome favor of July 25″ came to hand a week ago. Am pleased that you dont forget to write to me. Do please to keep writing as often as you can. that I may know how Father and Mother are.

I feel very bad to hear of their poor health, also that Aunt Mariette is so poorly.

How are Br [William] Frost and wife getting along? Do you ever see Henry Atkins and wife [Selina Richardson Atkins]?

When ever any of you write I wish you would please to mention Annies folks how they are getting along etc. as she is always anxious to hear like myself. How does John [Woodbury, Annie's brother] look after his long absense.

Any news about our old friends, and neighbors, is interesting. I think if I were there and you away I could find much to write about, but then I know how busy you all are. how are all the young folks? are there any more weddings in prospect. How are Sr [Eliza] Lund and family?

The weather is very different from last year. we have only had a few heavy rains, such as we used to have almost daily last season, so that the grass is not near so good as last season, though it is better for some things. farmers are getting their grain stacked without getting it spoiled with the rain.

I must close or I may lose the chance of sending this. From your loving sister.

Catharine J. Romney

9" August 1883
St Johns

Dear Father & Mother, Brothers & Sister   I dont feel to have time to write to each of you seperately unless I had letters to answer, so will write to you all together. On the 27" of last month, Friday morning early, Miles and I, with Br and Sr [Olive] Moffett (Rachel's cousin) started on a trip to Bush Valley. it had been raining hard in the night, and was raining a little in the morning, just enough to make it pleasant. We arrived at Round Valley about 5" P.M.   stopped at the Bishops [Peter J. Christofferson], who is brother to Sr [Rena] Keat. Br [James] Keat was sick with the chills. he asked Miles to "lay hands" on him, and he had'nt had any more as we came down, and was better, we had quite a long chat with them. Sr [Rena] Keat was quite homesick, and low spirited, and determined to go back to St George. went to see Christiana Riding Asey. I hear that she started to Utah this week. I never saw nicer looking vegetables, than they had in that settlement. Next morning we resumed our journey leaving Sr Moffett at Round Valley to visit with friends. got to the upper settlement on the Nutrioso before noon. ate dinner at Katie Pace's. they were all well. then started up the canyon for Bush Valley, distant ten miles, and arrived there late in the afternoon. Oh! how I would like to have you all there to admire the beauties of the country with me. I never saw anything half so grand, and beautiful. just imagine the road winding through a narrow canyon, with high mountains towering on either side, covered with the greenest grass, and the tallest, straightest pines, and quakenasps, the latter with their white bark, making a plesant contrast to their more sombre hued brothers of the forest. these interspersed with the grand, stately old oaks, and the beautiful flowers blooming about their roots, a clear creek deep down by the road side, overhung with green bushes, and grown up with grass and flowers, completed a picture long to be remembered. and I cant help but think since that Miles must have had a great amount of patience, to listen, and reply to my oft repeated exclamations of wonder and delight. for you see he has been there so many times, but he enjoyed seeing me enjoy it so much. however it came to an end as evrything else in this world does. We stayed with Bp. [Edward A.] Nobles, (nephew to Br Snow) who did all in their power to make our visit agreeable. next morning he took us in his team all over the valley, up in the timber and through the fields. Sr [Ann Jane Peel] Nobles and I got our arms full of flowers. the men kept getting out and gathering them until we had all we could hold, and crowded the babies out, till their Pa's had to take them. We had about 25 varieties of flowers, many that I had never seen before. Father the wall flowers would almost rival yours at the tabernacle. there were geraniums, and as beautiful larkspurs as I ever saw in the gardens at home.

After a good meeting, we rode down to Br Colemans to supper. had a chat with Br Copelon and son, and on monday morning started home again. took dinner with Will Lund, and saw lots of old friends. Br [Harrison Grey Otis] & Sr [Margaret Reed Angier] Peck, Lyman [Peck], George [Peck] and wife [Barbara Ellen Bryce Peck], Amelia [Peck Bigelow] and husband, Sr. Copelon, (who inquired about you all, and especially William.) Martha Campbell as used to be. Charlie and Maggie De Freiz, and El. & Annie Wiltbank who were there on a visit, and waited to see us. I was much pleased to see them all and had a good time.

They all seem to be doing well, and have a prospect of good crops and a chance of making good homes.

We got home tuesday night having had a splendid time.

We are all well except baby [Park]. he has been quite sick for a week past, teething. Kind love to yourselves and old friends. From yours in love.

C.J.R.

2" Sept 1883
St Johns
Mr. George T Cottam

Dearest Brother Your last welcome missive came to hand last week, with a few lines from Father. I feel very thankful that Father & Mother were better. George I feel it my duty to lecture you a little. Dont you know you are doing wrong by working so hard? havent you seen the effects of overwork in Fathers case? Dont my Brother make an old man of yourself, before your time. Dont think you are doing a good part by your family by overtaxing yourself. they will need you for a great many years, and you wont last out if you are not more prudent.

I am waiting anxiously for Ada's [George and Rachel's baby daughter] likeness I have heard so much of her beauty. I want to see if she comes up to my expectations. So you are back home with Father & Mother. now if you only had me there to torment you I suppose it would seem quite like old times. But I suppose Rachel is home again by this, and I suppose you would welcome her back again, for no matter how we enjoy being with Father & Mother there is yet one dearer than all. Is it not so? No place like home.

Pleas[e] write me all the news. What has become of Br [William] Trost? there are lots of old friends whom I never hear mentioned.

Br [Henry] Platt has gone to Snow Flake with Miles & Annie. Miles had to be there to fill a missionary appointment yesterday. they started friday, and expect to be back tomorrow night.

I went to Bush Valley last month with Miles. it is a most beautiful country, appears to be no end to grass, a splendid place for dairying. Br Daly from Harrisburg, who married Mary Wilson, lives there, also Br Coleman who used to live at Upper Kanab, and Joe Scott, old lady Lewis's son. I saw him in meeting but did'nt get to speak to him. I hear that he is a very good respectable man.

The St George folks at Nutrioso inquired about you, especially Will Lund. we had a plesant visit with them. they are doing well there and have good prospects. George Peck looks the very picture of a happy husband, but poor Lyman [Peck] looks rather disconsolate. his wife that used to be is married again (so she said) and gone to live down at Salt River. her Sister Jane is married and lives at Round Valley, where her parents live, and her sister Lucy lives here. she married Mr. Barich, the Probate Judge. they have had two children, and lost them both one died the week before last. Joe Lewis who used to work with Thomas, was at Nutrioso, and El. [Ellis] and Annie Wiltbank. they talk of moving to Lunis Valley ten miles below Bush, where Br Copelon is going to live, as she dont like Round Valley.

The boys are just digging us a cellar. The grass has been good here this summer. we have three good cows. they do well. one of them is an extra good one.

I must conclude with kind love to Father, Mother, Rachel, Emma, Thomas, and all their folks, with a large portion for yourself.

I remain your loving sister.

C.J.R.

15" Oct 1883
St Johns

Dear Father & Mother   Br Peterson and family are going to start to St George tomorrow and Caroline [age 9] wants to send the things she made for the fair. the wall packet she is sending to her Grandpa and Grandma, and the ruffle to her Aunt Emeline [Thomas P. Cottam's wife]. as she has not had a specimine of her work. she washed it herself so it isnt a very good color. she was going to make some pin cushions for Aunt Emma and Rachel, but the folks are starting sooner than we expected so I had to finish them.

I had to make a small basket of fruit only a taste for Father & Mother. I am afraid there wont be enough to divide with the boys and girls. I hope it wont spoil with the trip. I am also sending my ring. Emma said if I would William would mend it for me.[77]

I sent you a boquet for your vaces by Br [Lorenzo] Browns Granddaughter. I hope you got them all right. I dont forget your birthdays, [even] if I am so far away.

I wish I had something nice to send you.

Your loving daughter.

C.J.R.

23" Nov 1883
St Johns

Dear Father & Mother   I have written two or three times since I got a letter from you, and I ought not to spare time to write today, but I feel rather homesick from not hearing for so so long that I must scribble a few lines.

We are all well, but busy as usual.

Miles enlarged the paper last week, but he was not pleased with it as something was the matter with the ink, and it was quite blurred. I hope they will have better luck this week.

Caroline [age 9], George [Hannah's son, age 9], and Thomas [age 7], are going to school, and Annie will begin next week to teach night school at home three nights a week for the larger children, as they cant be spared from the type setting to go to day school. this larger paper is keeping them all very busy. they had to work till midnight two or three nights last week. There is soon to be a gentile paper started here. their handbills are out. they say they are "Anti Mormon", to the "hearts core."

I hope you still get our papers regularly.

Apostles [Brigham] Young and [Heber J.] Grant arrived here the night before last and held meetings yesterday, two in the day, and one in the evening. excellent meetings very good instructions were given.

I do wish Br [Erastus] Snow would come to Arizona again. I should so much like to see him.

I understand Br Brown got to Nutrioso about two weeks ago, but we have not heard any thing from him. Br [Harrison Grey] Peck came down, and has just started back but he didnt intend to come here when, he left home. Br and Sr Minerally have gone to Utah and were going to St George but I dont know whether they have been there yet or not. A young widow whom we are acquainted with from Round Valley has just started to St George. she is a very nice little woman, Mrs. Robinson whose husband was killed by the Apaches near Snow Flake a year ago last summer. she is going to marry a young man named of Peter Skousen. Peter Jarvis will likely be in St George by the time you get this. Sam [Jarvis] just called in and was telling us he has gone. Park [age 1] has just learned that he can run alone, and is so pleased that he wants to keep on the go all the time.

How are Grandma Romney, and Sr [Eliza] Lund, and Aunt Mariette, yourselves & all the folks. please give my love to all, and write as soon as convenient.

From your loving daughter

C. J. Romney

9" Dec. 1883
St Johns
Mrs. Eleanor C. Jarvis

Beloved Friend   I hope you will excuse me for being so dilatory in answering your last letter, and though I often think, and talk about you, my time is pretty well taken up.

This is sunday evening, conference is just closed. have had a good time, lots of company. Aunty [Elizabeth Hill] Swapp is here, also Miss [Mattie] Williams and ever so many men, Bp. [George C.] Williams, Bp. [Edward A.] Nobles, Bp. Holden, Br. Perkins, Br. Coleman, and Br. Heywood, as well as several others, off and on. so we have had a jolly time. it is really amusing to see their beds spread out and hear their joking and laughing, after they get to bed. Hannah gave up her room for the use of the men, and she and Sr Swapp, and Miss Williams, all stay in Annies room, so we have managed to make them all comfortable and had a good time. Swapps like Lunis Valley very much.

I suppose Heber [Jarvis] is in St George by this time, or nearly there.

Br. & Sr. Brown have been down to Conference

Angie Platt has a baby a few weeks old, her children are not very well.

There is considerable sickness just now among the children, measels, and bad colds. Br [Ammon] Tenney lost a baby yesterday and has another child very sick.

Sr. [Mary Jane Berry] Hales one of John Berrys daughters, had a still born baby this week.

Claude [age 3] has been having the measels, but is nearly well again. Hannah's two youngest have had colds and seem to feel quite badly.

13″ Dear Eleanor, Annie is at the Office correcting proof today. she is pretty well *considering*.[78] The children all have bad colds, and as cross as they know how to be, but no more of them have the measels yet. We got a fire place up a week before Conference, which has made us very comfortable. I dont know how we could have got along with company and the children sick, without it.

Junius [age 5] was just now throwing a rock with a sling and struck Claude in the mouth with it cutting his lips so he is feeling quite badly. so with one thing and another I expect I shall have to make my letter rather short.

Our Ladies Conference was slimly attended on account of sickness among the children, but we had very good instructions. we have an excellent President in Sr Smith [Emma S. Smith, wife of Jesse N. Smith].

Sr Ramsey is kept very busy.

The Outsiders here are as full of the Devil as it is possible to be. that is'nt bad talk is it? The Board of Supervisors have united our school district, with theirs, without our knowledge or consent. Our people will contest the matter I think we dont feel like sending our children to teachers of their choosing, nor yet pay taxes without receiving any of the appropriation.

But it is time to get supper so I must quit with kind love to all.

From your loving Friend

C. J. Romney

Dec. 30 1883
St Johns

My Dear Father & Mother   I recieved a few lines from you, with
one from Charles, written just at Conference time.[79] I dont wonder
Father that you had'nt time to write much, with all that you told me
of having to do. I think it is sadly too much for one person. I should
hate to have to clean, and fill 43 lamps to say nothing of all the rest
of the work. it seems to me it would be much better for them to get
some one to help you now, than to have you use yourself up and
then have to depend entirely on some one, who is not reliable. now
I consider this some of my business, as I want to see you again
sometime.

baby [Park] wont lie in bed without me in the morning, so I am
sitting up in bed writing, to keep him in till it is time to get up.
Claude [age 3] has just stuck his head up and says he wants a letter.

We have been having very fine weather. Christmas day was almost like springtime. We had a very plesant Christmas. on Christmas eve the boys and girls, Minnie [Hannah's daughter, age 15],
Mattie [Carrie's daughter, age 13], Willie [Carrie's son, age 15] and
Miles [Miles A., Hannah's son, age 14] went to the dance, and we got
the rest to bed, and filled their stockings (twelve of them), and then
Miles and I went down to the dance a little while. in the morning
the children had a happy time. George [Hannah's son, age 9] and
Thomas [age 7] each got a tin horse, and the little boys goats and
sheep, and their Pa amused them for a long time, by pointing out
to them their good points showing that they must be blooded animals and telling them which colt would be worth the most if they
had one.

We had Will [Platt] and Isabell [Romney Platt] here to dinner and
Br Anderson, as he has no one to get dinner for him. you know Miles
always had somebody of this kind, to invite to our Christmas dinners, so Br Anderson has taken the place of Br [William] Frost. How
are the old gentleman and his wife get along?

You will see by reading the Editorials in the "Era", how the Devil
is raging here among the outsiders. they have united our school District with theirs, so as to get all the appropriation, or compel us to
send our children to teachers of their choosing. they have a young
lady from the east teaching for them. we have Br [Willard] Farr and
Ida Hunt [Udall]. The doctor has threatened to have Sr Ramsey
fined, for going around doctoring, without having a diploma. They

will no doubt go to the full length of their rope. There is a comfort in knowing that "they can go just so far, and no farther."

I dont know why the gentile paper is so long in coming out. I understood that the Editor run off once, and they raised $700, and went to Holbrook and induced him to come back.

Dear Parents, we have had four weeks of sickness, most of the children have had the measels, and nearly well again.

I am worse ashamed of my writing, every time I write. I do it in too big a hurry, and a poor pen besides, but I flatter myself that you will be glad to get one if it is ever so poorly written. I am as ever your loving daughter.

Catharine J. Romney

10" Jan 1884
St Johns

Dear Father & Mother   I am expecting a letter all the time, but hav'nt had one since the one I got from Charles with a note in from Father.

Please tell the boys to be sure and put the small cross on the envelope; as Miles says he dont like to open letters which dont belong to him, though I assure him I have no secrets. he prefers my reading my letters first at any rate.

The "Apache Chief," the Anti Mormon paper of St Johns, started last week. It is a very weak feeble thing to what we expected, considering it has all the Gentiles to back it (four lawyers, one doctor, and a good many merchants, and saloon keepers.) He says in his Editorial, he hopes to be able to support his limited family with his paper when his contemporary can support such a numerous one." the paper altogether is so weak and contemptible, that I dont think the "Era" will reply to it at all, or take any notice of it, unless there is something of more importance, than in the last.

Dear Parents, last monday was my birthday. 29 years old you know. but as it was our "washday", I thought we would wash, though Annie did'nt like the idea of us washing on my birthday.[80] (Annie and I do our washing together)   It was a lovely day, just like spring. Annie got the children dinner when they came from school, and we thought we would [not] stop to eat ours till we got through, we always send Miles dinner. so presently Hannah sent for us to come in the house, and we found that she had prepared a very nice dinner of which we partook with relish. Hannah presented me with a nice wall pocket, and Annie, with a paper rack. in the evening as Miles had not yet come home, Minnie [Hannah's daughter, age 15] and I went to the joint meeting of the young men and ladies association, and when we came home Miles was there, and said he guessed he would go downtown a little while. in a few minutes he came back with a large chromo [chromolithograph], nicely framed, which he presented to me as a birthday present. It is called the "Surprise Party," and was indeed a surprise to me indeed. It is about 2 feet by 2-1/2 feet. it represents a winter night with snow on the ground, a beautiful country residence, with 4 or 5 sleighs full of people, who, are just alighting, with their baskets of picnic. a band of music is playing, and a lady has just come to the door. the lights are shining from the window, and all together it is a beautiful picture. Miles has always said since we came to Arizona that I must have some picture, as I did'nt bring mine with me.

How is Aunt Mariette getting along. give my love to her. I have not had a letter from her for nearly a year.

Eugene [Hannah's son, age 3 months] is just getting better of the measels.

Last tuesday, I went with some of the other sisters to the Meadows to hold a meeting with the Sisters. they still belong to our Relief Society, as there are not enough of them to have an organization of their own yet.

Please give my love to all, and keep a large portion for yourselves.

From your loving daughter.

C. J. Romney

[25 March 1884]

[*First part missing*] as there was here last night when those knives came. they were the centre of attraction till bed time. Oh such tickled boys Thomas [age 7] thinks there is nothing like his. he woud'nt begin to trade with his Pa.

This has been quite an exciting day. this morning, two gentiles were seen right in our town, digging post holes on Br Babbitts lot, with the intention of fencing, and jumping it. Br [Don C.] Babbitt and Br [Alexander] Nicoll came along, and tried to make them stop, when one of them struck Br Babbit and drawed his pistol on him. The Bishop and quite a number gathered, and began to build a fence, and dig up the posts of the outsiders, our folks also hauled a little board house that one of the brethren had built for a meat market, and placed it in the lot to try to keep it. by this time about a hundred gentiles and mexicans had gathered and did all they could to prevent our people from working there. a good many hard words and threats passed and one of our brethren, Br Malory was knocked down. this was almost more than he could stand, and some of our men had to take him off to prevent him from fighting. The Sherif finally came and ordered them all to leave. The gentiles left, but soon returned and tried to move the house away, when it fell to peices. They then pulled down the fence that our people had built, and proceeded to build another. Most of our men were in the field, so that only a few were on the ground. so they had to either give up; or resort to the use of firearms, and though many of the brethren felt that it was more than they could bear, the Bishop thought it better not to fight. Miles with all the rest feel that it is a hard pill to swallow. he has been up, to tell us not to feel alarmed. The field of operation is four or five blocks from our house, but we being on the hill can see quite plainly, and have watched the windows pretty closely ever since we heard of it. These are, in brief as near the facts as I have been able to get at them.

26" Afternoon.   When Minnie [Hannah's daughter, age 16] came home to dinner she brought us word that they have arrested nine or ten of our brethren. she thinks the Bishop is one of the number, but is not certain, however. I suppose they are out on bail as they were all at the office with Miles when she came away. I wont post this till I learn more about it. I dont know how Miles has escaped being arrested with the rest, as he took on a [illegible] part. I learn that the brethren will have their trial befor[e] a Justice of the Peace, next monday.

28"   just getting daylight. Annie had a fine son born at half past two this morning.[81] Please send the inclosed note to Sr. Woodbury [Annie's mother].

The Bishop has called on Miles to go to Salt Lake to represent our situation to the Presidency of the Church. he started last night about ten oclock and[?] take the cars at Holbrook. [Last part is missing.]

Church leaders in St. Johns had not complained of their situation to the authorities in Salt Lake City. But now six of the brethren, including Bishop David K. Udall, had been arrested for "unlawful assembly." Bishop Udall called on Miles to carry a letter to the president of the church.[82] As a result, a hundred more families were called to settle in the area.[83] The justice of the peace heard the charges of unlawful assembly and dismissed them as groundless.[84]

Apr. 17" 1884
St Johns
Mrs. Eleanor C. Jarvis

Dear Friend   I received your welcome favor a week ago and was much pleased to hear from you. I am owing some letters longer than that, but I feel that I must pen you a few lines first as it is so long since I wrote to you. I could easily tell that you had the blues when you wrote and when I read it I felt as if I wanted like to sit right down and answer it. not to scold you but see if I couldnt say some thing to cheer and comfort you. I feel to deeply sympathise with you in the way you are situated   it must be lonely for you indeed, but cheer up dear girl. for I do believe if it is for your best good to seek a new home, that the way will be opened so that George will be able to accomplish it. and though there are many difficulties to be encountered in settling a new country still I feel that you could lay a more permanent foundation for a living. still it wouldnt do to take us for an example. as we have had to buy almost evrything we have consumed. but then the Lord has certainly blessed us or we could never have got along with the drawbacks we have had. and you know Miles' labors have been required in other directions so that he has not been able to go to farming as yet to amount to any thing. though I think Miles A [Hannah's son, age 14] and the little boys will put in a little land this year. and I hope may raise something. for we have no garden, nor pig nor anything to help with. but live in hopes that we shall have some day.

You have no doubt seen by the papers that we have had quite a time here, land jumpers and all kinds of wickedness to put up with. a dirty lying paper as bad or worse than the "Tribune".[85] lawsuites, our rights trampled upon in evry possible way. so we get it in one way if not in another.

You have no doubt heard of Miles starting off suddenly to Salt Lake the night before Annie's boy [Orin] was born. It was urgent public business, and I feel that we have all been blessed in his going at the call of duty. for indeed it is the safest plan. and he never fails to respond to the call of the Priesthood. We have sent Miles [A.] and Gaskell [Hannah's son, age 12] to Woodruff to meet their Pa and expect him home the end of the week. We are all well. Annie has a nice boy. and I can tell you she is proud of him. she hurried matters so at the last that Sr [Rizpah] Gibbons did'nt get here in time and Hannah and I were alone with her but she got along well. I brought my bed into her room and slept till baby was two weeks old to look after her and tend to Alice [Annie's daughter, age 3]. and

I am sleeping in her bed to night   hav'nt exactly turned her out but just taken possession in her absense. she, and Hannah and I spent the day at Sr Gibbons yesterday, and it blew up [a storm] so that we all thought it best for her and baby to stay all night. I woke up and am writing in bed. I think it is near morning. I hear it raining but hope it will clear up so that Annie can get home or she will fret so. last Thursday morning was so plesant that Miles took Annie and I in the wagon to spend the day with Sr. Mary Ann Ramsey. (Sr [Elizabeth] Ramsey has gone to Utah. but dont expect to visit St George) but in the afternoon there came up such a storm before he came after us that Annie had to stay till the next day. so you see she has been rather unlucky. but she didnt seem any the worse for her out. though she hates to stay away from home. We dont know what the babys name will be until his Pa comes. Isabell [Romney Platt] and Maude [Crosby], and their boys are getting along all right. they are over a month old. Angie [Platt] was here and spent the afternoon with us a week or two ago. she has a baby girl 6 or 7 months ago. she tells me Jane lives down at Salt River. I am getting sleepy so must try and get another nap before daylight. so good bye. Yours with lots of love.

C. J. Romney

Kind regards to George [Jarvis], Rose [George Jarvis's plural wife], and all the dear children, and enquiring friends   excuse this dreadful writing

In January 1884, the anti-Mormons in St. Johns had begun publication of the weekly Apache Chief, its avowed purpose to drive the Mormons out of Apache County.[86] Their efforts were beginning to bear fruit. They began their campaign by pushing for the removal of Judge French. Not content to editorialize, they pressed charges against him. Petitions were circulated by his supporters, but his tenure was doomed.[87] His replacement, Sumner Howard, a native of Flynt, Michigan, had earned the praise of the St. Johns Ring and the corresponding disdain of the Mormons by his role in the polygamy prosecutions in Utah.[88] He would preside over the polygamy trials in Prescott, Arizona, in November 1884.

Pressing criminal charges against an enemy had proven a potent political tool to the St. Johns Ring, and they used it repeatedly. In the spring of 1884, they pressed a spurious charge of perjury against Miles P. Romney, David K. Udall, and Joseph Crosby.[89]

In May 1884, the Apache Chief called for use of the rope and shotgun as the only sure method to rid the area of Mormons.[90]

Short of such violence, however, they found they could be helpful to the federal marshals in rounding up polygamous men for trial. Raids by federal marshals, long dreaded in Utah, spread to Arizona. Plural wives went into hiding—among them, Catharine and Annie.[91]

The following letter was written on stationery of the "Office of the Orion Era, M.P. Romney, Ed. & Manager." In a letter of the same date, Annie wrote to her sister, Eleanor Jarvis, "Catharine and I are staying with Auntie Swapp in Luna Valley, as we were obliged to leave home in the night to avoid being supoenaed to appear as witnesses against Miles."[92] *They returned to St. Johns on June 25, 1884.*

June 1" 1884
Lunis Valley

Dear Parents,   We arrived in Lunas Valley [New Mexico] one week ago today, and have not had a word from home yet, but we are expecting a home missionary from there today and will likely get a letter by him. we are anxiously awaiting his arrival. The paper has just come from which I learn that Miles has gone with the Apostles to the Conference at St Joseph, to be held there yesterday and today. I am pleased to hear this as it will afford him a little rest of mind, which he must certainly need after being harrassed and bothered as he has been lately. We are still staying with Sr [Elizabeth Hill] Swapp [Hannah's aunt]. evrybody is very kind. The Swapp boys have all got homes here except James who is still in Utah. David Rogers Jr. live six miles from here, on a ranch. his sister Vade who used to be Dick Bleaks wife called to see us this morning. she lives here, and is married to one of the Allans of Toquer, a brother to Daves wife.

This is a fine little valley, and will no doubt become a nice settlement in course of time, as the facilities appear to be good, and in easy reach. there is an abundance of timber close by, such beautiful large pine trees close to town, and we saw a great amount of oak and juniper between here and Bush Valley. there are also quite a lot of cottonwoods growing on the stream here. they look quite old fashioned.

The Bishop [George C. Williams] and others have gone to Woodruff, and expect to be back in a week or two with a saw mill. Br Copelon is to run it; (they are living here.) this will no doubt be a great help in building up the place. There are about 45 families living here but only 20 of them have brought recommends, and belong to the ward.

Thomas [age 8] is with me and is going to school. Park [age 2], Alice [Annie's daughter, age 3], and the baby [Orin, Annie's son, age 2 months] are well, as also are Annie and myself.

Br Moffett came and brought us a letter from Miles. he says the children and all of them are well. he expects to come up as soon as possible. but dont know how long we will have to stay here. I hope it wont be long away from Miles and the children. but I suppose we must try to be as patient as possible, and feel very thankful that all is as well with us as it is.

The Swapp boys are some of them going down to Socorra for goods, so I may send this with them to post.

Goodbye from your ever loving daughter.

C. J. Romney

Miles says there are no letters come for us yet.

June 29" 1884
St Johns

Dear Father & Mother: I think it is about two weeks since I last wrote to you. and I think it is about two months since I got a letter from you if not more. But you will wonder so I must hasten to tell you what sad luck Annie and I have had about our letters.

Miles enclosed all that came for us in one large envelope, and sent them to Bush Valley by a brother who was going up. (to be forwarded to Lunas to us.) and I suppose Bp. [Edward A.] Nobles put them in his pocket and took them to Woodruff with him, where he has gone to work on the dam.

You may imagine our disappointment and anxiety, as neither of us have had a letter since long before we left home. Miles says he knows one of my letters was from Father. I do hope we shall soon get them. Sr. [Ann Jane Peel] Nobles said she would send them as soon as he comes home.

Dear Parents I got the parcel you sent me by Jerry Harndance. it came while I was away and I have not seen him yet.

I assure you my dear Parents that I feel more grateful to you than I can express for your kindness and thoughtfulness, but Miles and I are both afraid that you are depriving yourselves, to send to me. I could'nt have had anything come in better. I am so very much pleased with my shoes. good Salt Lake shoes are a treasure I assure you, and those are such nice ones. they will last me such a long time with care and shoes are no small item in our family.

Thomas and Junius's mouthes widened out as if they were made of the same material as their suspenders. there never was any to compare with them in their estimation.

I dont see how you spare the fruit, when you had such a poor crop last year, but it is just like my own careful Mother to always have something on hand.

A week ago tonight we were in Lunis, and had the blues all day, but after meeting we saw Miles coming   I assure you it was a time of rejoicing when he told us we could start home in the morning. we got home on wednesday. I expect we are running a risk but Miles hated so badly to have us away, and we felt bad to be so far away from home.

We found all well except Eugene [Hannah's son, age 9 months] who is quite young and delicate.

Prospects for Miles in this law business are very gloomy, at present unless the Lord opens up the way in some unforseen manner, which I hope and pray that he will. I suppose all we can do is to be as cautious as possible and trust God for the rest. I have faith to believe that he will protect us in striving to keep his commandments.

the newcomers here seem to be going to work with alacrity fencing, putting in crops etc. We took dinner with Br [Harrison Grey Otis] & Sr [Margaret Reed Angier] Peck the other day. Saw Will Lund & Wife & Annie Willbank [Wiltbank]. all well. heard that the jarvises are all well but did'nt see them as they live on the new town site, off the road.

I dont know whether or not it will be safe to send this through this office or not. if my letters are long between you must excuse it under the circumstances.

I hope I shall hear from you soon as I feel more anxious than ever since I got your note with the parcel stating that Father had been very sick. When I get the letters from Woodruff I will try to answer them.

please give my kind love to all.

I remain as ever your loving daughter.

C. J.

July 20" 1884[93]
Snow Flake   Apache Co.

Dear Father & Mother   You will see by this that I have again changed my location. you know there is an old saying "there is no rest for the wicked." so perhaps we are of that class. at any rate we hav'nt had much lately. However it is quite likely that we shall remain here for some time, and there is one thing about it I shall feel much better in writing and receiving letters, as they will not have to pass through the St Johns post Office. Please direct till further notice to this place to C. J. Cottam, and please tell Emma and the boys, and Aunt Mariette, and let Charles know when you write, so that I shall get my letters without delay. I have never got a line from Charles since he left St George.

You would likely see by the "Era" that a week ago last thursday Br Ammon Tenney was arrested on a charge of Polygamy and his wife Eliza Udall Sopeoned, quite unawares, to appear against him. She told the Officer she wouldnt go, and upon his leaving, she also left and went to our house, and from there to a place of safety. I had just gone to see Sr [Rizpah] Gibbons, and soon got word from Miles to stay till after dark. I was soon joined by Ida [Hunt Udall, plural wife of Bishop David K. Udall] as the Bishop and Miles learned that writs were out for them, only waiting a chance to procure the witnesses. About midnight Miles and the Bishop took us (Annie, Eliza, Ida, and I) three miles from home, to the lower end of the field, where we stayed with a Br White and family. we spent a very anxious time I assure you for the next four days, as we had none of the children with us except Annies baby [Orin, age 3 months]. The first Sr [Anna Eager] Tenney was brought down from their farm, 16 miles, and put under $1,000 dollar bonds to appear as a witness at her husbands examination, which was put off until the 22" of August, (which is entirely unlawful) and he was placed under $5,000 bonds to appear at that time. their house was guarded and watched, also the roads leading out of town, and of course Elizas prospects were rather gloomy, as that nasty filthy jail is not an inviting place.

Sr [Ella] Udall had a baby, six days old when Ida [Hunt Udall] had to leave, but she was doing pretty well when we last heard from her.[94]

Hannah packed up what things she thought we would need, and on monday night late, the brethren started with us four fugitives for this place, making quick time, and arriving here tuesday afternoon. they got counsel and instructions from President [Jesse N.] Smith and started back home thursday morning. Miles rented a house for Annie and I. of course Ida and Eliza are at Br Hunts [John Hunt, Ida's father]. everybody is very kind, and make us very welcome. but still it is quite a cross to be away from all the children. I feel so bad about having Hannah left with so much additional care and labor, and her health is not the best, but she is ever good, true, and faithful.

it is a great tax, and expense on Miles, and he feels so bad to have us away, but Br [Jesse N.] Smith thinks it best to be scattered for the present until something else takes the time and attention of our enemies. The children will be sent to us if we have to stay long. The District Court sits in St. Johns on the first monday in August, with Sumner Howard who used to be in Utah, as judge. his 4" of July Oration in Prescott was a bitter tirade against the "Mormons" so we cant look forward with much hopes to the justice of his rulings[95]

Dear Parents, I have written to you full particulars, so that you would understand how matters are, and not feel uneasy. of course I wouldnt have dared to do this if it had to pass through the St Johns Office. these details are in confidence to you alone, though the general items may be known to anyone.

Poor little Park [age 2], he is young to be left without a mother. Miles says the children are all very good while we have been away from them. we just got home for a few minutes before leaving but the little ones had all gone to bed, and we did'nt think it wise to wake them, so I just got to speak to Caroline [age 10] as she was awake. Poor little things, they have learned to keep a sharp lookout for the officers, and all suspicious characters.

Times would look very gloomy indeed if it were not for our faith in God, and his power and will to protect and bless us in striving to keep his commandments. this he has certainly done for which I feel very thankful.

We have not as yet recovered our lost letters. I still have faith that we shall do so. I have just had one letter from you, and none from anyone else for along time. I wrote to you about two weeks ago.

We were home from Lunis Valley just two weeks in peace.

Please give my love to all my brothers and sisters, (I wish they would write.) and friends, and keep a large portion for yourselves.

I earnestly pray that you may be blessed with health and strength, and that the blessings, and peace of God may attend you to comfort you at all times.

I remain your ever loving daughter.

Catharine.

I wrote this letter this morning. This is Sunday evening. I feel so lonely without the children, especially Park. We have been up to Sr [Lois Barnes Pratt] Hunts this afternoon. had a plesant time. listening to music on the guitars, and singing etc.

16" Aug" 1884
Snow Flake   Apache Co.
Mrs. E. C. Jarvis

Beloved Friend   Your letter of last May came to hand a little over a week ago. it has been following us around the country all summer, and just succeeded in finding us. so you will excuse our long silence. Annie will answer at another time so that you will hear oftener. I am deeply greived to learn of your bad luck and protracted illness.[96] had'nt heard a word of it till I got your letter. hope you have quite recovered your health.

Well my dear Friend we all have our trials. some in one way, and some in another. and some of us have pleasures instead. for instance, Annie and I have been taking some lengthy pleasure trips around the country this summer. last May some of our *kind friends* in St Johns did us the *honor* of desiring to make our acquaintance. and for that purpose issued invitations for us to attend a reception to be held at the Court House, but strange to relate—by some means or other the invitations failed to reach us and unlike your letter, have, as yet failed to find us:

On the 23" of May. Annie and I with Thomas [age 8], Alice [Annie's daughter, age 3], Park [age 2], and Orin [Annie's son, age 4 months], started for Lunis Valley, where we remained 4 weeks, where we were kindly treated, and enjoyed ourselves as well as circumstances would permit. at the end of that time miles came and brought us home. but after being at home two weeks it was again thought advisable for us to leave for a season, which we did, in company with two other fugitives. Miles and Br. [Ammon] Tenney brought us to Snow Flake, where we now are. We brought only Orin along but have since added to our family. on the morning of the 23" of July. I had a little daughter born. she weighed 8 1/2 lbs. just the same that Caroline did. We shall call her "Emma". She has light brown hair. and dark blue or grey eyes. cant tell which.

Last Friday Miles came over and brought Annies girls, and my three youngest boys (so we have them all but Caroline and Thomas.) Minnie [Hannah's daughter, age 16] came with him to tend to the children. they started back Monday morning. I hear that Hannah has been quite sick this last few days. and Eugene [Hannah's son, age 10 months] is quite poorly all the time. Bp [David K.] Udall called today on his way to Prescott where he has been summoned as a witness before the Grand Jury but he dont know on what case. he is to meet Miles at Woodruff tonight. when they will proceed together. Miles has to appear there to answer to a charge of perjury. So where these matters will end we know not, but trust to our Heavenly Father.

Park has diareah and very sore eyes. baby has sore eyes too. and Ann [Annie's daughter, age 5] & Alice each have one a little sore. Annie and all the rest well. they have gone to meeting, she and children. I got cold in my breast and had a fever this week but better again. There is much more I would like to say to you but cant send much paper, as I want to send you a pair of sleeve ruffles which I crotched [crocheted] when I began to sit up.

Dear Eleanor I pray the Lord to bless and raise you up unto perfect health and strength and bestow upon you evry blessing which you need.

Believe me to remain as ever your devoted friend.

C. J. Romney.

Please write soon and direct to C. J. Cottam. Snow Flake and if you write after we get back home direct to M. P. Romney.

Poor Caroline [age 10] has been away from me nearly all summer. wants to see the baby badly I know. Dont know when we can go home again.

28 Aug 1884   Thursday morning before sunrise
Snowflake

Dear Father and Mother   I wrote to you a week ago last Sunday I think or Monday, but I dont think you will feel that I am boring you if I write again now.

I am feeling just tolerable. I took cold and had a chill and fever Monday night and was quite sick Tuesday but am better again. Annies eyes are quite sore, also Claudes and Parks, but none of them laid up with them. baby's are not well but better. she grows a big girl, weighs 13-1/4 lbs yesterday just five weeks old, and gained 4 and 3/4 lbs.

I went to meeting last Sunday for the first time in Snowflake. After meeting I went to look at the new Stake meeting house which is being built here. it is a fine building, and reminds me of the Tabernacle at St George. though not quite so large, it faces the same way, has a spire on the same end, gallery and is the same color, being made of brick. The windows and doors are not in yet, but they are trying to get it ready to hold conference in, on the 13" of next month. they have to send for glass again as much of what came was found to be broken. President [Jesse N.] Smith is at present in the East selecting goods for the Coop Store. expects to be home before Conference.

Yesterday we got a letter from Miles, from Prescott. he said he and the Bishop [David K. Udall] were well, did'nt know how long they would have to stay but hoped not long. nothing had yet been done. Grand Jury had been in Session two days but had not reported any indictments up to that time. The Judges charge to them was very fair.

Yesterday afternoon Annie and I walked out and called on Br. and Sr. Oakley, found Sr Oakley about as usual. dressed, but lying on the bed. she dos'nt appear very [ill], but dont get around much if any. she inquired about you, and asked me to tell you when i wrote that she should never forget your kindness to her when her children died and shall ever feel grateful. she says she had nothing but an old muslin dress to bury her baby in and she thought that would'nt do, but Mother said, "it will do very well Sr Oakley. I will take it and do it up for you." And she says when mother brought it back, it looked beautiful just as nice as if it had just come out of the store. Which I dont doubt if Mother washed and ironed it. They said if we had come a day sooner, they could have treated us to a melon. I hav'nt seen such a thing, this year yet. just beginning to ripen.

When we got home I was give out. I wonder if I am getting old. I never was so easy to take cold, and so quickly tired in my life before, but the folks tell me when I have had six children I must'nt expect to be so strong. Annie has'nt allowed me to help wash yet, and I have to obey her a little as she has me to wait on when I make myself sick. Well I shall appreciate being strong and well once more.

I hav'nt heard a word from Hannah, nor the children since I wrote you last.

The people here are very kind we have not wanted for vegetables since we came, and scarcely for milk. I hope I may never forget it but return it to others if it is ever in my power to do so.

Dear Parents I pray for you daily, and I know the Lord will bless you for your goodness.

Jesse N. Smith Junr. started to Utah on Tuesday but I did'nt know till after he started. I think his business at the Temple is such that he dont wish it made public. so I would't like it to be known that I mentioned it. I had a little basket I wanted to send, but may have another chance soon.

I forgot to tell you that Rob. Jones looks very much the same as he did when he used to turn the big wheel for you, and carry a rose in his button hole, or an apple in his pocket for the girls.

John Hulet lives just across the street from us. he keeps the Post Office. he has one wife, and a little boy five years old. they have lost several.

I understand that Abram Perkins who married Lizzie Gublor of Washington is the miller at the grist mill, seven miles above here.

I must stop now as it is time to post this. Goodbye for the present. Please give my love to my Brothers and Sisters, and Friends, Aunt Mariette, Sr. [Eliza] Lund etc. and accept a large portion for yourselves.

From your ever loving daughter

Catharine

Father! I want to propound a conundrum. How many children will you be Grandpa to when Mother is Grandma to 20? Answer next week.

On August 31, 1884, Annie wrote to her sister Eleanor Jarvis, "Miles has been to Prescott to appear before the Grand Jury to answer to a charge of Perjury, and has been honorably acquitted. This Grand Jury was called more especially to investigate Mormon Polygamy and Perjury cases etc., and they have succeeded in making out seven indictments for Polygamy. Bp. Udall's name is among the number, and he has been given bonds to appear in November."[97]

7" Sept. 1884
Snowflake

Dear Father & Mother   I received your very kind letter the day before yesterday dated 26 or 27. you had'nt had but one letter from me since my sickness. I have written three or four times, which you have likely got by this time. I wonder if Emma and George hav'nt got letters from me lately.

I regret to hear of the sickness of Sr [Maria] Squire & Mary Alice Nelson. hope they are both better. I am sorry Mother's eyes are still sore   I often think about them. I often wonder how you get along with your new teeth and try to imagine how you look with them.

Last thursday was Fast Day so I took the baby to meeting and had her blessed (Emma Romney)   Miles spoke to Bp. [John] Hunt when he was here about having it done, and sending report to St Johns to be recorded.

We havnt heard a word from home since Miles got home from Prescott. Conference is next Saturday & Sunday, at this place, when I feel inclined to think Miles will come and take us home, but dont know.

I understand that Br. [Peter J.] Christopherson of Round Valley and Ammon Tenney passed through Holbrook this week with the U.S. Marshall on the way to Prescott under arrest for Polygamy, so you see the Officials in this Territory appear to mean business, and are quite zealous in the good work of persecuting or prosecuting the Mormons, but we know it is Gods work and we ought to feel proud of suffering in the good cause. I only hope that we may all hold out faithful to the end and be able to bear all our trials with meekness and patience.

The childrens eyes are better, but not quite well yet. Park [age 2] dont seem to feel very well, and is very cross and fretful.

Annie and children are well. The children have just come from Sunday School and are wanting their dinner so I expect I shall have to stop soon. This is a very windy day, dont know whether I can take the baby to meeting in it or not. We have had two very heavy rains this week, the streets swimming in a few minutes.

The people feel very much discouraged about their crops which they thought till recently were going to be exceptionally good, but they are mostly turning out very poorly.

I wrote to George & Thomas a week ago. hope they go all right. I have not had a line from Charles since before he left St George. I dont know any cause, as I wrote last.

I am sorry Uncle John & Aunt Sarah [Smith Burns] have such poor health. Please give my love to them when you write, also to Aunt Jennie and Uncle Thomas [Punter].

My love to Brothers, Sisters & Friends. And believe me to remain as ever your loving daughter.

C.J.R.

15″ Sept 1884
Snowflake

Dear Father & Mother   I have just got a letter from Charles, the first since before he left St George early in the spring.

This is Monday night. Been a busy time. Conference just over.

Miles came Friday forenoon. He brought Gaskell [Hannah's son, age 12] to tend the team.

We were very much disappointed as we fully expected to go home, as we thought the St Johns men wouldnt have anything to do with Polygamy anymore, but Miles says the Commissioner [George S. McCarter] has just the same power as ever and they feel just as vindictive. however Thank God, Pres[id]ent J[oseph]. F. Smith and Br. [Erastus] Snow will be in St. Johns in a week and he will counsel with them, in regard to the matter; so we will soon know what we are going to do. I feel so thankful that Br. Snow is coming. I believe they will come from St John, here, so we will likely get to see him.

Tuesday morning Dear Parents I got so sleepy last night, (which you will see by my writing) that I coul'dnt, go on writing. so must try to finish now. Miles started home yesterday morning. If we have to stay he is going to send Caroline [age 10] & Thomas [age 8] over. he would have stayed till today, but the Bp. [David K. Udall] came with him, and was anxious to get home. Sr. [Eliza Udall] Tenney and Ida [Hunt Udall] are well.

We were much pleased to meet some of our neighbors and friends from St Johns at Conference.

You dont know how badly I want to see the children and Hannah. Miles says she is very lame with the rheumatism, or something in her shoulder, and Eugene [Hannah's son, age 1] is sick and looks very bad all the time.

I sent you a little parcel (a basket) yesterday morning, by Mattie Williams, the daughter of the Parson [George C. Williams] as he is called, Bishop of Lunis Valley. they were very kind to us when we were there, and are very good people. The young man, whom she is going to marry Br Dilmon [Peter Dillman] was Thomas' school teacher in Lunis Valley. he seems to be a good young man. he was just baptized last fall. The Parson and wife were also here at Conference. I spok[e] to Sr East about bringing it but she hadnt started yet. I am sorry now that I did, as it may make you too many callers.

I am sorry to hear that Mother still has sore eyes, also Emma and the children. Parks [age 2] and baby's [Emma, age 7 weeks] have been better till the last two or three days when they have got a little fresh cold.

We had a very hard rain storm Sunday during meeting. we have had several lately so that storms run in the streets in a few minutes time.

I went to evry meeting except the Young Mens' during Conference. baby was very good.

You will see a report of the meetings in the paper.

I must now say goodbye for the present. from your loving daughter.

Love to all

C.J.R.

25" Oct. 1884
Snowflake

Dear Father & Mother   I got your very welcome letter of the 15"
ult. yesterday and thought I would sit right down and answer it, to
go out in the mail this morning, if it is saturday, or else it will have
to wait till Tuesday and I know you are anxious to hear often.

Miles came over last Sunday afternoon and has just gone back
this morning. he stayed longer than he expected to as the weather
has been very stormy. it has rained very hard the last two days and
nights, and still looks very threatening. I hope he wont get wet and
make his cough bad again, but he couldnt wait longer as he has to
print tickets for the Election which will come off in a week or two.
He just learned by the paper since he came here of the death of his
Mother, and was pleased that your letter came while he was here so
that he could learn a little more of the particulars. Poor dear soul
she has suffered a long time and it is no doubt a happy change, and
a joyful meeting with the loved ones gone before.

I felt bitterly disappointed that the children did'nt come but
Miles expected to have to move us to Taylor or somewhere (but
Charlz Defreiz has'nt brought Maggie [Jarvis DeFriez, his wife] so
we can stay here a little longer) and as it is nearing court time he
thinks we are less secure, and it might be that we should have to get
around in a hurry, and would be very much encumbered with so
many children.

Oh, I do hope the time will soon come that we can live together
again in peace. Hannah wrote that she wants to see us very badly
and especially this little stranger, and her Pa says Caroline would
give her ears to see her. just think of her being three months old,
almost big enough to shorten and never been home. If our team had
been in good condition I think Annie and I would have been to pay
you a visit this summer, but it is too poor for so long a journey.

I expect Br East is on his way back, as they only intended to stay
a day or two in St George. I was afraid of sending too many too you
for fear they might impose on your generosity.

A brother Reidhead of Woodruff have been staying in Br Halls
house a long time but I guess they have started home. Bp. Owens of
Woodruff has gone back now so perhaps you may get to send the
bonnet curtain with him. there is no bother about getting things
from Woodruff as there are teams going back and forth all the time,
so if you send it in care of Br. [Joseph] Fish we will get it all right.

We are all well except that the children have bad colds.

I hope you are both well. With kind love to all I subscribe myself your loving daughter

Catharine

Looking on theirs as test cases, five of the brethren went to trial for polygamy in November. Because they believed that the statute of limitations had run and that the law did not apply to marriages that had been entered into outside the Arizona Territory, they felt optimistic that they would be acquitted.[98]

9" Nov. 1884
Snowflake

Dear Father & Mother I must write a few lines to acknowlege the receipt of the nice present you sent me. I regretted that Br [Peter] Dillman and Mattie [Williams Dillman] could not come this way so that I could hear all about you, but perhaps it is well for them as we should no doubt have almost worn them out with answering questions. however they sent the parcels, all right. I felt almost like crying when I opened them to see how thoughtful and kind you are all the time. the children were almost wild with delight. Oh! the talk about Grandpa and Grandma and how the boys and Ann discussed the merits of their respective Grandparents is as good as a theatre, and you ought to see Junius's big eyes bung out when he tells how Grandpa & Grandma used to give him apples grapes and sweetcakes, just as if he [age 6] could remember it for himself.

We got two notes from Miles last week. they were all well at home. he said Thomas [age 8] & Caroline [age 10] are well and happy. he sent word that the Court at Prescott will not convene till the 17" instead of the first Monday as announced, so it will make it still longer till we know what we are going to do.

There is but little doubt but the Anti Mormon ticket will win the day, as they have resorted to evry kind of fraud, to forward their purposes. The "Era" that should have been here a week ago has not come yet, detained no doubt at the St Johns post office for fear of it influencing voters. Br. Harris was in St Johns last Tuesday at the Election and got here on Thursday he said the Era was out on time as usual and he brought one in his pocket the only one which has come here as yet. If we were in a civilized country I think such offenses of Post Masters would be punishable by law, but here nothing can be done, by way of justice, for Mormons. And there is little doubt but if those wicked men at St Johns come into office again they will be more bitter in their feelings than before, as our people have unitedly voted against them, and the paper has strongly advocated their being retired from office, but if our people do all in their power to maintain their rights, I believe the Lord will do his part and it will come out all right, though we cant always understand it at the time.

We are all well at present, and I hope you are enjoying the same blessing and that Rachels breast is better by this time.

I have got letters from Aunt Mariette, and George which I will try to answer in the course of a week or two.

Br. & Sr. Roundy who live next door to us have gone away for a week or ten days and we are feeding their pigs, and milking their cows. we would have plenty of milk now if the cows would only come up regular.

I must conclude with kindest love.

From your affectionate daughter

Catharine

11" Nov 1884

Dear Parents   I received your welcome letter yesterday. Am sorry you did not see Br & Sr East. she is a nice little woman. I should have pressed her to call as she had no friends there but was afraid of causing you extra work.

John Clark and Charlie Dodge from Nutrioso, one by the name of Earle, from Round Valley, Alic Nicoll, and John White of St Johns have all gone to St George but I did'nt see any of them, but they will all have to pass through Woodruff so if the parcel was sent in care of Joseph Fish he would forward it. one of the young ladies from St Johns gone to get married is Miss Babbit a relative of J. E. Johnson and will likely stay there.[99]

Bp. Udall brought us a letter from Miles   he [Bishop Udall] and the other brethren indicted for Polygamy are on their way to Prescott. I Pray that they may return all right.

I am very busy coloring braid this morning to make the girls some hats. All well.

4 months yesterday since I saw the children.

C.J.R.

16" Nov 1884
Snowflake
Mr. George T. Cottam

Beloved Brother George   Your kind letter dated Oct 19" came duly to hand and was thankfully received.

I was very sorry to hear of Rachel having a gathered breast, and the children being sick but I trust you are all quite well again by this time. We are all well except bad colds. we got a letter from Miles last Tuesday. he said they were all well at home. Thomas & Caroline well and happy, and good children. of course it is a great comfort to know that, but still we often long for the privelige of living peacefully in our own home once more with all the loved ones. it is a long *long* four months.

The Court in Prescott will convene tomorrow. the Bp. [Udall,] Br. [Ammon] Tenney, Br. [Peter J.] Christofferson, Br. [William J.] Flake, Br. [C. I.] Kemp indicted for Polygamy and another Brother, by the name of [John] Milner, a Lawyer from Provo, all started for Prescott last Tuesday morning   the[y] went with a wagon as they thought it would be less expensive for them than going by "rail" and "stage". I earnestly pray that they may all come out all right. I suppose Br. Milner will assist them what he can. Miles writes that they are threatening to bring up the Perjury case again against him and the Bishop, but I do hope the[y] wont succeed in making him any more trouble.

You say you wish we could have come and made you a visit, if we had known in the Spring that we should have had to stay away so long, I think Miles would have tried hard to get us home to you for a visit but there are so many children, that I dont see any chance and especially now the weather is getting cold. I wouldnt have felt that I could possibly staid away from any of the children long enough to go to Utah and back, but we never know what we can do till we are tried and I expect I should tire you folks all out if I came with so many little ones.

Oh you would be surprised at the fraudes that have been perpetrated at our County Election last week. I expect the same old Anti Mormon ring are in Office again, and the people will continue to suffer.

You say you are getting old and grey headed. I too sometimes find a grey hair in my head. Miles is getting quite grey.

So each baby is an improvement on the others is it? You didnt tell me the name of your last. is he as pretty as Ada [George and Rachel's daughter]?

We have done very well for milk since we have been here. those who have had plenty have shared with us. we have been milking cows for the folks who live next door, for the last two weeks nearly, while they have been away, that is whenever the cows would come up. Love to all. From your loving sister

Catharine

The polygamy trials at the November term of court were already underway when Miles P. Romney arrived in Prescott to appear before another grand jury in the perjury case involving the Kitchen Springs Ranch. Romney, Udall, and Crosby were all indicted. Udall and Crosby pleaded not guilty, and their trials were set for the June term of court. Miles's attorney argued that the jury had been improperly instructed in his case and moved to quash the indictment. The judge quashed his indictment and "respited" the bonds, postponing further action to the next term of court.[100] James Stinson and a Mr. Bagnal supplied the bonds upon the guarantee of William J. Flake that he would reimburse them if the bonds were forfeited.[101]

In the polygamy trials, Ammon M. Tenney, C. J. Kemp, and Peter J. Christofferson were convicted of unlawful cohabitation. They were fined and sent to the Detroit House of Corrections, the "American Siberia" over a thousand miles away.[102] William J. Flake and Peter Skousen pleaded guilty, thereby receiving a lesser sentence.[103] They were fined and sentenced to six months in the territorial penitentiary in Yuma, Arizona. The trial of David K. Udall for polygamy was postponed for lack of evidence.[104]

On December 7, 1884, Miles and Udall saw the men off for prison. They then rode through the snow for six days to Snowflake, where they met with Apostle Seymour B. Young, emissary of the First Presidency.[105] The First Presidency counseled that it would be better for polygamists to seek refuge in Mexico than to go to prison.[106]

There followed a major exodus of church leadership from the Little Colorado area the winter of 1884-85. Some of the brethren traveled to Utah or Mexico briefly, then returned to Arizona. Others left Arizona, never to return.[107]

Before Miles left Snowflake, a federal marshal appeared at Hannah's home with handcuffs and a gun. He demanded that Miles surrender and "save himself and the country a lot of expense." (Perhaps, in those days, communication was such that the marshal did not know that Miles had already appeared in court in Prescott and had been released under bond.) Hannah sewed all her money in the clothes of her son, Miles A., and sent him to warn her husband. The younger Miles rode all day and part of the night before reaching his father in Snowflake.[108]

Having made the decision to leave Arizona, Miles left Catharine and Annie in Snowflake to prepare for the trip while he returned to St. Johns to bid Hannah good-bye and settle his business affairs. Miles told Hannah to remain in Arizona until she could join him later in Mexico, where he intended to establish a place for all of them. Hannah packed provisions for him with a heavy heart, fearing that she would never see him again.[109]

When Miles arrived back in Snowflake, he, Catharine, and Annie finished their preparations and then loaded their children and provisions into a lumber wagon to begin the journey to St. George. A short distance out, they met a fellow traveler with room in his wagon who agreed to take some of the children with him. On New Year's Eve, the travelers camped in several feet of snow on Buckskin Mountain. Icicles formed on their hair. They tried to start a fire, but the sticks and brush were too wet to serve as kindling. A straw hat Catharine had made for Thomas was set ablaze to start a fire that warmed them through the night.[110] *Fortunatley, they were almost home. In a few days, they would enjoy the warm winter sun of Utah's Dixie and a joyful reunion with family and friends.*

NOTES

1. The story of the founding of St. Johns is found in many sources, including Joseph Fish, "History of the Eastern Arizona Stake and of the Establishment of the Snowflake Stake," typescript, George S. Tanner Collection, BYU Archives, and Special Collections, University of Utah Libraries; John H. Krenkel, ed., *The Life and Times of Joseph Fish, Mormon Pioneer* (Danville, Ill.: Interstate Printers and Publishers, 1970); Manuscript History of the St. Johns Ward, LDS Church Archives; James H. McClintock, *Mormon Settlement in Arizona: A Record of Peaceful Conquest of the Desert* (Phoenix: Manufacturing Stationers, 1921), reissued with a foreword by Charles S. Peterson (Tucson: University of Arizona Press, 1985); Charles S. Peterson, *Take Up Your Mission: Mormon Colonizing along the Little Colorado River, 1870-1900* (Tucson: University of Arizona Press, 1973); Jesse N. Smith, *Journal of Jesse N. Smith* (Salt Lake City: Deseret News, 1953); George S. Tanner Collection, BYU Archives, and Special Collections, University of Utah Libraries; David K. Udall and Pearl Udall Nelson, *Arizona Pioneer Mormon: David King Udall, His Story and His Family*

(Tucson, Ariz.: Arizona Silhouettes, 1959); David K. Udall Papers, LDS Church Archives; manuscript histories and minutes of the local units at the LDS Church Archives.

2. Peterson, *Take Up Your Mission*, 1-14.

3. Andrew Amundsen, Journal, May 28, 1873, quoted in Peterson, *Take Up Your Mission*, 12.

4. Peterson, *Take Up Your Mission*, 9-10, citing *Journal of Discourses*.

5. Leonard J. Arrington, *Brigham Young: American Moses* (Urbana: University of Illinois Press, 1986), 382-83.

6. Ibid., 383; Erastus Snow to Father, January 30, 1878, typescript from *Deseret News*, Lot Smith Collection, BYU Archives.

7. Udall and Nelson, *Arizona Pioneer Mormon*, 71; Letter to the Editor from Amram [Miles P. Romney], *Deseret News*, May 18, 1881, quoted in Thomas C. Romney, *Life Story of Miles Park Romney* (Independence, Mo.: Zion's Printing and Publishing, 1948), 121-23.

8. McClintock, *Mormon Settlement in Arizona*, 177-78.

9. Krenkel, *Life and Times of Joseph Fish*, 200.

10. Wilford Woodruff to A. M. Tenney, May 26, 1881, typescript, LeSeuer Papers, George S. Tanner Collection, Special Collections, University of Utah Libraries.

11. Wilford Woodruff to Lot Smith, November 24, 1879, Lot Smith Collection, BYU Archives.

12. Ibid.

13. Udall and Nelson, *Arizona Pioneer Mormon*, 74. Regarding the Mormon exodus see Arrington, *Brigham Young*, 66-71.

14. McClintock, *Mormon Settlements in Arizona*, 179.

15. Fish, "History of the Eastern Arizona Stake," 60.

16. Wilford Woodruff to A. M. Tenney, May 25, 1880, typescript, LeSeuer Papers, George S. Tanner Collection, Special Collections, University of Utah Libraries.

17. Krenkel, *Life and Times of Joseph Fish*, 215-17; Smith, *Journal of Jesse N. Smith*, 248; Peterson, *Take Up Your Mission*, 220-24.

18. Wilford Woodruff to Lot Smith, December 14, 1880, Lot Smith Collection, BYU Archives.

19. Udall and Nelson, *Arizona Pioneer Mormon*, 66-71. For more information on the Udall family, see Appendix 1.

20. Fish, "History of the Eastern Arizona Stake," 58; Udall and Nelson, *Arizona Pioneer Mormon*, 69.

21. Udall and Nelson, *Arizona Pioneer Mormon*, 77-79.

22. Ibid., 76-77.

23. Wilford Woodruff to Lot Smith, December 14, 1880, Lot Smith Collection, BYU Archives.

24. Carrie's two children, Will and Mattie, had returned to their father following Carrie's death on September 11, 1879. Thomas C. Romney, *Life Story of Miles Park Romney*, 75; Arthur K. Hafen, *Devoted Empire Builders: Pioneers of St. George* (St. George, Utah: N.p., 1969), 113, 114.

25. "Erastus Snow had been called to aid in the colonization of Arizona, possibly that was a better place, and the move was on." Albert E. Miller and Mary Ann Cottam Miller, *The Immortal Pioneers, Founders of the City of St. George, Utah* (St. George, Utah: N.p., 1946), 202. For more information on some of the families who moved to St. Johns, see Appendix 1.

26. George T. Cottam, Diary of George T. Cottam, 1875-1928, April 11, 1881, photocopy, Special Collections, Southern Utah University, Cedar City, Utah.

27. Ibid., April 12, 1881; Thomas C. Romney, *Life Story of Miles Park Romney*, 116.

28. The United Order was a cooperative movement intended to promote unity and self-sufficiency among members of the church. Its practice took various forms and was eventually discontinued. Leonard J. Arrington, *Great Basin Kingdom: An Economic History of the Latter-day Saints, 1830-1900* (Cambridge, Mass.: Harvard University Press, 1958), 323-49; Peterson, *Take Up Your Mission*, 91-122; Andrew Karl Larson, *I Was Called to Dixie, the Virgin River Basin: Unique Experiences in Mormon Pioneering* (Salt Lake City: Deseret News Press, 1961), 290-313; Lot Smith Collection, BYU Archives; St. George United Order Record Book, 1870-1903, LDS Church Archives.

29. George Woodbury, brother of Annie Romney and Eleanor Jarvis, married Elizabeth Rowena ("Roz") Romney, daughter of Miles's brother, Joseph Gaskell Romney, on April 13, 1881, two days after Miles and Catharine left for Arizona.

30. While Miles was on his mission to England, he became very ill and was informed by the doctor that one of his lungs was entirely gone and the other was in the process of disintegration. Thomas C. Romney, *Life Story of Miles Park Romney*, 29.

31. Miles became a member of the Arizona Bar and specialized in criminal cases. In one incident Miles acted as counsel for two defendants charged with assault with a deadly weapon. One of the defendants, Juan Perera, was acquitted; the other, Sylvester Padilla, was held under bail of $500 to appear before the Third Judicial District Court. *Deseret News*, March 28, 1883, quoting the *Orion Era*.

32. Willard Farr married Mary Ann (Minnie) Romney as a plural wife, April 29, 1886.

33. Udall and Nelson, *Arizona Pioneer Mormon*, 187, 188; Thomas C. Romney, *Life Story of Miles Park Romney*, 150.

34. Bp. is an abbreviation for *Bishop*.

35. An infection at the end of a finger.

36. Thomas C. Romney, *Life Story of Miles Park Romney*, 114, quoting *Deseret News*, November 10, 1881.

37. Quoted in Krenkel, *Life and Times of Joseph Fish*, 226.

38. St. Johns Ward Record, Book A, September 5, 1881, cited in Udall and Nelson, *Arizona Pioneer Mormon*, 86.

39. This is the only letter in this volume written to Miles.

40. Andrew Gibbons was one of the original group of Mormon pioneers to enter the Salt Lake Valley in 1847. Udall and Nelson, *Arizona Pioneer Mormon*, 70.

41. Catharine was in the first stage of pregnancy and likely experiencing morning sickness.

42. George's wife, Rachel, was from Hamblin in Mountain Meadows, not far from St. George. Mary Ann C. Miller, "Biography of George Thomas Cottam," in William Howard Thompson, ed., *Thomas Cottam 1820, and His Wives, Ann Howarth 1820, and Caroline Smith 1820* (St. George, Utah: Thomas Cottam Family Organization, 1987), 2:195.

43. Catharine's and Annie's children referred to Hannah as "Auntie." Catharine and Annie were known to children of the other wives as "Aunt Catharine" and "Aunt Annie."

44. David K. Udall recalled, "Times were hard and we lived in a primitive way, but we were not longfaced or sad about it for we found many blessings to appreciate and we were young and full of zeal, full of fun, too. There was fine talent in our community. . . . Brother August Mineer was a fine violinist, his father before him having played in the Royal Orchestra in Denmark." Udall and Nelson, *Arizona Pioneer Mormon*, 89.

45. Benjamin Franklin Pendleton (1818-81) was a blacksmith who helped prepare wagons for the trek west. He died November 17, 1881. Hafen, *Devoted Empire Builders*, 103, 104.

46. Jesse Johnson, a brother of Maude Crosby, died on November 3, 1881, at the age of twenty-one.

47. That is, this was the second time in Arizona that they had cooked potatoes from their garden.

48. As ward architect, Miles P. Romney would have designed the schoolhouse. His drawings for a similar building, the St. Johns tithing office, are located in the LDS Church Archives.

49. Minutes of school business meeting held January 8, 1882, Record of the St. Johns Ward, LDS Church Archives.

50. Catharine served as first counselor in the St. Johns Ward Relief Society from February 1882 through the remainder of her time in St. Johns. St. Johns Ward Relief Society Minutes, LDS Church Archives.

51. Nathaniel Ashby, Jr., died on March 19, 1882, at age forty-six, on his way home from a mission to the Hawaiian Islands accompanied by his wife and son. Hafen, *Devoted Empire Builders*, 4, 5.

52. Mt. Trumbull, Arizona, was a source of timber from which the St. George pioneers built beautiful homes and fine furniture. Miller and Miller, *The Immortal Pioneers*, 151. James William Nixon, Sr., who operated the saw mill at Mt. Trumbull, died on February 19, 1882. Hafen, *Devoted Empire Builders*, 99.

53. When the Romneys left St. George, Hannah was determined to take the organ with them. "I said I would take it if I had to walk. So we took it, but I did not have to walk. We found it a source of pleasure and refinement in raising our children." Hannah H. Romney, "Autobiography of Hannah Hood Hill Romney," photocopy of typescript in author's possession, 9.

54. Hannah was president of the ward Primary, the local unit of the church's auxiliary for children. Record of the St. Johns Ward, February 5, 1882, LDS Church Archives.

55. Park Romney was born on March 25, 1882.

56. Matilda Thompson, daughter of William Thompson, married James G. Bleak as a plural wife on February 3, 1882. Bleak authored the Annals of the Southern Utah Mission, LDS Church Archives.

57. In the early days of the church, home missionaries were appointed to preach in local wards.

58. Besides helping out by boarding the men Miles hired, Hannah raised chickens and rented several cows. With the extra milk, she made butter and fed a pig. Her two oldest daughters, Isabell and Minnie, took in sewing and laundry, and the boys helped their father. Hannah H. Romney, "Autobiography," 10.

59. Ida F. Hunt married David K. Udall, bishop of the St. Johns Ward, on May 25, 1882, in the St. George Temple. The "Sister Udall" referred to in the letters is Bishop Udall's first wife, Ella. Ida Hunt Udall kept a journal of this period of her life, including the trip with David and Ella Udall to St. George for the wedding. Portions are quoted in Udall and Nelson, *Arizona Pioneer Mormon*. A photocopy of the handwritten original is located in the LDS Church Archives. The entire journal appears in Maria S. Ellsworth, ed., *Mormon Odyssey: The Story of Ida Hunt Udall, Plural Wife* (Urbana: University of Illinois Press, 1992).

60. After President Wilford Woodruff issued a manifesto in 1890 that polygamy would be prohibited where it violated the laws of the land, most members of the church reasoned that, since the church was based on continuing revelation, if God could give a commandment, he could also revoke it. Leonard J. Arrington and Davis Bitton, *The Mormon Experience: A History of the Latter-day Saints* (New York: Random House, 1980), 244-45.

61. Fast day is a monthly day of fasting and prayer on which a church meeting is held at which members express their feelings for the gospel, and babies may be given a name and blessing.

62. The Young Men's and Young Ladies' Mutual Improvement Associations were church auxiliaries for the youth.

63. Hannah had had a miscarriage, losing twins at about three months. Hannah H. Romney, "Autobiography," 10.

64. Nathan Robinson was one of the first settlers in the Little Colorado area, having gone with Lot Smith to settle Sunset in January 1876. That fall, he returned for his wife and children. They stopped at the dedication of the St. George Temple on their way to Arizona. He got a contract to work on the railroad in the San Francisco Mountains. While looking for a cow, he crossed a hill on his horse and came across some Indians slaughtering a beef. They shot him, but his horse continued on home, alerting the family of difficulty. The family spent the night in the barn protected by an embankment. The next day a search party found him dead. Recollection by Annise A. Bybee [Mrs. Robinson], Roberta Clayton Collection, BYU Archives. The next year, Mrs. Robinson married Peter Skousen, one of the

men convicted of polygamy in 1884. See Catharine's letter of November 23, 1883.

65. This incident was reported in the *Deseret News*, September 6, 1882, quoted in Thomas C. Romney, *Life Story of Miles Park Romney*, 156-58.

66. Charles A. Franklin (also known as A. F. Banta) published the *Arizona Pioneer*, Apache County's first newspaper. It lasted only a few months. In January 1883, the Mormons formed the St. Johns Publishing Company, bought Franklin's printing press, and began publishing the *Orion Era*. Fish, "History of the Eastern Arizona Stake," 62. Family members state that Miles P. Romney owned the press. Hannah H. Romney, "Autobiography," 11; Thomas C. Romney, *Life Story of Miles Park Romney*, 150-51; Letter from Miles P. Romney to Thomas P. Cottam, December 27, 1885, in possession of Edward L. Kimball, Provo, Utah, complaining that the purchaser of the press had not made payments.

67. The Jarvises would have been visiting their children, who had moved to the Little Colorado area. Josephine was their daughter.

68. Children are baptized and confirmed members of the LDS Church at age eight.

69. In an "Address to the Members of the Church of Jesus Christ of Latter-day Saints," dated August 29, 1882, the First Presidency of the church responded to a requirement of the Edmunds Law that to vote, a citizen must swear that he did not cohabit with another person in the marriage relation. The First Presidency pleaded for those who could truthfully take the oath to do so and not let apathy keep them away from the polls and thus further disenfranchise the people. They noted that insertion of the phrase "in the marriage relation," which was not required by the statute but was inserted by the commissioners who wrote the oath, allowed the promiscuous to vote while disenfranchising polygamists. James R. Clark, *Messages of the First Presidency* (Salt Lake City: Bookcraft, 1965, 1970), 2:342-47.

70. Miles had delivered "a very spirited discourse on the principles of honesty, integrity and family affairs in general." Record of the St. Johns Ward, September 17, 1882, LDS Church Archives.

71. Sam Adair was the leader of the first group called to go to Washington, Utah, to produce cotton in 1857. Larson, *I Was Called to Dixie*, 67.

72. An allusion to Numbers 11:5 in which the children of Israel complained to Moses, "We remember the fish, which we did eat in Egypt freely; the cucumbers, and the melons, and the leeks, and the onions. . . . "

73. Sarah Elizabeth Smith, Catharine's cousin, married William Thomas Noall on December 15, 1881.

74. Five issues of the *Orion Era*, all from 1883, are located in the University of Arizona Archives, Tucson. For excerpts from it, see Appendix 2.

75. Henry John Platt married Harriet Angeline ("Angie") Lang on December 24, 1878, and William Erastus ("Will") Platt married Isabell Romney on January 4, 1883. Br. Henry Platt was Henry's and Will's father. The Platt family would have been returning to St. Johns after having been in St.

George for Will and Isabell's wedding. For more details on the Platt family, see Appendix 1.

76. Charles S. Cottam married Beata Eliza Johnson on January 8, 1884.

77. William Thompson was a jeweler before he moved to Dixie. William Howard Thompson, "Emma Cottam: Pioneer, Wife and Mother," in Thompson, *Thomas Cottam*, 2:6.

78. Annie was pregnant with Orin Nelson Romney, born March 28, 1884.

79. The annual and semiannual general conferences of the church are held during the first week of April and the first week of October.

80. An essay entitled "Wash Day," which was probably written by Catharine, appeared in the *Orion Era* on November 10, 1883. It is reprinted in Appendix 2.

81. Orin Nelson Romney was born March 28, 1884.

82. This letter, dated March 27, 1884, is printed in Samuel W. Taylor and Raymond W. Taylor, eds., *The John Taylor Papers*, vol. 2, *The President* (Redwood City, Calif.: Taylor Trust, 1985), 327-29.

83. A list of the numbers of families to be called from the various stakes is attached to a letter from Wilford Woodruff to Lot Smith, April 15, 1884, advising Smith of this action, Lot Smith Collection, BYU Archives. See also Udall and Nelson, *Arizona Pioneer Mormon*, 106.

84. The defendants were arrested again and appeared before a grand jury, which dismissed their case. Fish, "History of the Eastern Arizona Stake," 64; *Deseret News*, April 4 and 8, 1884, cited in Thomas C. Romney, *Life Story of Miles Park Romney*, 136-41.

85. The *Tribune* was the anti-Mormon newspaper in Salt Lake City.

86. In a "Retrospective" dated December 4, 1884, the *Apache Chief* bragged about accomplishment of its "avowed purpose of fighting Mormons and their methods."

87. *Apache Chief*, May 9 and December 5, 1884.

88. Ibid., April 4, 1884.

89. The perjury case arose from an incident in which Miles P. Romney attempted to finalize his claim to a 160-acre ranch at Kitchen Springs. By continuous residence on the land for two years, he could claim legal title to the property. Miles had kept members of his family on the piece of land and had hired others to work there, although he had not personally lived there. Miles appeared in court with his two witnesses, David K. Udall and Joseph Crosby. Alfred Ruiz, the clerk of the court, asked Udall if Romney had continuously resided on the land. Udall answered, "No." Ruiz then said, "Has he abandoned the place for six months at a time?" Udall replied, "No, he has not. I have passed by the place and been there on the place at different times and have seen members of his family and hired men there making improvements, and I saw nothing that indicated an intention to abandon it." Ruiz told him that under the law those activities constituted continuous residence. Udall then said, "If that is so, I can answer 'Yes.'" Joseph Crosby entered his testimony based on the same understanding of the law. Udall and Udall, *Arizona Pioneer Mormon*, 119.

Upon learning that this testimony had been given, members of the St. Johns Ring pressed charges for perjury against Miles, Crosby, and Udall on the grounds that they had lied about Miles's continuous residency. In June 1884, the defendants appeared before U.S. Commissioner McCarter, who released them because the documents containing the evidence were in the United States General Land Office in Washington, D.C. In August, the defendants appeared before a grand jury in Prescott, which listened to Udall's and Ruiz's statements and refused to indict them.

At the November 1884 term of court in Prescott, however, the case was presented to another grand jury, and all three defendants were indicted. Udall and Crosby pleaded not guilty, and their cases were continued to the following summer. Miles's indictment was quashed after his attorney argued that, in his case, the judge had failed to properly instruct the jury. The judge then "respited" or reapplied the bonds and ordered Miles to appear before the next grand jury.

The perjury trial was held July 1885. By this time, Miles had gone to Mexico. Joseph Crosby was tried and acquitted. At Udall's trial, the jury was not allowed to hear that it was, in fact, the court clerk, Ruiz, who had instructed Udall that Romney's activities constituted continuous residence on the land. As a result of the exclusion of this evidence, Udall was found guilty. Following his trial, opinion toward him began to shift. The prosecutor listened to Udall's side of the story and said that he would be satisfied with whatever sentence the judge meted. He asked the court to give Udall any benefit of the doubt. Judge Sumner Howard, however, sentenced him to three years in the House of Correction in Detroit, Michigan. After serving five months of his prison term, Udall received a "full and unconditional" pardon from President Grover Cleveland and returned home.

Udall and Nelson, *Arizona Pioneer Mormon*, 114-43; Fish, "History of the Eastern Arizona Stake," 37; Thomas C. Romney, *Life Story of Miles Park Romney*, 141-42; Letter, Annie Romney to Eleanor Jarvis, August 31, 1884; *Apache Chief*, November 14, 1884; "Account of the Defense Fund in the Perjury Cases of Miles P. Romney, David K. Udall and Joseph Crosby," in David K. Udall, "Journal of the L. D. Saints Arrested and Tried," LDS Church Archives.

90. *Apache Chief*, May 30, 1884, cited in Peterson, *Take Up Your Mission*, 229-30.

91. On one occasion, a group of women was quilting when the marshals arrived. The plural wives hid under the bed while Hannah answered the door. The officers presented her with subpoenas for Catherine Woodbury and Annie Cottam (their last names reversed). Catharine started to laugh. One of the other women, who failed to see the humor, began to cry. When Hannah sent the marshals away to get a proper warrant, the plural wives had time to escape. Catharine's daughter Lula remembered hearing her mother and Eliza Tenney laugh over their recollection of the scene. Fragments of this story are related in Lula R. Clayson, "Catherine Jane Cottam Romney—B," photocopy in author's possession, 3; and Thomas C. Romney, *Life Story of Miles Park Romney*, 168-69.

92. Original letter in possession of Ella F. Bentley, Provo, Utah; photocopy in author's possession.

93. This letter was written three days before the birth of Catharine's daughter Emma.

94. Ida Hunt Udall described these events in her Autobiography and Diary, 1873-1905, photocopy, LDS Church Archives.

95. The *Apache Chief* reported Judge Sumner Howard's Fourth of July address given at Prescott: "There is little danger which menaces this beautiful territory equal to that black cloud that follows the blasting approach to a polygamous priesthood, and which has already cast its withering influence over the most beautiful portion of your territory. . . . it is not only the design of the foul and unscrupulous priesthood to seize upon this Territory and those adjoining it but that it will be an accomplished fact unless there is a rising of the people of this Territory. . . . " *Apache Chief,* July 18, 1884, quoted in Peterson, *Take Up Your Mission,* 229.

96. Beginning in 1884, Eleanor Jarvis became very ill with milk leg (clotting and inflammation of veins in the leg after childbirth). She was often bedridden and unable to care for her family. Her husband's second wife, Rose, who had no children of her own, helped care for Eleanor's children and taught school. Her health was restored some seventeen or eighteen years later following a blessing she received in the temple in St. George. Diary of Eleanor C. W. Jarvis, typescript, Utah State Historical Society, 3-4.

97. Original letter in possession of Ella F. Bentley, Provo, Utah; photocopy in author's possession.

98. They argued that, under the Edmunds Law, entering into a polygamous marriage constituted a felony but that subsequent cohabitation was only a misdemeanor. *United States v. Tenney,* 2 Ariz. 29, 8 Pac. 295 (1885).

99. Joseph E. Johnson was a horticulturalist, founder of the Gardners' Club in St. George, medicinal expert, and publisher of Dixie's first newspaper. Larson, *I Was Called to Dixie,* 335-43, 431-36, 442-43. He was Maude Crosby's father.

100. The author of a contemporaneous account of these events concluded, "The respital of these bonds were considered illegal and if Bro. Romney does not appear to await the action of the Grand Jury, the bonds cannot be collected according to the judgment of good attorneys." "Account of the Defense Fund in the Perjury Cases." Perhaps he reasoned that his bonds had been spent by his appearance in court and that some other legal process, such as issuing of a warrant, would be required before he could again be placed under bonds.

101. When Miles failed to appear for his trial in July 1885, William J. Flake, who had just returned from serving six months in the territorial penitentiary in Yuma for polygamy, paid the bonds at great hardship to himself and his family. Omer D. Flake, *William J. Flake: Pioneer—Colonizer* (n.p., n.d.), 102-3, 109-10.

102. A term used in a letter of the First Presidency to presidents of the stakes at Eastern Arizona, Little Colorado, St. Joseph and Maricopa, dated December 16, 1884, in Taylor and Taylor, *The John Taylor Papers,* 329.

103. Flake and Skousen were advised that Judge Sumner Howard had agreed to the lighter sentence if they would plead guilty. *Deseret News*, March 6, 1885, quoted in Thomas C. Romney, *Life Story of Miles Park Romney*, 163-64.

104. Udall, "Journal of the L. D. Saints Arrested and Tried."

105. "Account of the Defense Fund in the Perjury Cases."

106. "Better for parts of families to remove and go where they can live in peace than to be hauled to prison. . . . " First Presidency to Presidents of Stakes at Eastern Arizona, Little Colorado, St. Joseph and Maricopa, December 16, 1884, in Taylor and Taylor, *The John Taylor Papers*, 329.

107. Smith, *Journal of Jesse N. Smith*, 296-321.

108. Hannah H. Romney, "Autobiography," 11, 12.

109. Ibid., 12.

110. Thomas C. Romney, *Life Story of Miles Park Romney*, 173-76.

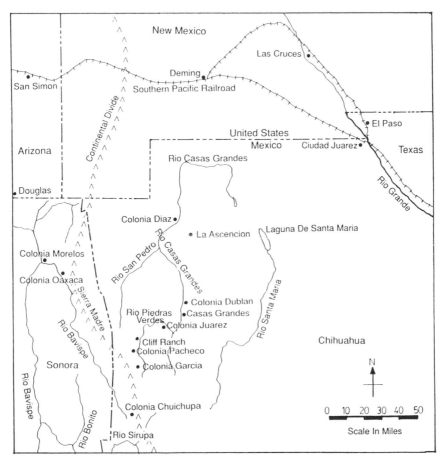

The Mormon colonies in Mexico. (Map drawn by Jolane Moulton)

This photo of Catharine and her children was taken in St. George prior to their departure for Mexico in January 1887. It was especially prized by Catharine because it was her only picture of Claude, who died shortly thereafter. Catharine refers to the photo in her letter of February 27, 1887. *Standing:* Thomas and Caroline. *Sitting:* Claude, Junius, Park, Catharine, and Emma. (Courtesy of Special Collections Department, University of Utah Libraries)

Olla Cave Cliff Dwellings, Cave Valley, Mexico, which Catharine described in her letter of September 11, 1889. Catharine said that the vessel was "built of mud made of clay mixed with straw or grass, about two or three inches thick." (Courtesy of the Church Archives, Church of Jesus Christ of Latter-day Saints)

Mill built by William R. R. Stowell. The house was occupied by the family of Brigham Stowell, whose daughter Gertrude married Junius Romney. (Courtesy of Genevieve Moulton)

Annie Maria Woodbury
Romney. (Courtesy of the
St. Johns Stake Family
History Center)

Annie and her children. *Back (left
to right):* Erastus, Alice, Ann, and
Orin. *Front (left to right):*
Eleanor, Erma, Annie, and Ivie.
(Courtesy of Ella F. Bentley)

Catharine and her children taken about 1895. *Back row (left to right):*
Caroline, Junius, and Park. *Front row (left to right):* Emma, Ethel,
Catharine, Lula, and Ida. Thomas would have been on his mission.
(Courtesy of Genevieve Moulton)

Miles, Hannah, and their children. (Courtesy of Jasmine Romney Edmunds)

George Frederick and Eleanor Cannon Woodbury Jarvis family. *Back row (left to right):* Annie, Clarence, Orin, and John. *Front row (left to right):* Eleanor ("Ella"), Frank, George, Eleanor, and Rose. (Originally published in *George Jarvis and Joseph George DeFriez Genealogy* by Margaret Jarvis Overson)

Home of Junius Romney in Colonia Juarez. Catharine had a home built on an adjoining lot. (Courtesy of the Church Archives, Church of Jesus Christ of Latter-day Saints)

PART THREE

Mexico

The simple fact that the Mormons could escape the anti-polygamy laws of the United States by moving to Mexico qualified it as a logical retreat for those desperate families that winter of 1884-85.[1] Beyond that, a mild climate and arable land allowed a reasonable hope of securing a livelihood. Perhaps overly friendly to foreigners, Mexico's president, Porfirio Díaz, believed that the economic future of his country depended on foreign capital and initiative.[2] By 1912, Díaz's policies would lead to a revolution that would drive the Mormons from Mexico.[3] In the meantime, Mexico would provide a haven for a generation of polygamous Mormon families.

Ultimately, the Mormons established eight colonies in Mexico. Six were in the state of Chihuahua and two in neighboring Sonora.[4] But in the winter of 1884-85 the church's contact in Mexico was limited to a few missionary and exploring parties. It would take time, energy, and diplomacy to cultivate relationships, rent and buy land, and build towns, farms, and industries.

With no end to the polygamy prosecutions in sight, the Romneys decided that Miles, Annie, and her children would go to Mexico. Catharine and her children were to remain temporarily in St. George with the Cottams.[5]

Miles and Annie traveled by train, Miles disguising himself so completely that even members of his own family did not recognize him.[6] They stopped in Salt Lake City, where Miles disposed of his remaining real estate holdings. After heading west to San Francisco, they went south, stopping at San Simon, Arizona. There they were met by Will and Miles A., who had brought a team, a wagon, *and provisions from Hannah.[7] After traveling another ninety miles by team, across the international border, they arrived within a week of the first Mormon colonists and settled in a temporary camp a few miles from La Ascencion, site of the customshouse.[8]*

Among those already there were old friends from Arizona and St. George, including President Jesse N. Smith, who was presiding over the camp. Jesse N.'s brother, Lot Smith, founder of Sunset, Arizona, gave Miles a pair of boots and a wagon cover, saying, "Use these to protect yourselves from the weather."[9] The Romneys built their first shelter in Mexico by driving four posts into the ground and covering two sides with burlap sacks sewn together. The wagon box and some brush made the other two sides.[10]

Within six weeks of the first arrivals, their numbers had reached 350.[11] Alarmed at this influx of Americans, local officials concluded that they intended to invade. The chief magistrate at Casas Grandes dispatched a letter to the Mormons ordering them to leave by April 25, 1885.[12]

Church leaders immediately requested a stay of the order until they could dispatch representatives to confer with federal officials in Mexico City. They contacted a young Mexican lawyer, who presented their position in a well-written document.[13] By the time they were able to meet with President Díaz, he had completed discussions with his ministers regarding the Mormon question. The outcome was favorable to the Mormons. General Pacheco, minister of colonization, issued an order that the Mormons not be molested, and the local official who had issued the expulsion order was relieved of his position. President Díaz welcomed the Mormons, saying that his administration wanted "a class of colonists that will build up and help develop the resources of the country, and we feel assured that this is the object of your coming among us." He also introduced them to people who could sell them land. General Pacheco said he felt confident that the Mormons could practice their religion if they would quietly go about their business.[14]

At the end of June 1885, Miles and Annie moved into a small Mexican house about a mile and a half from La Ascension. They used the wagon box for a bedroom. Their garden supplied them with vegetables, which Annie cooked over the fireplace. On July 5, 1885, Annie wrote to her sister, Eleanor Jarvis, "I would find it very lonesome here if I had any spare time, but I have too much to do to think about it very often. I generally feel worst when I try to write, for a long time I always had to have a good cry, but I am getting hardened now so that I don't mind it so much. . . . some of the brethren have gone now to see about purchasing some land up in the mountains. . . . "[15]

About sixty miles from the temporary camp near La Ascencion and only twelve miles from the Mexican town of Casas Grandes, explorers had found fine timber and soft water in "an excellent mountain stream . . . running over gravel and cobble rock" with "rich alluvial soil on the river bottoms."[16] Here they surveyed a townsite for "Colonia Juarez" and were still negotiating its purchase in December 1885, when a few settlers, among them the Romneys, relocated there. The Romneys' new home was a twelve-by-fourteen-foot dugout in the bank of the Piedras Verdes River.[17]

On December 27, 1885, Miles wrote long and discouraging letters to Catharine and her brother Thomas. He had been advised to return to Arizona to save his bonds, but while making preparations to leave, he had learned that they had been forfeited and that he was now subject to arrest in both the United States and Mexico. To Thomas, he related:

> The other day I went out Deer hunting   saw a herd of about 100 Antelope and followed them 6 miles and at night returned home loaded with—disappointment and no meat, but I'm going to try it again before long. . . .
>
> I sometimes think that I am only an injury now to both my family and my friends. I have borrowed my friends money, and my family receive no support from me. and the prospect ahead seems as black as midnight darkness. I would not trouble so much if my family had a comfortable home and I was out of debt, but it worries me to be in debt and helpless to work and repay, but such are my unfortunate circumstances today.
>
> So far as my faith is concerned in the Gospel it was never better   I know that truth will triumph, though some of us may be sacrificed in its establishment.
>
> I feel grateful to you for what you have done for my family and hope if I am not able to return the kindness that Catherine will teach her children to remember and repay in years to come.
>
> If the Marshalls come here I do not know whether I will fight or not. If I can dodge I will. If I cannot time alone will tell what I may do. It is pure malice that makes them pursue me so relentlessly and if old Judge Howard would come in person he might get sick and return.
>
> The climate here is lovely, warm and pleasant. We have not had a storm in the last three months.
>
> It is hard to tell where I will be when you get this. I may be here and I may have left Mexico or I may [have been] captured. I hope not the latter.

> *I have written to Catherine today a good long letter, but I hate to write such letters, no good news, but the same old story of trouble and a stormy looking future.*
>
> *Annie and Children are all well and join in kind regards.*
>
> *Bro Thomas may God bless you is the sincere prayer of your friend and brother in exile.*[18]

In February 1886, church leaders in Mexico City finalized the purchase of 60,000 hectares (about 20,000 acres) for Colonia Juarez from the Ignacio G. del Campo Company.[19] The Jefe Politico, the judges, and a Catholic priest from Casas Grandes, the county seat twelve miles away, joined the Mormons in their celebration of the birthday of the Mexican patriot, Benito Juarez, March 21, on which occasion they named their town "Colonia Juarez." Miles P. Romney was orator of the day.[20]

Miles soon sent his son Will back to St. Johns with a team and wagon to bring Hannah and her children to Mexico.[21] Hannah had been alone with her children in St. Johns for over a year, struggling to provide for them. Fearing for her children's safety, she detested the wickedness surrounding them. When Will arrived, she sold her household belongings and purchased another team and wagon. Hannah's daughters, Isabell and Minnie, who had married, stayed in St. Johns along with Will, who found work in Arizona. In March 1886, Hannah left for Mexico with her other children. She had planned to travel with the Skousens, but they were not quite ready, and she did not want to be apart from her husband for another two weeks. When she stopped in Nutrioso to visit her dear friends the Paces, they told her she must be crazy to cross the territory where Geronimo was on the warpath. She replied that she would trust in the Lord.

Hannah and her children traveled on unfamiliar roads through hazardous ice, snow, and mud. She sat up all night holding her baby. One morning, they woke to find they had spent the night at a recent Indian campsite. When she finally reached the border, customs officials declared a twenty-five dollar duty on her cookstove. She did not have the money. As they tried to lift it out of the wagon, they broke two of the rods and decided she could keep the stove and return with the money later.

Miles was delighted to have Hannah and her children safely in Mexico. He had built her a small house with a mud roof and dirt floor. Two boxes fastened together formed a table; log stumps served as chairs. Hannah remembered, "I was thankful for it, as my dear children and I would be with their father and we could *live in peace, with no marshals to molest us or separate us again. . . . "[22] When Hannah arrived in Mexico, Annie's baby was three weeks old. Annie resumed teaching school, and Hannah tended the children.[23]*

The colonists had planted crops, built homes and a few public buildings, and dug a canal when they learned that, through a faulty survey, their settlement encroached on the holdings of the land and cattle baron Don Luis Terrazas. They had to relocate five miles upstream. Survey of the new townsite for Colonia Juarez began in November 1886.[24]

Finally it was time to send for Catharine. Miles asked Hannah if she thought they would be able to feed so many. Hannah replied that "the Lord would open the way for us to get food if we would do right and put our trust in Him."[25]

Catharine and her children had lived in St. George with the Cottams for two years. They tried to be helpful to the relatives. George Cottam noted in his record book, "Thomas Romney helped me haul corn today."[26] Thomas, Junius, and Claude contracted to herd about thirty head of cattle for the neighbors at a cent and a half a day.[27]

Thomas and Caroline Cottam's family had grown while Catharine was in Arizona. Thomas P., Catharine's younger brother, had married Emeline Jarvis, sister-in-law of Eleanor Jarvis. When Catharine arrived in St. George, they were the parents of Emma, age 2, and a baby, Thomas. Catharine's youngest brother, Charles, had also married. His wife of one year, Beata Eliza Johnson, a young convert from Sweden, was expecting their first child. Emma and William Thompson had eight children, including Amelia and Matilda by William's first marriage, and Emma (15), Nelly (13), William (10), Mary (7), Joseph (4), and George (1). George and Rachel had Mary Ann (9), Rachel (7), Caroline (6), Georgie (4), Ada (2), and James (3 months). More little nieces and nephews were added during the two years Catharine and her children stayed in St. George. Charles and Beata, who made their home in Salt Lake City, were spending the winter of 1886-87 in St. George to be in the warm climate for Beata's health. Family gatherings would have seen the young cousins enjoying each other's company. Still, Catharine and her children were anxious to join Miles.

On Christmas Day 1886, a Saturday, Thomas and Caroline Cottam hosted a family dinner. Apostle Wilford Woodruff, who was in hiding from the federal marshals, joined their celebration. A week later, the family gathered at the home of George and Rachel for New Year's dinner.[28]

The next Monday, Catharine and her children were ready to leave for Mexico. Apostle Wilford Woodruff gave them a blessing,[29] and they bid their family good-bye. Then George Cottam drove them in his wagon to the train station in Milford in central Utah. The wagon trip to Milford lasted four days. On Friday, January 7, 1887, George wrote in his daybook, "go to Milford by 4 am   very cold started Catharine off."[30] It was Catharine's thirty-second birthday. The train traveled north to Salt Lake City, east through Denver, and, finally, south to Deming, New Mexico, where Catharine and her children were met by teams to cross the border into Mexico.[31] They still had several days' journey ahead of them.

When they finally arrived in Colonia Juarez, Catharine would have been disappointed that there was no news from home. She wrote home but heard nothing. It would soon be six weeks since she had left St. George, and there was still no word. The following undated letter was found in an envelope postmarked Casas Grandes on one side and El Paso, Texas, Feb 15 10 AM 1887 on the other side.

Dear Father and Mother   I am just going to write you a line or two thay [that] you may know I am still in the land of the living, if you havent forgotten that there is such a person.

What is the matter? have you all left the country, or are you too busy to write? Still I can hardly beleive you have neglected to write for so long. if I knew it was the fault of the Post Masters. I should ache to give them all a good "going over"

Please give my kind love to all. and accept the same

From your loving daughter

C. J. Romney

10 Feb. 1887
Juarez near Cases Grande

Dear Father & Mother   We recieved your most welcome letter of Jan. 28" the day before yesterday, the first word I had got from you since I left home, so you may imagine how anxious I was. I am so sorry to hear that you have both been sick, but I hope you are reasonably well again   you say Aunty and her baby are well. what is the baby and when was it born, and who did they get to stay with them? You know they spoke to me about staying with them.

I wrote to you the day after I got here. hope you got it.

The paper has never come yet. I dont know what can be the matter. Miles sends his love to you. he feels very grateful to you all and often speaks about you. he says he knows you both miss me. he says he knows by the way he missed me himself, while we were so long seperated. he is well with the exception of his cough. Hannah is not feeling well lately. I think that some of the children had the scarletina when we got here as two or three of them were quite sick on the road, but I did not then know what it was. it has gone through nearly all the family. Thomas [age 10] is quite sick now and has been for three days, but they have all been able to walk about, so it must be a mild form. One of our brethren who lives at Casa Grande has lost three of his children, and have several more sick, with some disease which is raging among the mexicans at that place. I suppose it is the scarletina in an aggravated form, and perhaps other diseases with it. there is only the one family of our people there. This is thought to be a very healthy climate. Miles says the only objection he sees to it is the sudden change of temperature when people are apt to take cold unless they are careful.

The children started to school the second day after we got here. the term was out last Friday and commenced again on Monday.

There are some little things that I forgot to bring. I saved some nice peach, apricot and plum pits, and am so sorry I did not bring a few of them. Miles has been planting some almonds today which Emma gave me. I wish I had brought a few of the soft shelled ones as well, and some onion seed. I also forgot to bring that stick of brimstone out of the cupboard, and you know Annie wrote, and asked me to bring some indigo, but I forgot that too, this is about the hardest of any thing to get here. Br. [George C.] Williams who came from Demming with us paid 50 cts for a box of pepper box blueing containing three dozen boxes, and the duty on it was $1.23 cts. I could have put a chunk of indigo in my pocket if I had just thought of it.

The boys have shot a duck tonight. there are lots of them on the river.

Miles is going to Casa Grande tomorrow to take a grist and I expect to go with him.

Poor old Sr. Johnson will be missed by a great many people.

My dear Parents I feel so thankful that Charles and Beata are with you this winter. please give my love to them, also to George and Thomas and families, and to my dear sister. (I shall be thankful to hear of her being right well again) and family, how are the [Thompson] girls, Matilda, Amelia, Emma and Nelly. Who has Br. [William] Lang taken with him, and is he coming here?

Br. & Sr. [Erastus] Snow are well. he comes in quite often.

We have potatoes, and plenty of beans, plenty of corn meal and some flour. We killed a fine pig just after we came, weighing 150 lbs. and a week after we had a family party   21 of us all together. had a splendid dinner, lacking only the fruit. we felt very grateful to our heavenly father that we were permitted to be once more together. the other day Miles bought a deer, which we enjoyed very much. he has been plowing, making a coffin, and planting peas today. he finished his portion of the ditch for the new town site last week. Gaskell [Hannah's son, age 15] and Thomas helped, and worked well, so their Pa said. Miles A. [Hannah's son, age 17] has not been able to use his arm much yet, so is going to school. We have a good team, and feed to keep it till grass comes. This past week has been quite stormy, wind and some rain, the first of the season. The children do not forget you. Emma [age 2] has fine times with Eugene [Hannah's son, age 3] and Orin [Annie's son, age 2]. I thought of writing to Uncle John Burns [in Salt Lake City], but you may please tell him of us as he said he should feel very anxious to hear. Good bye and much love.

C. J. Romney

I feel very happy and comfortable in my new home. I think I have one of the best and kindest of husbands. Miles says he hopes you will sometime be able to pay us a visit as the journey can be made in a short time and the expense not very great.

21" Feb. 1887
Juarez near Casa Grande   Chihuahua   Mexico

My Dear Father & Mother   Before you get this you will have heard through Miles' letter to George, of our sad loss, our dear little Claude [age 7] has gone and left us, and we sorely miss him and it was hard to reconcile ourselves to part with him, but still we feel to acknowlege the hand of God in this great affliction, as well as in the many blessings which he has bestowed upon us, and we certainly have much to be thankful for, that we were able to get what he craved while sick which was fruit and milk and such medicines as we thought would be good for him. Br. [Erastus] Snow very kindly sent us some dried fruit for him, so that he had all that he needed. I feel great satisfaction in the thought that he was laid away very nicely. as it happened, Hannah had a piece of beautiful linen, just enough to make him a pair of pants, waist & shoes, which together with a pair of nice white stockings and garments, and a white ribbon bow at his neck made up his burial cloths, and he looked very natural, and had such a sweet expression on his dear little face.

I feel from circumstances connected with his sickness, that he had to go. his Pa administered to him many times, as well as calling in others of the brethren very often, and the little fellow had great faith in this ordinance, often saying, when suffering so intensely, I want Pa to pray for me, and sometimes making the same request of me when I was lying by him in the night. he always wanted either his Pa or me to lie down by him as long as he was concious. he was unconcious most of the time for the last day and night. he suffered intensely the latter part of his illness [scarlatina] and had a great many spasams, but still our faith was strong that he would recover, and we held on to him, until it seemed cruel to do so any longer. it is needless for me to tell you how hard it was to part with him, since you have several times passed through the same ordeal. I cannot tell you how thankful I am that I am here with my dear husband. the trial would have been a much more bitter one without him to comfort and console me. I always prayed earnestly that their lives might all be spared until we should be priveliged to be reunited with our loved ones, for your sakes also I am thankful we were here, for I know what an anxiety it would have been to you, if anything had happened while we were there. Park [age 4] is much better again his bloating has entirely gone, but he is quite thin. Hannah is very sick today. she was taken very sick while waiting on Claude on Monday night when he was first taken with spasams. she has been some better since for two or three days, but is worse again. I do hope she will soon be all right again.

When we got home from burying our little boy I found your letter awaiting us, and were very pleased to hear from you as I had felt quite anxious about you. we are so sorry to know you have both been sick but thankful to know you are better again. I think of you so often and wonder how you all are. How do you get the washing done, etc. I am so glad Emma is so near you and that Charles & Beata are with you.

Do you hear anything of Br. [Frederick William] Foremaster? Did Br. [William] Lang get the order for the things and is he expecting to come here?

When you write if you know anything of Annie's folks [Orin and Ann C. Woodbury], please to mention them as she dos'nt hear from them very often. The folks send kind love to you.

So poor Br. [George] Baker has gone to rest at last   it must be a happy release to him after being in such a state for so long.

Park and Emma [age 2] stood the journey well, so did all of them except Caroline [age 12], who was quite sea sick. we didnt any of us really suffer with the cold, as we had plenty of wraps, and the cars were nice and warm.

I had about 100 lbs of freight over weight but I dont know how much it cost as Geo[rge]. Romney [Miles's brother in Salt Lake City] very kindly attended to all such things so that I had no trouble about it. I heard Br. Snow say that he had dried fruit shipped from Milford [Utah] to Demming [New Mexico], and it only cost him five cts per lb. so freight cannot be so very high from Salt lake through [though?] this same fruit he got through the Custom House free of duty by opening and taking a little out of each sack. they should not charge duty on anything which a person is using out of, but they cannot be depended on very much. some people get through easily, and some have to pay enormous prices. Miles says that after living in the country for two years he knows very little more about duty than when he first came, as they are so changeable. we were very fortunate and did not have to pay a cent of duty on anything except a shovel which we got at Demming for another person, but if they had searched our wagon as closely as they do some peoples we should have to have paid. they only opened one box lid and looked among the bedding a little. if a person has a little tact they can bring many little things medecines etc. by tying them up in a rag and throwing it in their provision box, or something of the sort.

Br [Ralph] Ramsey has been to Demming to meet his wife, who went back from here. they are expected back now. the old lady did not come with us. Two sisters Spencer from the Seiver [Sevier] with their four children, Sr. [Dora Wilcken] Pratt, and her five children, a brother from the 1" Ward S.L. City and myself and children, travelled together. they were very agreeable, and our journey was as pleasant as we could reasonably expect.

Miles thought we all looked well considering the journey etc.

We wondered why the paper did not come. thanks for the one you sent. I dont know how it is, as the Utah papers come all right. All births and deaths are required by law to be registered, the cost of each registration being $1.00. There is a premium of 20 or 25 cts on american money over the mexican currency, showing a bad state of affairs when they discount their own money. In regard to citizenship, Miles tells me it is optional with an individual the same as in the U.S. of course if they do not become citizens, they cannot enjoy the priveliges of citizens.

Two or three weeks ago Miles took me down to Casa Granda for a ride when he went after the mail. this is the nearest town to us. it is 12 miles off. it is much like other mexican towns which I have seen but rather better looking. it seems to abound in hogs which run at large in the streets, is devoid of trees, shrubbery or any green thing almost, though it is said to be 150 years old. there is not a fence nor anything to make it look homelike. The country is beautiful. [*Last part is missing.*]

Catharine was grief stricken over the loss of her little Claude. For many days, her only consolation was to gather flowers along the banks of the river and weave them into baskets.[32]

Feb 27, 1887
Colonia Juarez

Dear Father & Mother, I always felt very thankful for having our pictures taken, as also was Miles, who appreciated them *very* much, but now we feel doubly so, it is a priceless treasure. To have our dear little son's form and features where we can look at them, is indeed a blessed privelige, and a great comfort to us both. Claude was always a great favorite with his Pa who is very fond of his children. he was always such an independant little fellow and so full of life and activity. The train hands on the road seemed to take quite a notion to him. one of the conductors gave him 20 cts. others an apple, orange etc.

There has been a brother Wm. N. Fife here the other day from Sulphur Springs Arizona. he says he and his first wife whose name was Davis, were well acquainted with you both in the early days of Salt Lake. he built the house which Sutton afterwards owned, above Cumberlands. he is scotch and his wife welsh. she was killed by a Mexican a year or two ago. I remember reading an account of it in the paper; he talks some of moving out here.

If you happen to see Mary Lund [Miles's sister] you may please to tell her about how we are.

With kind love to my brothers & sisters I remain as ever your loving daughter

Catharine

Has Aunt Mariett's affairs been settled up yet? Kind love to Grandma Pymm   Miles sends kind regards to all.

6" March 1887
Juarez near Casa Grande   Chihuahua

My Dear Parents   It is only a week since I last wrote to you, but I am certain that another letter, though following so soon on the last will not be unwelcome, and I am certain you will feel very anxious to know how we all are. We are all much better. Hannah is able to be around again and as well as can be expected. Park [age 4] is improving nicely. Miles' cough is some better. I think he will continue to improve as spring advances. he has lost considerable in weight in the last month, owing, partly at least to care and anxiety. We all feel very thankful to the Lord for opening up the way for me to come when I did. I doubt not but our dear little Claude is happier and better off, but it seems so lonely without him. oh how I miss him when I get them washed or ready for Sunday School.

We are having lovely weather lately no storms except wind. this is the only disagreeable weather we have had.

Please tell Charles that I found one of the keys and will send it when I get a chance. it was among my cloths in the box.

In regard to the paper Father! if you wish to send me one, I should very much like to have one which Eleanor Jarvis takes. I think it costs only 50 cts per year, and is a splendid ladies paper. I believe it is called the "Farm and Fireside."

Mother if you have a coarse darning needle to spare would you please to put one in your next letter, as I forgot to get any. I think if it were wrapped in a bit of thin tissue paper to keep it from rattling about, it would come all right. Dear Mother, how is your rheumatism? Hannah says when she had the rheumatism in St. John after I left, she cured it by taking half a teaspoon full of soda in a little water evry morning before eating. Wont you try it? as it is so simple and handy.

Have you had any more of your bad spells Father? I feel so anxious about you both, and we all pray for you that you may enjoy health.

I hope the children and all are better than when you wrote last.

Please give my love to Emma and family, girls and all, to the boys and their wives. I should very much like to hear from any of them.

The birds begin to sing sweetly, and the cottonwoods are putting forth their green buds; if we could only have some nice rains to bring up the grass for our stock, and insure a good harvest we should feel very thankful.

If it were not for our great loss, I should feel very happy indeed, blessed with one of the best and kindest of husbands, my dear children and Parents, Brothers & Sisters. I have much to be thankful for, and sometimes feel that it is wrong for me to grieve, because the Lord has seen fit in his providence to take one of our treasures for a season.

Miles got up a new milk cow yesterday, which will be a great help to us.

With kindest love I remain as ever your affectionate daughter

Catharine J Romney

Dear Mother I enclose a lock of our little boys hair which I cut from his head when I combed him just before putting him in his coffin. also a bit of linen of which his cloths were made, thinking you will be pleased to have them.

Miles wishes me to tender his kindest love to you. also Hannah and the rest of the folks. Please forward the enclosed note to Uncle John Burns

20″ March 1887
Juarez

Dear Parents   It was with feelings of joy and thankfulness that I perused your most welcome letter of the 6″, received last evening. I had suffered considerable anxiety since receiving your previous letter, informing us of Mothers serious illness, though Miles tried to encourage me all that he could as he felt impressed that she was better, and thank God that his impression has proved to be correct. I do hope and trust that by this time you have both regained your usual health and strength. I know just how attentive and good Emma and Beata and all the girls have been in taking care of Mother and I am so thankful to know they are all so near to look after you both. I am glad Aunt Mary called to see you while you were sick. The children have all had bad coughs but are about over them now. Hannah is quite poorly but better than she was.

Miles his wrist is well again. he and Gaskell [Hannah's son, age 15] are hauling posts to fence our city lots. Miles has been working on the new water ditch evry day the past week, trying to run the water through and has worked too hard and nearly used himself up, as he has had very little help, and he being one of the committee it has depended on him, as most of the brethren are at work on the road up the mountain, where the saw mill is to be set. it has been here a week or more. Miles was to have gone this week with Br. [Apostle Moses] Thatcher and others on the mountain this week but could not leave.

Annie is still teaching school though she has'nt many scholars as several families have moved up to the new town site. people are beginning to do some gardening. our peas, onions, etc. are up. There has not been any snow here, and very little rain, so we shall have to trust to the summer rains to bring up the grass for our stock and also for assisting in raising crops. I trust the Lord will abundantly bless us to this end.

Miles was called on to lecture again last evening to the Mutual. I went and enjoyed it very much.

We killed a pig this week which weighed 135 lbs. we have one new milk cow and one or two to come in soon. We got your letter yesterday and thank you for it.

How is Emma's health. And the girls. I must try to write to her soon. How is Emma [Thompson Squire] and John [Squire] getting along?[33]

Is Br. [William] Lang intending to come on here   I supposed he did when he offered to get my things from Br. [Frederick William] Foremaster. did he get the order for them. Miles, Hannah and all send their love. they are all very thankful to know you are better. Hannah says tell Mother she is so thankful for and pleased with her towel. she says you could'nt have sent anything which would have pleased her better.

We get our mail twice a week from Casa Grandes. the brethren go after it in turns. Miles acts as Post-Master for the camp. [*Last part is missing.*]

May 1" 1887
Juarez   Mexico

My Beloved Parents   I have been looking so anxiously for further word from you. I hope however that I shall not be disappointed next mail. the last word I had Mother was still very sick. I do hope that her recovery will be sure and speedy. Oh that I could know that Mother was bustling around today as she has nearly always been getting dinner and waiting on Father, and doing a score of little odd jobs. I cannot bear to think of you dear Mother as being confined to a sick bed for so many weeks, and suffering as you must have done, and the great anxiety of all in regard to you. We are all tolerable well at presant except Annie's baby [Erastus] which has been quite poorly with his teething for a week past.

Miles sends his best regards to you. he says to tell you that water is getting scarce and not a very good prospect for crops at presant, but still we hope for the rains to come soon. March was a lovely month and Miles planted the garden thinking he could bring it along while there was plenty of water. it came up beautifully when there came [a] cold snap and froze it off, so that it will have to be planted over again. Miles planted the almonds which I brought. there are 12 or 14 of them up and I hope they will grow and do well. There were seven head of horses stolen last Sunday two of them right out of camp. truly there are many things to discourage the people here, as well as some to encourage. it seems to be a time of disappointments and uncertainty and people who have been struggling on here for two years and over and living on faith as it were, have to continue to so live, seeing but a short distance ahead of them at a time but still I have no doubt but there will be a brighter day in the near future. There are a good many coming lately but they mostly seem to be people who are hard pressed, which dos'nt help the circumstances of those already here. Teams started from here yesterday to bring 57 Mexican Mormon converts from the City of Mexico, we expect them here in a few days.[34] this will be an extra burthen on the people here, but of course it is a work which is necessary to be done, and must have a beginning and which will undoubtedly result in great good, sooner or later. We expect that Br. [Erastus] Snow will be back here before long. he was in the city of Mexico when we heard from him last. Br. [Henry] Eyring and family are well.[35] they talk of moving up to the townsite in a few days. they have been staying in Br. Snows house since they came. his son Ed. [Eyring] and Joe Breyner started back to the States yesterday.

Horses and stock are very poor as the grass is so dry and of course the hay and corn fodder is nearly done.

We have not suffered for the necessaries of life and I think we shall not if we can only have good crops. Miles thinks some of moving me up to the townsite in a few days, but not certain. Leo [Hannah's son, age 3 weeks] is a fine bright little fellow. School will be out next friday. the children are busy learning recitations dialogues etc. for the last day.

I have been busy this week making baskets, one of the neighbors found out I could make them and came to see if I would make her two or three. she let me have some soap grease which was very acceptable, as we were just out of soap.[36]

I think I must have left my gingham skirt as I can only find the waist, (the one Mary gave me.) I have been wondering if, as it is not very heavy, you could send it to me by mail, if there is no one coming. I hate to ask you but I shall need it this summer, and I think it would not cost much and would not be liable to make trouble if it should be opened, as it is dirty and has been worn. parcels of small articles often come through the mail. I will enclose three 2 cent American stamps. they are no use here. Postage seems high from here to the States, but strange as it seems, it costs 10 cents to send a letter from one point to an other in Mexico, be the distance ever so short.

I hope the children are all better. I hear the whooping cough has been in St George. nearly all of the children here have had it, one baby, Mattie Dillmans, died from it.

The "Farm and Fireside" has come all right, many thanks for it. Please give my love to all my brothers and sisters. I have been expecting letters from some of them, but as yet in vain. Good bye for the presant, and may God bless, preserve, and heal you both is my prayer, for my dear Father & Mother. How I should like to see you.

May 1887
Juarez
Mrs. Eleanor C. Jarvis

Dear Friend   I think I have not answered your kind letter recieved some weeks ago, so I will proceed to do so. we are all pretty well now except Erastus [Annie's son, age 1] who is teething and not feeling very well. Annie wrote to you about a week ago, so I suppose she told you about the earthquake etc. forty persons are reported killed in a town in Sonora about a hundred miles from here, so we may consider ourselves very fortunate in escaping without injury to people or damage to property in this part of the country.

A week ago yesterday Miles moved me up to the townsite, and I have got quite comfortably located in my new home. It seems a long week since I saw Hannah & Annie. I have just come down this morning to spend the day and go to meeting we left Caroline [age 12] & Thomas [age 11] at home to keep house. I have a large mexican wagon box and a nice large shed made of green willows, which makes me very comfortable. I have a cow and some chickens. Miles and the boys plowed and planted a garden patch yesterday, so if we have good luck I hope we shall soon have some garden stuff.

Br. [Henry] Eyring and Dessie [Eyring] are camped about a block from us. she has been down two or three days this week and I have been showing her how to make baskets. she got along splendidly. they seem to feel quite contented. Br. Eyring rode down with us this morning. We have had quite an adventerous time of it this week. on Wednesday evening one of the neighbors called in to see me, and while sitting talking we saw a scorpion crawling up the fireplace. but we didnt get to kill it. the same night, I woke up in the night and heard a rustling among the leaves in the roof of the shed. I lay and watched and listened and feared it might be a snake but as it was moonlight I could finally discern the shape of it enough to know that it was not a snake but could not tell what it was. when it came daylight I found it was on some sacks and went under the wagon box. I could see it was spotted black and white. Gaskell [Hannah's son, age 15] was sleeping there so I called him and Thomas up and they poked it with long sticks but it would not come out. we found it had killed a hen which had roosted at the side of the shed in the willows and concluded it must be a skunk. I sent for one of the neighbors who came and shot three times with his pistol and once with his shotgun, which latter blew its head out into the house. the boys got the rest of it out and buried it. you may imagine the smell but the wind blew hard and the place being so open, soon carried the worst of it away. the same day in the afternoon there was a large snake in the shed which run under the wagon box, but we have not seen it since. I hope you are all well. give my love to Rosie [plural wife of George Jarvis,] Ellie [Eleanor's daughter] and the children and your Ma [Ann Cannon Woodbury] and accept a large portion for yourself. From your loving friend

Catharine J. Romney

22" May 1887
Juarez

My Dear Parents   I sit down to answer your most welcome letter of the 4 ult. I felt thankful indeed to learn from it that Mother was on the mend. I hope and pray that it may be permanent this time. oh what a seige you have had. it makes my heart ache to think of it. I was so thankful to know that my dear sister had got through with her trouble and was doing well. may God bless and strengthen her, and you all.

I went yesterday afternoon to visit my dear little Claudie's grave. the fire which burned over so much of this country two or three weeks ago, had passed over the graveyard, burning up all the grass, but I was thankful to see had not injured or disfigured the head-boards. his was just as his Pa left it when we buried him   name and age quite distinct. It seems to me that I miss him more than ever since I have had them up here where there are not so many of us. Please give my love to my brothers and sisters. I need not tell you how I should like to see you all. Miles has put up a temporary fence and he says I ought to tell you how high toned we are. we used to think we were doing well if we could get black walnut furniture, but we now have a black walnut gate. what do you think of that for style? Mary says in the children's letter that Uncle Charles has got the porch almost done   I didn't know he would be able to work on it at all while Mother was so sick. How has Beata's health been. I suppose little Mary [Charles and Beata's daughter, age 1] has grown very interesting. my girl is a real [*last part missing; the following was added as a postscript at the top of the first page:*]
May 25"   Dear Father & Mother,   I got your letter of the 11" yesterday with 3 envelopes and one in the last. many thanks for them   I am thankful you are no worse. we are all well.

The following is an undated fragment.

I hope our people will be able to start a tannery here as well as other home industries for our benefit and wellbeing, in the near future.

A good many have got discouraged and occasionally a family moves back to the states. still people on the whole have lived better a great deal than in the early days of Dixie. and I feel confident that those who stay here will in time become very comfortable. though of course we are all subject to disappointments. the bean crop which in the early part of the season promised to do splendidly were visited by a kind of bug. which stripped and killed the vines before the beans were full grown. and indeed the later ones scarcely formed. so that our bean crop will be very light. where we had expected to have five or six hundred lbs. just on these two lots.

The following is another undated fragment.

Br. Whipple and Miles were going up the river last Monday to where they are surveying for a new ditch. so they took Hannah Annie and I along for a ride. and a very plesant time we had. the whole country is covered with beautiful green grass, fine rolling hills, at the back of which ar[e] high mountains, but not much timber, except what grows along the river   cottonwood, sycamore, black willow and a little black walnut, but there is plenty of timber a few miles up the mountain. We heard in meeting yesterday how the people can obtain clothing, shoes etc. by buying cattle and sheep to eat up the grass the Lord has blessed us with, and raise our own hides and wood, and work them up, and I think there will be efforts made to that end as soon as people are able. so it will likely be but a few years till people will be more comfortable

9" June 1887
Juarez

My Beloved Parents,   Your dear letter of May 28" came to hand the other day, and I was truly thankful to learn that my dear mother had been able to again breathe the pure air of Heaven, to ride around and enjoy your new porch. I hope it will prove a great comfort to you. I can imagine how you will enjoy sitting out there this summer when your days work is done. that is if you can only enjoy health, which I pray God you may. Over three long dreary months of constant pain and suffering, and me so far away that I could not help to wait on you. but I feel so thankful evry time I think of it that you have been surrounded by kind and loving ones ready and willing to aid and assist you through that trying ordeal. No wonder the children were all so delighted to see Grandma out once more.

The children talk of you so much. Emma [age 2] called out the other day "Ma—ma—ma—" I answered and she said—"When I get a big girl I am going to make Grandma a little basket and Grandpa a little basket," and went on building a lot more "castles in the air." Park [age 5] had a large swelling on his cheek for over two weeks, which finally developed into a very bad carbuncle. we had it lanced and it is now well, but he has a very severe cold for two or three days past. You ask me about writing paper. I dont know how it sells but Miles has got it here. Dear Parents I shall never forget your constant kindness and thoughtfulness. I have been looking at my dear little Claudes likeness. his Pa and I both feel that we cannot be thankful enough to you for having it taken, it is such a comfort. Miles says sometimes he would'nt take a hundred dollars for it if he could'nt replace it.

21" Dear Father & mother. This is Carolines birthday. 13 years old. she has grown considerable since we left St. George. I quit writing on Sunday to go down to the other town as Miles sent up for me. I went to meeting and had a good time. we had a large mess of splendid green peas for dinner off our own lot, and will have plenty of green beans in a week or two. evrything is much more forward there than here, as it was planted much earlier. Miles brought me home in the evening. it looked very stormy and rained on us some but cleared up without doing much good. Miles sent after lumber and fixed my house up a little for rainy weather (which we expect soon in good ernest) only temporary, but so as to shelter us from the weather. I churn a little butter evry other day, and we have about a quart of milk night and morning besides the strippings.

Thomas [age 11] went with Will [Carrie's son, age 19] up to the saw mill yesterday morning for an out. he was very anxious to go and see the country. I expect them home tomorrow. Some of the brethren have began to harvest their wheat. Hannah & Annie are both well. Annie's baby is teething and keeps quite poorly lately. Sr. Minerva Snow came last week. she looks well and as natural as life. she and Br [Erastus] Snow, Erastus [B. Snow] and wife [Ann S. Snow] are up today to Br. [Helaman] Pratts. I expect them to call on me. Br. [Henry] Eyring has built him a nice log house. they expect to move into it soon. Sr. Croft has called a time or two. she is well. lost her baby on the road. With kindest love to my brothers and sisters, I remain your loving daughter

C.J.R.

I got a letter from Mary Whittaker & Carrie Smith [Catharine's cousins in Salt Lake City] last week. they told me that James [Smith, Catharine's cousin in Salt Lake City] was starting on a mission to Indian Territory and Cha's [Charles Cottam] had bought his cow. The envelopes have come safe. many thanks

20" June 1887
Juarez   Mexico
Br. [Frederick William] Foremaster

Dear Sir   Before leaving St George last January, hearing of your severe illness at Johnson Kane Co[unty].[37] and that there was a prospect of your not going to Mexico, I wrote a Postal card to you, asking you to send my quilt, aprons, hood, socks and stockings back to St George if you had a chance, that I might bring them with me, but they did not come. As I am needing those articles I thought I would write and see if you will please to do me the great kindness to forward them to my husband at this place, if you find anyone coming this far, and if this is impracticable, please send them in to my Father in St. George when there is an opportunity and I shall feel greatly obliged to you. With kind regards to yourself and wife, and trusting that you have regained your health, I remain respectfully
                                                                C. J. Romney

3" July 1887
Juarez   Chihuahua   Mexico
Mr. Thomas P. Cottam

My Dear Brother   I was very pleased to receive your welcome letter of June 12" and to learn that you were all as well as you were. I hope your little Heber is quite well again. I suppose he as well as Emma & Thomas [Thomas and Emeline's children] have grown considerable since I saw them. Caroline [age 13] & Emma [age 2] have both grown a great deal. Br. [Erastus] Snow told me yesterday he had got word from Sr. Elizabeth [Snow], and Sr. Patty Perkins was supposed to be dying with a cancer on her face, poor soul. what she must have suffered. Sr. Minerva [Snow] is here. I have not seen much of her yet as they still live down at the other camp. The harvesting is mostly done and threshing has began. it is turning out very poorly, and as one sixth of what there is has to be paid for rent of land, it will leave but very little for our people, as the wheat is all on rented land. the brethren have become pretty well satisfied that this is poor wheat land. Our stack of wheat off three and a half acres, is about as large as a chicken coop, (not the same shape of course) and Miles hardly thinks there will be ten bushels. of course this is very discouraging after so much hard labor, but still we hope the corn and beans, sugar cane etc. will turn out well and help us out. our gardens look well now, but of course, up here it was put in late and is rather backward.

We had quite a nice rain last night so I am in hopes the rainy season which has been threatening for some time, has really set in, so that there will be green grass for the teams, as most of them are very poor, our poor old horses are almost give out   they look like nothing but skin and bone, and they have had so much work to do.

Miles gets very little work to do, as few people have anything to pay out. he is going to build a rough lumber house this next week, for one of the brethren, and this last week he and Miles A. [Hannah's son, age 17] who is working with his Pa in the shop, have put up a lumber room on the lot here for Annie, who I think will move up soon, as her dugout is very uncomfortable for sleeping in in summer. I think likely if our team picks up soon, that Miles will be able to put up Hannah and I each a lumber house before winter, when Hannah will likely move up here. I am fixed very comfortable for warm weather. I do not think the weather is as warm here as in St George, as there is nearly always a breeze.

Br. Croff and wife are well I believe. they have got a lot and moved up on the townsite. Br. [Henry] Eyring has built quite a nice little house of hewn logs, with a good floor in etc. and are living in it.[38] he has worked hard since he came here, has his lots planted and looking well. I think he and E. B. Snow [son of Erastus Snow] are soon to start on their missions.[39] The earthquake increased the water in the river so that we have not been short. For and in which we acknowlege the goodness of God.

I have no doubt but in one way or another we shall be able to make a living in spite of many discouraging circumstances, but Miles often feels very blue on account of his debts. still I trust that matters ere long will assume a brighter aspect. I am expecting Miles up to meeting today. there are to be meetings and Sunday Schools at both places until the rest of the camp move up here, when the crops are all gathered in. We are all well. Give my love to Emeline [Jarvis Cottam, Thomas P.'s wife] With kind love and best wishes to the Bishop of the 4 Ward [Thomas P. Cottam] I remain your loving sister

July 31″ 1887
Juarez

Dear Father & Mother   I received your most welcome letter last
week dated July 11″ which was full of interest to us, since I wrote
last I think. We have recieved three papers from you with envelopes
in, and the old book you spoke of, all right. how kind and thoughtful
you are my dear Parents. I am very sorry to say my skirt has not yet
come. but I have not quite given up hope. if it does not, I shall be
very sorry for the loss of your money and trouble in sending it as
well as for the skirt. We also read something in regard to this new
law, that any small article would come through the mail without
being subject to duty. if carried into effect this would be of great benefit to the people here.

I am so thankful to know that my dear Mother has so far recovered and trust that you may both enjoy health and strength for many
years yet. What does Emma [Cottam Thompson] call her baby? I
have not had a line from her, and in fact have only written to her
once since I came here. I have been very busy lately since the straws
were ready for use, in braiding and making hats for the children, as
they need them this hot weather. I am now at Hannahs. Gaskell
[Hannah's son, age 15] brought Annie and I down in the team to go
to meeting as I fear it will be the last time, at least for the present,
that we shall have the privelige of hearing him [Erastus Snow]
preach. he and Sr. Snow expect to leave in a few days, and it is doubtful if he ever gets down here again. we feel bad to part with them. I
suppose the illness of President [John] Taylor [president of the
church] is the cause of his going.

Miles has picked a beautiful large water melon. they are not doing
near so well as last year. we have green beans in great abundance
and will have corn ready this week. we have lived well lately with
our gardens and cows. we average about half a pound of butter per
day from each cow since the rains started. Br. [Erastus] Snow had
word that Br. [Henry] Eyring and Erastus [B. Snow] and wife [Ann S.
Snow] arrived in Mexico all right.

We celebrated the 24″ last Monday, and had a splendid time.[40] Br.
[Erastus] Snow delivered the best speech on the Pioneers that I ever
heard in my life on that subject. there was singing, recitations & dialogues, and dancing in the afternoon for the children and in the
evening for adults. Miles was chairman of committee. The weather
is very close and warm lately, between the rains, but not near such
warm weather as St George, as a usual thing.

I recieved Emma [Thompson] Squire's letter and will answer it as soon as I can. please give my love to them all.

Will [Carrie's son, age 19] started back to the States last Tuesday. dont know whether he will go to Salt Lake or Arizona. he thinks he can do better than in this country, and his Pa thinks it best to not try to persuade him to stay when he is not contented.[41] Yours in haste.

Catharine

Miles joins me in love.

14" Aug 1887
Juarez near Casas Grandes   Chihuahua   Mexico
Mr. & Mrs. Charles S. Cottam

Dear Br. & Sister   It is a long time since I parted with you, and I have never recieved a line from you, nor written one to you either but I suppose you hear of me as I do of you through Fathers letters. still I think we ought to be a little more sociable. Annie is going to write to her brother Frank [Woodbury] so I will send this in his, for I am not sure of your address.

One of the lost keys I found among my cloths after I got here. I forgot to send it with Sr. Elizabeth Snow [wife of Erastus Snow] when she went back, but I have sent it by Sr. Minerva Snow [wife of Erastus Snow], who left here last Tuesday. it is quite likely that you will not be able to see her as it may be wisdom for her to keep quiet nor does she know when she will be in the city, but she promised when ever she shall go to the city to leave it at Sr. Bathsheba Smiths[42] house, also three little baskets which Caroline [age 13] made and was very anxious to send. one is for Mother, one for Carrie Smith and one for Aunt Beata. she thinks it will please Mary [Charles and Beata's two-year-old daughter] to carry around in her little hand. she could have done better if she had known sooner of a chance to send. The first time you see cousin Mary [Whittaker] and Carrie [Smith], please give my love to them and tell them I have not forgotten that I owe them a letter and intend writing the first opportunity, but I do not know the address of either of them.

How is my dear sisters [Beata, Charles Cottam's wife] health, and little miss Mary [Charles and Beata's daughter]. I suppose she grows more interesting evry day. she and Emma [age 3] would have grand times if they were together. Emma has a kitten for her baby, which she is very fond of. she kisses and fondles it as if it were a real baby.

The children are all well except Annies oldest boy Orin [age 3] he has been feeling quite sick all day, and Thomas [age 11] has had a sore foot for a few days. I dont know but it is going to be a stone bruise or what.

I have chosen a bad day for writing as I am suffering severely with toothache and neuralgia all last night and today so that I feel in very poor trim for writing but must not always excuse myself for evry trifle.

We had a very heavy rain storm yesterday, and it bids fair to be repeated again today. we are having green corn, beans, potatoes, and other vegetables, and though our wheat was almost a failure I hope the corn crop will turn out well. We are milking four cows among us now, so that we do very well for milk and butter. I was pleased to hear that you had bought a cow how is she doing. How is Uncle John Burns? give my love to him. I feel very sorry for him in his loneliness, and feeble health. Though over five months since my dear little Claude died, I still miss him very much, and I suppose the void will never be filled, in this world. it was a sad blow to his Pa and me and to all the family, though we realize that he is better of[f] and would not come back if he could.

Beata is your Mother [Johnson] & Hilda [Johnson, Beata's sister] still at Virgin City? and how do your sister Annas poor little motherless children get along. Poor mother! what a hard seige she has had of it. I fear she will never be as well able to work as she used to be, but thank God she has partially recovered. Caroline is a great help to me. she went to a dance last night with Mattie [Carrie's daughter, age 17] and the big boys all join in kind love. Yours lovingly

Catharine

Your kindness is remembered with feelings of gratitude. Miles and Gaskell have been out hunting today and just brought home two deer.

20" Aug 1887
Juarez

My Beloved Father & Mother It is almost three weeks since I wrote last and I fear you will think me very careless. I got your last kind note over a week ago I think, with one from Willie Thompson [son of Emma and William Thompson] to the boys if they can I want them to write to him in this. Junius [age 9] is off herding with George [Hannah's son, age 12] today. the herding of all the cows in town is done together, each family taking their turn, of one or more days according to the number of cows they have. The cows are doing well just now and will do I suppose till the frost kills the grass. I make about a pound of butter evry other day from my cow. some of our beans have began to ripen. Thomas [age 12] has been down with the other boys today to gather some and their Pa has been threshing and cleaning them. The day before yesterday 18″ was Miles birthday. 44 years old. we had Bishop [George] Seevy and wife & Br. [Helaman] Pratt and wife and Dessie Eyring to dinner, and a very nice dinner though plain. nearly all of our own raising. potatoes, corn, beans, cucumbers, tomatoes and onions, with good bread and butter, and some squash pies and molasses cake. no meat though nor knick knacks. pretty good for Mexico was'nt it. Our melons are not doing near so well this year.

Br [Erastus] & Sister [Minerva] Snow send kind love. they left here a week ago last Tuesday. Miles got out a plan for a house from him which he is to build an adobe house.[43] Miles will do the wood work. Br. Snow let him have his stove on his work, which Annie and I have together. it seems very nice to have a stove again. Hannah moved up over a week ago, in a temporary house till we can get adobies made. she lives across the road from us. it is much more plesant than living so far away, and Miles feels so much better to have us where he can see us all evry day. he has put up a shed to work in, has done some turning and made a lounge yesterday and today. We are all well at present. I was so thankful to know that you were both some better. also that the boys had raised such good crops. I think we shall pull through all right if Miles could only get work for cash to pay his debts. but I trust the Lord will open the way before long. I fear times will seem more dull than ever now that Br. Snow has gone and there is no certainty of his coming back. we felt bad in this out of the way place to see him go. I hear that postage is reduced in coming from the States here but it is still the same in sending from here. we cant get the postmaster to send a letter for less than 5 cts. I hope there will be a change. We got a paper with envelopes in by last mail and thank you very much for the same. I fear my skirt has been lost. one of the brethren lately got a package of tea lately without even a stamp on it. and Hannah got a little bit in a small paper box from Isabell. but E. W. Snow sent his mother [Minerva Snow] two packages together which never came. so it seems like chance work though your papers and letters have come all right. With kind love and gratitude I remain your devoted daughter

Catharine.

If George [Cottam] and family have had their pictures taken I wish they would send me one. The boys have just shot two deers. it will be a treat.

4" Sept. 1887
Juarez   Mexico

Dearest Father & Mother   I must answer your last dear letter, received about two weeks ago and dated 13" August, also a paper and envelopes. I got the old book, all the papers and envelopes, and evrything you have ever sent so far as I know except the skirt, and in this country of cranky officials there is no telling what has become of it. it may turn up yet however, as the laws seem to be administered just as suits the whim and humor of the officers of the law. Our people have petitioned for mail service to be put on and a post office established here   when this is done I think it will make our mail matter more sure and satisfactory perhaps. I was much pleased to learn from your last letter that Mother is still improving, and that Emma [Thompson] Squire [daughter of Catharine's sister, Emma] has presented you with a great granddaughter. I suppose its Pa & Ma are very proud of it. what is its name. I have never yet heard the name of your last grandson. How is Emmas [Cottam Thompson] health now and Amelia's [Thompson]? also Matilda [Thompson Bleak] and children. please give my love to them all.

Hannah got a letter last mail from Sr. Minerva [Snow]   they reached the end of their journey in safety and all well only tired and anxious.

The children are all gone to Sunday school. I went last sunday but staid at home today to write. am going to meeting this afternoon. Miles has gone to a business meeting. we are all pretty well at present. We have four cows between us and they are doing very well now the grass is so good. so we thought we would try to make a few small cheesse for winter use when the cows dry up. Miles made us a press and we got some instructions from a neighbor and last Thursday tried our hand though we had neither of us ever seen one made. we had good luck. it seems very good and when dry will probabally weigh five or six lbs. we made another yesterday about the same size. we will only be able to make two or three a week as we will have to make a little butter to use. we are doing very well at present as far as a living goes, and trust the Lord will open the way before us in the future. How are you getting along my dear parents. I think of you so often. I fear you are pretty hard run after doing so much for me, and mothers long and severe illness, but I thank God you are better, if you can only enjoy the blessing of health, my mind will be much more easy in regard to you. I feel so thankful all the time that Emma and the boys live so near you.

I often talk to the children about you and ask Emma [Catharine's daughter, age 3] where you are etc. the other day I was speaking about you when she said, "Grandpa said, here's some grapes and gave me some, and I went over to auntie's and she gave me some." I was surprised to hear her talk about grapes as I didn't think she would remember about them so long.

I understand the saw mill has had to stop running as it was found to not be on our purchase of country. there may be some trouble about it but I hope not as it would be a great drawback to the mission here. the lumber which has been sawed has been a great blessing enabling the people to become sheltered from the rain, which visits us evry two or three days. about two weeks ago we had a terrific rain storm. the rain came down in torrents in a huge sheet of water, breaking our city ditch and bringing streams of water in evry direction. The largest flood I ever saw came tearing down a wash on the river. I think it must [have] been two or three times as large as the river which carries a great deal of water since the rains began. My house which had been quite comfortable before, leaked very badly on this occasion. so the next morning Miles took what lumber he had and put me up a lumber room and I was moved in soon after noon it stands the rain famously and I am very comfortable in it. I have only a ground floor as yet but Miles is going to lay one as soon as he can get some lumber seasoned. it is only a few feet from Annie's they being joined by a small lumber stove room so that we can both use the same stove quite conveniently. It seems quite homelike to have a house where I can have my looking glass and what few pictures I have left put up, and other trinkets which help to make a house look cozy. I have one door and one window, shelves for my dishes, books etc. etc.

How is Grandma Pym. kind regards to them. Sr. [Eliza] Lund, Br. [William] Langs folks etc. has he settled down in St George again. Please give my best love to all my brothers and sisters and families and accept a large portion for yourselves. Your loving daughter

Catharine

Br. & Sr. Croft and Sr. [Mary Bonelli] Eyring all well

The boys have just been finishing a dugout for us to use as a cellar to put vegetables milk etc. in which will make us still more comfortable. I wish I could know how you are just now.

18" Sept 1887
Juarez   Mexico

My Beloved Father & Mother   It is over three weeks since I got your last letter, though I feel certain that it is on account of the irregularity of the mails. the last mail did not come at all on account of high water, caused by the frequent and heavy rains to which this country is subject. I wrote a long letter to you less than two weeks ago and sent to Demming to be posted by a brother who was going out. also one to Br. [Frederick William] Foremaster, and to Cousin Mary Ann [Whittaker] & Carrie [Smith] in Salt Lake. there will be a chance to send to Demming again in about a week, so I may write again then if I get a letter from you before then. I feel very anxious always to know how you both are but hope you are much better. Dessie Eyring was down and spent the day with me last Tuesday. she and children were well and all right also Br. [Henry] Eyring when she heard last   was expecting a letter from her sister Hannah [Fawcett Nixon]. she told me Sam Jarvis was to start here this month. I wish I had known in time to get Br. Foremaster to send those things to you and perhaps he could have brought some of them.

   Miles went to Casas Grandes one day this week and took Annie & Mattie [Carrie's daughter, age 17] for a ride. he bought four little pigs, for $4.82, to make a little meat for this winter when the cows dry up. they will likely weigh about 75 or 80 lbs apiece by the time we want to kill them. we have two others, one we will kill and the other is part american so Miles wants to keep her, to raise pigs. these mexican pigs are runty little things. the owners ear mark them and let them run loose in the town. I suppose they never see a pen, and know no restraint so it is hard to keep them in the pen for awhile. The grass is still nice and green. so the cows are yet doing first rate. we have made seven small cheese, and will likely make a few more yet though when we do we have to go without milk for one day, as it takes all the nights and mornings milk. most of the people here are making their own cheese. some neighbors who dont have milk enough join together.

I thank you very much for the envelopes and papers which you are ever so thoughtful about sending. we got one by the last mail that came. I will just suggest dear Father if it is just as convenient for you, you might please to substitute a sheet or two of note paper for the envelopes as I have several on hand now. I am not out of paper and have no doubt but we shall get more when we need it. still I just mention it.

I have made Miles and Hannah each a pair of slippers this week with rawhide soles. they will answer very well to save shoes after the rainy season is over, though it is the first time I ever tried to work with such material though many people here have had to wear such things for a long time, as mexican shoes are very poor. our cane in the field still looks well, but our late corn which was put in about the 21 of July just after the rains began, and which has been our main dependance for cornmeal is I fear going to prove a failure. Miles got of one of the brethren what he had bought for early corn, white flint, which would mature quickly have plenty of time before frost, but by some mistake it has turned out to be mexican corn, and though it has grown very fast with the rain it is not near ready to tassel out yet and will likely not make roasting ears, though it will be fodder for the animals. Br. [George] Seevy whom Miles got the seed off, planted the same kind and of course will suffer loss as well as us. A week ago the river was very high, higher than I ever saw it before, but thanks to the high rock bank, which here keeps it within bounds, it would have to rise many feet higher before it could overflow on us. Miles said on Sunday he should judge there were more than ten times as much water in the river as there is in the early part of the summer, and it is always a respectable sized stream.

Tuesday Morning. this is the day the mail goes out so I must hurry and finish this to post. Miles [Miles A., Hannah's son, age 17] is helping his Pa on a small frame building, to be used at present for a store etc. Gaskell [Hannah's son, age 15] and George [Hannah's son, age 12] started away yesterday morning to Elvia with the team to bring some wheat for some of the brethren for which they will be paid in flour. they will be gone a week, and the roads are reported very bad with the rain. We were afraid yesterday morning that our horses had been stolen during the night. the boys hunted several hours but finally found them, and we felt quite relieved. Thomas [age 11] Junius [age 9] and Ernest [Hannah's son, age 9] have been stripping cane yesterday and today, for a brother who is up in the mountain. ours is not ripe yet. so you see they are all busy. The boys have fine fun making the calvs swim the river night and morning. I think I told you that Mattie Dillman lost her baby last spring. she and all her Fathers [George C. Williams] folks soon after moved up in the mountain country, where her Mother and her Fathers other wife both lost their babies within a few days of each other. her brother went to Utah and got married and was called to take his wife and fill a mission to the city of Mexico. but his health has been so bad lately that he has not been able to go yet. they are up at his Fathers. I must conclude with kindest love to yourselves and all my brothers & Sisters.

C. J. Romney

I should like to hear from Matilda, Amelia, Emma, or Nelly [daughters of Emma Cottam Thompson] or any of them, if they think it worthwhile. Your letters will come for 2 cts now and papers for 1 I think.

26″ Sept 1887
Juarez

My Beloved Parents   I have been writing to Emma so will enclose a few lines to you, though I can hardly think of anything to say as I wrote to you only a few days ago. Thomas, Junius and Ernest are down stripping cane again today. they strip it as it stands, we expect to have it made up soon. Gaskell and George have not yet got back. the roads are said to be very muddy. The river is very high again today. I think the rainy season must be nearly over.

I do not know if I told you that Will [Carrie's son, age 19] went back to the city and is working in the Deseret News Office. he dos'nt have steady work, but part of the time, when they need an extra hand. Miles' brother Joseph is suffering with a cancer on his face. I did not see him when in the city as he lives 12 miles south, but Violet told me about it.[44] it has broken out in two or three places, and we hear he has been to San francisco to be doctored. Poor man. he must suffer terribly with it. Young Joseph [Romney] went with his Father. Do you ever see or hear any thing of Aunt Mary [Smith Taylor], or how they get along? Kind love to Sr. Lund, Grandma Pymm etc. We have a hen just starting to hatch today   I hope she will do better than our others have   we have set a good many hens this year but had poor luck. We made another small cheese today, but the cows dont give so much now and we will have to quit. Br. Eli Whipple buried his baby yesterday. How did Thomas [P. Cottam] spend his birthday this year? Lovingly yours

C. J. Romney

Miles and all the children join in kind love and best wishes.

3 Oct. 1887
Juarez near Cases Grandes   Chihuahua, Mexico
Br. [Frederick William] Foremaster

Dear Bro.   I wrote a note to you, in relation to those few articles which you were going to bring here for me, and enclosed three portraits of your children. I hope you got them all right.

Br. George Seevey is starting to Utah on a visit and expects to come back by way of Johnson, and has promised to bring the things for me if they are sent to Br. Johnson, of Johnson[,] Kane Co. Now could I get you to please to send them there, with a note to Br. Johnson asking him to be kind enough to deliver them to Br. Seevy, or any other responsible person who might call for them, and you will greatly oblige

C. J. Romney

I am sorry to put you to so much trouble. still I shall feel very grateful if you can do me this favor.

9 Oct 1887
Juarez   Mexico

My Beloved Father & Mother   I think it must be nearly morning, but I woke up a long time ago, and commenced to think about you and could not go to sleep again so having a little oil in my lamp, I felt I must write to you. In two more days it will be my mothers birthday, and as I sat down to write my eyes caught sight of some lines in the exponent I got to lay my paper on, inscribed, "to my mother"   I was just thinking of her in connection with my father, so I glanced them over and finding they express my feelings better than I can myself, I have cut them out and will enclose them.[45] I only wish I could find something as appropriate to my Father. but you are so inseperable in my mind that what does for one, will almost answer for you both. there has been no division, no pulling apart. All has been union, love and peace. The tenderest care of each other and those who were given to you, as well as to all who came in your way, to whom you could lend a helping hand. And I cannot express the pleasure it affords me that such is my knowlege of my dear Parents. My great regret is that [I] did not do more for your comfort. when I was with you. I so often think about the time I was with you and how I might have let you both do less hard work perhaps. it seems to me if I were there now I would not let you do a thing that I could do for you. How often do I wish that I could do Fathers sweeping and Mothers washing housework etc. I do feel so thankful that you have Emma [Thompson Squire] and Amelia [Thompson], and the rest of the girls so near, as well as the boys, for I know they will all save you all they can if you will let them. The children cherish a most affectionate remembrance of you both, and look as anxiously for a letter as I do almost. Our last word was nearly three weeks ago I think after fathers accident, and mother in bed with the chills. I have written to you since also to Emma[,] Charles, & George, to thank him for his picture. it is splendid. I was so pleased to get it. I told the children the other day that Tuesday would be Grandma's birthday. Park [age 5] said "what are you going to send her ma! a card?" I was asking Emma [age 3] where she would rather live. She said "With grandpa & grandma and you get another little girl like me." she grows very fast and so does Caroline [age 13]. she is such a help to me, but she will be starting to school soon. I think Annie will teach our own children in her room, and I will take care of her little ones. We have no schoolhouse up here yet but as soon as the harvesting is over, an effort will be made to build one. A great deal of public business devolves on Miles now as the Bishop [George W. Sevey] has gone to Utah on a visit to his family, besides his own labors to preform, in providing for the many wants of a large family, directing the labors of his boys, and looking after all the little odds and ends, so you may be sure his time and thoughts are well employed. he gets letters from Br. [Erastus] Snow pertaining to his business and other matters. he is well. The rains stopped some little time ago and the weather in the daytime has been very warm, but yesterday and the night before a very cold wind blew, and last evening it began to rain and has rained quite hard and steady nearly all night and is raining now. I heard the clock in Annies strike three a little while ago, and I thought it was getting daylight a longtime ago.

Miles is afraid we shall have frost when this storm clears off, and if so it will do considerable damage to us as well as others, as our cane is all standing yet as well a[s] a good bit of corn, much of which we have no hopes of ripening, but if it could only make roasting ears so we can dry a lot of it we shall be glad. our other corn is turning out well. They will begin to make our molasses tomorrow. The boys all work so well, and they are kept very busy, gathering in crops, taking care of the animals etc. our cows have done so well this summer, but are failing fast now. like all ranch and mexican cows they are of very little us[e] in the winter even if they are well fed. still we hope to have a little milk along. We made 12 small cheese, which will be very nice through the winter. we have had very little meat this [summer], but we got a piece of beef yesterday from a brother who killed one, which will be quite a treat. we also managed to get some soap grease from him and made up two cans of lye. it seems like nearly evry one has been almost without soap lately and no grease to be had, but the store has sent for soap.

I wish Emma would please to find out from Agnes [Thompson, another wife of William Thompson] how she makes gympsum salve and what it is specially good for, as plenty of it grows here, and where there are children, salves is always useful, as they get so many stubbed toes, cane cuts etc. either Agnes or Lizzie [Thompson, another wife of William Thompson] once told me how to make it, but I forget.

We are all well at present. I wish I could know that you are the same. I hope to get word when the mail comes. it should have come yesterday but failed to. a mexican has undertaken to bring it to us for $5.00 per month, twice a week. a white man would want at least twice that amount but they can live on so little. still we shall have to watch him or he will likely steal enough to make up. last Wednesday I went over to help Hannah make the boys some overalls, and he came with the mail for the first time, as there was a good bit of business to be done, receipts to sign, interpreting etc. Miles asked Hannah to set him something to eat as he would be detained so long. after eating he noticed me sewing on the machine, and made us understand that he was a tailor and wanted to try the machine. we let him do so and he sewed quite awhile. he sat and smoked his cigaretts one after another, stood by the stove wher[e] Hannah was getting dinner, and looked in the kettle. Miles thought he was getting most too sociable, so he took him by the shoulders and walked him off into the shop with him, and stayed there with him while we ate dinner. the fellow took no offense seemingly but laid down there and had a nap while his horse was feeding about on the grass. we hope he is not going to be such a nuisance all the time or we shall want to change mail carriers, as Miles wont want to waste half a day in watching him nor have to go without his dinner.

Hannah got a letter from Minnie [Romney Farr, Hannah's daughter living in St. Johns] last mail, and two papers, one containing a necktie and the other a pair of gloves for her Ma. I expect it would grieve the officials of Mexico if they knew of all the little notions which come without them having a chance to tax them, when one of our big men was here, he got a beautiful silk handkerchief and gold ring in one paper, but of course it dont do to say anything. Isabell [Romney Platt, Hannah's daughter living in St. Johns] sent her ma a small parcel about two months ago, after reading of the new postal law, and it is still at the Office at Casas Grandes, waiting till the[y] get the new law on duties to know what to charge. several have parcels there waiting and when they went down to try to get them he let them open and see them but not take them away. Br. [Henry] Eyring sent his wife a small package of medecine by last mail and there was no trouble nor duty, also a little pastboard box with teas for Hannah from Isabell. she has only one child and very poor health. Will [Platt, Isabell's husband] is postmaster of St John. Minnie is well, and in Ogden been learning dress making. Br. [Willard] Farr [Minnie's husband] was there this summer. With kindest love to you all and wishing you both many happy returns of your birthdays   your loving

Catharine

Thursday morning   Dear Parents   I read, your long looked for letter of Sept. 10. the day before yesterday. but oh! what bad news it contained. Mother with those horrible chill which she has suffered so much with in her life. it makes me feel so bad to think about it. and I so far away, so powerless to lend a helping hand. I used to take such pride in doing the washing and hard work. the two long years that you had them before. and now you are so little able to stand the chill in your weak state. I do thank God that Emma and Amelia are so near you for I know how good they are. Now my dear Father I must tell you how grieved I am to hear of your accident, but Father wont you be careful and not get in such dangerous places. I do feel so anxious about you all the time. I am sorry to hear of Sam Jarvis losing his baby.

I am so pleased that George [Cottam] is going to send me their photos   I hope it will come safely.

I have not had a word from my dear sister since I left home. and have never heard what she named her baby. I suppose John and Emma [Thompson Squire] are wrapped up in their baby. what do they call her. tell them I shall expect a picture of her soon so that I can pass my judgement on her. so they must have her looking her very best if they want it to be favorable. How do you get along with your new Bishop [their son, Thomas]?

Dear Father & Mother I think I prize your letters more than ever. Caroline was going to write to Mary Ann and Rachel [George Cottam's daughters] but there is no room this time. I hope I shall not tire you out completely with this long letter. with kindest love and best wishes to you all and praying God to heal you both I am as ever your loving daughter

Catharine

30″ Oct 1887
Juarez   Mexico

My Beloved Parents   I wrote to you and sent by the last mail just as I recieved your last letter and should not be writing again so soon, but I am anxious to get a little plaster of paris as my lamp burner has come loose and I cannot use it. could you please dear father send me a little in a paper if sufficient for that would not make it too heavy. Thomas [Catharine's brother] would know how much it would take. if it would be too heavy for a paper, I think it would come all right in a small sack or box, as Isabell sends her Ma a little tea in a small pastboard box and it comes all right without duty. still papers seem to be the safest way, as they dont seem to be molested for Minnie has sent her Ma several small articles gloves etc. in that way. I hate to trouble you so much for I know how fully your time is taken up. the paper you send is anxiously looked for, not only by me. the big boys are specially interested and I see many little items of interest and useful information in them and though I seldom read a story, I was reading a detective story today in the last one which I got quite interested in. I hope the next number will come so I will know how it comes out. You say you have had some very heavy rains. we had two nice showers a week ago, quite unlike the other years that Miles has been here. but I hope we will have more rain this winter so that the grass will come up earlier than last spring.

I feel very grateful to you for trying to get the things to us from Br. Foremaster (I hope he will get them) and also for the nice present you are sending, but I feel sure that you need evry dollar you have got so dont worry about us my dear parents. though I think he could have brought a few lbs of fruit perhaps and had them open as if using out of them. and you would not have missed that so much. if I had thought in time I would have asked you to send me a few fruit stones for seed. some of our almond trees are living. they are hard shell like Emmas and I should like some like yours softshells. I got the photos all right. Annies Br. Frank [Woodbury] sent her some U.S. stamps and she gave me two or three so we could send letters to Demming to be posted when anyone goes out from here, but we have mostly been able to get postage stamps though of course it is worth saving three cents on a letter when we can.

Miles had the Epistle read in meeting today.[46] The Saints had a genuine surprise at conference I see. I hope the Apostles wont fall into the hands of their enemies. I was sorry to hear about Br. Parker. what other post masters are they who have got into trouble. one of our brethren in Savoya New Mexico, Br. Pitkin who travell[ed] part way with us when we went to St George, the man whom Miles sent the team back to Arizona by, has been found out to have robbed the Government of four thousand dollars. Miles says he is liable to be sent to prison for 15 years. how strange that men can become so dishonest. we are all well at present, except colds, and the children's eyes are not quite well, but much better than a week ago. Mattie [Romney Brown, Carrie's daughter] has been down several times and seems to be getting along firstrate in her new home. but I have been so busy I have not been up to see her yet. I have been fixing up our hats for winter this week. I generally find something to do to keep me out of mischief if I have got a big girl to help me. Hannah has quite a hard time of it now with so many boys to sew wash and cook for and so little help, and a young baby too. but Caroline [age 13] will be able to help her some and perhaps I will be able to help her a little with her sewing occasionally. I have been looking for a letter from Charles but have not got one yet.

We have had some hard frosts the last two or three nights a little ice on the water bucket and some cold winds, but quite a lot of sun in the daytime.

We have quite a bit of hay and plenty of corn fodder for winter had between 70 and 80 gallons of molasses of very good quality, and Miles has sold some furniture for beans so we have plenty of them to last us a year, and eat as many as we want of them and we all feel that the Lord has blessed us very much.

With my best love to your selves and all, and prayers for your health and strength I remain your loving daughter

Catharine

Nov 13" 1887
Juarez   Mexico

My Dear Father & Mother   I was expecting to get a letter from you by the last mail but was disappointed but hope to next mail. I was also looking for one from Charles. I have written to him twice, and not had a word from him since I came here. We got a paper from you last mail. we are very glad of them. I think it will be better not to send anything at all in them in the future, not even envelopes, as Miles says it would be a penitentary offence if found out. Minnie [Romney Farr, Hannah's daughter living in St. Johns] has been sending her Ma some little notions which have come all right, still it might make trouble. in my last letter I asked you to please send me a little plaster. if you have not done so when you get this, will you please to send it in a little package or box as there will then be no risks to run and if there should be a little duty on it we can pay it, but I think there wont be. I am glad you did'nt send clothing or anything of that kind by Sam Jarvis as there can't be any trouble about that unless it should be the things from Br. Foremaster and I think they will come all right.

We are all well and doing first rate. Thomas [age 11], George [age 13] and the little boys have been digging our peanuts lately and have got done. we had about three and a half bushels I think. Miles says we could send you a peck and hardly miss them, but as there is no chance I must tell you that he shall have me eat them for you. The boys have also been digging our potatoes down at the other camp. they are very small, and turned out very poorly. still they are a nice change and all help. and Miles & Gaskell [Hannah's son, age 16] have been up in the mountain this week and dug what we had there. 12 bushels of very good potatoes so as we have plenty of beans you see we shall get along nicely for provisions, if nothing happens more than we know of. I think with the blessings of the Lord we shall be able to make good homes and a good living in this country. at any rate we feel quite hopeful for the future, so dont worry about us in the least. How do you get along for the necessaries of life? and how is your health now. I do hope you are both better. I cannot tell you how thankful I feel that Emma and the boys [Catharine's sister and brothers] are so near you. how is her health now? I am in hopes it is better. I suppose her roses are all gone. has she had such a nice flower garden as last year, and how are your geraneums doing. In imagination I often look in at the old familiar place and see the chairs, the pictures and the many objects so well remembered, and above all the forms and faces so dear to me. Annie will commence school tomorrow morning in her room, and as our crops are gathered I think all of our children who are old enough will be able to attend this winter. it seems good to be all together again as a family. Miles keeps very busy with ward business and the building of Br. [Erastus] Snows house and the last two days he has been moving up and planting out our little fruit trees from the lower camp, as that land does not belong to us. we have over 40 peach trees, a dozen almond, 6 apple and 4 plum trees with about 9 little grape vines started. the peach trees Miles took to look after this summer of a man from the Gila, and was to have half for taking care of them.

Dessie Eyring commenced school at her house last Monday morning, with 10 small scholars, as we have no school house yet, private schools is the only way of having our children taught at present.

Our cows are failing fast but still we make a nice bit of butter, and Miles got some nice beef this week, which is quite a treat as we have not had much meat this summer.

I have been to meeting today. we have splendid meetings here the people turnout very well and seem to have a good spirit. the Sunday schools and primaries are well attended.

There is much public work to be done here this winter, besides the school house there is a canal to make on the other side of the river to the farming land so that we wont have to rent, though the gentiles are very anxious we should work their land again.

Good bye for the present with kind love to yourselves and all. I am as ever your loving daughter

Catharine

We have been having 4 or 5 days of cold stormy weather with a drizzling rain, but it has cleared up and is very warm in the day again with hard frost at night.

4" Dec. 1887
Juarez Mexico

My Dear Parents I was five weeks without a word from you, and had began to feel very uneasy, when last mail I got the envelope with the plaster of paris and a line or two saying that you were both as well as common, which was joyous news. you said you had written two or three days before, but I have never got it. this I think is about the first letter you have sent me which I have missed getting that I know of. I guess it has gone to hunt the one Miles wrote to George when Claude died. however I hope I shall get it yet.

I am so thankful for the plaster. I have fixed my lamp, and it is as good as new. I wonder who would have been so prompt and good to send it to me as my own dear Parents. I do appreciate your kindness I assure you. I got a letter from Charles last mail and if I get time I may answer it and send in yours, if so will you please to forward it when you write to him.

Sam Jarvis has not come yet. I think he must have stayed some-time with his folks in Arizona.

We are all enjoying pretty good health in fact very good with the exception of slight colds occasionally. I think this will prove to be a very healthful climate, and a most delightful clime all the year round with the exception of the wind which blows a good deal. still when we get good fences, tight houses and trees around I am satisfied we shall not notice that so much, though we had about as hard a wind as I ever experienced the day before yesterday. Miles says it is about the worst he has seen in Mexico. I had a nice ride down to Casas Grandes on Thursday.

The children are doing well in school. Annie is certainly a splendid teacher. she has 20 scholars and three or four more coming tomorrow, so that he[r] house will be packed full, and many disappointed because there is not more room. Sr. Croft started a small school for a few little ones last Monday, and Sr. [Dora Wilcken] Pratt will start in another week, all in their own houses, but there are none of them willing to take large scholars except Annie.

Miles got a quarter of beef the other day, about the fattest and best I ever saw. I do wish you could have a roast of it. it is just the kind of meat you would both enjoy, so fat, juicy and tender, and I know Father would enjoy a bowl of our nice soupe. We have the suet, and are just lacking the raisins to make a nice Christmas pudding, but then we shall have to make a suet pudding, and imagine it is just as nice.

I wish you a merry Christmas and happy New Year in which Miles heartily joins, and I know the children would but they are all at Sunday school. Hannah and Annie are well.

We are not favored with any of the twelve [apostles] here at present. Br. & Sr. [Erastus] Snow were well the last letter Miles got. his house is going on slowly. Brethren all very busy, plenty of work to be done as in all new places. Kind love to all, your loving daughter.

Catharine

11″ Dec. 1887
Juarez   Mexico

Dear Father & Mother   I got a letter from George a week ago with the Sulphate of zinc and stamps in from you, for which, many thanks, also the piece of muslin from Emma. please thank her for me. The lost letter has not come yet, the one you spoke of having sent two or three days before you sent the plaster.

Sam Jarvis called last Tuesday. he got in the night before to the old camp where they are staying for the present in his old house. he said they had a very good journey and are all well. have not seen Fanny [DeFriez Jarvis, Sam's wife] nor Sr. DeFreiz [Fanny's mother] yet   I thought perhaps they would be up today but it is so cold and stormy that they likely wont. He brought the little sack you sent me all right for which my dear Parents I feel truly grateful. I was so pleased with the buckles, thread etc. as well as the money. Br. Taylor has gone after goods and I want to get me some factory [unbleached muslin like that made at the cotton factory near St. George] with it as soon as he comes back.

Miles thinks you have better judgement than most people. Will Platt and Isabell [Romney Platt, Hannah's daughter living in St. Johns] sent a parcel by a young man, who came without a family, some shoes for her Ma and the children, which had never been worn, and they daubed them all up with mud, thinking I suppose that that would help them to pass, but the Custom Officers could of course see that they had not been worn, and took them for smuggled goods, threatened fine and imprisonment, but finally sent them up, but the[y] cost Miles much more than they were worth besides a great deal of trouble and anxiety. Sam [Jarvis] was very lucky I think   he said he did'nt have to pay any duty. he did not get the things from Br. Foremaster as a Br. Johnson had already started with them. he thought I had got them as the man had been at Diaz, (our first town 70 miles away) thre[e] weeks when he got there. Sam says he is going to live there, but I think he will soon send the things up.

Br & Sr. [George C.] Williams were here this morning but were in a hurry to start home on account of the storm which they think will be severe in the mountains where they live   Mattie [Williams] Dillman is down too but she has not called yet.

Just two weeks from today will be Christmas. I wonder how you will spend it, likely in Thomas's   a Merry Christmas to you one and all, and many returns of the same.

Emma [Catharine's daughter, age 3] wants me to tell Grandpa & Grandma that she just fell over Ma's rockers and cut her mouth and chin and made them bleed. the children are busy studying their lessons for tomorrow, and Park [age 5] has been studying his letters out of Claudes linen book. he says Claude will want it again when he comes to live with us again.

We are all well. This is miserable writing my pen is so poor. if you could send me one or two in a letter some time please, as they seem to be one of the little articles not to be got here. though I am ashamed to ask you for so many things. I must now say goodbye. Miles and the children join me in kind love.

Catharine

Dear Parents, this is Friday. the mail should have come on Wednesday but has not come yet, owing I suppose to the extreme cold and stormy weather which we have been having. there is two or three inches of snow on the ground and the mountains all around us ar[e] covered with it. the most snow that has been seen here since our people settled in this country.

Br. [Helaman] Pratt and Miles I think will start to the mountains today to be gone two or three days. will take guns and try to get some deer. It is fine and sunshiny today and the snow will likely soon disappear. I have been having toothache for two or three days.

8" April 1888
Juarez Mexico
Mrs. Eleanor C. Jarvis

Dearest Friend   Your most welcome favor of Mch [March] 11" came to hand only this week, owing to the irregularity of the mails recently. I heartily sympathize with you in the gloomy prospect before you of being left alone for so long in your poor state of health, but I have better faith for you. I do firmly believe that you will be abundantly blessed while George [Eleanor's husband] is away [on a mission to England], that your health will improve, that Rosa [plural wife of George Jarvis] and the children will enjoy good health, and that ways and means will be opened up, that together with your united industry and frugality will enable you to live quite comfortably. now these are my feelings, and I hope you will write me occasionally and let me know if I am right or wrong. give my love to Rosie[,] Ellie, Annie and the boys [Eleanor's children]. I suppose George has started before now. is it to England he has gone? Now do cheer up, and take courage. and I am satisfied all will be well, while your husband is in the missionary field. In regard to Sr. [Mary Ann] DeFrieze, whenever I have seen Sam and enquired in regard to her eyesight, I believe he said it was no worse, and I think once he told me a little better. I have not seen either she or Fanny

[DeFriez Jarvis] as they stayed down at the old camp until they moved to Corallas.

I wrote a note to your Ma [Ann Cannon Woodbury] a week ago informing her of the birth of another granddaughter [Eleanor Romney, Annie's daughter], which [you] will likely hear of before you get this. it is eleven days old and is a very good, pretty sweet, cute little girl, all of which its mother will no doubt inform you. Annie is doing remarkably well. couldnt be better in the length of time. she walked into my room this morning. I have to keep cautioning her not to be too ventursome. Ann [Annie's daughter, age 9] is getting to be a great help to her Ma. they all think a great deal of the baby as a matter of course. Erastus [Annie's son, age 2] has been a very good boy, and comes to me to be waited on just as good as to his mother when he knows she cant do it.

We have had some very warm weather the past week or two, so Annie has thought while she has had to be in bed. The cottonwood trees up and down the river have donned their beautiful mantle of green, and the grass has began to spring up, to please the eye and gladden the heart.

I received a Farm and Fireside the same time as your letter. I am so glad to get them, but I am afraid my year will soon be out.

I saw Dessie [Eyring] last Sunday at meeting she was well. I did'nt go today. Dessie has just called in from meeting to see Annie and the baby. she wishes to be kindly remembered to you, and wishes you would please tell Sr. [Mary B.] Eyring they are all well.[47] she is still teaching school.

We have not started to garden yet as the springs are backward and uncertain, frost coming quite late last spring and killing our early vegetables, so that we lost much of our seed.

We set 5 hens lately but have had rather poor luck. one has not come off and the other four have only 23 between them.

The [Young Men's and Young Women's] Associations have held some very creditable conjoint sessions this winter. the last one for the season was held last night. Caroline [age 13] had a recitation, "The Foreclosure of the Mortgage," and once before she had the "Schoolmasters Guests," both in Ellie's [Eleanor's daughter's] book. I am so glad Thomas got that book, as it has some very nice selections

I must now close with kind love to yourself and all the girls   I remain as ever your loving friend

Catharine

13 May 1888
Juarez

My Dear Father & Mother   I have got baby washed and dressed and to sleep and the rest of the children are all gone to Sunday School so I will try and write you a few lines. Miles wrote on the 2" to inform you of the birth of a new daughter to us. you see we determined to have a "May day" celebration for children and grown people, a picnic up the river under the trees, all of us were going except Miles and I. we were going to keep house but I concluded to change the programme a little and keep Annie at home, however she did'nt seem to feel very bad about it.

Baby was born at 20 minutes to 3 oclock in the morning, she weighed 9 lbs. and is a very fine little girl. I think we shall call her Ethel. How do you like her name? She has been troubled with snuffles and colic some so that she has not be[en] quite as good as my babies generally are but I think she will soon be all right as I hardly think it is crossness. The children are very much delighted with this little sister, perhaps the more so because Ma hasn't had a little baby for so long. I have had good nursing and attention and have got along well. I had only our own folks with me. Hannah is as good a hand as we have here, and I felt I would rather have her than anyone. I was out in the garden for a short walk yesterday and again today so I am in a fair way to regain my strength, if the weather continues fine. Caroline [age 13] has taken hold and done so well with the work while I have been sick, and it seems so nice to have a girl old enough and so willing to wait on me. she was the "May Queen" chosen by the young ladies association and Primary. they all seemed to enjoy themselves very much. they finished off with a dance in the evening.

A little over two weeks ago Miles started to build Hannah a house, one large room with an upstairs for the boys bedroom. he has finished the mason work yesterday, has laid it all up himself with the boys to tend him. they have all worked like beavers. their Pa says he never saw better boys to work than ours all are, even Park [age 6], Eugene [Hannah's son, age 4], Orin [Annie's son, age 4] & Emma [age 3] have had their little buckkets and carried water, all feeling a great interest in Aunty having a house. she certainly needs a floor badly as her baby creeps all over in the dirt. Miles can soon finish it if he can get the lumber and nails.

Our gardens are looking pretty well, but my flower garden does not look as promising as I should like to see it. I am afraid I planted too soon and shall lose most of my seed as only a few have come up as yet. still some more may come. If any of the little girls have time and feel like gathering me a few petunia, verbenia or any other kind of small flower seed that could come in a letter at any time when they are ripe I shall be glad to get them. How are your geraniums and other houseplants doing I often think of the windows full of beautiful flowers. I think in time I shall be able to raise nice flowers here. We have beautiful wild flowers here. the gardens and some of the streets have been covered with such a pretty white lilly, which comes out in the evening and closes about noon every day for the last six or seven weeks. I have had such a plesant view from my door while I have been in bed. the green lucern patch thickly dotted with these beautiful white flowers, with the green trees on the river in the distance, and still farther in the background some very pretty hills and mountains. Miles and Gaskell [Hannah's son, age 16] have been trying for two or three days and nights to get the water on our farming land but as the ditch is new it soaks up the water and breaks occasionally.

I received your most welcome letter of Apr. 19" by last mail and was so glad to hear you were both well but so very sorry to hear of Emma [Catharine's sister] and some of the children being so poorly. I hope they are all well ere this. I also regret to hear of the trouble the people are having.[48] it will go very hard with those in poor circumstances. thanks for the envelopes and paper. I also got a Canada paper last mail we like them very much. I wrote and told you of getting the Bible a long time ago. perhaps you never got my letter. you speak of sending some ribbons and a silk handkerchief. is it long since? I am sorry to say we never got them, but hope we shall yet. Thomas [age 12] feels very badly about his handkerchief he knows it was one of the prettiest ones that ever was and can't hardly feel reconciled to the loss. I dont know why we should be so unlucky about our parcels, when Hannah has had such good luck. The children feel very hard at the Mexicans for keeping them.

Hannah got a letter from Sr. Minerva [Snow] the other day. she feels very badly at the loss of Erastus W. [Snow] and her health is not very good as she is worn down with watching and anxiety.[49] so we shall not see her as we had hoped to soon. We are all pretty well at present, and unitedly send our love to you all.

Have Rob [Lund] and Mary [Romney Lund, Miles's sister] moved to the city yet? have they and Wooleys sold out?[50] I have been helping Emma [age 3] to write a letter to you. she wanted to do it herself, and wants you to know that she folded and put it in the envelope herself. Good bye and God bless you both and all the dear ones.

From your loving daughter.

Catharine

Baby [Ethel] has woke up and claims my attention   she is just as sweet as she can be.

Dear Father if you can sometime will you please enclose in a letter, a package of light blue diamond dye for blueing my cloths. Isabell sent us some and it did very well while it lasted.

Mrs. Eleanor C. Jarvis,

Dear Friend,   [*illegible*] I had a little daughter come to help me celebrate mayday. Miles and I were going to stay at home [*illegible*] keep house, and all the rest were going to a picnic up the river, but we [*illegible*] stay and help us eat the chicken which we had intended to have all to ourselves, so we had a good time at home and all those who went seemed to enjoy themselves very much. [*Parts of two pages are illegible.*]

Eleanor it is two weeks since I began to write. I have been having sore eyes and been trying to take care of them but they are still bad so I must try and write anyway. If you see any of our folks please tell them we are well and I will write when my eyes are better, but I must finish this as it is began.

Annie got a letter from your Ma and Nona yesterday, from which we hear of the death of Rosies [plural wife of George Jarvis] father. give my love to her and all the girls also to Allie when you see her. your Ma, aunt Alice, Ellie and the children. Do you get good news from George, and how do you get along since he went?

The death of Br. [Erastus] Snow has been a heavy blow to us as to all the people here, as no doubt it is to you in St George, and wherever he was know[n]. we were expecting him here this month. it is a great loss to us. he will never need his house now which Miles has worked so hard to finish.[51] Caroline and another girl are up cleaning it today. Caroline will try and answer Ellies letter soon, but I keep her pretty busy since baby came. I find my time is not my own now, and I can't get along with the work like I could last summer, but stil[l] I made Annie and I each a nice large cloths basket last week, besides helping Caroline with the house work, washing and ironing   my eyes were too bad to do much sewing. I have made a good many mens and boys hats this spring, for our own family and some others, but my straws are getting low and I dont know what chance there is going to be to get many this coming harvest as there is very little wheat being raised here this season.

We are having pretty warm weather just now. we had a nice rain three afternoons last week, which makes evrything look much fresh.

We have planted a good many flower seeds   some did not come up. but we have lots of zenias, some of them in bloom. we also have morning glories, cyprus, sweet peas four oclocks marigolds and coxcombs coming along. we each had a pink given us. Annies has blossomed, and Miles got us each a rose bush   mine had a pink rose on and Hannahs a white one   I fear Annies is dead. Good bye. write soon.

Catharine.

I am sorry to hear of the brethren being convicted.

24″ June 1888
Juarez   Mexico

Dear Father & Mother   Your last letter, dated June 1″ came last mail. I feel very bad to hear of my dear mother being sick again but hope she is quite as well as usual again long ere this. The news of Br. [Erastus] Snows death was indeed a great blow to us, as we were expecting him here so soon, and he seemed like a father to the people here. Miles said he never felt so lonesome in his life as he did after recieving the news. he was hurrying to get his house finished in hopes he would soon occupy it, but alas, vain hope! But then we realize the truth of a remark made at his funeral, "Our loss is his infinite gain." My eyes are [sore] and have been for a long time, about two weeks I think, and I have not done much reading nor sewing and ought not to write but I know you will feel anxious if you dont hear. Park [age 6] has been quite sick for several days but I trust he will soon be better. I think perhaps he is troubled some with worms. You spoke of sending me some shoelaces in a letter. I never got it.

Now I have some good news to tell you. I have at last got the quilt and hood which I sent so long ago by Br Foremaster all right, and no trouble at the custom house, and I assure you it comes in good now. We had a nice rain three days in succession a little more than a week ago and we thought our rainy season had commenced but we have not had any since, and the weather is pretty warm.

I will try and answer Thomas's [Cottam, Catharine's brother] letter today if my eyes will permit, and Emma [Thompson] Squires as soon as I can.

Good bye for the present from your loving daughter

C. J. Romney

I got a paper last mail. do you have much trouble to read my poor writing

19" July 1888
Juarez   Mexico

My Dear Parents   It has been quite a while since I wrote to you owing to having very sore eyes, but I am very glad to be able to say they are very much better though still weak and dim. it has thrown me so behind with my work as sewing mending etc has had to go undone except what Caroline [age 14] has had time to do. the last letter I tried to write was to Thomas and my eyes were worse after it. I have not had a letter from you for some time and feel very anxious. had a paper a little more than a week ago. Br. [Alexander F.] McDonald came a few days ago. he told me of seeing you but I have not had a chance to talk with him much yet. We have had considerable sickness in our family lately and there have been two or three other cases in town [of] a malarial fever or dumb ague, owing to we think to the river being so low and so full of moss, which has made it unhealthy, but the rains have started and the river rose so I think the cause is pretty well removed. Park [age 6] took sick over four weeks ago and was very bad. Ernest [Hannah's son, age 10], Junius [age 10,] Thomas [age 12], Miles [Hannah's son, age 18] and last of all Eugene [Hannah's son, age 4] followed, six of them, so we have had quite a time of it, but we think it was partly caused by our own neglect and ignorance in not purifying their systems and by allowing them to go in swimming so much, but it will be a lesson to us another spring. we think going in the water so much must have had considerable to do with it, as none of the girls have come down with it yet. the boys are all better and have not had fever for several days except Miles, though they keep weak and languid   it has made it quite hard on Gaskell and George [Hannah's sons, ages 16 and 13] they being the only well ones. but my boys are all able now to milk and help with the chores again. Our gardens and everything look so well now since the rains started and I think better health will prevail.

Br. [Apostle Moses] Thatcher and Sister Elizabeth Snow [wife of Erastus Snow] came to visit us three weeks ago. they have made their home at Hannahs all the time they have been here. they will leave again tomorrow. their coming caused rather sorrowful feelings, as Br. [Erastus] Snow had intended taking this trip with them and perhaps making his home among us a good part of the time. You will likely see Sr. Snow after her return home and if so she can tell you all about us. they went up in the mountain to Corallas to camp a few days last week. Br. Thatcher wanted Miles to take all of our sick boys and me for my bad eyes and go with them. we almost concluded to go but when we considered the rains and no tent with so many sick we thought it best not to risk going, so Miles went after a load of lumber and to weed the potatoes. he took George to help him and Thomas for his health. he had one very sick day while he was gone but is better again.

My eyes feel rather bad again now so I must close with out writing as long a letter as I wanted to.

Love to all. lovingly

Catharine

I have such beautiful zennia's or Old age and youth some very double almost like a rose and such a variety of colors. I have had Caroline pick some of the leaves to send you but likely they will fade and not look so nice.

5" Aug. 1888
Juarez Mexico

Dear Father & Mother Your very welcome letter of July 10" came with last mail. contents a good newsy letter, one sheet of paper one envelope, two pens and one awl, a letter worth having was'nt it? Thank you for them all. you say it was so very warm or hot the day you wrote it is so here some days when it dos'nt rain, it is especially so today in the house though there is usually a cool breeze out of doors. if it were not for that I do'nt know how we could stand the heat sometimes. I am sorry to know you have both been so poorly again. our boys are all better though Park dos'nt feel very well today, my eyes are much better but still not strong and well as I could like to have them. baby [Ethel] is not feeling very well for a few days. she is a very delicate looking child, and seems to be very nervous. quite different from most of my children. her Pa thinks her a perfect little beauty but we should like to have her more healthy looking. I rejoice to hear of Beata [Cottam, Charles's wife] having a son and of Charles [Catharine's brother] having plenty of work now. I am sorry to hear of Uncle John Burns being so poorly. I regret that my letter was so pale and hard to read it is the fault of the ink it is so poor. I never write to you without thinking of it, and as soon as I can find any any better I will try to get some.

As far as a living is concerned we are doing well, our gardens especially. Hannah's has done splendidly we have had some peas, and potatoes a few, plenty of string beans of the best quality and an abundance of summer squash. plenty of the last two for us all and Miles has given away lots of it to those who had none. it seems so nice to have good gardens of our own and I scarcely know how we could have got along without them while Br. [Apostle Moses] Thatcher and Sr. [Elizabeth] Snow [wife of Erastus Snow] were here, and we have a nice lucern patch started. it almost kept our mules alive in the spring when they had to work so hard. We do very well now for milk and butter, and we have not been entirely without flour for a long time though we use mostly corn meal and shall have to eat more of it in the future I think, but that is'nt so bad when we have milk and butter to go with it. if we only had a way of changing some of our butter for other little notions that we need sometimes we would often this season of the year, spare some. still we do not suffer for anything, and these things will no doubt work around all right in time. markets will be found, and money become more plentiful. when the time ever comes that we can get enough to pay our debts we shall feel to rejoice and be very thankful.

Miles had some pieces of window glass left from Br. [Erastus] Snows house, so he cut it and made us each three nice picture frames and framed, Father, Mother, and Thomas for me and says he will frame Charles and perhaps George and family next time, they look so nice. Hannah and Annie each have mine and the children done. and Hannah has Mary and family and Br. [Apostle Moses] Thatcher and Annie has her brother George [Woodbury] and family and her uncle Angus [Munn Cannon]. Br. [Alexander F.] McDonald went back to Demming to meet his team. he is expected back in a day or two and Br. [John M.] McFarlin with him I think. they may be in before I post this. The families of the brethren who are in prison no doubt feel very badly about it, and what is the prospect when they come out.

We do indeed miss Br [Erastus] Snow more than words can express and no doubt shall do so for years to come. I dont know who could fill his place.

We shall have ripe tomatoes soon, have had a good many cucumbers and lots of melons. the boys picked 29" yesterday, some of them nice large ones, and today Br. [Helaman] & Sr. [Dora Wilcken] Pratt and children came over and had a feast with us. Our gardens would have done much better than they have if the boys had not been sick but we have had to neglect them till they have grown up with weeds.

I must now conclude with kind love to brothers & sisters, and a large share for yourselves. I remain your loving daughter

Catharine J. Romney

7" Aug 1888

Dear Parents Br. [John M.] McFarlane got in yesterday [from St. George] he was soon down to see us and told me to go up and see Lizzy [wife of John M. Macfarlane] and get a parcel and dollar you had sent me. I went up but she could'nt get at her boxes so I will get it today. they are all well except the baby. who has been rather poorly for a few days. Br. Mc had the melarial fever on the road but is well again. he has lost 20 lbs since he left St. George. so he looks much thinner. Sam Jarvis was at Annies to supper last night he says Sr. Defriez [Sam's mother-in-law] is entirely blind can't tell light from darkness. and is quite feeble. fanny [DeFriez Jarvis, Sam's wife] has a little girl about two weeks old. she and baby doing well. he would like some of his folks to give him Georges address.[52] I dont think I ever saw a child so fond of flowers as Emma [Catharine's daughter, age 4] is. she hovers around them like a humming bird or a butterfly which she is so fond of trying to catch. evry morning she goes in the flower garden. looks it all over and then calls out Ma please can I have a cypress and a four o clock and a big morning glory and a little morning glory and a cream colored flower etc. going through the whole catalogue till she gets them. The mail came last night bringing me a letter from Eleanor [Jarvis] and one from Mary Ann [Whittaker] and Carrie [Smith, Catharine's cousins]. all were pretty well.

Ury Mcfarlane [son of John M. Macfarlane, age 16] has just brought the sack. and such a sack. I can hardly keep from crying just as loving hands have put them up. evrything so nice and thoughtful. I cannot thank you in words. Good bye and God bless you I wish I could send you something.

the mail is here

15 Aug 1888
Juarez Mexico

Dear Parents I wrote a week ago but as Dessie [Eyring] has kindly sent a letter to see if I would like to enclose a note I will do so if there is time before the mexican comes for the mail. My eyes are better and worse as I use them or let them rest. and of course I feel that I must do some sewing when I have been nearly all summer with sick boys and sore eyes. The boys being sick has been a great drawback to their Pa with his work. and our gardens have grown up to weeds. they seem so week and have so much headache now that they are better. I told you about Br. McFarlane having brought the parcel you sent us. Thomas [age 12] says Grandpa and Grandma know just what folks want. I assure you it seemed so to me. there had not been any coarse white thread in the store for a long time, and shoe thread could not be got at Demming as we had sent two or three times. I find the eye salve is going to help me. Who worked the pin cushion cover and Emmas [age 4] handkerchief. she was very much delighted as well as was Caroline [age 14] with the beads and bracelets etc. babys dress I feel certain is one of Emmas [Cottam Thompson] make and is a perfect beauty   if I am right please thank her for me. the buttons, shoe thread, laces, pins needles and in fact evrything come in very usefully. and I assure you I feel more than pleased with the little bellows. it seems like an old friend. Br. McFarlane has taken dinner with us two or three times. he and Lizzy [Macfarlane] and the children were all here on Sunday evening and had a feast of melons with us.

The mail has come so I must close.

22" Aug 1888
Juarez   Mexico
Mrs. E. C. Jarvis

My Dear Friend,   Your most welcome letter came duly to hand, for which, and the sweet william seed I thank you very much. I am thankful you are getting along as well as you are and that your health, though not the best, permits you to oversee the labors of the children. tell Orin I think he has done remarkably well, and he will certainly be blessed in helping his ma, and Clarence too, as well as Ellie and Annie, and no doubt Frank does all he can by way of cheering and comforting his ma. I know what a help Ellie is by what she was when I was there and by my own girl now. give my love to them all, and to Rosa [George's second wife] and all the girls. I am pleased to hear of Nona having a girl. she has as many kinds as anybody now. what is her name. dont forget to give my love to Polly and Roz

[Romney Woodbury] when you see them. How is Aunt Alices health and eyes. I have had quit[e] a seige of sore eyes this summer. they are much better but I dare not read scarcely at all, which is quite a trial when I nurse the baby. the boys are all much better but do not recover their strength very fast. they dont feel able to do the hard work they could before. Junius [age 10] has just come home from the field   he has been there all night with Gaskell [Hannah's son, age 16] and George [Hannah's son, age 13] to water. they brought home some prickly pear apples about as larg[e] as eggs. they taste very nice. I never tasted any that I liked till this year.

We are all well at present. Annie is feeling quite disappointed as she did not get the letter you spoke of having sent her. she has a very nice portrait of your ma of which she is justly proud. I feel so sorry to hear of her lameness. give my kind love to her as well as my sincere sympathy. Annie has a very nice and interesting little family. Ann [Annie's daughter, age 9] braids very nicely now and Alice [Annie's daughter, age 7] is learning to knit and does better at that than any little girl I ever saw after only a week's practice.

The last mail brought me three Farm and Firesides. thanks for the trouble you have been to. how is it they are still coming?

I have had some beautiful flowers this year though not much variety of kinds: we have any amount of zenias almost evry color, and as double as roses, I never saw them so pretty in my life before, and any amount of the most beautiful cypress, and french morning glories marigools etc. I had just one seed of burgamot come up and I wish you could see it. it is over a foot high and a foot and a half in diameter and is now covered with seeds. I wish I could have got more kinds of seeds to come up.

We have had a great many melons in the last month for ourselves and neighbors but they are nearly gone now. we have had plenty of string beans, summer squash, some potatoes and peas, and Hannah has had some tomatoes. some people have had corn for sometime but we hav'nt yet. I have got the sweetest baby that you can imagine. we are not having anything like as much rain as last summer. Good bye and may God bless and prosper you is my earnest prayer.

I remain ever your loving friend

Catharine J Romney.

Address C. J. Cottam. Sam [Jarvis] was down. all well. Fanny [DeFriez Jarvis] has a fine daughter. Sr. DeFriez [Fanny's mother] is entirely blind. he wants Georges [Jarvis, Sam's brother] address so he can write to him

28" Aug 1888
Juarez   Mexico

My Dear Parents   I suppose a short letter will be better than none
at all. I intended to write you Sunday but your old neighbors came to
see us, so I did'nt get time, and with our washing and ironing in addition to the baby being cross the last two days I have not had time,
but as Dessie [Eyring] has sent a letter in to see if I want to enclose
one I am tempted to try to write a few lines. We are all tolerable well
except that Miles has a cold, and Ernest [Hannah's son, age 10]
keeps rather poorly ever since he was sick. The great event of the
season came off last night. Miles, Annie and I, as well as Caroline
[age 14] and the four oldest boys went to a dance in the new school
house. the first time in Mexico we enjoyed ourselves real well, but
all feel tired and used up since. I suppose we are getting too old for
such pastimes. or else it is because we are so out of practice. Dont
you think my ink is an improvement on what I have been having? I
made this out of some brown diamond dye which I brought with
me. I believe you would find it much cheaper than buying your ink,
just dissolve a little bit in a very little warm water. Gaskell [Han-
nah's son, age 16] has started to learn the carpenter trade with his
Pa. George [Hannah's son, age 13] and Thomas [age 12] are doing the
team work now though of course the big boys will have to help them
at harvesting and busy times. Miles says he wants all of the boys to
learn some trade as the younger ones get old enough to do the farming, whatever trade they fancy the most. if we were near enough I
should like to have one of them learn their Uncle Thomas' trade
[plastering].[53] Junius [age 10] went with his Pa and some other of the
brethren yesterday to help survey a new graveyard. when the mexican authorities were here they said the law would not allow us to
have our graveyard where it is as it is on the side of town where most
of the wind comes from. we are sorry for this but must conform to
the law. I think I answered Emma Squire's last letter. please ask her.
I got your last letter July 30" with the sad news of my dear Father
having hurt his eye. I do hope and trust it is well again, and that you
are both enjoying good health again. our mutual friends here are all
well so far as I know. Br. [Alexander F.] Mcdonald gave us a raking in
meeting for mentioning people in our letters to friends. I know it
does no harm to mention them to you still I must try to conform to
counsel. Do you ever hear from Uncle Thomas Punter? The mail
has come in, one paper but no letter from you. I feel so anxious
about you both. we are having a very dry summer quite unlike last

season. crops are suffering for rain. I feel like writing a long letter if time would permit, but must not be late for the mail. love to all. lovingly yours.

C. J. Romney

The following is the last two pages of a letter.

able to be around and look after things a little now and I think we shall soon all be much better again   Miles has been feeling quite poorly but I do hope he won't get sick. he and the two oldest boys and Br. [John M.] Mcfarlane started to the saw mill Friday morning. Miles A [Hannah's son, age 18] took a horse and gun in hopes of brin[g]ing home some game   we dont expect them home till Tuesday. Miles main object in going is to look at the place and see if it is advisable to buy a place in the mountain. if he concludes to do so I shall move up but of course I dont [know] anything about it yet. however I should be glad to go if we could have better health. There are a great many cases of malaria in town besides ours. one man and his wife, near neighbors are very bad. I think the lack of rain and the river has become so full of moss and the water so foul that it has created this sickness.

Thueday morning 6"   Dear Parents   Miles and the boys have got home. Miles A. shot a Doe and a fawn and a turkey   how we did enjoy it this morning for breakfast   the vension was as tender as chicken. I wish you could have enjoyed some of it too. Miles hardly thinks now that we shall go in the mountain but are not quite sure. we are all some better   children and all. we have succeeded in getting the fever broken and think we shall soon be all right again. skunks took one of our hens who had some little chickens last night. Thomas [age 12] knocked one over with rocks Monday morning but it got in our cellar, and is there yet I guess. your loving daughter

Sept 12" 1888
Juarez   Mexico

Dear Father & Mother   Your most welcome letter of Aug 13" and one from Thomas with a note from you and two papers came last mail. I was so very thankful to hear you were both better also that your eyes were better. I am pleased to hear that you had been having such a pleasant visit and a rest from your labors. and to hear of Br.

& Sr. Holt. and of all old friends. please return my kind regards when you see them again.

I can well imagine what a help George and Rachel are to them in this busy time. the enjoyment of Georgie riding horses and the girls hunting eggs, tending calv[e]s etc.

I am glad to hear of Emeline [Jarvis Cottam, wife of Thomas P. Cottam] having a fine boy and doing so nicely. of William, Emma [Thompson] and children being so well at present. I can realize how busy my dear sister keeps all the time for I never remember seeing her when she was'nt busy either working for herself or someone else. I often think of her great kindness to me and mine when I was there. give my best love to her. I should write but I can say with her that it seems as if evry hour is fully occupied. in one way or another. with having sick boys and very sore eyes nearly all summer I have got behind with my sewing hat making etc. so that it is crowding me and baby [Ethel] is not quite a[s] good to be down as most of my babies have been. and the time is well taken up with house work sewing braiding. coloring etc.   yesterday I made two cans of lye into soap. we were just out and wondered what we were going to do. but the way always opens when we really need anything very badly, so that we get it. we have got three hens set. one of them has commenced to hatch. Dessie [Eyring] sent a letter yesterday to see if I wanted to enclose a note to you but if I can write one long enough to be worth while I shall not send in hers as it looks stingy to send with someone else's stamp so often. but she always sends it for me to post lately thinking I may want to put a note in. and of course five cents a letter is quite an item sometimes. and Miles tells me never to neglect writing to you and I know you are anxious to hear as we are from you. your letters and the news you write is always very interesting to us. What kind of an arbor is there over Grandpa and Grandma's grave. do you mean those Tamarac trees and reed cane or has something else been planted? Have Rob [Lund] and Mary [Romney Lund] moved to the city yet? If you know anything of Annie['s] folks and think of it when you write you might please to mention them as she dos'nt hear very often. we are sorry to hear of Sr. [Ann Cannon] Woodbury being so lame. Br. Mc [John M. Macfarlane] and Lizzy [Macfarlane] send kind regards   he is here in the shop nearly evry day. ate supper with us Saturday night. I am writing with baby so please excuse imperfections. Annie will begin to teach school next monday in the school house. the trustees have engaded [engaged] her for six months. I must close with kindest love. I remain your devoted daughter.

Catharine J. Romney

Caroline wants Nelly [Thompson] and the rest of the girls to write to her.

Sept 30" 1888
Juarez Mexico

My Dear Parents   Your most welcome letter of the 10" ult. came to hand about a week ago. I regret very much to hear of your being so poorly, but trust you are well again. I write nearly evry two or three weeks, seldom more than three weeks between as I know you feel anxious if you dont hear.

We are all well at present. George [Hannah's son, age 13] & Thomas [age 12] went to the saw mill after lumber. they were to lay over there today start home in the morning and expect to get here on tuesday. Caroline [age 14] and the smaller children all who are old enough are going to school to Aunt Annie. she has been teaching two weeks in the school house. Hannah was up at Matties [Romney Brown, Carrie's daughter] all night. she had a little girl [Carrie] born at nine oclock this morning, and is now feeling as well as can be expected. The weather has been much warmer this summer than last on account of the lack of rain, but it is much cooler for a few weeks and is drizzling with rain today. I think we get all the papers you send. one came last week. they are welcome visitors. I am very sorry we did not get the blueing. Br. [John M.] McFarlane and Lizzy [Macfarlane] and children are all well. we see him nearly every day as he often comes to read the papers. they both wish to be kindly remembered to you both. Ury [Macfarlane] has gone with our boys to the mountain.[54]

About 6 P.M. Sunday. I had to stop writing on account of a heavy rain storm, as it leaked in on the table, and I feared it would wet my paper. I intended going to meeting but it rained too hard to take the baby. Miles and Caroline and the boys went. since meeting it stopped raining and Caroline and I took the children and went for a walk up to the graveyard taking a beautiful wreath and some boquets of flowers out of my flower garden and put on Claudies grave. The dear little fellow. I never look at his picture without feeling to thank you for it. it is worth a great deal to me I assure you.

Here is this sweet little Ethel [age 4 months] laughing at me. she often gets a good hugging and kissing for her grandpa & grandma she is such a pet. I know you would like her ever so much. she has such pretty dark eyes and is very lovable.

Hannah has not heard from the girls lately. Minnie [Romney Farr, Hannah's daughter] is in Snowflake I believe   they were both pretty well at last accounts. Hannah got a letter from Sr. Minerva [Snow] a few weeks ago   she says her health is very poor. she is working in the San Pete [Manti] Temple. Caroline has just been writing to Nelly [Thompson]. she says she will answer Marys [Thompson] letter as soon as she can. she will have to answer it for me too.

I wrote to Mary A Whittaker and Carrie Smith [Catharine's cousins] and sent last mail. I have never had but one letter from Charles since I came here. I dont know if I told you that an old gentleman died here a few weeks ago, and his wife has gone back home to northern Utah.

It will puzzle you to keep track of your grandchildren if they keep on increasing as fast as they have done lately. Walter [Charles's son], Arthur [Thomas P.'s son] & Ethel [Catharine's daughter], yes and Ezra [Emma's son] I had almost forgotten him, since I left and perhaps another by this time. Well it is getting late so I must say good bye and love to you all. From your loving daughter

Catharine.

Emma is teasing to write but it is too late tonight.

3 Oct.   I went the door this morning just before light and there stood a skunk licking some cream off the ground that splashed out of the churn last night. Miles called one of the boys up to bring the gun but just before he could fire it ran under Annies house and is there yet.

About thirty-five miles southwest of Colonia Juarez, high in the Sierra Madre Mountains, Helaman Pratt purchased a several-thousand-acre tract, "Cliff Ranch," along the Piedras Verdes River and Spring Creek.[55] *The land was excellent for grazing, and it was possible to grow crops there, although the growing season was short. The mountains were covered with giant pines and oaks, with an undergrowth of wildflowers. Crystal clear water flowed down the rocky gorges. The sight and sound of exotic birds, parakeets, mockingbirds, and blue jays filled the air. Refreshing spring water could be dammed up to create a cooling pool for milk and cheese. There was an abundance of wild game. Helaman Pratt stocked his ranch with dairy cows. His wife, Dora Wilcken Pratt, and their children operated the ranch and manufactured cheese.*

Desiring companionship for those of his family living at Cliff Ranch, Helaman Pratt invited Miles P. Romney to locate part of his family there. Miles saw an opportunity to contribute to his family's

livelihood and agreed. Catharine and her children were the first to live there, arriving in November 1888. A few months later, Miles, Hannah, and the boys joined them for a time to work on a dam and canal that would bring water from the mountain stream onto the ranch itself. The Romneys manufactured furniture, Miles turning the spindles and legs on the lathe in his carpentry shop in Juarez and Catharine weaving the bottoms from strips of rawhide.[56]

Companionship was limited but congenial. Catharine had traveled by train with Dora Wilcken Pratt from Salt Lake City to Deming, New Mexico. The Williams and Dillman families, acquaintances from Arizona, located two miles away at the Williams Ranch. Cave Valley Ranch, the cite of ancient Indian ruins, was located another two miles beyond the Williams Ranch. The families met together for church meetings and held Primary for the children. The young people enjoyed picnicking or swimming in a pool made by damming the mountain stream. Catharine often took her children for walks in the mountain, pointing out to them the beauties of nature.

Although there was plenty of wild game, food was often in short supply while the Romneys lived at Cliff Ranch, because they were not good hunters. The Romneys returned to Colonia Juarez in the fall of 1890; the Pratts remained there until the spring of 1891.

27" Nov. 1888
Sierra Madre Mountains

Dear Father & Mother   Two weeks ago tomorrow morning Miles and I with the children and Gaskell [Hannah's son, age 17] left Juarez for this place with Br. [Helaman] Pratt and part of his family to try and make a home where we can raise a little stock. we shall try it for a while any how. we dont know yet whether we shall sell out in Juarez or just what we shall do. we shall be able to tell better after awhile. I felt very much encouraged the first week after we left home as I improved evry day. but I took a billious spell and for a week past now have been having the fever again every other day. but hope to soon be weel [well] again. Caroline [age 14] has'nt had the fever since we left but she bloats up considerably, and dos'nt feel very well yet. Emma [age 4] has had some fever once but seems to be feeling pretty well now. Miles' cough has been bad since we came up here   I am afraid this is too high an altitude for his lungs. he started home this morning on mule back, and if he has good luck will get ther tonight. he had to go to Casas Grandes to make his monthly report to the post master, and will likely have to stay at home two or three weeks to attend to some business and work he has on hand there when I expect him back to stay while the big boys go down to go to school. I expect Miles A [Hannah's son, age 19] up in two or three days to stay till his Pa comes back. We got in our house last Monday   a very comfortable lumber room 12-14 feet, by far the best I have had in Mexico. I think I shall like here very well when we all get well again. I tried to write yesterday to send down by Miles but I did not feel able, so thought I would write this to send down by Br. Pratt who will start this afternoon. he is going to Chihuahua to try to sell his cheese about 1500 lbs and expects to be gone about a month.[57] the Sr. Pratt who is here is the one who came to Mexico when I did. I like her very much   she makes a splendid neighbor, and we have no other neighbor nearer than two miles. we are about 4 miles from the saw mill. we hav'nt heard from home since we left. I expect a letter from you when Miles A comes. Br. Pratt killed a beef yesterday and Miles got 100 lbs so it will last us quite awhile. You often ask me what you can send. I dont like you to risk send[ing] anything when it is so uncertain, but it seems to me I remember a lot of old Juveniles in the cloths cupboard. now I have been thinking if you dont intend keeping them to have them bound, perhaps you would not mind sending a few of them in a roll like other papers, for the children to read, as it would be pretty sure to come and the children will miss the Juveniles now we have left home, as they have had Annies to read. Frank [Woodbury, Annie's brother] has been sending them to her. dont send them if you want to keep them. I feel very anxious to hear how you both are. Please give my love to all and accept the same yourselves. I wish you a happy New Year and a Merry Merry Christmas all of you. Good bye and God bless you.

Catharine

13 Dec. 1888
Cliff Ranch   Sierra Madre Mountains
Mr. George T. Cottam

Dear Brother   I expect you have heard by this time that I have changed my place of abode. it will be four weeks tomorrow since we arrived here. we were three days coming up, as there is a very hard mountain to pull up, and we had to take one wagon up at a time, and Br. [Helaman] Pratt had a large herd of stock to drive up. the ranch belongs to him and Miles has bought an interest in it hoping to be able to raise a little stock, our potatoes etc. I do not know whether we shall all move up or not yet. The two big boys have been up here fencing but they are going to school to Aunt Annie the rest of the winter. Gaskell [Hannah's son, age 17] went down a week ago and Miles A. [Hannah's son, age 19] will start home in the morning. he and Thomas [age 12] have gone hunting today   he wants to get me a turkey for Christmas and one or two to take down home. I hope he will be successful. about six weeks ago when he was up here with his Pa he shot one turkey and two deer a doe and a fawn. Br. [George C.] Williams told me the other day that since he came up here, I think about a year and eight months, he has killed between 80 and 90 deer and another family where there are several grown boys have killed over two hundred in about the same length of time. Br. Pratt killed one about two weeks ago. Miles went down a little more than two weeks ago. I expect him up again before long. Emma [age 4] Caroline [age 14] and I were pretty sick when we left home but have got quite well and strong again, but we all have bad colds. We have had very nice weather most of the time, considerable rain and the rest of the time the nights have been clear and cold, and the frost so heavy that it looked like a light fall of snow. One of our mexican brethren is herding sheep at the foot of the mountain, one night a week or two ago a mountain lion took two or three of the sheep, in the morning he tracked it up to a cave, he looked in and saw it, and though he only had two cartridges he fired and then ran and got on a big rock, the lion came out roaring loudly, and soon lay down and died. A boy in Hop Valley a few miles from here came in sight of three bears last week. he shot and killed one of them and last Friday night they caught one of the others in a trap. Miles A was there at the time. he went over to get a colt of his. [*Last part is missing.*]

23" Dec 1888
Cliff Ranch   Sierra Madre Mountains   Mexico
Mrs. Eleanor C. Jarvis

Dear Friend   I think I will sit down and have a chat with you this afternoon for I am [sure] you will want to know how I like my mountain home. we started here on the 19 of last month. Caroline, Emma, and I had been sick for several weeks and were still very weak and miserable. Caroline was bloated up till she was a sight to see. but I am thankful to be able to say that we are beginning to feel like ourselves again, though we have all had bad colds.

Miles staied two weeks and then went [down to fin]ish some work. I expect him up again in a week or two. the two big boys Miles [A.] and Gaskell have been here fencing but have gone down home to go to school. I have not heard from there for two weeks. Annie forwarded your welcome letter, and she has likely answered hers, so you will know how they all are. I should like to see them all but we shall have to spend our christmas apart this year. I have been busy making some little presents for the children. we hope and intend to have a good time on Christmas. our whole town expect to eat dinner at Sr. [Dora Wilcken] Pratts, and on Christmas eve all the children in the town are invited to a candy pulling at our house, when we expect to have doughnuts, cookies etc. and a general good time. now you see we do'nt do things up shabily in this part of the country. evrything is done on a grand scale, a sort of wholesale business you see. Our town consists at present of Br. & Sr. Pratt and six children, Sr. Romney and her six children. We have Sunday school every sunday and in the afternoon usually take a walk. I like living here very well only that I miss the meetings and the society of the rest of the family. but I keep too busy to get lonesome as I got so behind with my work while I was sick. Our nearest neighbors live about a mile and a half from us and the saw mill and settlement is three or four miles from here. this is a very pretty picturesque place, and I have a very nice and agreeable neighbor in Sr. Pratt. Give my love to Rosie [plural wife of George Jarvis]. I feel to deeply sympathise with her and their family, Allie and all. I am so glad you are as well as you are, and that George is getting along so well. Remember me kindly to your mother and all the girls. I often think of you and hope and pray you may have health and strength. How is your Aunt Alice. I felt very sorry to hear of Roz's [Romney Woodbury] misfortune and sickness but hope she is well again. Good bye from your loving Friend

C. J. Romney.

I enclose some moss ferns, leaves etc.   hope it will not get spoiled on the road.

7" July 1889
Cliff Ranch
Mrs. E. C. Jarvis

My Dear Friend   I am so used to answering my letters when I get them that I did'nt think but I had answered your last till the other day and I fear I have neglected to do so, but I have been quite busy and Caroline [age 15] was gone 17 weeks, she got home last Wednesday and Alice [Annie's daughter, age 8] & Orin [Annie's son, age 5] came up with her. Gaskell [Hannah's son, age 17] went down and brought her home, and I assure you I am glad to have her here once more. Annie had a bad cold and was not feeling well when they left. the children will likely stay some time. Miles A. [Hannah's son, age 19] and his Pa are both down there at work now. Annie's school was out on the 28″ I went down with Miles the last of May and was gone a week. Annie says she seldom gets a letter from any of you. I quite enjoyed a visit with her and Mattie [Romney Brown, Carrie's daughter]. Mattie has such a fine large baby, and Ella [Annie's baby] is considerable larger than Ethel [Catharine's baby] and Caroline says she believes there never was a better baby. Ethel suffers by comparison in her estimation as far as goodness goes though she has to acknowlege that Ethel is very cute. she says a good many words and walks all about but she wont be friends with Caroline yet. she had quite forgotten her. We walked over to Br. [George C.] William's ranch to meeting this afternoon a mile and a half and back, so am pretty tired. last Sunday it was held here and the Sunday before at Cave Valley. I go to Sunday school and Primary and generally to meeting so do'nt get very lonesome. Monday 8″. I was writing last night when it was so dark and baby cross that I have made a great botch of it. Caroline wants to know if Ellie [Eleanor's daughter] will please to answer her last letter, and sends her love to her aunt Rosie [plural wife of George Jarvis] and yourself as well as Annie [Eleanor's daughter] and the babies. Junius [age 11] sends his love to Orin & Clarence [Eleanor Jarvis's sons]. he is just saddling up the little poney to go after the cows. Caroline is just having a ride on it, and he is going to take the baby for one before he starts. Give my love to your Ma and the girls Roz, Polly, Nona, Rosie and all the children. Ellie must be quite a young lady now. she was so much larger than Caroline. I am glad Rosie is so good & kind, and that George is meeting with such good success. How is your Aunts Alice, Willie, Josaphine etc. getting along?

We have such lovely wild flowers here and a great variety but have had very poor luck with my garden flowers this spring. some people are having green peas and new potatoes now. Some people in Juarez have fruit trees and grape vines bearing, and a good many black berries and strawberries there I hear. there are a number of cases of malaria so I am glad I am in the mountains. Is there any prospect of Josaphine [Jarvis] getting married?[58] Tell me all the

news when you write. Dessie [Eyring] was well when I was down. Minnie [Romney Farr] is in Arizona she had a boy [Lorin Miles Farr] born on the 3 of April. Isabell [Romney Platt] has very poor health. I should like to visit with you this afternoon. lovingly yours
Catharine.

What do you call your baby?

July 7" 1889
Cliff Ranch   Sieree Madre Mountains

Dear Father & Mother   I have not had a word from you for over five weeks so that I am feeling very anxious to know how you are. I think I wrote to you last when Miles started down to Juarez to work. he is still there. I got a letter from him the other day and he has the headache a good deal and dosn't feel so well as he does in the mountains. Miles A [Hannah's son, age 19] has gone down to work and Gaskell [Hannah's son, age 17] went down to bring Caroline [age 15] home. they got here on Wednesday, bringing Alice [Annie's daughter, age 8] and Orin [Annie's son, age 5] with them to stay with us awhile. there are a number of cases of malaria down there now and I fear it will be worse if the rainy season dos'nt set in soon. it has been threatening for several weeks but has only resulted in a few showers.

I assure you I am thankful to have Caroline at home again, and she seems just as pleased to be here. was gone 17 weeks. she has grown considerably. The boys are busy in the field as there is a fine growth of weeds since our showers started.

We have been bothered with some breachey stock which persist in getting in, in spite of the fence and our efforts and have eaten off considerable of our corn. Park [age 7] goes to the field evry day, and dosn't seem to mind it. Ernest [Hannah's son, age 11] & Junius [age 11] take turns in going to the field and tending to the cows, week about. they have a little horse and drive the cows off in the morning and go after them in the afternoon. we are milking eight. they dont do very well but will as soon as the rains come as that will bring an abundance of grass. Ethel [14 months] has just got up and is sitting enjoying some pancakes which Caroline is just frying for breakfast. dont I wish you were just going to eat some with us. the boys are out milking. Miles dos'nt believe in women and girls doing such work if it can be avoided so George [Hannah's son, age 14] and Thomas [age 13] do it most of the time. Ethel and Ella [Annie's baby, 16 months] both talk some but Ella dosn't walk yet. Annie had a bad cold and was not feeling well when the children came away. Emma [age 4] is having a good time with Alice and Orin, they are such nice quiet children. she loves to hear about you and talks about you as if she could remember you. We are all well and trust you are the same. How is Aunt Mary [Smith Taylor] getting along. Grandma Pymm etc. Love to Emma, the boys and all the folks and a large portion for yourself. Your loving daughter.

Catharine

28" July 1889
Cliff Ranch   Mexico

My Dear Father & Mother   I recieved your last letter this past week, and am very sorry to learn of my dear Mothers sickness. I do hope and pray to the Lord that you are much better again.

Hannah went down to stay at Juarez in Annies plas [place] for two or three weeks till Annie had a visit and rest up in this mountain country. she got here last Tuesday, and is enjoying herself firstrate. the day after she came the 24" [Pioneer Day] we took the team and all the children and went over to the field where we ate our dinners, and the children played games under the trees, and Thomas [age 13] and Ernest [Hannah's son, age 11] caught 10 fish. we should have enjoyed ourselves so much only that we had the misfortune to break our wagon bows under an oak tree. Baby [Ethel] is climbing over me, standing up on my lap etc. while I write so you wont expect perfection in writing.

We went over to Br. [George C.] Williams to meeting yesterday and last Sunday had meeting here. We had almost despaired of having any good rains here to bring up the grass, till a week ago last Saturday just as we were dismissing primary when it began to rain, it soon came down in sheets and torrents, and lasted between two and three hours before it entirely stopped. the whole surface of the ground was covered with a running stream, and a torrent was coming down through our pasture about waist deep to Gaskell [Hannah's son, age 17] and Thomas who had to cross it as they came from the field, right in the wash. we found next morning it had swept over our garden like a river washing up some and covering up much more of it with dirt and rubbish which we have since cleaned off the best we could and the rain we have had since have helped to wash them clean so it looks pretty well again   it washed away some of our fence. the whole country since the rain begins to look beautiful and green. we had need of better grass for our cows. they have began to increase in their milk nicely. Br. [Helaman] Pratt's have began to make cheese. we are milking eight cows now. Most people are having new potatoes. some have had since the first of this month, but we had no early seed. so ours are later but they look lovely. and I think we shall have plenty of them. we are having the first mess of summer squash this morning will soon have beans, corn and cucumbers. I wrote and told you of getting the blue dye. the calico has made me a pretty basque.

Miles and the folks were well when we heard last. Ethel would worry Grandma nearly to death if she were there she is such a climber and so mischievous. I hope Emma [Cottam Thompson] went to the city to have a rest. only I dont know how you would get along without her. So Sr. [Clara] Bowman has gone to rest. I see by the paper that Sr. Tiax is dead.

My Dear Parents I should like so much to see you, and all my brothers sisters and children. the children join me in kind love to you. I remain as ever your loving daughter.

Catharine J Romney

Gaskell says they had a good time at Juarez on the 24" [Pioneer Day]. Miles was the Orator of the day.

11" Sept. 1889
Cliff Ranch

My Dear Parents It is about three weeks since I wrote last. the day after I sent it off, on Saturday, Hannah came home, bringing with her Sr. Agnes McDonald, and Mattie [Romney Brown] to pay us a visit. we were very pleased to see them and had a nice time, though Mattie only stayed 6 days as she wanted to get home to dry corn. while she was here we went down in the field one afternoon to gather hops. we have got I think enough to last us till they grow again. such nice large hops and right in the field. and the same day we went up the mountain to see some caves and natural curiosities. just above the field, among the rest are two large arches formed of the solid rock. I expect they would be from 50 to a hundred feet from one side to the other and fifty feet high and since then Gaskell [Hannah's son, age 17] took us over to Cave Valley to see two large caves there. they are large caves in the solid rock running away back in the side of the mountain, and have been inhabited by some ancient people. in one of them have been about 30 rooms, though many of the partition walls have fallen to decay. the dividing walls have been built of mud or clay, and then plastered, and some of them are covered with rude drawings, of men, animals etc. there are indications of fire as there are ashes on the floors and the walls and roof are black with smoke the doorways, or openings for gaining entrance to the different rooms are quite small, only about three feet high and perhaps two wide. in the front of one is a large vessel [*a drawing is sketched in here*] about this shape built of mud made of clay mixed with straw or grass, about two or three inches thick. it is about 12 or 14 feet high and perhaps 8 or 10 in diamiter it is round, and many suppose it has been made for storing grain in. in the other there are remains of two or three smaller ones which have been similar to the large one. this cave is also divided off into different apartments some of the rooms look to be 8 or ten feet square. visiting these ancient dwelling places caused me to have strange feelings, and to wish I could know who the people were who the inhabitants were. The night before Mattie started home, we went over to Cave Valley to a surprise party. while there I got your last letter which Miles had just sent up. it was dated Aug. 14″ you were both tolerable, for which I feel thankful. sorry to hear of Mary Ann [Cottam, George's daughter] being sick. was glad to have the plan of Charle's new house. I hope William and Emma [Thompson] got home all right. I hope you will have rain as the heat must be very oppressive. Last Sunday meeting was over at Cave Valley. Gaskell went and Caroline [age 15] went with Br. [Helaman] Pratts folks, and I started with Thomas [age 13] and the children down the river for a walk and to find some grapes but had'nt gone far when Eugene [Hannah's son, age 5] came running to tell me [*page missing*]. boys and Emma would like to read this. With love to all I remain you[r] loving daughter

Catharine

22″ Oct. 1889
Cliff Ranch   Mexico

My Dear Father & Mother,   I feel that I have been rather neglectful as it is over three weeks since I wrote last. Miles came up on horseback two weeks ago last Friday. he left Annie and children all well, but a great deal of malaria and other sickness in Juarez this summer and fall. he brought me your last letter dated Sept 22″ just a month ago. you were both middling, so much better news than I often get. Miles was saying Sunday evening he wished you could just come in to see us, and I assure you I felt to say amen to it. I should so like to see you. I regret so much to hear of George Woodburys [Annie's brother, age 29] death. such a helpless little family. Miles says Annie feels very badly.

I am very sorry to hear of George getting hurt with lightening. hope he is all right again. it was certainly a providence that it was no worse. We got some mail last Sunday among the rest the St. Louis and Canada papers you speak of sending, but the wrappers were pasted on as usual, no braid on them. the parcel you sent me, gingham and shoe thread, were at Casas Grandes the last time Miles was down and he tried to get it but they refused to let him have it saying there was something wrong about it and it would have to go back to Paso Del Norte first. so I am in hopes of getting it the next time he goes down. the laws and customs of these mexican officials are past finding out and very annoying sometimes. You ask me if there is anything else I would like to have you send me. you are so very kind and good my dear parents but I get along very nicely as a rule, and the risk in sending as well as the expense to you is so great. still reading matter is always very acceptable, of any kind, papers, Juveniles, a history, or anything that may ever be convenient, and is pretty sure to come. I wish you would both send us a lock of your hair when you write again please.

Miles has done such a lot of hard work since he came up, and the kind of work he is not used to is so hard on him. he has built me an other large room, and to save having to pay out so much for lumber, has built it of rock, with a nice fireplace in. he will try and put a shingled roof on, and a floor in as soon as he can. I may not get much use of it this winter except the fireplace to sit by of an evening, as Annie will come up to teach the children and we may have to use it for a schoolroom. it is possible that I may go to juarez to take care of Annies place this winter but dont know yet. Miles took us up to Corallis the Sunday before last about ten or twelve miles one of the plesantest rides I ever enjoyed saw Sr. Defreiz it made me feel very sad to see her she is stone blind. sends her love to you all, and all old friends. Sam [Jarvis] and wife had gone to Juarez last Sunday we went to meeting at Cave [Valley]. began yesterday to dig potatoes a good prospect. We are all well. Miles has also built a rock chimney for Hannah and a large rock cellar for the potatoes. The boys have shot three deer lately, and one as they went to Juarez last time. Please direct to Colonia Juarez as there is another Juarez in Mexico.

The following is an undated fragment.

27" Sunday

Dear Parents. I recieved your last welcome letter with the fish hooks enclosed the night before last—also a paper all right. many thanks. the boys much pleased. I do hope Miles will be able to get both parcels next time he goes down.

People waiting to go.

22" Oct 1889
Cliff Ranch   Mexico
Mrs. E. C. Jarvis

My Beloved Friend   It is some time since I recieved your last welcome letter. I regret very much to hear of your continued poor health, but feel that you are indeed blessed in having so good and helpful a daughter, and also that Rosie [plural wife of George Jarvis] is so good and kind, and I believe she appreciates you as much as you do her. I trust the Lord will continue to bless you both as he has done. give my love to her, Ella [Eleanor's daughter] and all the children. I felt so shocked to hear of the sudden death of your Br. George [Woodbury]. Miles says Annie feels very badly, it is so long since she has seen him. I am sure it has been a sad blow to your Mother and all of you. and poor Roz [Woodbury, George's wife] with her helpless little ones. I cannot express my feelings when I think of them. the God of the widow and the fatherless, alone can afford them the comfort and consolation which they so sorely need, and she could not have a better friend than your ma. please give my love to them and tell them I offer my sincere and heartfelt sympathy in this the hour of affliction. May God bind up the broken hearts and may we all be able to acknowlege his hand in all things as we should.

The people in Juarez were very anxious to have Annie teach again this winter   she has given such good satisfaction, but I think she is tired of such a large school   it is such hard work for her and she has declined for which we are very glad as we could'nt send all of ours down, and I think Annie will come up here this winter and just teach our own and perhaps Br. [Helaman] Pratts, so I think she will enjoy the change as she likes this place, and can be very warm and comfortable and of course will only need to hold a short session each day with so few. Br. [John M.] McFarlane I suppose will teach in Juarez.[59]

I have weaned Ethel [17 months]. she is little but as "smart as a steel trap," says almost evrything, and has run alone nearly six months. our family are all well but there has been a great deal of sickness and some deaths in Juarez this summer.

Our potato crop is turning out well. it will be a long tedius job to get them all harvested. we started yesterday. we also have a good many squash as well as some corn. it didnt quite all get ripe.

Miles took us over to Corallis a week ago last Sunday. one of the plesantest rides I ever had. The rugged mountain scenery was glorious in its autumnal tints. I went into raptures over it nearly the entire distance. one huge juniper tree we passed of the darkest green had a vine running through it which the frost had turned a bright scarlet. it looked like a huge boquet. I wish you could enjoy such an out and such a sight.

Last Sunday we went to Cave Valley to meeting. next Sunday it will be here. Caroline wants to write to Ella so I must quit and take her place at the ironing. excuse this terrible writing. I remain your friend as ever.

C.J.R.

3" Dec. 1889
Juarez   Mexico

My Dear Parents   I wrote to you a few days after I came down and the next mail brought me a letter from you, and last week I got another with a note in from Emma [Cottam Thompson], and have got two papers by the last mail. I sent your letters up for the children to read so must answer from memory. Emma [age 5] & Ethel [19 months] were wonderfully pleased with their little letters. Miles told me I had better put them away and take care of them for them till they get big. I feel very badly about Amanda Cannon.[60] her poor mother will be almost heart broken. I hope Eliza Lund is all right again.

I am more pleased than I can tell to hear of you both being so much better lately.

Br. [Apostle Moses] Thatcher is expected in this evening. I have the mail to attend to now which is quite a new experience for me. tomorrow is mail day, so I must not leave this to do then. Miles & Miles A are working on the grist mill, the[y] go about sunrise, take their dinners, and come home about dark. they expect to finish in a week or two. Miles was called on to lecture to the young people last sunday evening, on the conquest of Mexico. I went and took the children, but Ethel was naughty and I had to bring her out. she has been very poorly with a bad cold.

Miles is not feeling well lately. he has the canker or something the matter with his mouth. Yours in love

C.J.R.

26" Jan. 1890
Juarez   Mexico

My Beloved Father & Mother   This is January but a person might almost believe it to be two or three months later, judding [judging] by the weather the past few days. it is perfectly delightful. I have been to Sunday School with Emma [age 5] and Ethel [20 months] this morning. My dear parents it is such a long time since I have had a letter from you, nearly two months I think, so you may judge how anxious I feel. I expected the mail in last night but the brother who took the order forgot to call for it. it comes to Casas Grandes twice a week, but we only have a weekly service here. they send it up every Wednesday, and then if any of the brethren go down on Friday or Saturday we send an order and have it brought up.

Br. [Helaman] Pratt came down from the mountain [Cliff Ranch] yesterday, bringing me letters from Miles, Hannah, Annie, Caroline [age 15], Junius [age 11] and Park [age 7]. I thought I would keep the latter as it is the first letter he ever wrote and it is very precious to me, but I believe I will translate it and send it to you. Caroline had a very sore throat. And Miles was quite poorly with bad cold and cough. it will be two weeks next Tuesday since he went up home. had been here about two months and a half. Miles A [Hannah's son, age 20] took a load of potatoes to sell but did'nt have very good luck. he was gone 17 days, had a stormy time, muddy roads and had to sell for beans and whatever he could get, as he did not want to haul them back, and one of our old mares lost her colt while he was gone. Frances [Turley Romney, wife of Miles A.] went with him, they got back last Saturday and went up to the mountain on Monday.[61] they would be thankful to get home again.

Caroline has embroidered and made Ethel a new white petticoat   it looks real nice, she has got it on today for the first time and is quite proud of it. she is the greatest little talker. when I was getting breakfast the other morning while they were both in bed, I said, "Emma would you and Ethel like an egg for breakfast?" Ethel spoke up quickly and said, "No! porrige, porrige, I like it." so you see she is like her Grandpa, she likes milk porrige we often have it for breakfast. we have a good little cow and she does well considering we have nothing to feed her except a little bran sometimes, she goes in the herd.

I hav'nt heard how you spent the holidays, nor whether Charles has been to see you. it seems so lonesome not to hear from any of you for so long. So Aunt Ann [Smith Cottam] is dead.[62] it seems sad to think of her and Uncle John being estranged from each other. How are Emma [Cottam Thompson] and the boys getting along? I got two papers from you about two weeks ago. We have had no stamps for three or four weeks, and there are none at Casas Grandes. we have had to send letters and the money with them to be stamped at Chihuahua. this is a specemine of the speed with which business is transacted in Mexico. they seem to think that a few stamps ought to last a long time, and so they do the mexicans, for I suppose they dont write letters like our people do.

Annie writes me that the children are all good and learning fast. It would be difficult to find a child of more importance, in her opinion than our Emma. she seems to think that she has a lisence to do whatever she sees me do. I feel the necessity of being circumspect in what I do and say, with a child of her disposition. if I can only train her properly she will no doubt make a very smart woman. she asks questions about almost everything you can think of.

There are three or four bad cases of rheumatism or rheumatic fever among children here. Sr Fife has concluded that the linament is not doing any good now and has began to use a strong solution of salt and Salt petre in cold water, rubbing it in well and thinks it helps her. did you ever try it?

I was sorry to learn of the destructive floods along the Virgin.

Has Br. Robt. Parker ever come home? How are Alice Woodburys eyes now?

Have you seen the "Christmas Star"? it must be a grand thing, judging by the notices of it in the paper.

Br. [Henry] Eyring is to start for the city of Chihuahua on Thursday to purchase goods for the store.[63] it is doing well considering the drawbacks to contend with. they have declared a dividend of 25 per cent for the year they have run it. of course the duty on some articles is very high, for instance the duty on a pair of shoes of any kind large or small is one dollar, which makes a pair of baby shoes, when brought from the states, cost about $3.00 per pair, placing them quite beyond the reach of most people. I have been making some for our babies. I have made baby a little pair of sunday shoes, the tops out of a little piece of black velvet that I had with toe caps and pieces around the heel of thin mexican leather something after the style of the cloth shoes we used to wear, and they really look quite nice.

The duty on dress braid which they have got in at last is a dollar on a dozen of those small rolls, so they sell at two for 35 cts.   calico is 20 cts a sara 3 inches less than a yard. My Beloved parents, how I should enjoy the privelige of looking in at you, and still I ought not to complain for it is a longer time since Annie saw her folks and very much longer since Hannah saw hers. How are Aunt Mary [Smith Taylor] and family getting along? we never hear from them. Good bye for [now]   letter just come but havent had time to open it   Dear Father could you please send me three or four shoe or harness needles. I think they would come in a letter all right. I believe they could be got at the harness shop.

Catharine's mother, Caroline Cottam, died on February 19, 1890, in St. George.

15″ Apr. 1890
Juarez   Mexico

My Beloved Father   I wrote a letter to you and sent by Br Eyring a week ago, but will write a few lines again now as I am going back home again in a day or two and it may be some time before I get a chance to send a letter down. Miles came down last Friday and brought Caroline [age 15] and Junius [age 12], and Frances [Turley Romney, wife of Miles A. Romney] came on a visit to her folks. Annie has not come down yet but may do in a few weeks, so we will shut the house up for the present, as the boys are anxious to have ma at home again, and this will be a very busy season of the year, for Miles and the boys, indeed they have been very busy in the field ever since he went up the last time. they have made a long flume across the river to get the water on some more of his land.

I do hope your health is at least reasonably good and that the rest of the folks are all well. please give my love to them. Miles joins me in love and good wishes. We are all well except George [Hannah's son, age 15], who was going after lumber two or three weeks ago and got his foot badly sprained and bruised up, so that he has been laid up and not able to walk when his Pa left, a great misfortune especially just now when his help is needed so badly.

Now dear father in regard to the $50.00 in the store as soon as you mentioned it to me, I thought of a disposition I should like to make of it, but fearing it would not meet with Miles approval I thought I would try to gain his consent before I mentioned it to you, and that was that it should be paid over to the boys on the debt owing to them, George and Thomas [her brothers].[64]

Miles felt just as I was afraid he would on the subject, utterly refused to use a cent, even for that purpose, as he claims that any such means left to a woman, belongs solely to herself and children. still as he is so anxious to begin to pay the debt, he has consented on one condition to let me turn this over, if it meets with your mind, which is that he transfers to me his capital stock in the Juarez coop store amounting I think to $65.00 which being Mexican money will be equivalent to $50.00 in american money. this store is doing a good business, paid I believe 25 cents [per cent] dividend last year, but Br. Eyring can tell you particulars about it. I think myself it will be quite as good for me, as I can then draw the dividend without the risk of losing in the mail or at the custom house. Now if this is satisfactory and the boys are willing to take this kind of pay, please turn it over to them, $25.00 to each.

With best love I remain your devoted daughter.

C. J. Romney

9" June 1890
Cliff Ranch Mexico

My Beloved Father, I have scarcely a moment to write this morning as Miles and Hannah are just going to start to Juarez but I want to send Ethels [age 2] picture for you to look at, and perhaps you will be able to have one taken from it or if not you may please to send it back to me sometime as it is the only one of her and in fact it is the only artist that has been in this part of the country since we came, and I guess if I had had photographs taken instead of the tin type I should never have got any, as the last time I was in Juarez the people had never got their likenesses, he had sent them away to be finished and had gone off himself, but the tin ones he finished right away.

Annie got a letter from her mother, yesterday. I have had one since I came from Juarez, telling of Georgies [son of George and Rachel Cottam] death.[65] wrote to George and Emma [her brother and sister] a week ago.

Annie had a little girl born on the 4" she is doing well. we are all well. Miles is taking a load of furniture down a bad road to haul it over. Miles says he will try and send this out to Demming to post as it will go safer. Good bye and may God bless you is my constant prayer. Your loving daughter

Catharine.

No rain   very warm in day time and freezing at night.

15″ June 1890
Cliff Ranch   Mexico

Dear Father   Your welcome letter of May 29″ came to hand last evening. Miles & Hannah have been to Juarez this week with a load of furniture and came back yesterday. Miles has got a job of work to do there, a house to build for Br. [Henry] Eyring so he will move either Annie or I there in about two weeks, likely Annie as my boys are needed here on the farm. Miles finds that he cannot make all ends meet by our farm work alone. he must get work at his trade, and it is a bad road to haul furniture over.

Mattie [Romney Brown] is with us on a visit perhaps for two or three weeks if she can content herself. Carolines ankle is getting some better, but not near well yet. she thinks four weeks is a long time for it to be bad. I am very sorry to hear of Alice Isom being so sick. hope she is well again. Glad Matilda [Thompson Bleak] has got a son. please offer my congratulations. You say you would like to change places with Br. [John M.] Mcfarlane for a week. Oh Father! how we should all like to have you pay us a visit. Miles says he would send a team out to Demming to bring you from the railroad if you could come. you dont know how delighted we should be. Miles often speaks about you, how you would enjoy the childrens little cute tricks.

In regard to the dividend you speak of, please let the boys draw it, though it is but little it will be better than nothing to them. the capital I will leave as it is for the present. I got the $20 dollars from Br. Eyring, put $20 in the store and Miles put enough with the $5.00 to get Caroline & Thomas each a pair of shoes. the premium had come down from 30 to 25 cts [cents] by the time he got here   I got all the things just as you sent them I think the black sateen[66] dress, one light delaine[67] dress, a calico skirt, 2 ladies ties, 2 boys ties, 1 neck handkerchief, 1 pair gloves, 4 packages diamond dye, 3 lasts, fish glue one hymn book, 2 photographs hair buttons, needles etc. all very nice, and much appreciated. I think I got the papers all right, got two last Sunday and one yesterday and thank you very much for them also for the envelopes in your last letter. you are ever the same kind thoughtful Father. I wrote to you a week ago and sent Ethels likeness   also wrote to Emma and George a few days before.

I believe you would enjoy a visit to our sunday school   we have about 40 names enrolled with a good attendance, indeed nearly evrybody here goes. Br. Pratt is superintendant and when he is not there, Gaskell [Hannah's son, age 18] who is secretary, takes charge, administers the sacrament and goes right ahead like a man   they are all good steady boys so far, and seem quite contended here. I saw Br [Peter] and Sr. [Mattie] Dillman last Sunday   they send kind regards. Please give my love to all the folks. Ed. Eyring and another man were here last night   left this morning. Miles joins me in kind love to you. yours in love

C. J. Romney

I am glad Charles has got your likenesses enlarged   should like much to see them.

13" July 1890
Cliff Ranch   Mexico
Mr. George T. Cottam

Dear Brother   I cant for the life of me remember whether I answered your last letter or not, so what am I to do, run the risk of not answering it at all, or the worse one to you, of answering it twice. I scarcely know how to decide in the matter, but I suppose I had better write a line or two to show [that even] if I am so forgetful that I have not forgotten you.

I got your letter about four weeks ago, while we were over to Cave Valley to a meeting, called by Apostle Brigham Young who paid us a flying visit. he staid here one night.

Miles moved Annie back to Juarez two weeks ago. he has gone to work there at his trade part or all of the summer. Miles A. and Gaskell [Hannah's sons] will go down to help him in about two weeks. I feel sorry to see him have such a hard life of it, but it seems impossible to get ahead with so many though we have got the best kind of boys to work. breadstuff is not near so cheap as it used to be when we first came to this country, and our people have not yet been very successful in the raising of small grain. many difficulties to be met and overcome as there is wherever our people settle, a great deal of trouble and expense, and loss of time, caused our people by Custom house officers and other officials. sometimes people are fined through not understanding or complying with the law in regard to the registering of births, or not getting permits for burying the dead or something of the kind, but I suppose it will be better as we get to better understand the laws of the country, which seem so strange to us.

Corn has risen one half, is just double what it was 4 months ago. flour has been $6.00 a hundred for a long time, but I hear it is $8.00 but dont know whether it is true or not.

We have had one mess of new potatoes and I think in a week or two we shall be able to begin using them often. no other vegetables yet as our springs are very backward, but everything is growing nicely now since the rains have started and the grass is growing well now though it was all dried up as it had been such a dry winter, and our cows did'nt do scarcely anything, but they are increasing nicely now. we are milking eight. Br. Pratts folks will begin making cheese tomorrow morning. they made five hundred dollars worth last summer and have got a good many more cows this summer, so you see these large stock owners can do well in this country. I am sure you and Rachel both miss your boy very much and I sincerely sympathize with you. Is Charles intending to move down this fall. Give my love to Emma, Thomas and families, to Rachel and children. tell the girls to write to Caroline. I remain as ever your loving sister

C. J. Romney

Aug 10" 1890
Cliff Ranch   Mexico
Mrs. Eleanor C. Jarvis

Dear Friend   I have been rather dilatory about answering your last letter, but I had written just a short time before, and thought I would wait till another time, and for several weeks I had forgotten that I had not answered it until this morning when I resolved to do so at once. many thanks for the nice cards. the girls were very much pleased with them. and the boys thought some must be for them so I gave them some of the small ones. they were very pretty. I am so sorry to hear of your continued poor health and also the news I read in the paper of Georges arrest.[68] it seems too bad when he has been back so short a time, and you sick too, but I pray the Lord to bless and strengthen you for every trial. Oh Eleanor if you could only enjoy good health once more how thankful I should feel.

When we got your letter, Miles and I were at Juarez to attend the funeral of Matties [Romney Brown] little Carrie. I received word while there of George losing his oldest boy. he followed close after Mother.

As we came home up the mountain, you may tell the boys we saw a bear, and Uncle Miles shot at it but we were too far away to hit it, and about four weeks ago Miles A. went a few miles to hunt a cow and saw a mountain lion and a deer, he wounded both but did'nt get either of them. he also saw a theif who on seeing him was running away from a beef animal of Br. [George C.] Williams, which he had just killed. he came back and told the brethren, and went back that night with three of them to show them where it was they found the beef with just a little of it gone. Miles came back but the rest followed the thieves, which they found by their tracks to be four and seemed to have gone to Casas Grandes so I suppose they were Mexicans. you can also tell them that one of the brethren and two young men were up here and went across the mountains and were gone five days, when they came back they had killed one bear, five deer, and nine turkey, but our boys dont kill much as the game is more shy around where people live, but they have caught lots of fish. I suppose they are growing to be large boys and a great help and Master Frank was always a large boy. The girls would enjoy hunting moss and gum and wild flowers with Caroline and Emma. give my love to them all. also to Rosie [plural wife of George Jarvis]. tell Ellie [Eleanor's daughter] to write to Caroline when she can. she has written to all the girls last and feels almost discouraged she went over two weeks ago on a visit to Juarez. Annie moved down six weeks ago, but you have doubtless heard from her. she has a nice baby girl. she calls it "Ivie." I hear it is very cross lately. we have been expecting Miles up for a few days, but he has'nt come yet. have been having some hard rains lately. how I should enjoy a visit with you this afternoon. Last Sunday we went over to meeting and were out in a big storm. We are all well. Hannah hears that Isabell [Romney Platt] has another baby three living and two dead. Minnie [Romney Farr] has one fair boy. Your loving friend,

Catharine

9" Oct. 1890
Cliff Ranch

My Beloved Father Miles A came up the night before last and brought me your last welcome letter dated Sept. 16" and he will start back this morning. is moving his wife down. their baby is growing nicely. they call her "Pearl". I am so sorry to hear you have had another bad spell. we are all well with the exception of colds. but we are very busy. corn to harvest, husk and shell, before we move, and potato harvesting will begin in about two weeks, but I fear we are going to be sadly disappointed in our potato crop as Hannah went over yesterday and had the boys try them in a number of places and found them very small, though the vines have looked splendid all summer. still they may grow some yet if it dont freeze too hard.

Where is Rob Lund and his bride living. they were married on my wedding day and also Miles A and France[s]'s.

I am pleased your grapes have done so well   I should like to be helping you to dry them.

Dear Father you often ask me what you can send me. I am almost afraid of sending by mail for fear of losing, but if you choose to risk it I thought I would mention that I should be so glad of three or four yards of black selisia for lining, as what lining they have in the store at present is very poor calico and perhaps a few large hair pins, if convenient, but do as you think best as there is a risk to run. Caroline has got five of her papers   she is delighted with them. she was going to write to you this time but wont be able to now as they are to start in a few minutes.

I often see you in imagination, the dear old home which was such a good house to me for the two years when I was seperated from Miles, and the dear mother so kind and good, but though we shall likely not meet again in this life, still if we all prove faithful the parting cannot be for very long, but I should like so much to see you.

Please give my love to Emma and the boys. If you ever come across a patent office report or any such old book wont you please send it to me to make a scrap book. Good bye and god bless you.

                                                                Catharine

The Romneys moved back to Juarez in the fall of 1890. Shortly thereafter, Miles purchased a hundred-acre farm near the Mexican town Casas Grandes, about ten miles from their home in Colonia Juarez. Miles built a Mexican-style adobe house for Hannah, who volunteered to live on the farm to care for the boys who would be working there. Catharine and Annie both lived in Juarez. During this time, the family began to prosper.[69]

10" Dec. 1890
Juarez Mexico

Dear Father   This is mail morning and I have neglected writing, so must write a few lines in a hurry as it is three weeks since I wrote, and I fear you will feel anxious. I have not had a letter from you since I wrote, but I got the scrap book all right, and was very glad of it. I spent all the Sunday after I got it in pasting scraps in it. I think likely the parcel is down at Casas Grandes before now. Orson [Brown] is going to see and get it for me when he goes down this week if it is there.

I sent to Demming [New Mexico] to be posted there, a pair of sockes, a little Christmas gift from Caroline and I, a trifling thing, but I know you will appreciate them just as much as if it was something of more worth, as I carded and spun the yarn and Caroline knit them. I hope they will help to keep your feet warm and comfortable this winter.

I assure you dear Father you are often in my thoughts. O how I should love to see you, and all the dear ones at home. How are they all? If it were not for you I would seldom ever hear from or about any of you, though I have not yet answered Georges last letter. I have not got Charle's promised letter yet.

Miles and I and some of the children have very bad colds just now. otherwise we are all well. Hannah and children got down here a week ago today, but we still have some potatoes and our stock there   the boys started up yesterdsay to hunt and drive them. I hope they will find them all right. Miles A, Gaskell, George, Thomas, Ernest & Junius have all gone. it will likely take them two weeks. I told you of a brother [Almon B.] Johnson having the smallpox and his being quarantined. I am sorry to relate the sad sequel so far as it has gone. he died. in four days, after his wife was confined. (she was a Hilton sister in law to Maria Parker.) since then the whole family have come down with it. and the mother, babe, and next youngest child are dead. only three children left. they were doing well the last I heard. I trust it will spread no further. everything has been done that could be done by the authorities and the people in such disease, nurses and all the comforts that could be procured here have been provided for them. Miles has felt much anxiety and spent a great deal of time about it but feels much relieved the last few days since the Bishop [George W. Sevey] came home. I am looking anxiously for a letter from you. Your loving daughter

Catharine

19 Jan. 1891[70]
Juarez, Mexico

My Dear Father   I wrote to you two weeks ago last Sunday and had it ready to send off on Wednesday so Caroline added a note to apprise you of the important event which happened that morning, namely the birth of another little granddaughter for you, and as it was my birthday we thought it quite an eventful day. she is a nice little thing, weighed 8 lbs. we call her Ida. she will be two weeks old to-morrow. I am sitting up in bed, writing, as it is very cold to get up early, so I wait until the children get off to school. They all go down to Ethel [age 2], except Caroline [age 16] and she will start next Monday I expect. She has been a good faithful nurse for me, doing all the work just as good as a woman could, as Hannah and Annie have not been able to come much since the 5 day, when school began. Annie is teaching all our children in her house, and Hannah is taking care of her little ones. There are two more cases of smallpox but they are very light. The patients not having felt much inconvenience from it except having to be quarantined. bad colds and coughs have been very prevalent,—we have all had a turn of it and Miles has been very poorly with his cough for about three weeks.

We expect Miles' brother George down on a visit sometime in February. I hear that Br. [John M.] McFarlane has sent for one of his wives to come out soon [to Mexico]. he is clerking in a store at Casas Grandes.[71] they are all well I believe. The children tell me Br. [Henry] Eyring is not very well, a cold I suppose. I sent a transfer for the stock in Co-op store, hope you will get it all right. Miles tells me, my dividend is ready to draw, what he has turned over to me and on the $120 that you sent me by Br. Eyring   it is 25 per cent for the past year, so you see the store has been doing a pretty good business.

I hear Br. John R. Young is here but dont know whether he has come to stay or not, our Colony has increased very much in population in the past year. but unless more land is purchased I dont know how all are to be sustained.

I feel very anxious to hear from you, and know how you are getting along. we got two packages of papers from you since I have been sick, with the end of the story. Caroline and the boys were much pleased to get them, they are in great demand when they come.

We are having a very cold, stormy winter. there is more snow on the ground now than there has been in Juarez at any one time since we came to mexico. it snowed all day yesterday, so I dont know when I shall dare go out of doors. I must now say goodbye for the present from your loving daughter,

Catharine J. Romney

23″ Friday   Dear Father,   I didn't get this sent off and as I got a letter from you I will answer it. it is dated 8 Jan. I am so glad to hear you were all well, and had such a nice time on Christmas. it was no doubt a day long to be remembered by the young folks as well as the older ones. The children were all much interested in reading your account of it, and of course there are many speculations as to what each one got. I am thankful to hear that you are able to take such a walk as to middleton and back. The last mail brought us another scrap book, for which many thanks. I have given it to Caroline. also two papers came, but one of them is the same number as one you sent a week or two ago. you are very kind to take so much trouble for us. Sr. Lizzie McFarlane has a son born a day or two ago.[72] I have had to write this with our new baby [Ida] on my lap, by the stove so it may be hard to read.

Miles is feeling quite unwell with his cold and cough. This severe cold weather is very hard on the sheep herd, ten or fifteen dying every night, a great loss to Orson [Brown, Mattie Romney's husband], who has the herd this year.

Catharine C. Romney

25″ March 1891
Juarez   Mexico

Dear Father   I wrote to you a little more than a week ago, but must put a few lines in with the girls letters, though it will soon be time to send this to post, and baby is crying   she was quite sick for about a week but is much better though she still has very bad cough. I am certain you must have written to me but have not had a letter for about two months, so was much relieved to get one from the girls the other day, but sorry to hear you were not very well. we got two papers last mail. thanks for them. there is a great demand for them whenever they come.

We have nearly all been more or less sick lately with bad colds or something of the kind.

Lizzie McFarlane was down with the children to see me on Sunday   she is going to move down to Casas Grandes for the present as Br. Mc is working there. Br. [Alexander F.] McDonald has gone to Salt Lake to conference. Br. [Henry] Eyring and family ar well so far as I know. We are beginning to do a little gardening, most of the early fruit was frosted, very changeable weather.

Not much building going on, but Miles and boys working in shop some. must stop as baby is crying. From yours in love.

Catharine

3" May 1891
Juarez Mexico

Dearest Father   I am writing or rather have written to Thomas, and will enclose a few lines to you. I have not had a letter since I wrote last, but got two papers the other day. I think we get them pretty regularly. The day before yesterday being the first of May, we all went up the river on a picnic excursion which was got up by the Sunday School, except Miles & Hannah, Leo [Hannah's son, age 4] and Ethel [age 3]. he coaxed her to stay and eat her birthday dinner with him. we had a very nice time, nearly the whole town turned out, to have a holiday. about 30 wagons went. there was a good programme consisting of Songs, recitations, speeches etc. Miles A. [Hannah's son, age 21] had a speech on the origin of May day which he delivered in a very creditable manner, for a young fellow. Ann [Annie's daughter, age 11] had a comic recitation. Junius [age 13] had to have a recitation for Sunday School this morning. I wanted to go but did not get ready in time. The boys have been down to the farm the first part of the week and have plowed and put in about five acres of corn, and if they have good luck hope to get considerable more in this coming week. our garden seeds are beginning to come up, but the land needs manuring so may not do so well as we could wish this season, though we hope to have some early potatoes, our old ones are nearly gone. the St George folks have not arrived yet. We are all well and trust you are the same. Miles and the rest of the folks join me in kind love to you. lovingly yours,

C. J. Romney

The man who has our stock on shares has found two of them dead in the past two days.

31" May 1891
Juarez Mexico

My Beloved Father   I recieved your last welcome letter about a week ago, just after I had posted one to you. am thankful to hear that you are moderately well, and that all our folks are enjoying pretty good health. George [Catharine's brother] was away at the drive, and Thomas [her brother] just got home when you wrote. you speak of a dividend being due me, which leads me to think that some of my letters cannot have reached you. I wrote to you I think in January and enclosed a transfer of the $50.00 to George & Thomas, and asked you somewhere near the same time to please to pay to them the previous dividend, as you wrote me about sending word to Emma [her sister] what I would like her to get me for it. Miles transfered his on this store to me about the time I speak of, and I drew a 25 per cent dividend for the year, so I had better send another transfer. This store did a good business last year, but likely will not do so well this season, as much of the mexican trade has been cut off, by some of our brethren starting one at Casas Grandes. Be assured that Charles [her brother] shall have the benefit of our faith and prayers only two days till he shall start. May God protect and bless him and his family in his absense.[73]

You are certainly a devoted Father. I trust the boys and all of us appreciate and always shall your self sacrifices, and labors my dear Father. I must be brief this time as my letter is going to be full. so good bye and God bless you.

C. J. Romney

The following is an undated fragment.

not persecute you any more by writing with such pale ink as he could scarcely read what I wrote to him.

Now dear Father, many thanks for the parcel you spoke of sending. I have not got it yet but hope to soon.

Miles has got Br. Eyring's house so far finished that they have moved into it. it is a very pretty brick house. they are all well. also Br. [John M.] McFarlanes family. he ate supper here Sunday night, told me about meeting Charles. I have not had any letters from Charles since the time of Mothers death. I am very sorry to hear of Beate having such poor health.

I am always pleased to hear of Emma and the boys, and how they are getting along.

Is there any prospect of Amelia [Thompson] getting married? tell her she must'nt live to be an old maid.

I ha'vnt answered George's last letter yet, but will do so at my earliest convenience. Please give my love to them all. and to old friends. how is aunt mary getting along. and Sr. Lund.

Agnes Mcdonald has come here to live.

Miles got a letter from Br. [Apostle George] Teasdale a day or two ago. he is at Diaz and expects to be up here soon.

I am so sorry to hear of your poor health lately. and so wish I could see and help you.

Good bye and may God bless you always. is the constant prayer of your loving daughter.

Catharine

4" July 1891
Juarez   Mexico

My Beloved Father   This is the glorious fourth, and I suppose it is being celebrated in grand style all over the United States, and likely in Utah as well, a day like this almost makes me homesick, to see the dear old stars and stripes floating out on the breeeze, and to hear the lively strains of martial music, that I have been used to in the days of "Auld lang syne" but I see the Mexican flag, the red, white and green is waving over our schoolhouse, where a new flag-pole has recently been put up, also a bellfry now surmounts the schoolhouse ready for a bell as soon as our little town can afford one, and an addition of another large room will soon be completed, which will make such public gatherings much more comfortable. Miles has had charge of the work. Today has been devoted to the enjoyment of the children. the Primary gave an entertainment this morning at 10:00 and this afternoon they are having a dance. I went in the forenoon but have stayed home to write this afternoon. I hav'nt sent to the post office today, but scarcely expect a letter. I got one from Charles by last mail, dated Alabama, June 16"   he had not heard any word from home, but was expecting letters, had not yet held any meetings. I must answer it soon. I also got a letter from Mary Ann Whittaker [Catharine's cousin in Salt Lake City] a few weeks ago, but it had been over two months on the road. I have not answered it yet.

This is a very warm day and the flies are so bad that I can scarcely write, and baby [Ida] claims considerable of my attention today. she will be six months old in three more days. she is a very smart child of her age. she sat alone at five months old, and the other day she pulled herself up on her feet by a chair. her Pa thinks she is the smartest baby we ever had, and I guess she is for she has made me take her out of Primary the last two or three times I have gone.

Br. [John M.] McFarlane was here to supper the night before last and then Miles took him up to Hannah's to stay all night. he and family are well, as also Br. [Henry] Eyring, so far as I know. Sr. Fanny McDonald has gone on to Demming [New Mexico] to meet and bring home Br. [Alexander F.] Mc. [Macdonald] who has been sick in the city for so long.

Our garden is looking pretty well though the potatoes are turning out rather poorly but still what we have are a great help to us. we have had one mess of corn, and a few string beans, and shall soon have plenty. Sunday morning 5″ Hannah & Annie called just as I was writing yesterday. they live three or four blocks away. Two weeks ago today was Carolines birthday. 17 years old but it was a very sad one to her, as her dear friend and companion was buried on that day. Miss Edie Pratt. she was nearly eighteen and a very sad case, as her brother Parley 16 years old died four or five days before, supposed to be diptheria. they were our neighbors in the mountains and moved down to the foot of the mountain 12 miles from here this spring. Br. [Apostle George] Teasdale was here on a visit two weeks ago. I ate dinner with him at Hannahs. With love I remain your devoted daughter

Catharine.

love to all.

4″ Aug 1891
Juarez   Mexico

Dearest Father   The last word I had from you was a note in with one from Mary [Thompson, Emma's daughter, age 13], and two papers last week. I think it is about time for me to write again but will have to be brief this time as it is almost dark and Miles will soon be home to supper, and the mail goes in the morning. We are all pretty well. Ethel [age 3] is much better than she was.

I have sent an answer to Charle's letter and written to Beata. I owe Emma Squire and Mary [Thompson] each a letter but must write them as soon as I can.

I have sent a transfer for that capital stock to the boys, at two different times now but never heard whether you got them. One was sent in January and the other not long ago, but do not know if you got either of them   please tell me when you write as we feel so anxious to get even that small amount paid. it is such a worry to be in debt, and so far away. if we were nearer we could pay a few dollars at a time, and I believe in that way could have had it all paid before now.

Those who have grapes say they are doing splendidly. Orson [Brown] & Mattie [Romney Brown] brought me a nice taste from their lot on Sunday. some people have a good many plums, but peaches and apricots were mostly destroyed by late frosts. I think this will be a good place for fruit. melons are getting ripe. wheat is going to be very scarce and dear this season. The boys are down at the farm. we expect to plant wheat this fall. have some corn growing   should have had lots more in but could not get the land broke. it so hard and our team was very poor. From your loving daughter

Catharine J. Romney

29" Aug. 1891
Juarez   Mexico

Dear Father   I find I have only a half sheet of dirty writing paper, but it is raining so that I can't send to get any and must use this if I write to send by next mail, and it will have to be written in a hurry. your last letter came a week ago last wednesday, just at the time that Ethel [age 3] was very low. some of the folks thought she was dying, and indeed there seemed small chance of life though I did not lose faith in her recovery, and through the blessing of God upon the administration of the Elders, Together with the remedies which we applied she has been restored to a degree of health again. though not well yet, she is much better. thank the Lord. It is two weeks yesterday since she was taken and since that time I have not been away from the house. it was membraneous croupe. we thought at first it was pneumonia. Br. [Henry] Eyring has been doctoring her with home[o]pathic pills and has been very kind and attentive. Miles and Hannah were here almost night and day, and Annie what time she could be while she was so bad. baby [Ida] is not very well. she has lately cut three teeth. we believe her to be the smartest girl of her age in all Mexico. the boys make so much of her. this is just our private opinion you know.

We are having a splendid rain today, but it is too late in the season to do the good it would have done a month or two ago. this has been an unusually dry summer, making up for the heavy floods of last summer. on account of it breadstuff is very high this season, and likely to be a great scarcity of it. our new schoolhouse is almost completed, and next Saturday and Sunday have been appointed to

hold a conference, for the Saints in all the settlement to meet together in it. when it will be dedicated, Br. [Apostle George] Teasdale
is to be here. it is plastered inside and they are now plastering the
adobie part on the outside. Miles has had charge of the building of it.
he got up a party to raise means to help finish paying for it, but Ethel
was taken so sick I was afraid we would'nt any of us be able to go but
she got so much better that they all went but me. it was said to be
the best party ever held in Juarez. the white walls and nicely finished house with plenty of room, adding very much to the enjoyment of the company, and then there was a choice selection of
songs, with reading, speaking etc. interspersed with the dancing.
Grapes have done well here this season only that the bees and bugs
made sad work with them. plums also did well. I shall be very glad
when we can have fruit. Love to all. I remain as ever your loving
daughter,

C.J.R.

13" Sept. 1891
Juarez   Mexico
Mrs. Eleanor C. Jarvis

Dear Friend   Your welcome letter dated Aug. 2" came duly to hand.
I recieved it four weeks ago yesterday, while up at Hannah's spending the day, and read it to her and Annie. while there that afternoon,
Ethel [age 3] was taken quite sick and kept getting worse, until it
developed into membraneous croupe and she was a very sick child.
in fact some thought that she would scarsely recover but somehow
I did not lose faith and I thank God that our little girl has been
spared to us. Hannah stayed with us a good part of the time for over
a week both night and day, and Annie [did] what she could, but of
course she had her own baby to look after and the mail to attend to.
she was three weeks in the house and is now pretty well again
though quite thin and pale. Caroline [age 17] took her to Sunday
school this morning, and the children took her from there up to
Annies and a sudden rain storm came up, so when I went up after
her about noon her Pa objected to my bringing her till it should clear
up so I must go up again after awhile.

I heard the other day that Dessie Eyring had got word of your having another daughter. I am very pleased to hear of it and trust that
your health will be greatly improved now. when you write again tell
us what you call her. So poor old Br. [James] Keat has gone to rest. it

seemed so sad to hear of him having that dreaded disease. I too feel glad to hear of Miranda McArthur settling down to what I hope will prove a happier life. Truly "the way of the transgressor is hard."

Our school house is nicely finished now. when it was done, Miles who has had charge of the building of it, got up a party to raise means to help to defray the expenses of the finishing, but it came off after Ethel was taken sick so I could not leave her, but Miles, Hannah & Annie and the young folks went as she was much better that night, and they had a splendid time, the best party there has been in juarez. Miles was surprised during the evening by the reading of an address expressing the appreciation and satisfaction of the citizens of Juarez at the way the house had been built and the appearance of it etc. and tendering him a vote of thanks for his faithful and enerjetic labors. A week ago yesterday and today, a conference of the saints in the various settlements of this mission was held at this place there was a splendid turnout, and we had a good time. Br. [Apostle George] Teasdale was with us. there is to be another one held in November.

Baby has been very poorly for a week past with teething. she has four through. Many thanks for the lace pattern we have been too busy to try to pick it out yet but want to soon. Good bye for the present from your loving friend

C.J.R.

27" Sept. 1891
Juarez Mexico

My Dear Father I received your most welcome letter of the 7" ult, a week ago, and was thankful to hear you are able to be around, though your health you say has not been so good lately. I trust it will improve as the cold weather approaches. the tabernacle will look nice I am sure with the cleaning, new carpets etc.

We got a paper when the letter came, and the last week brought me a letter from Charles. he was getting along well and seemed to be in good health and spirits. he says he expects Beate has sent me their pictures, but if so I have not recieved them. I do hope I shall get them and that they will not get lost on the road.

Hannah has been down at the farm for over two weeks cooking for the boys. Thomas [age 15] went down with her but will be back tomorrow with his Pa who went down the day before yesterday. We are all pretty well now except Ida [8 months] she is teething and was very sick for a week or two. then got better but has been very poorly for the last three days, with quite a high fever at nights. but it is her teeth bothering her I think, nothing serious.

You mention that the band are to have a benefit at conference. I hope it will prove a success, which of your grandchildren are taking parts on the stage.

Br. [Apostle George] Teasdale came in day before yesterday and, will likely be preaching today but I can't go on account of baby. our Sunday school is much improved since the schoolhouse is finished and there is more room. the small ones are all in one large class in the basement, where they are taught by telling bible stor[i]es etc. Orson [Brown] is the teacher and Caroline [age 17] assistant teacher. The day school is to begin tomorrow. they are going to try to have three grades this season. Br. [Dennison E.] Harris[,] Principle, will teach the more advanced classes, his wife the second grade and as soon as enough go to justify I expect Caroline will assist with the primary scholars. this will help us, if she does teach, about paying the tuition of the rest of the children, so I hope she will be able to do so.

Bread stuff is getting scarce and high priced, owing to the increase of immigration. I fear Juarez will never be a self supporting community, unless some new industries are established, as farming land is rather scarce and poor for grain. still it is building up, and has become a very pretty little place.

The mexicans from different parts bring peaches and apples to peddle, but I expect they find money rather scarce here, however I hope it wont be many years till we can raise what we want of fruit. I have just quit gathering a boquet for a mexican, who came to the door and wanted to buy 10 cts. worth of flowers, the first time I ever sold flowers in my life. they are lovely this summer. a row on each side of the path from the gate, and two little gardens in front.

If you happen to think some time and have a chance to send the children a reading and recitation book they would be very much pleased with it. With the best love and ever praying for you dear father. yours in love.

Catharine

13″ Dec 1891
Juarez   Mexico

My Beloved Father   It is two or three weeks since I wrote last, and quite a while since I last heard from you. have been looking anxiously for two or three mails. Thomas [age 15] and Junius [age 13] have been writing and so I will just write a note. I see Thomas is up to his nonsense, telling you about corn bread,[74] but you must not think that is all we have to eat, still bread stuff is going to be very scarce for most of the people, before harvest, and I should feel very thankful if we had corn enough on hand to see us through, but we have never gone without yet, and I do hope and trust that our efforts at wheat raising will prove successful. We are all well except bad colds. Miles coughs badly as usual in winter. he went down to the farm yesterday. will be back tomorrow. Hannah and her Father [Archibald N. Hill] were up last Sunday. the old gentleman says he remembers you well. he is 75 years old, and is very grey. he will likely stay till spring. We are having very cold, windy weather for a week or two.

It makes me feel very thankful when I think about you, that you have such a warm, comfortable home. I often see you in imagination, and should so like to in reality. I suppose Amelia [Thompson][75] is married before this. should like to hear all particulars. Please give my love to all the folks. Miles joins me in love. Yours as ever,

C. J. Romney.

have not got the parcel by Sr. Mc. [Fanny McDonald] but they are going to get their things in a few weeks. A merry Christmas to you all.

20" Feb. 1892
Juarez   Mexico

My Beloved Father   I recieved your long looked for and most welcome letter of the present month, last night, and as I had not sent off one that I wrote last Sunday, I will answer it in short. you may imagine how thankfully it was recieved when I had not heard from you for about two months, and none of the rest write to me any more.

I am thankful to hear of their prosperity, buying farms, etc. and trust that they as well as us will raise good crops.

Miles came back yesterday from the farm. he and Thomas [age 15] have been ploughing a little trying to break some of the land ready for a corn crop, but it is a very heavy sod, full of mesquit and other roots which break their plows and cause a continual expense, as well as being very hard on the animals who are very poor and need more grain than they get. you know the old saying, "poor people have poor ways." however we must do the best we can and trust in the Lord for his blessing on our labors. a number are moving from here and the mountains over into Sonora. Br. [George C.] Williams & [Peter] Dillman among the rest. all is peace in this neighborhood at present. I dreamed of you the night before last, and had such a good long talk with you. how I should like to see you. Expect Br. Hardy's will be in, in a few days. Thanks for all you send me. got two papers last night. Br. M [Alexander F. Macdonald] is much better. Br. Hill [Hannah's father] started home day before yesterday. we are all well. I did'nt know Emma [Thompson] Squire had three children.

24" Apr. 1892
Juarez   Mexico
Mr. George T. Cottam

Dear Brother   It was with much pleasure that I recieved your last welcome letter, and intended to answer it last Sunday when I wrote to Emma [Thompson] but did not get time so kept hers till now. Emma [age 7] and Erastus [Annie's son, age 6] have been out of school all week with the chicken pox but have got pret.y well again. Ethel [age 3] and Ida [age 1], Ella [Annie's daughter, age 4] and Ivie [Annie's daughter, age 1], are all having the whooping cough, so we have had quite a sickly time of it. Mattie [Romney Brown] lost her baby, two weeks ago today, a fine big boy, poor girl. her house is again left unto her desolate. and Orson [Brown] is having such bad luck too. he took the company sheep herd, and the first year did well with them but afterwards some disease came among them and they died by the hundreds, and the severe wind and dust storms of this spring have scattered them so that there are several hundred missing, sheep and lambs together, but he is a very enerjetic young man.

There was a splendid prospect for fruit early in the spring but late frosts have cut off most of the peaches. still it is expected if the frost dont visit us again that there will be some left.

Miles and I were looking this morning at our little trees and found there are about 30 peaches and a few little plums. Miles says he hopes we will be able to find a market for our surplus fruit this season, and we have discussed the advisability of hiring a wheelbarrow to go and peddle it. You say you are "as gray as a rat and not very fat"   I fear I am in the same box as you. Thomas [age 16] is up here the past week working in the garden and hauling wood. George [Hannah's son, 17] and Junius [age 14] are working at the farm. they will only be able to get a few acres broke for corn this spring as it is terrible land to break, and they have broken three or four plows on it. our teams are in poor condition this spring, for hard work, as feed is very scarce. indeed for both man and beast. I dont know that there has been any actual suffering among our people yet but it is hard to tell how they will bridge over the time till harvest, for it is not in the country, and many have nothing on hand, and many are in debt for what they have been living on for a good while. Our wheat looks well so far, and I do hope and pray that we shall reap a good harvest, but there are many drawbacks and it will require watching while it is ripening for the mexicans are great thieves. they have stolen five or six ropes off our horses as they were staked right in our own field.

I do hope we shall have rain this summer to bring feed for the stock as there has been great suffering among them this winter.

Give my love to Father, when he comes home, Rachel [Cottam, George's wife] and the children, Thomas [P. Cottam] & family & all write again soon. I like so much to hear from you. may God bless you all. From your loving sister

Catharine J. Romney.

June 18" 1892
Juarez   Mexico

My Dear Father   This is wash day and I ought to do a little planting also while the garden is damp, but it is also mail morning so I feel that I must answer your last welcome letter which came a week ago. it was dated May 2" so was nearly a month on the road and you tell me in that, that you had written before and told me of your journey, so it must have been lost as we never got it. I had not heard a word from you except a postal card since you came from the city [Salt Lake City], so you wont wonder I was feeling uneasy. I think it is only seldom that a letter is lost lately. was the dollar you mention sending me in that letter? if so perhaps that accounts for my not getting it, as either letter nor money ever reached me. I am very sorry about them both as I always did hate to have anything lost, but thank you very much for sending it. but I shall get the eye salve you sent by Sr. Hardy, as I spoke to Sr. Meecham about it when she was here at conference time and she said her Mother has one in her trunk but could not remember who sent it. they have another kind at the store which has helped my eyes the last time or two they were sore. your letter is such a good newsy one. I take pleasure in reading it over. I am glad to hear you are all as well as you are, that Emma is better.

Very sorry indeed to hear of the sad accident to George Holts baby. I am glad to hear of Charles family doing so nicely. how is it that he is likely to stay so long [on his mission]? A week ago today the news of Br. [John M.] McFarlanes death came. it came quick. funeral services were held in the schoolhouse on Sunday Br. [Alexander F.] McDonald and Miles were the principal speakers. I feel very very sorry for his helpless family here. they feel very badly of course. they dont know yet what they will do, till they hear from home, but I feel certain their folks in St George will want them to return, and I think likely they will do so, as this would be a hard place to get along for women and children, but of course if they go they will likely have to sell out and especially their household goods at a great sacrifice, as money is very scarce here just now and is very low compared with american money.[76] Our children are all getting better, for which I feel very thankful, for it is over two months since they took sick and Ida [age 1] has been very bad. she got as poor as a crow. Miles and the boys are very busy this week harvesting the wheat. Miles went down on Sunday evening and sent Junius [age 14] up on Monday for Thomas [age 16], who was working in the shop with Gaskell [Hannah's son, age 20]. My children are all there but Caroline [age 17], Ethel [age 4] and Ida [age 1]. the mail has come so must close. will write to Emma [Cottam Thompson] next time. There is more I would like to write but cannot send today if I do. I hope the letter that is lost will come yet. Your loving daughter

Catharine

19" June 1892
Juarez Mexico
Mrs. Emma C. Thompson

My Beloved Sister   I was much pleased to recieve your last welcome letter. Though it was without date it came in Father's which was dated May 2" and I think I got it on June 4" so it seemed I came near losing it as I did the one before it, for Father said he had written me about the incidents of his visit to Salt Lake and I had recieved nothing but a postal card, so you may know how worried I was getting. however this is not often the case as they generally come in about eight or ten days, and I dont think we often lose any.

Dessie Eyring was in this afternoon. we had quite a chat about the folks at home. they are going to have quite a lot of peaches, and a great many grapes this year, as well as a few apples. I went to Sunday School this morning, and afterwards to see Sisters [Tilly and

Lizzie] McFarlane. Tilly was quite sick with sick headache. they are both feeling as well as can possibly be expected. funeral services were held last Sunday [for John M. Macfarlane]. Miles and Br. [Alexander F.] McDonald spoke and after meeting Miles and Ernest [Hannah's son, age 14], Maggie [Hannah's daughter, age 12], Park [age 10] and Emma [age 7] went down to the farm. they are very busy harvesting as the grain was getting so ripe that Junius [age 14] came up on Monday to get Thomas [age 16] to help, and we have not seen any of them since, and Gaskell [Hannah's son, age 20] went down on horseback this morning to see his Ma so my family is rather small, but I expect Gaskell home tonight. Father told me a long time ago that you had had the La Grippe [influenza], but I had never heard of the other diseases troubling you. I am thankful you are so much better. I am sorry Father is so weak and miserable. Fanny McDonald went out to Demming [New Mexico] and when she came home told me there was a parcel there for me. she could have brought it for me, if I had asked her to and is sorry now that she did'nt and so am I. must send by the first Sister who goes out. she thinks Joseph Bently brought them that far, but he didnt say anything to me about it the few minutes I spoke to him. Caroline wants me to ask you why Nelly [Thompson, Emma's daughter] never writes. she has written two or three times since she got one. she will be 18 years old the day after tomorrow. dos'nt it seem funny to think of her being that old? Please give my love to all the girls and in fact all the folks! what has been the matter with Matilda [Thompson Bleak, Emma's step-daughter]? My baby [Ida] has been sick for over two months but is gaining nicely now.

This has been quite a hot day 102 in the shade. I am so sleepy I must close. From your loving sister

Catharine J. Romney

Francis, Miles' [A. Romney's] wife had a son born on Thursday. she has two nice children now. I think Sister Mc[Donald]. made some mistake about the parcel. my chromos are still there.

3" July 1892
Juarez

My Beloved Father I came home last Thursday from the farm where I had been nearly a week on a visit to and to cut straws. on my return I found a letter from you, also a paper, with one in to Caroline from Mary Ann [Cottam, George and Rachel's daughter], which she will answer soon I think. I have just been looking for yours to see the date but dont see it as Thomas [age 16] had it to read, so must answer from memory. You spoke of having had Br. & Sr. Woodruff [Wilford Woodruff, president of the church] to see you, of your good conference, of Emma and the boys etc. I am so thankful you are all as well as you are, that Emma [Cottam Thompson] is so much better   I will enclose a letter to her which I wrote about two weeks ago, but forgot to send off. Dear Father you speak of having sent me a dollar at two different times. I am very sorry to say that I have not recieved the money nor the letters it was in, that is if you sent it by mail which I suppose you did. it is strange how they can tell when there is money in a letter. I feel very bad to have you deprive yourself of what you need, and send to me, and especially when it is lost, but I appreciate so much your loving kindness. I feel that we have much to be thankful for. our threshing was done while I was at the farm and we raised I think about three hundred and seventy five bushels, a share of which belonged to Miles A. [Hannah's son, age 22.]

26" Sept. 1892
Juarez   Mexico

Dearest Father   I have not heard from you for a long time. I have written two or three times since, but feel that I must write again, to send out tomorrow. The past week or two I have been looking for a letter by every mail. I wrote to Charles and Beata [Cottam] not long ago, and last week I wrote to Beata and Carrie Smith [Catharine's cousin] last week and sent with Gaskell. he started for Salt Lake City last Thursday. it is his intention to go to work, and earn means to go to the [Brigham Young] Academy at Provo. he has quite an ambition to make something of himself and I do hope he will succeed. he started out with a most excellent reputation, and a good trade. he is well thought of by all who know him, and is a good boy or rather man, for he was 21 years old the day he started. the night before he went we had a farewell supper and evenings entertainment for a number of his and Carolines young friends and companions. they had a very nice time. he has lived with me for nearly a year, so I miss him very much. Thomas [age 16] came up from the farm this morning to help his Pa in the shop for two or three weeks till he starts to school. Caroline [age 18] began her seasons work in the school room two weeks ago, and 7 of the smaller children are going. the older ones will start later. the brethren have in the last two weeks decided to adopt the free school system, taxing themselves on their income for the support of the school in order that all children may go whether parents are able to pay or not. Miles has been elected chairman of the board of trustees for three years, has also been appointed assessor, and collector of school taxes. A military organization has also been effected in the past few days, on account of Indian excitement, which is not without grounds this time, though it was believed by many to be only rumors till last Monday, a week ago yesterday, when a terrible tragedy was enacted, an account of which you will no doubt read in the news before you get this. it happened at our old home, in the mountains, Cliff Ranch. Br. Thompson (a Danish brother) and family took Br. Pratts farm on shares and were living in one of his houses. on Sunday night Br. Thompson had gone over to Pechaco, to work on the thresher, leaving his wife (an old lady) two sons and a little granddaughter, the only ones on the ranch. the next morning after breakfast the boys went out to feed the pigs, on their way to the field, the little girl was with them, without warning the oldest boy 17 years old was shot dead and the younger one, 15 years old wounded by indians concealed behind the stable and cellar. the little girl 8 years old ran screaming to the house, the old lady came out in the yard and was shot three or four times and then finished by being hit in the head by a rock. they likely saved the child to carry her off, but she and the little boy hid, till the indians five men, a squaw and one child, robbed the house of bedding, clothing, provisions, firearms and ammunition, and left. they have eluded the men who have been scouring the country since, but another company were sent out yesterday. and I do hope they will be captured. they are Apaches, escaped from the reservation.

It will be a terrible strain back to the mountains, as people can not attend to the duties of life when in fear of their lives. indeen [Indeed] it is unsafe to live there or to travel.

There was a child died here last week.

I must close with kind love and best wishes to all I remain your loving daughter.

Catharine J. Romney

4″ Dec. 1892
Juarez Mexico

My Beloved Father   This is Sunday evening   baby [Ida] and I are the only occupants of the house. she is in bed nursing her doll and singing at the top of her voice something about her papa. she is devoted to her Pa, and has always been since she could notice   he is the object of her thoughts, her songs, and her talk. she wants to follow him around, just as Emma did you. The older ones have gone to S[unday].S[chool]. teachers meeting, and the rest over to Aunt Annies. George [Hannah's son, age 18] came up this morning to start to school in the morning. I have been expecting Br. & Sr. Meecham and George Hardy up this evening but they hav'nt come yet. they are going home tomorrow, are all well. she has a nice baby girl. I recieved your long looked for letter 10 days ago. was so pleased to hear from you once more. our letters must miss sometimes, for I write quite often. the last two that I got from you were written exactly two months apart, Sept. 13" and Nov. 13" and you had just been sick both times. this gives me sorrow dear Father. The lines you sent me are very touching. where did you get them? I started to read them to the children, but broke down and had to go in the other room and let Thomas [age 16] read them. We are indeed far away. when shall we all meet again? Not until we meet on the other side. I trust I may prove worthy to meet my dear Parents in the great beyond. and that I be able to raise my children as well as you have done yours.

So Rachel [Cottam, George's wife] has her tithing [tenth] baby [Bertha Jane]? well please offer my congratulations to the happy Father & Mother and love to all the folks. I wrote to Thomas [P. Cottam, Catharine's brother] the last time I wrote to you.

We have had another period of expecting the Presidency [of the church], but again they have not come. our conference was a week ago. had a very good one, and finished up with a social party in the evening on Monday   Hannah staid and we all went and had a splendid time. the best party I have been to in Mexico. we dont often go but Br. [Apostle George] Teasdale called on Miles to get it up, and manage it and the proceeds to finish paying for the new organ. so we had a splendid assortment of songs, recitations, etc. Joseph Bently recited   his wife sang and played on the guitar. Annie read the "Bells." Caroline [age 18] recited, and we had a good many beside.

Miles has consented to assist in putting on a play or two this winter. he and Caroline & Miles A. and Joseph Bently are among those who will take part. we have never had a theatre here yet.

Three weeks from today is Christmas. six years ago we were all together except Miles, three are gone since then and I wonder what changes will take place in the next six years. it matters but little if we only remain faithful.

There is some talk of our people chartering a car to take those who wish to go from here to the dedication [of the Salt Lake Temple]. a good many will go if they can raise the means. there are several young married couples who would like to go to the Temple to be sealed.[77] Miles A. and his wife, [Frances Turley Romney] and Mattie [Romney Brown] and her husband [Orson Brown], among the number, but I dont know if they will be able to get the money or not, but hope they will. We got a paper from you the other day. they are a great help to Caroline as there are nice little stories in that do to tell to her school children. many thanks for them.

We are all well at present. Junius [age 14] and Park [age 10] are down at the farm. after awhile they will come up to school, and Thomas & Ernest [Hannah's son, age 15] go down. I was down on a visit two days last week.

Good bye for the present   From your loving daughter

Catharine J. Romney

4" Jan. 1893

Dearest Father   I wrote to you on Christmas day but have been waiting for some of the children to write, but they have not had time, and I have since got another letter from you, dated Dec. 19"   was very sorry to hear you had had such a sick spell. there have been a great many cases of the kind here, or bad colds, coughs etc. Emma [age 8], Ethel [age 4] Ida [23 months] and Caroline [age 18] were quite sick last week and the two little ones are still quite sick, earache etc. and Miles was [*six lines are illegible; a piece of the paper was torn off.*]

had come all the way from Dublan to go to it [a performance of "The Charcoal Burner," directed by Miles], but Br. [Apostle George] Teasdale administered to him on Saturday morning and he was much better, played then and again on Monday. it was a complete success. Caroline, Miles A. [Hannah's son, age 23] and George [Hannah's son, age 18] took parts and gave great satisfaction. Miles of course was the Charcoal Burner and Jos. Bently as Abel Cole "brought the house down"   Hannah came up on Monday and went [*the next five lines are illegible; page torn.*]

The following is an undated fragment.

went to a wedding reception yesterday. Br. [Apostle George] Teasdale preformed the ceremony. there was a dance in the evening for the young folks. We have been having some lovely rains the last two days or rather nights. Ernest has got the melaria. the rest of us are well. Junius, Park, Emma, Alice and Erastus are going to school. Sometime you might please to put a pen or two in when [you] write if you like as these seem so poor. I fear you can scarcely read my writing. Good bye my Dear Father. Yours in love.

Catharine

12 Feb 1893
Juarez   Mexico

My Beloved Father   One of the children had your last letter and has mislaid it, so I have forgotten the date, but I think I have written since I recieved it, but I feel that I ought to write oftener than I do.

We are all tolerable well at present, though it has been a general time of sickness this winter, with very bad colds, almost like the "Grippe," and other things. Sr. [Margaret ("Maggie") McKean] Bently lost her baby over a week ago after a severe sickness of four or five weeks. Please tell Rachel [Cottam, George's wife] that her cousin Sister Olive Moffett, has lost her oldest child, a few weeks ago, a bright, smart girl of 13, after a very lingering illness of many weeks. she had been sick more or less for about two years, a few days before she died she recieved a beautiful hymn book, the first prize for a story about animals, from the Juvenile Instructor.

I have quite a sad thing to tell you about. Br. [Apostle George] Teasdale, and his wife Sr. Tillie started on a visit to Diaz, less than two weeks ago. while there, on last Monday morning before daylight she died very suddenly. was gone before he could get a light. cause supposed to be heart disease. she leaves two boys, the oldest 14 years old today   the other wife and the children were sent for the same day and went down to the funeral. and all got back home last night. but I have not seen them to speak to them yet. We have had a very dry winter again. I dont know what will become of the country if this drouth continues much longer. We have had considerable wind lately, but this is a very fine day. the fruit trees are commencing to blossom. I hope the frost will not kill them but we had ice last night. Miles A [Hannah's son, age 23] will leave here next month for a mission to Europe. expects to take his wife with him as far as the city to go through the [Salt Lake] temple. I got a letter from Gaskell

[Hannah's son, age 21] yesterday. he says he hopes he will see you if you go to conference, but he says he expects there will be such a crowd that it is doubtful. I hope he and Miles A. will both be able to see you, for I do hope you can go, and only wish Miles and Hannah could go. I have just been out a few minutes, and came to find miss Ida [age 2] up, with the pen, trying to finish this letter. I have just recieved the first valentine I have had for 20 years. Junius [age 14] has brought me one, quite pretty. they are the first ever brought to this place.

I have not heard from Charles [Cottam] for a long time, nor in fact from any of the boys, Dear Father, if it ever comes handy to send me another scrap book I should be very glad of it as Caroline [age 18] is getting hers pretty well filled. From yours devotedly

Catharine J. Romney.

Had a nice rain last evening and snow all night   from five to eight inches   a great blessing   this is the 15"

9" Mch. 1893
Juarez   Mexico

My Dear Father   I have not had a letter from you since I wrote, but got one from Thomas [her brother] over a week ago, that you had directed, so I will write a few lines to you now and Ill answer his as soon as I can. will enclose a letter from Caroline [age 18] and Emma [age 8] to the girls [their cousins].

Miles, Thomas [age 16], Junius [age 14] and Caroline are all down at the farm this week. we thought a change would do Caroline good after being in school and working so hard all winter. I dont think she will teach any more this winter, as it has been closed three or four weeks on account of sickness in Br. Harris's family. they have lost two of their children, supposed to be diptheria; if they teach any more only two teachers will be required. Miles A. expects to start from here about the 27" but he will not be able to take Frances [his wife] with him to the temple as he expected on account of the scarcity of money. Orson [Brown] and Mattie [Romney Brown] expect to go but are not certain yet. I do wish Miles could have gone to conference [General Conference in Salt Lake City] for a rest and change, for he needs it very badly. he has never been out of Mexico since he came here, and it has been nothing but hard work, both public and private, hard living, and anxiety for him since he has been in this country. You would be surprised to see how grey he is. still we have very much to be thankful for. Our wheat and lucern are looking well. we have had two nice storms lately, which was sadly needed as everything was about dried up.

Br. [Apostle George] Teasdale will start today on his way to conference, quite a number will go from here during the next two weeks. Brs. [Helaman] Pratt, [Henry] Eyring, [Alexander F.] McDonald and others.

The fruit trees are in full bloom and it froze ice the night before last but I hope the fruit will not be all killed.

Gaskell [Hannah's son, age 21] was going to school in the city the last word we had. We are all pretty well but there has been a great deal of sickness this winter.

Please give my love to all the folks and a large portion for yourself. From your loving daughter

Catharine J. Romney

23″ Mch. 1893
Juarez   Mexico

My Dearest Father   I think it is a week yesterday since I got your last letter. it was as your letters always are read with pleasure. I will try and write more plainly. Miles feels quite annoyed with me for not writing plain enough for you to read without trouble. I was pleased to hear that you and all the folks were well. Several of the children have very bad colds and are quite poorly. I never saw a time of so much sore throats as there has been lately. Br. Harris has lost two children with that or croupe lately.

Caroline got a postal card from you yesterday, and a photograph of Mary Ann and Rachel [Cottam, George and Rachel's daughters] last week. I tell you she was pleased, and so were we all to see them. I recognized Annie [Mary Ann Cottam] but should not have known Rachel if they had not been together   they are two fine looking young ladies. I should like to see Nelly & Mary [Thompson, Emma's daughters]. We have also got two papers from you lately. many thanks for them. I sometimes think that you go to more trouble for me than you ought, but still dear Father there is one thing that I have thought for a long time that I should like eventually to have for a keepsake, that is if you were willing and Emma don't want it and that is your's and Mother's pictures in the cases, that were taken when you were young. I think the boys would not care so much for them as I should, but of course I would not want to have them if Emmie wishes to.

When do you expect Charles home?[78] I wrote to him some months ago but have had no answer.

It was snowing on the mountains yesterday, and raining some here, but we have so much wind that it dries up what moisture does fall. This is a very cold day and I fear we shall have frost, but hope the fruit will be spared and that our wheat and other crops will be a success this season.

Ethel [age 4] is down at the farm with her Aunty [Hannah]. they will be up next Saturday. Miles was down there a day or two last week and walked up on Monday, for the team is so poor, and have to work so hard on the farm as well as keeping us in wood. Good bye and may God bless you is my constant prayer   From your loving daughter,

Catharine

21" April 1893
Juarez   Mexico

My Beloved Father   For the past month we have had considerable sickness, and there is still a good lot in town. My children are all better now but Junius [age 15] still has a bad cold, and I have one myself. Yesterday afternoon Erastus [Annie's son, age 7] was playing by the rock wall, when something bit or stung him on the little finger. he did not see what it was but we think it must have been a rattlesnake. we applied what remedies we could but it swelled terribly. his Pa administered to him a time or two, and late last night he and Jos[eph]. Bently administered again, so he has rested as well as we could expect, and I hope he will get all right soon.

We had a hard frost the night before last, ice thicker than window glass, and the grape vines yesterday was a sorry looking sight. they were just in blossom and a promise of a splendid crop. Sr. [Mary B.] Eyring says she never in her life has seen vines loaded as heavy as hers were, and even our little vines were full of blossom, but we are higher up on the hill and it does not seem to have served ours as badly as those lower down in town. people tell me that many of the large peaches were frozen right through, and I fear all the fruit has suffered more or less but I hope there will be some of each kind escape. I have just been reading your last letter over and though I think

I have written since, I have not answered it in full, for Ethel [age 4] was very sick and so have Caroline [age 18] and Emma [age 8] and all the boys been none escaping but the baby [Ida, age 2]. I have written to George and Thomas [her brothers]. Miles got a letter from Miles A. [Hannah's son, age 23] by the last mail he was having a good time with Gaskell [Hannah's son, age 21] and the folks [in Salt Lake City]. said the [Salt Lake] temple is beyond description. I hope he will see Beata [Cottam, Charles's wife]. I gave him a letter to her. I was married on the 15″ Sept. 1873 in S.L.City by Joseph F. Smith. Caroline C. Romney born on 21″ June 1874, St George, Thomas C. born Apr. 3 1876, in St. George, Junius born 12″ Mch. 1878, in St George, Claude born 10″ Jan. 1880 St George, died in Juarez of scarletina on the 24″ of Feb. 1887, Park born 25″ Mch. 1882 in St. Johns Arizona. Emma born 23″ July 1884 in Snow Flake Arizona. Ethel, born in Juarez Mexico in 1″ May 1888, Ida born Jan. 7″ 1891, in Juarez Mexico.[79]

Dear Father I hope you will excuse me for being so slow in writing this. for it had slipped my mind with so much sickness. We have had two or three papers from you lately and Caroline got the scrapbook, and was very pleased with it. Are they very much trouble for you to get or expense? If not sometime when it may come handy, if you could send me another one I should be so glad, for we have saved the papers you have sent us so long, and the mice are destroying them and as there are so many useful things in them I like to save them for the children to read, and especially as reading matter in the shape of books is so hard to get here.

Miles has just been out and found the rattlesnake and killed it where Erastus was playing. it was a little thing with three little rattles I am glad it is dead. we are just going to wash and dress his finger. Love to all, and a large portion for you.

Catharine

26″ Erastus is much better. all well.

8″ May 1893

Dear Father Orson [Brown], Mattie [Romney Brown] and Orson's mother got home [from Salt Lake City] last night, all well. I had them here to supper. Mattie just got time to call on Beata [Cottam] for a few minutes the day before she left the city, and she sent me Mary and Walters [Cottam, Charles and Beata's children] pictures. they are splendid. I am so pleased to see them. I got a letter from

Beata she had been sick but was better. expects Charles home [from his mission] in six weeks or two months. I never hear anything of Aunt Ellen [Cottam Pilling] and boys, nor of Uncle John [Cottam]. do you? Ida [age 2] is the cutest child. her Pa says sometimes he wishes you could see her. he thinks she would amuse you ever so much.

From your loving daughter

C.J.R.

11" June 1893
Colonia Juarez   Mexico
Mrs. Eleanor C. Jarvis

Dear Friend   Your welcome letter of Apr. 30" came duly to hand. I am very sorry to hear of your eyes being bad. I have had so much of it that I can certainly able to sympathize with you. mine were very bad last summer till Br. [Joseph C.] Bently came and he brought me some of Johnsons eye salve that Father sent me, which always helps me. No, I had not heard of George [Jarvis] being Bishop. Father seldom tells much news except just about our own family. I hope he will soon entirely recover, as you as a family have had so much sickness. Annie was just reading me a letter she got from your ma [Ann Cannon Woodbury, Eleanor and Annie's mother], she speaks of your having been sick. I feel so sorry to hear this, and hope you are well again.

Annie is quite poorly, but there is a cause for it, and I trust she will soon be better.[80]

I am glad the children are getting along so well in school. Our boys don't have a very good chance on account of the farm for some of them have to be there all the time, and so they have to take turns. the boys are all there now but Thomas [age 17], who is helping his Pa at carpenter work, and Erastus [Annie's son, age 7]. they have started to harvest and are and will be very busy. Park [age 11] and Orin [Annie's son, age 9], are not willing to come up for fear they will have to stay. they get plenty of milk and butter there, while the cows here do very little as it is so dry that there is no grass for them, and that is quite an attraction to children, you know, and then their Aunty [Hannah] is so good to them. We have not been able to get water to water our corn land yet, but I trust that the rains will not be witheld [withheld] from us much longer. the weather is very dry and hot at present, as it has been the past two years.

Miles A [Hannah's son] and Mattie [Romney Brown, Carrie's daughter] and husband [Orson Brown] were at the dedication [of the Salt Lake Temple]. the latter went for the purpose of having their endowments and being sealed [in the Salt Lake Temple], and Miles is labor[ing] in the Manchester Conference.[81] I got a letter from Gaskell [Hannah's son] by the last mail. he seems to enjoy himself there. said school would be out in two weeks.

Dessie [Eyring] was in here awhile this forenoon. her baby is 21 months, a large bright child and one of the worst mischiefs I ever saw. Dessie has such a pretty convenient house all done but plastering. Milly [Eyring Snow] and children [Theresa and Beatrice Snow] are all well I believe, poor girl, it seems so sad, to be left alone as young as she is.[82] There was a splendid prospect for fruit early in the spring but the frost played sad havoc. still there will be considerable granes [grains]. I should so like to see you. love to all. From yours lovingly

C.J.R.

19" Aug. 1893
Juarez   Mexico

My Beloved Father   I just scribbled a short note to you a week ago while i was tending to the mail, because I thought you would feel worried. Your last letter was dated 11" July. we have had several papers lately, but none since I wrote. It must be very hot without rain for so long, it was here, but has rained a good bit now for the last five weeks, which makes the hills green and the hearts of the people as well as the animals to rejoice. I hope George [Cottam] & Thomas's [P. Cottam] babies are well again, and that Charles [Cottam] has got home [from his mission] all right—before now. Annies baby [Erma] has been quite sick for about a week, but is better again. the rest of us are well. Miles is going down to the farm today so that Geo[rge]. [Hannah's son, age 18] can come up tomorrow. Hannah was up last Sunday. Next week is conference. Miles is having the schoolhouse whitewashed and cleaned up as school is to start in two weeks, he is one of the trustees, and has lots of public labor to preform. Yesterday was his fiftieth birthday, so he commemorated it by giving Caroline [age 19] a beautiful bedstead, the first one Thomas [age 17] has made all himself, so she feels quite proud of it. I expect to lose her in about a month now. If nothing happens to prevent, they [Caroline Romney and Edward Eyring] have concluded to go to Utah to

Conference and will likely be married in the Manti temple as his sister lives near there.[83] of course it will be a great sacrifice of means to go back when Mexican money is so low, but I hope they will be able to get enough, as it is so much better to start right, and they would have to go sometime. I shall feel very much disappointed if she dos'nt get to see you. I hope you will be up at conference so she will meet you at Charles's [in Salt Lake City]. If she goes to the temple she ought to have I suppose, a record of when she was blessed, baptized etc. I have sent to Minnie [Romney Farr] at St Johns to get the latter from the Ward books, and have thought dear father I would see if you would please to learn from the same sourse when and by whom she was blessed, if it is not too much trouble but I fear it will be considerable, and any of the rest if it came handy, as my record I left in St. John when I had to run away, and I guess the mice eat it up a[s] they did some of my things. Caroline, Thomas and Claude were blessed in the Tabernacle and Junius in the first ward school house, in 74, 76, 78, and 80. I shall be so pleased if you can do this for me and if not time to send here she could get it when she gets to the city. if you would send the word to Charles she wil have to leave here about the 21" of Sept. if they go. We appreciate the papers very much. The folks all join me in love to you and all the folks. Yours in love,

Catharine.

19" Sept. 1893
Juarez   Mexico

Beloved Father   Your last welcome letter of Sept 2" came last mail. It was read with feelings of mingled joy and sorrow, sorrow at hearing of your poor health your frequent bad spells and joy that you are still able to write to me. Hannah was up, and she with Miles & Annie as well as the children join with me in sympathy and love, and our prayers and desires are that you may not suffer, nor have any accident. Dear Father dont run any risks, such as cleaning those high windows in the tabernacle, or lighting lamps etc.   you dont know how much I think about you lately and how I should love to see you. I cannot account for your getting a report [of Caroline's engagement] instead of a letter. I have written twice to tell you that Caroline is soon to be married but I suppose you can't have got the letters. she and Ed. Eyring also Ida Eyring and Ed Turley will start for Salt Lake about the 28", a week hence. Sr. [Mary B.] Eyring is going with them. Ed. intended to take Caroline down to see you, but his Father [Henry Eyring] has been gone to the city of Mexico for two months and is needing Ed in the store so badly, that he dos'nt feel that he can possibly spare him long enough to go so far as St. George.[84] I as well as she are quite disappointed. I wish you were going to be up at conference, so she could see you. If you should have a chance to send the likeness of aunt Jenny [Cottam Punter] and Uncle Thomas [Punter], to Charles [Cottam], by some one going, she can bring it for me. I think Caroline will get a good husband, and I know she will make a splendid good wife. he is just having his house started to be built. they will live about three blocks from us. Miles has just been in and wants me to be sure and give his best regards to you. he and Annie and I, George [Hannah's son, age 18] and Caroline, all [*page missing*] best love to all.

6" Nov. 1893
Juarez Mexico

My Beloved Father I have been waiting to write to you till two things should happen. one was to get a letter from you. this I have not had since before Caroline went to Utah. the other was till she should come home so I could tell you some news. she came the day before yesterday, is looking well.[85] they are staying for a few days at Br. [Henry] Eyrings, but are going to rent until their house is done. We also had a great surprise. Gaskell [Hannah's son, age 22] came back with them, quite unexpected to us. times are so hard in Salt Lake just now and work so scarce, that he could not get the means to go to school this winter as he expected and desired to, so he will likely stay here at least for this winter. he looks fat, and well. Miles was doing well the last we heard from him. Caroline went to see Charles & Beata [Cottam] three or four times   they were very kind and wanted them to come and stay some of the time, but she said her aunt Beata was quite sick and she was afraid it would make her more work. she went to see Aunt Ellen [Cottam Pilling], she was very pleased to see her. also Aunt Elizabeth [Fovargue Smith], Becca, Sarah and Carrie [Smith, Catharine's cousins], all were well I believe. she did'nt get to see Uncle John [Cottam]. I am sorry she couldnt but the City is such a big place and so many to see who lived so far apart. They were married in the Salt Lake Temple on the 11" of October, on Mothers birthday. also on the day that Ernest [Hannah's son] was sixteen years old. I was pleased it happened so.

Some of our brethren have been in prison, Orson Brown among the rest, for catching some Mexican horse thieves, and Miles and Br. [Helaman] Pratt had to go to El Paso to see about it. he was gone a week.

I have had four or five papers from you since I got your last letter. one of them had some pens in it   many thanks or them. Emma [age 9] was sick with some kind of a fever for five weeks. there has been a great many children down with fever lately. one little girl died yesterday. We are all pretty well now. I feel anxious to hear how you are, and all the folks. Please give my love to Emma and the boys and families. With best love I am as ever yours,

Catharine.

By the mid-1890s, the privation of the early colonists had given way to their united industry and thrift. Through mostly cooperative efforts, they had established grist, saw, shingle, planing, and lath mills; a tannery; a cannery; a harness and saddle shop; two shoe shops; four cheese factories; and five orchards. They had also built a meetinghouse for school, church, and recreational uses and established the Juarez Cooperative Mercantile Institution.[86]

7" Jan. 1894
Colonia Juarez   Mexico

My Beloved Father   I recieved your most welcome letter of Dec. 19" a little over a week ago, and was very sorry to hear of your sickness, but hope you are quite well again by this time. Those bad colds have also been prevalent here amounting almost to an epidemic. I am glad you are in a comfortable home, so that I dont have to feel that you are suffering with cold this winter weather. we have had four very windy disagreeable days but today has been a lovely day almost like spring but very cold this morning as there was a hard frost last night. This is my 39" birthday and Ida is three years old today. she was born the day I was 36.

The children all remember their grandpa, and I assure you I do not forget you, and my dear mother, brothers, and sisters, and your kindness to me and mine when I was with you. please give my love to all the folks. Father do you have all you need to make you comfortable? I would so like to see you and often do so in imagination. in my fancy I see you and mother as you used to sit by the fireplace on winter evenings. I was dreaming of her just a night or two ago. You speak as if you had not had a letter from me for a long time. I am sorry my letters do not reach you as they should do, for I try to write quite often. I wrote you a long letter at the time of the trouble with the rebels, and must have written twice since, also wrote to Thomas [P. Cottam]. How did you spend Christmas and New Years, for everyone but you have stopped writing, even the children no longer get letters from their cousins. We had quite a plesant time considering that Hannah lives so far away that we cant be all together anymore. some of the boys went down and Hannah came up part of the time. we dare not leave the place all alone. one of the brethren from here who is farming a few miles from our farm came up with his boys to spend christmas, and while he was away had over fifty dollars worth of property, consisting of plows, grain, carpenter tools, stolen out of his house.

Between christmas and New Year[,] Gaskell [age 22], George [age 19] & Maggie [age 13] went down to visit their mother [Hannah] as there was no school, and the boys hunted. they shot 30 ducks, so we have had quite a feast. they came up New years morning and in the afternoon Miles took Ida and I down. we had a splendid time and came home on Wednesday. how are Lizzie and Tilly McFarlane getting along, and where do they live? please remember me to them. How is Aunt Mary [Smith Taylor]? Love to Sr. [Eliza] Lund and all old friends. We are all pretty well at present. Junius [age 15] and Park [age 11] at the farm. Carolines house soon be done.

Good bye and God bless you dear father. I am as ever yours in love.

C.J.R.

27″ Jan. 1894
Juarez   Mexico

My Beloved Father,   I wrote to you three weeks ago, and we learned since that the mail which it went out in was attacked by the rebels between here and the railway station, and searched for official letters, the horses taken and passengers relieved of their firearms etc. but Br. [Henry] Eyring says he understood that some of the mail matter was allowed to go on. so I dont know whether you would get my letter or not. there was also one to you from Caroline. You had been having a touch of epizootic when you wrote last, but I trust you are entirely well again ere this. also some of the children were poorly. We are all well except that some of the children have a touch of canker, and I have quite a bad cold.

Miles is busy this week, helping the bishop [George W. Sevey] to settle tithing.[87] public business of one kind and another takes up a great deal of his time. Br. [Apostle George] Teasdale wants them to have a theatre at conference time and show "Damon and Pythias" so they are going to put it on, in a little over three weeks. they had a rehearsal last night.[88] Ethel [age 5] is going to take the child's part.

Miles doesn't like to go on any more but there don't seem to be anybody else to take hold of it yet, and they think it best to have some such amusement for the young. There have been th[r]ee pairs of twins born here in the past two or three months. the first, two boys, were premature, and died soon after they were born. then Alma Spillsbury's wife had a pair of twin girls, which are both alive and doing well, and three weeks ago, one of our near neighbors, Sr. Cluff, had a little boy and girl born, but the[y] both died last week, just four days apart.

A letter came last week for Park [age 11] from George Thompson [Emma's son]. I sent it to the farm to him. there was also one from James [Cottam, George and Rachel's son] to Emma [age 9]. I expect they will answer soon. Junius [age 15] has got the first prize again for his story to the Juvenile Instructor [a church magazine]. the book came last mail. it is called "Famous Boys," contains sketches of Benjamin Franklin, Daniel Webster, and other noted men who were poor boys. his other prize was the history of "John Taylor."[89] I am so glad of him getting these good books, as they are so nice for them to read, especially as such things can not be got here, and I think there is nothing like having good reading matter for the children. you don't know how much good those "Juvenile Instructors," which you sent them when we lived in the mountains have done them. they often look in them now for readings for school, deacons meetings etc. This Ida [age 3] of ours is a great girl. she is about as shrewd as Claude was. the other day she wanted to go with me to the funeral. I said, "No you must stay and play with Ethel." Pretty soon she looked up and said, "When I'm your ma, I'll say, no you can't go." She seems to think it is only a matter of time till she will be my mother. I expect we will have a job to train her properly. With love to all I remain your devoted daughter.

C. J. Romney

29″   I will add a few lines before posting this. I expect you have heard of the death of Br. Josiah Hardy.[90] he died two weeks ago last Friday. cause supposed to be blood poisoning, resulting from a bad food. he suffered a great deal with his foot for a few weeks before he died. with that exception he seemed quite hale and hearty the last time he was down in August. Hannah was up yesterday. and we were invited over to Br. [Apostle George] Teasdales to supper and spend the evening. Apostle Brigham Young and some of his family are expected some time this week. will likely spend some time here, also John Henry Smith is expected in about two weeks.

I have heard that your coop store has failed. Is it true? and did the boys and Emma lose what they had in it? I do hope not. Our store has declared a dividend of 25 per cent for the past year. so you see mine is doing me considerable good. Good night. and may God bless you. I am getting sleepy. so must close.

29" March 1894
Juarez   Mexico

My Beloved Father   It is several weeks since I last heard from you, and I think it is three weeks last Monday since I last wrote to you. the same day that Thomas [age 17] and Emma [age 9] were vaccinated. it made them quite sick for over two weeks. they could hardly use their arms. the rest would have been done but there was only enough matter to do one or two of a family, but Br. [Henry] Eyring has gone to Chihuahua and will bring more. it costs 20 cts apiece. this is such a smallpox country that a law has been passed compelling evrybody to be vaccinated. We had a week of very warm weather, almost like summer, and the peach and apricot trees were loaded with bloom when up came one of our terrible wind storms lasting about two days, and followed by a light fall of snow and a very hard frost. ice in wash tub over half inch thick, which I suppose killed most of the fruit that was out. but though there were some blue looking people here at the time, still I think if no more hard frosts come that there will still be quite a bit of fruit, as a good many of the peach trees are putting forth a few new blossoms, and the plum trees were not out enough to be hurt much. In consequence of the great reduction in value of Mexican money which is now only worth 40 some odd cents on the dollar, the Mining camps and moneyed men who used to get their flour from the States, have had to stop as it would now cost including duty 12. dollars per cwt. [100 pounds] and have lately been buying of the mexicans, which threatened to cut off our supplies, so that last week the Bishopric [the bishop and his two counselors] had to take the matter in hand and appoint men to hunt around and buy up wheat and corn to last the people till harvest. It is a bad thing when a community dos'nt raise its own bread.

We have been living in hopes that we would soon get our heads above water, as one hundred bushels of wheat this year would finish paying for our farm, and they put in a good many acres of wheat which looked lovely in the fall, better than it ever had done, but for some cause or other it has killed out this winter until Miles says there is not half a stand and one big patch is entirely dead, and it is so uncertain about getting water for putting in any quantity of corn, as the mexican water masters have the power to dictate just what crop you must use the water on at a certain time, and when our wheat is killed and no use to put it on that we cant use it for corn land. Miles feels almost discouraged about the farm sometimes, and disgusted with these rediculous rules, but we have to put up with them I suppose while we can do no better. we have put out a good many fruit trees and grape vines on the farm to try and make something of it, and Hannah is trying bees there now. she has four hives. I am thankful to be able to say we are all pretty well just now and I trust you are better than when you wrote last. How is Emmas [Cottam Thompson] health? I never hear from her nor the boys either except through you, and I have written last to every one of them. Did Thomas [Cottam] ever get my last letter? it must be four or five months since I sent it. How is Charle's [Cottam] place at Middleton doing? does he talk of moving down there?

Miles A was getting along very well [on his mission to England] when we heard from him last, only very short of means.

Caroline is getting along very well, has a nice little home. she was up yesterday helping me. I trust Sr. [Ann C.] Woodbury is well again. Please give my love to all the folks, and accept a great portion for yourself. though absent you are not forgotten dear Father. Good bye and may God bless you is the prayer of your loving daughter.

Catharine J. Romney

13" Sept 1894
Juarez Mexico
Mr. Thomas Cottam

Dearest Father Caroline's letter to the girls is waiting for me to put a piece in to you. I recieved your most welcome letter a week or two

ago but cannot see it just now and have forgotten the date. I have
had very sore eyes part of the summer, but they are better, so I can
see to read and write again. baby [Lula] has a bad cold just now. otherwise we are all pretty well. she weighed 18½ lbs. before she was 4
months old. Miles has gone to Casas Grandes with Brs. [Apostle
George] Teasdale and [Henry] Eyring today on some kind of land
business. Saturday the 15″ is a National holiday [Mexican Independence Day] and Br. Teasdale thinks it ought to be celebrated. Miles
is to be Orator of the day.[91] Br. Black who used to be the miller at
Washington was here to dinner when your letter came and asked to
be remembered to you   also Br. [Peter] Dillman inquired about you
and sent his and his wifes' regards. I can tell you you are not forgotten by your old friends. much less by us who love you so dearly.
Miles tells me I ought to write to you every week, but I am too slow
to get at it I guess. I hear that Sr. [Maggie] Bently is going to Utah on
a visit so I must see her as she will likely see you. Miles is building
them a new house. There was a very heavy hail storm above here
two or three weeks ago which did much damage to the crops in the
field. people made ice cream with the hail stones, which were [*last
part missing.*]

*In the following fragment, Catharine is reporting to her father
her conversation with a missionary recently returned from England, probably Hannah's son Miles A.*

name and now he thinks he was mistaken about the name, but he
says they were very kind to him. there was a woman one son and
two daughters, nice girls. the mother belonged to the church but
was wavering, and not considered a very good staunch member. I
think he only met them once or twice. I asked him if he knew anything of Br. John Ormerod [Thomas Cottam's lifelong friend in Eng-
land]. he says he did not see him but heard of him and knew there
was a member of the church by that name in the Liverpool conference but he only labored in that conference a short time just before
he came home and did'nt get very well acquainted there.

It seems strang[e] that you have not seen Charles for so long when
he lives as near as he does, but I suppose it has been a hard time for
money since he came off his mission. I never hear from him any
more.

21″   Well, I guess I must post this. Caroline was up yesterday.
she has had a bad cold and been poorly for a few days but is better.
Sr. [Maggie] Bently [gave] me a letter and photo yesterday from

Emma Squires of her children. I am very much pleased with it and will try to answer it before long.

Your loving daughter,

Catharine.

Although scattered between the home in Juarez and the farm ten miles away, all branches of the Romney family occasionally gathered at one of the homes for visiting, singing, a reading or two by Annie, and evening prayer.[92]

Now and then, friends were invited for a special occasion. In June 1895, they celebrated the return of Hannah's son Miles A. from his mission to England. "Some forty-seven souls of his family and a few friends," reported the Deseret News, *"sat down to tables which groaned under the weight of the viands which covered them. The turkeys, chickens, fruits, vegetables etc., which graced the table, were raised themselves on the farm. After an enjoyable repast the young folks amused themselves in games and outdoor sports; the visitors inspected the farm, and it was a lovely sight to see about twenty acres of golden grain, just ready for the reaper, waving in the breeze. In the evening there was an excellent program of speeches, songs, essays, and recitations. . . . "[93]*

This celebration would have been especially meaningful for Catharine's eldest son Thomas who, at age nineteen, had recently received his own call to serve a mission. After working on the farm a couple of years, Thomas had returned to Juarez where he was working with his father and brothers as a carpenter. Initially, Thomas was assigned to serve in England, and he was thrilled to be going to the land of his ancestors, where his father, grandfather, uncle, and brother had served. A few weeks after receiving this call, he received another letter reassigning him to the Southern States Mission. He was disappointed but not unfaithful. He was gone for three years, traveling without purse or scrip, as his father had.[94]

27" Oct. 1895
Colonia Juarez   Mexico

Dear Father,   Your last letter of Sept. 25" was a long time coming, as we were shut off from communication with the rest of the world by high water. the Santa Maria river was so high that the mail could neither go nor come for quite awhile. so I dont know whether you got my last letter or not. so I must go back for a month. We have had three St. George papers in the last month. the last one was Oct. 5.

thank you very much for them. Br. [Joseph] Bently and Millie Snow generally borrow and read them besides our family. so they are pretty well read.

Thomas [age 19] left home for Salt Lake on the 23 of Sept. and we have not had a line from him yet. but Pres. [Apostle George] Teasdale and Br. [Henry] Eyring returned from Conference a week ago today. they both saw him and Br. Teasdale says he went through the Temple, and he thinks he started on his mission about the 11" of this month. he says he was appointed to Virginia. I am so anxious to hear from him. I suppose he was too busy while in Salt Lake. as it was conference. and he has so many relatives. I told him to try and see Aunt Ellen [Cottam Pilling], Uncle John [Cottam] and all the folks if he could. I am sorry to hear such an account as we do of the strife and animosity which politics is creating among our people in Utah.

Miles has been to Diaz on busines[s] for over a week. Park [age 13] went with him. he got home this morning   I fear this is very poor writing as my eyes are quite sore and have been for nearly two months. so have the childrens been but they are better now.

Ida [age 4] was quite sick all last night with a hot fever, headache and sick stomach. but she seems better today.

We are having a nice rain today.

Tuesday evening 29"   I must finish this tonight as tomorrow is mail day and I have to do my washing. Ethel [age 7] is quite sick today and has very sore eyes. she can scarcely bear a ray of light. they just started to be sore on Sunday. Caroline [age 21] also has been quite sick for two or three days, with a severe cold, but is some better.

I do hope and pray my dear Father that you are much better. Please remember me in love to Emma, George, Thomas, and all their families. I hope your arm and shoulder are quite well again. it seems so bad for you to have such an accident. Yours in love.

Catharine J. Romney

1" Jan. 1896
Colonia Juarez   Old Mexico
Mr. Thomas C. Romney

My Dearest Son, I have recieved a very welcome New Years present today in the shape of a letter from you, which I have looked for so long. I have written to you I think at least five times if not more, so our letters must get lost. perhaps you have not got any which were addressed to Bandanna? This is the first letter we have got since you got any from us. Junius [age 17], Ann [Annie's daughter, age 16] and Emma [age 11] have been looking very anxiously for answers to theirs. Aunty [Hannah] got here today just after her letter did. she seems very pleased to get it. she and Pa have gone to the party. Aunt Annie did'nt want to go as she has been quite sick ever since school closed for the holiday vacation, and I have my usual cold, cough and hoarseness, but I hope it wo'nt last me all winter. There is a kind of epidemic going around in the form of severe colds or distemper and nearly evrybody seems to have more or less of it Ann had to come out of the party sick with her lungs last night and has not gone tonight. Ernest [Hannah's son, age 18] is almost sick with sore throat etc. but ventured to go. if he is well enough he will go after wood tomorrow and again the next day. he has been after wood, and watering the wheat during vacation. Park [age 13] and Orin [Annie's son, age 11] are alone on the farm tonight. Miles [A., Hannah's son, age 26], Gaskell [Hannah's son, age 24] and Geo. [Hannah's son, age 21] persuaded Pa and Aunty to sit for a family group this afternoon, as there are two artists here from Utah, and all of them were here except Isabell [Romney Platt] and Minnie [Romney Farr]. The boys pay for it. it is a large one to frame. I am glad they have had it. of course photographs come too high for us to afford it. Miles [A.] had his two children [Pearl, age 5, and Miles, age 3] taken and Caroline has got Camillas [Caroline and Ed's daughter, age 1] taken. I feel so sorry about yours, but I fear they are entirely lost. I am thankful you are getting along so well, and feel well in the work of the Lord, and are in the enjoyment of his Spirit. with that all our labors and trials may become easy to bear. but be wise my dear boy, and do not provoke enmity when it is not really necessary, not that I doubt the Lord being amply able to protect and preserve you. still you may save yourself some persecutions and trouble by being a little more cautious. I am thankful you were able to control your temper. that is a lesson we should all learn if we would attain to greatness. The children had a party this afternoon. [*Two pages are missing.*]

Gaskell has moved Annie [Pratt Romney, Gaskell's wife] up here into one of Sr. Cordons rooms I believe, and he and Miles expect to start to Carolitos to work in a day or two, at $5.00 a day and board themselves. I dont like to see them go although they do get such high wages. Miles will be missed very much in mutuals [Young Men's and Young Women's associations] and Sunday schools. I read in Carolines letter of your having to sleep in the woods. it makes me feel bad to hear of this, this cold weather. still you are in the service of the Lord and he I feel will protect you from permanent injury.

Now my dear boy, I am your Mother, and consequently must be pardoned if I watch you with a jealous eye, for your welfare, both temporal and spiritual are very dear to me. so if I caution or criticise you, you will take it in the spirit in which it is offered, will you not my dear? In the first place my son: I think that either in speaking or writing we should avoid the too frequent use of the name of Deity. we have been taught this from the fact that the Melchesidic [Melchizedic] Priesthood was named this in order to avoid this very thing.[95]

In the next place my son, though I see no harm in your accepting the socks, I think you should avoid call[ing] young ladies sweet. do not get girls to thinking much of you, only as a man of God, preforming your duty humbly and quietly in his fear. I pray continually that your faith and trust in our Heavenly Father may continue and increase. and that you may not get to thinking too much of yourself, but have wisdom and humility at all times.

I had a beautiful album for a Christmas present from Caroline, Jun[ius], and Park, and glass dish from Emma, am very proud of them.

Monday 13. I think this will be a funny letter, written at so many different times. Orson [Brown] has been home a week and gone off again today. he and Pa are going in partners in a small store at the farm, as see [soon] as they can get a room built for it. Sr. Fife wishes to be remembered to you   she says to tell you she has not forgotten her promise to pray for you. Now my dear son I can tell you what I had reference to in what I wrote yesterday, but I do not like to spread evil reports. still I suppose I ought to tell you. if you refer to it in answering this, do so on a separate scrap of paper please, as I would rather no one knew of my mentioning it. Last night in the evening meeting the Bp. announced to the people the sad news that Br. Neilson and Sr. Burnham had been disfellowshiped from the ward by the Bishopric, for adultry and lying, and further action will be taken by the High Council when they will likely be cut off the Church. this crime was committed over two years ago, while she was yet the wife of another man. Isn't this terrible: it has made me almost heart sick to think of it. We had some very good speaking last night. Orson [Brown] in his admonition, quoted the Scripture which says, "He that thinketh he standeth, take heed lest he fall." This struck me very forcibly, for if we do not both watch and pray, how liable we are to stray from the fold and be overtaken in sin. May the Lord bless us all, and make us strong to resist temptation of evry kind & death is nothing to be compared to anything of this kind. it would be welcome indeed, in preference. Good bye and may our Heavenly Father abundantly bless you my dear boy.

28" Mch. 1896
Colonia Juarez
Mr. Thomas C. Romney

Dear Son, I recieved your long looked for letter by the last mail. I think some of my letters must miss reaching you as I have written quite often, still I have not written for perhaps two or three weeks. there has been so much sickness. Anna [Pratt Romney, Gaskell's wife] has been sick for three or four weeks. Ray [Mattie and Orson Brown's son, age 3], and Clyde [Mattie and Orson Brown's son, age 16 months], and Camilla [Caroline and Ed Eyring's, daughter, age 15 months] were sick and about twelve days ago Mattie [Romney Brown] was taken very sick. for several days it seemed doubtful which way it would turn with her, but she is now improving, but slowly. she is very weak and can not bear much noise. Sr. Fife takes care of the baby with Emily Burrell to help her and we have Ray here. Orson is away out at Demming and has been for some time. Br. Taylor and his wife Hannah, her mother and Jim started to Utah last Wednesday to conference, and do some work in the Temple. I think the old gentleman is to meet them in New Mexico and go on with them. Bp. [George W.] Seevey was very sick a week ago at Magdalina, with pneumonia. We did'nt know but he would have to be buried there, but the Lord has so far spared his life and he was at the farm yesterday and got here in the afternoon. Pa has been down to see him this morning he is still very sick Pa says. Pa says to tell you that he expects to get some money in a few days, and will send you some. we had had another streak of our usual luck with stock. last Monday while Aunty was up here, the little durham cow got bloated on lucern and died. that is over a hundred dollars at one blow, but of course we shall survive that as we have done previous losses. I am glad your valise escaped the fire but I can't think how the contents got burned, and that escaped. no word from Grandpa lately. Park was 14 last Wednesday, and today is Orins [Annie's son, age 12] and Ellas [Annie's daughter, age 8] birthdays Yours will soon come. I wish I could send you something. would send you our family picture, but perhaps you would rather have it here safe than run the risk. Caroline sent you the picture of her house by the last mail. This is a busy day, as the children are to bathe and prepare for the matinee at two o clock, and you know what a busy time theatre days are at our house, and Ray is here extra to bathe etc. Yesterday and today we are having hard wind. Ann [Annie's daughter, age 17] was disappointed at not getting a letter. Camilla is quite poorly with her teeth again this week.

We have got Auntys big cow Daisy milking now as your cow dried up nearly and is turned out.

Is it since you went that Brig. Whipple took Harry [Whipple, his brother] back to Arizona. Sarah [Hawkins Whipple, Brig's wife] feels very much discouraged her mother says. they are in very poor circumstances, and no way of making anything as Brig. has to stay with Harry. he has a fit evry night now, so is not crazy as he was. I feel very sorry for them. what a sorrow and affliction for a family.[96] Sr. [Dora Wilcken] Pratt has been here taking care of Anna [Pratt Romney, Gaskell's wife] for two weeks. Gaskell took her home this morning. Ira was fooling with some powder the other day and got his face badly burned. nearly all the skin is off it I hear. Do[?] clerks in Bently & Harris's store. I expect Gaskell will stay at the farm tonight, and Ernest [Hannah's son, age 18] and Maggie [Hannah's daughter, age 15] will come up to the theatre, and Sunday. the store is doing nicely. I must now conclude as it is near mail time. We pray for you constantly my dear boy and may the Lord continue to bless and preserve you. Your loving mother

C. J. Romney

17" April 1896
Juarez   Mexico
Mr. Thomas C. Romney

My Dear Son   I think I will write to you this morning if only a few lines, though I have no letter to answer as I answered your last one some time ago. Pa sent $22.00 mexican money to Br. Kimball [president of the Southern States Mission], the address you sent, I think two weeks ago tomorrow. I hope you have recieved it all right. Pa says he expects with so many writing that you get all the news, and I feel about the same, that I hardly know what to write, still it wont do to think that too much, or others may think the same, and you fail to get lots of items at all, and your mother ought to be able to write something of interest and perhaps benefit if not very newsy.

The last letter I got from Grandpa, he was quite poorly. got a paper last mail perhaps I will send a clipping to show you how the weather is there. We are having a terrible wind storm here today and last night, one of the old fashioned sort. my paper is covered with dust as I write, and the apricots which are some of them larger than the end of your thumb are blowing off by the wholesale. yesterday we had a lovely prospect for fruit, but of course what will be spared to us is all uncertain, as you know these hard winds generally precede a hard frost, but the elements are not under our control, so all we can do is to hope and pray for the best, and then feel satisfied. If the weather will permit, Ed [Eyring] and Caroline [Romney Eyring], Sr. Snow and her children are going down to the farm tomorrow afternoon and stay till Sunday afternoon one night on a visit to Aunty. Pa will go down tomorrow. Caroline has had a bad cold and felt quite poorly for a day or two but is better. Mattie [Romney Brown] poor girl, is still quite sick, some days able to sit up a little, but not to walk a bit. you ought to write to her. Orson [Brown] is not back yet. she was speaking the other day of the good times you and her used to have together. and it would please her perhaps to know that you remember them. Anna [Pratt Romney, Gaskell's wife] is getting pretty well again I believe but have not seen her for several days. Ray [Mattie and Orson Brown's son, age 3] has lived with us ever since his mother has been sick. I have been shingling Pa's hair this morning. who does yours? your companion, or a barber? Do you wear dickies as they do in England, or white or colored shirts. We are expecting Ernest up, as there is to be a party in the school house tonight.

Now my dear boy, I believe I have your interests at heart as much, or more, than anyone else on earth, and I watch over you with a jealous care, so you will take it in the spirit in which it is meant if I criticise your writing a little, will you not my dear son. I think you are improving very much in your penmanship, with one exception, too much flourishing. do you know I had a hard job to read the last one the tails of some letters were so interlaced with other words. Too much of this makes writing look superficial, and as I have read some people judge of a persons character by his or her handwriting, though I very much doubt if this method of judging would be either just or correct, and certainly so in your case, as I believe you to be ernest and straightforward. still it is well to avoid extremes even in this little item, and it is only right that we should make writing as well as evrything else which we do a source of improvement. and to be a really good correspondent is really a fine accomplishment.

another thing which in my judgement we should avoid in writing is too many I's. It makes a person appear conceited, though they may have [no] idea of feeling so at the time of writing.

I recieved a letter last week from Cousin Mary A Whittaker. she spoke of your spending the evening at her house [in Salt Lake City on the way to Virginia] and spoke very highly of you. she said Carrie would be 30 years old the next day. still teaching school. she sent regards to you. Have you written to Grandpa yet: take time and write plainly when you do as he says he can hardly read my writing when it is dim. I believe Pa would be real pleased sometime to get a good paper from the part where you are laboring, as a specemine. when you write to him I would describe the places of note cities wher you labor or public buildings. And your new companion, how do you like him, compared with the old one? Br. Harris delivered a very good discourse on Sunday. had been to Diaz. gave a rather bad report of the youth there. working at Demming and other places, losing the faith etc. some of them. also rebuked the conduct of some of the boys here at the S.S. [Sunday School] entertainment the night before, and how he was annoyed with it. excuse these blotches. the pen is to black. Good bye and God bless and preserve you my dear boy, is the constant prayer of your mother.

Catharine J. Romney

May 5, 1896
Colonia Juarez   Mexico
Mr. Thomas C. Romney

My Dear Son   I have not been able to find your last letter this afternoon as I carried it around in my pocket and may have lost it so I don't remember the date and am not quite sure whether I have answered it in full or not, but certainly I have written a note since at any rate it was very interesting, so was Pa's which came over a week ago. I heard him reading it to Miles & Gaskell the other day. they were up to spend mayday [May Day], which is being celebrated today. this being a national holiday of this country. We have had a very enjoyable time today. Meeting in the "Park"   Maggie [Hannah's daughter, age 16] queen, Emma [age 11] one of the maids, Jos. Bentley orator, speeches by Brs. [Apostle George] Teasdale and [Henry] Eyring and Miles [A., Hannah's son], national song, Maggie Bentley, song by Lilly [Burrell, Thomas's "sweetheart"], Ann [Annie's daughter, age 17] & Annie Eyring, one by Nellie [Millie?] Turley and others, and recitations by Marcus Tanyia, C. [Charles] E. McClellan, and Will Clayson. they did splendidly. Charleys was "The Actors Story," and Wills "Sams Letter," a good comic. We invited Miles [A.], Gaskell & George, with their wives to join us in a picnic in Aunt Annies arbor. also Ed. & Caroline. and we had a fine time. only that Pa is away as he generally is at the farm. and Aunty [Hannah] and Park [age 14] went down to help Pa talk in the store. We wanted Mattie [Romney Brown] to come too but Sr. Fife had asked her before to go there to dinner. so Junius took her down to the Park in Taylor & Browns buggy where she sat till it was out and he brought her up to Sr. Fifes. It is seven weeks today since she went to bed and her first out of her room was the day before yesterday when Pa took her for a ride in the buggy Sr. Taylor got home yesterday from Salt Lake, and Sr. Fifes granddaughter, Miss Ethel Snyder of Ogden came with her. I have not met her yet. Orson [Brown] has not come yet, has gone to Kannas [Kansas] but will likely be home in a few days. I think Br. Hyrum Harris will likely board at Aunties a while to get a knowlege of the language from the mexicans. he was there two days last week. Pa, Aunty, Aunt Annie and I went to Br. Harris from meeting and spent the evening a week ago last Sunday. they inquire about you; send kind regards. The young folks were invited to Annie Eyrings to dinner today, but they, Ann and Junius [age 18] did not like to go when we invited the folks to come here, so they stayed at home. There has been a childrens party, but it is out now, and there are games and outdoor sports in the Park. children all gone. no one on the hill here but me just now. Br. Harris has had snow stored in the mountains and has made ice cream today Miles [A.] has invited the boys and Caroline to his house to an ice cream supper, and there is to be a dance this evening. Will Turley is very sick with pneumonia. there have been several bad cases of that lately. I am so sorry the gourd you sent me has never come, but I would hardly think such a large thing as that would come through the mail. I got a nice long letter from Grandpa by the mail. he was quite poorly and his rheumatism bothered him so that he had to write at two or three times. Aunt Emma [Cottam Thompson] had been with Willie [Thompson] to Milford [to the train station] to meet Uncle William [Thompson] who had been to conference. They had just got wall paper etc. from Salt Lake to finish their new home with. he says it will be very nice. I am so glad, for I don't know of anyone more worthy of the comforts of life than your Aunt Emma. She has always been so patient and uncomplaining

Well! I have let Emma go to the party tonight, as the rest of the maids were going. I [don't] want her to begin to think of going at nights, for a long time yet, except on this occasion.

Caroline has had a very nice present made to her today in the shape of a very pretty little gold watch. she has got it on tonight and looks very pretty in her new buff lawn dress. Sr. [Mary B.] Eyring has given each of her three daughters and Caroline a watch. sent to Salt Lake by Sr. Taylor for them. she has earned them with her grapes last year I think. I am very glad that your valise and cloths did not get burned. Br. [Apostle George] Teasdale expects to start for Utah with his family about the 20" I believe. Br. Taylors mother has come home with them. also Luanna Baker has her mother and her husband here on a visit. Br. Trejo, he preached last sunday. so did Miles and Pa had a splendid meeting. Mattie says she is going to send you one of her pictures and write to you. Good bye From your loving mother

C. R.

6" the coyotes came last night and I find the rooster and two hens gone this morning leaving just seven hens.

Catharine's father, Thomas Cottam, died November 10, 1896, in St. George, Utah. Catharine had not seen her parents since moving to Mexico in 1887. In February 1897, Miles married a young widow, Emily ("Millie") Eyring Snow, daughter of Henry Eyring and daughter-in-law of Erastus Snow.[97] She was the mother of two young daughters, Theresa and Beatrice Snow. That summer Catharine joined Hannah on the family farm, where she lived in a new house Miles had built for her. The following is a fragment of a letter to Catharine's son Thomas in July 1897.

engaged in the ministry, in preaching the Gospel of Salvation. I think we are indeed fortunate and I hope that evry son I have will fill an honorable mission. I do trust my dear boy that you will be preserved from evry evil, and be enabled to return home in peace and safety. The 4" of July,[98] Sunday, while we were in meeting, we had a very heavy rain storm, which detained us in the school house sometime after the close of the meeting. Caroline went home with me and helped me about packing up. Ernest [Hannah's son, age 19] with our team and Erastus [Annie's son, age 11] with Georges' [Hannah's son, age 22] got off with their loads, quite early. Pa and the children followed with the buggy an hour or two later. I enjoyed the ride and when we got to the farm I saw the new store for the first time since it was finished and furnished, but the greatest place of interest, of course was our new house, and as it looked like raining,

Pa and the boys, helped me to lay the carpet, and move the things in, though it was two or three before I got fully straightened around. I have three adobe rooms, and a rough lumber room for a summer kitchen. they are all in a row and face Aunties house, the back being on the fence line, which runs from the big barn, north and south. The first room on the North is about 14 feet square. it is the girls bed room. the next, 14 by 18 or 20, I use for sitting room and bed room. I have a good notion to tell you how I have got it fixed [even] if you are a boy.[99] on the walls I have the large picture of yourself and the group of elders which Caroline and Junius got framed for me with a very nice deep frame a large bust picture of Pa. The group of Pa and Aunty and their children, the old picture of Pa, Joseph Smith, Grandpa, Grandma, and Uncle Thomas, & the large chromos which I had up before you remember, with three nice corner shelves hung up in one corner, the bed, and bureau on one side, with a washstand in one corner behind the door with a bowl and pitcher on   in one end is the small table I had in Juarez in the front room, with an improvised book case fixed on the back against the wall, with the cradle, chairs, and centre table on which I keep the album etc. and the same old carpet on the floor, completes the furnishing   there is one nice large window in each room, in the dining room which is 14 feet square, I have the cupboard, table and a lounge bed fixed on boxes for Park [age 15]. but in the winter will have to have the stove in. then the summer kitchen joins on to this is made of the lumber which yours and Gaskells rooms were built of. it has the stove in, cupboard for tins etc. so you can see I am very comfortable. it seems so nice to have plenty of room and white walls. The day I wrote, Aunty [Hannah] and Maggie [Hannah's daughter, age 17] had gone to Juarez. Ernest and I had a little Sunday school for the children, and after we went up in the summer house and ate water and musk melons and passed a very plesant day. Pa has been down [from Juarez] two or three times since I moved. the last time he built us a new out house, he is so good and thoughtful.

20" Mch. 1898
Romney Farm near Colonia Juarez   Mexico
Mrs. Eleanor C. Jarvis

Beloved Friend,   Your most welcome and interesting letter of Jan 17 came to hand some weeks since, and was more than welcome I can tell you. And I am very glad to hear of you all being as well as you are, so thankful that your health is some better, and trust it will continue to improve.

Very sad about those young women of Washington dying. I guess you remember Fred Jones of Pine Valley. he lives at Dublan, and his oldest son went on a mission last fall when George [Hannah's son] went? his wife and baby have died since he went away. George is doing well [on a mission]. so is Ed [Eyring, Caroline's husband on a mission to Germany]. learning the language and beginning to preach. Caroline [age 23] has had a very bad sick spell about five weeks ago. Junius [age 20] came down [from Juarez] with a buckboard and took me up one evening. she had been very bad all day. was three hours at one time that she never got a breath without gasping for it. The asthma and other things and in her condition it was hard to doctor her for it. she was easier when I got there. I found Millie [Eyring Snow Romney] with her, and she had had evry care. I and Junius sat up with her that night, and I stayed right with her for five days. she is now pretty well again. but Camill[a] [Eyring, Caroline's daughter] is not very well.[100] they don't know but she has the whooping cough. I got a letter from Thomas [age 21] last evening. he is feeling well, and very strong in his faith and zealous in his labors. he and com[panion]. have quite an experience in the city of Buena Vista lately, where they were holding many meetings and baptizing some. the mother of one of their converts was so bitterly opposed to her daughter being baptized that she gave them poison in their supper. her daughter and her husband and the two elders all felt the effects of it but Thomas not so bad as the rest. he administered to the other three when they all recovered, and he went and baptized the lady at half past ten oclock at night. On the 24" of last month as they were going home with a gentleman to spend the night after organizing a sunday school, they were attacked by a mob of about 30 men, who forced them to get their things guarded them and insulted them till the train left in the morning, when they put them aboard, purchased tickets for them to a place 44 miles away, and tried to make them take an oath that they would never enter the city again. this they positively refused to do, as they had an appointment to baptize some on the 3" of this month. so they set out on their return, preaching as they went, and when he wrote were within twelve miles of the place from which they had been expelled. What news do you get from Orin [Woodbury, Eleanor's brother]? give my best regards to him when you write. Junius came down last evening, and has now gone back. we had such a plesant visit. Annie and the children are all well, except Frank he is teething and not very well. I was up two weeks ago. have been busy making a new carpet this winter. expect it will soon be done. You will no doubt have heard of the shocking death of Sr. Agnes McDonald. Murdered in her bed and her house and store robbed by mexicans. the murderers have not been captured yet.[101] Lizzie Macdonald has just come from her home in Arizona to take her place. Miles tells me. I have to use glasses all the time when I read, write, or sew now, and am not as young looking as I was when you first knew me. I seldom hear from my brother or sister but got a letter from Carrie Cottam [George and Rachel's daughter] about three weeks ago or more and Park [age 15] got one from Emma [Thompson Squire, Emma's daughter] lately. I sometimes see Fanny [DeFriez Jarvis, Sam's wife] in meeting and two or three months ago I took the time when in Juarez, to call there to see Sr. DeFreiz [Fanny's mother]. the poor old lady seemed so pleased. she looks quite aged. has the palsy or something that causes her head to move all the time. she is stone blind, but played three tunes for me on the organ.

Love to yourself and all the folks. I remain as ever yours

C.J.R.

14" Aug. 1898
Romney Farm   Chihuahua   Mexico
Mr. Thomas C. Romney

My Dearly Beloved Son   As Emma [age 14] is writing, I too will write if it is only a few lines. I got your last letter to me three weeks ago and answered it a few days after. I hope you got it all right. Two weeks ago Pa got a letter from you bearing the welcome news that you will be released sometime next month, not unmixed with sadness that we shall not likely see you, perhaps for a long time to come, but then I think perhaps that will be the wisest course for you to pursue [trying to find work in Salt Lake], and I pray ernestly that the Lord will guide and direct you for your best good, for your temporal and spiritual welfare, and give you wisdom humility, and integrity. now, and through all your future life. I care not so much for your acquiring wealth or renown, as for your ever remaining a true and faithful Latter day Saint and in time becoming the head of a worthy family, though of course your success in whatever avocation you may choose will be hailed with pleasure. however my dear boy let me give you a word of caution. do be careful about getting in debt, for it makes a person a slave indeed, and is a cruel task master. perhaps I am too extreme in my views in these matters, but I have a great dread of debt. I wish I could help you to make a start, but thank the Lord that you have health and strength, and pray God that you may have wisdom to assist you in retaining these great and inestimable blessings be strict my dear son, whereever you are in the observance of the Word of Wisdom, the law of tithing, however little you may have; and in all the laws of the Gospel, returning good for evil etc. and the blessings of our Heavenly Father will surely attend you. may his spirit be with you to cheer and comfort your heart. I have not yet recieved the letters you spoke of. I was most thankful for the [*the rest of the letter except the postscript is missing.*] put our washing away and had a lovely time. but was sorry Aunty was not here to enjoy it too, but of course she had a good time too. The children have been having sore eyes.

Sept. 28 1898
Colonia Juarez   Chihuahua   Mexico
Mr. Thomas C. Romney

My Beloved Son   I feel ashamed that I have been so long without writing to you this time, but I believe you will feel to excuse me when you know that our little Vernon [age 2][102] has been sick for over five weeks, and is still not able to walk. about six weeks ago he had a fever for three or four days, but as he was cutting teeth, and was in the habit of being sick at such times I thought it nothing serious. on the Saturday he seemed better and we came up here with Pa, as he sat on the seat and appeared pretty well. on the next day Sunday, he seemed fretful, but was around, and I noticed as we rode home after meeting that he seemed distressed when we drove over the rough places. the next day or two, he felt like lying down and sleeping a good deal and I soon discovered that he could no longer walk, but on trying would fall over. still I thought it weakness, until in a day or two I found that he could scarcely use his arms, to feed himself. we nursed and cared for him. Pa administered to him and we washed and anointed him and he began to improve in health but was helpless in his limbs so the next week Pa thought I had better bring him up and see if any one knew what ailed him. I had been rubbing him with consecrated oil, and was advised to keep on with that once a day and also rub him with salt and whisky twice a day, but after another week he was still so helpless that we took him to Doctor Keat a young man from St. George, Sr. Ivans brother in-law, who had just come, he said it was infantile paralysis, that he had seen many cases of it in Boston where he graduated, so he is doc-

toring him. expects to get an electric battery to use for him and also
for Sister Harpers little [one] who has had something similar and
has one lame ankle. he is in good health now, only for his limbs,
cannot stand at all and though his arms are much better than they
were, are not natural yet. I wish my dear that you would send his
name in to the Temple to be prayed for, and also be faithful yourself
in praying for him every day, that he may soon be restored to perfect
health and strength with the full use of his legs and arms. I had a
letter from you dated Aug. 30", and since then Junius [age 20] has
written, and sent you some more money, and a week ago your letter
to Pa and I came bringing the welcome news that you are again in
the "City of the Saints," [Salt Lake City] among friends and relatives. please give my love to them. you did not say when you arrived. The children are not at all suited that you are not coming
home at present, and indeed it makes me feel lonesome to think
that I cannot see you after so long an absense. I feel more thankful
than I can tell, that you have been able through the blessings of God
to fill an honorable mission and return in safety, and I hope and pray
that the same Spirit may be with you in your everyday life, to keep
you in the line of your duty, "in the straight and narrow path which
leadeth unto life eternal," and I shall ever pray for your success in
every worthy aim, and that you may be preserved from every evil
and temptation. Now my dear boy, build well upon the foundation
which you [words missing], do not fail to strictly keep the word of
wisdom, do not be led into breaking it in the smallest particular, because it is common to do so, or for any other excuse. always pay a
strict and honest tithing, and keep out of debt as much as possible,
and never neglect your prayers or any duty pertaining to our holy
religion, and you will be blessed, and prospered of the Lord.

Metias [Artemesia Redd Romney, George Romney's wife] brother
is here on his way home from the Southern States. preached on Sunday. a very sensible, humble man, seems to be. I met him. says he
has heard of you that you were a very successful elder. I am staying
with Aunt Annie. all well. but am anxious to get home as it is so
lonesome for Auntie [Hannah]. Mattie [Carrie's daughter, age 28]
has been very sick but is better. Caroline [age 24] well except cold.

Heber Davis and Steenie Thompson were married on Friday they
have bought Br. [George] Seevey's place. he lives in the field. Sr.
Spencer who used to live in the mountains, now at Galiana has gone
crazy I hear. very sad isn't it? Hope she will get better soon. A number of people are going to conference [in Salt Lake City]. Br. [An-
thony W.] Ivins, and Gaskell [Hannah's son, age 27] & Annie among

the rest I hear. It is time to post this so good bye for the present. in haste from your ever loving Mother

Catharine J. Romney

I had a letter the other day from Br. [Benjamin E.] Rich, congratulating me on having a son who had done a good work in the missionary field, which I appreciated very much.

Sunday Apr. 30' 1899
Romney Farm   Colonia Juarez near Casas Grandes
Chihuahua   Mex.
Mr. Charles S. Cottam

My Dear Brother   I received your letter with the unexpected and unwelcome news which it contained last Wednesday. I was not at all prepared to hear of my dear Sister Beata's death.[103] for although I knew she had been sick for so long I had no idea of the nature of her disease which I learn from the "Herald" and also from Emmas letter which I received since yours, was supposed to be consumption [tuberculosis]. I am very sorry for yourself and those poor motherless children, and sympathise greatly with you all in the great loss you have sustained, and I also grieve on my own account for I loved Beata very dearly. still I cannot help but feel that it is her infinite gain and that on her account we can have no regrets, for though my personal association with her was of so short a duration, I feel quite sure that she was as fully prepared to go as we can any of us hope to be. I was very thankful to note the good peaceful spirit of your letter, that you felt to submit without complaint, to the decree of our Heavenly Father and to feel reconciled to the great loss which you have sustained. I trust that we may all live worthy to be reunited with her again in eternity.

What a help Beata was to me when I was getting ready to come to Mexico. I shall never forget, so kind, thoughtful and helpful. How do the children feel? is Mary [Charles and Beata's daughter, age 13] able to take hold of the work and keep house for you. or what shall you do? Tell me when you write. I am so glad Hilda [Beata's sister] got there in time to see her alive. it must have been a great satisfaction to them.

I sent your letter right up for the boys and girls to read and have not heard from them sinse, but I know they too will regret her death. It seems to me there are a great many deaths in St. George of late. how many changes have taken place since I saw you last. Father,

Mother, Claude [Catharine's son], Georgie [George and Rachel Cottam's son], Ruth [Charles and Beata Cottam's daughter] and now Beata—all gone, just in our own family. it makes a person wonder whose turn it will be next. I hope we shall all be prepared when the summons comes. after all, as I often think when I hear of young people turning out badly, there are many things worse than death.

My little Vernon [age 2] is much better but still his legs are far from well. Lula [age 4] has a bad cold and earache today. the rest of us are better of our colds, as several of us have had quite bad ones for a few days, but all pretty well now. Isabell [Romney Platt, age 36] paid us a visit of four weeks about two months ago. she had all of her children (five girls), but Will [Platt] was so busy with his patients, that he could not come. it is the first time we had seen her since we left St Johns, so it was quite a treat. Caroline [age 24] is getting along very well. she gets good word from Ed [on his mission in Germany]. he feels well in his labors. Anns [Romney Clayson, age 20] husband [William Argent Clayson] has just been called on a mission to the Southern States.[104] Miles A. [Hannah's son, age 29] and Thomas [age 23] are doing the carpenter work on Br. [Anthony W.] Ivins new house. Br. Ivins returned from conference a week ago last night I heard. Junius [age 21] & Ernest [Hannah's son, age 21] are still with Br. [Henry] Eyring in the store. What have you done with your home in Salt Lake. have you sold or rented it? I must now close with best love to yourself and the children. I remain your affectionate sister.

C. J. Romney.

Please send the enclosed letter to Emma

In 1899, Miles sold the Casas Grandes farm and the Juarez property and bought a hundred-acre farm near Colonia Dublan in the bottomland of the Casas Grandes River, which would be the headquarters of the Romney family for the rest of his life. At last they could all be together. Catharine and Annie lived in a large, two-story adobe house, each with her own apartment but sharing the parlor. Hannah and Millie each had their own homes a short distance away.[105]

The farm was the scene of pleasant memories for the Romney children. On moonlit evenings, Miles and the wives would visit and sing old songs, while the children played such games as "Run, Sheep, Run." Each year, the family held a celebration for Miles's birthday, Christmas, and New Year's. The children began weeks ahead of time to prepare their recitations for the Christmas program.

Annie's daughter Ella remembered, "Early Christmas morning we arose excitedly and cleaned ourselves for the Christmas Parade just before sunrise. The Christmas tree was always placed in front of the big east window at Aunt Millies because the room was large and safe from prying eyes. At the signal we marched in a line over to the house and round and round the beautiful tree with the morning sun lighting up its homemade trimmings. Then Father, himself, delivered the gift with many a joke and chuckle. Old Santa himself could not have made things more merry."[106]

The wives shared responsibilities for domestic chores. Among other things, Hannah sewed and took care of chickens; Annie supervised molasses making, took care of the cream, and made the butter; and Catharine separated the milk and made hats and slippers. Ella, Annie's daughter, wrote, "We used to sit for hours cleaning straws with Aunt Catherine or sewing carpet rugs. During these hours we always sang a great deal. Every once in a while Aunt Catherine would say, 'Girls, I'll just have to nap a minute.' She'd lean back in the old rocking chair and sleep for five minutes then wake up apparently rested. After the straws were cleaned and separated into bundles they had to be braided into hats."[107]

24 Mch. 1901
Colonia Dublan   Chihuahua   Mexico
Mr. Charles S. Cottam

My Dear Brother   Your welcome letter of Feb. 26" came duly to hand. it certainly was the bearer of very sad news. it is so sad to think of dear Carrie [Cottam Webb] being taken right in the bloom of her young womanhood, and I sincerely sympathize with her poor young husband and her Father & Mother.[108] I hope little Bertha [George and Rachel Cottam's daughter] is entirely well before now. how old is she. I don't know the four smaller girls one from the other, only I think when I look at the picture that I know which is Maggie [George and Rachel's daughter].

Dear Brother it is past the time now that you expected your young lady down. I hope you have not been disappointed this time, but that you have changed your state of loneliness for one of co-partnership with the lady of your choice and that it will prove a happy union as well as a great blessing to the children.[109] what a time you must have had with the children sick, and poor Mary [Charles's daughter, age 15, who was taking care of the household]. I dont wonder that she gets discouraged at her age, for the many duties and cares of a household are enough for a woman of mature years, to have devolving upon her.

I feel so sorry to know that Emma [Cottam Thompson] is having such poor health for so long, but hope she will soon be right well again.[110]

Who keeps house for Mary Ann [Cottam Miller, George and Rachel's daughter] while she is in school, and where does she teach?[111]

Miles has had a long sick spell for over a month, but he is much better again, but still has a cold and cough. he has been to Juarez this week on business. Hannah went with him and they stayed at Mattie's [Romney Brown] and had a nice time visiting with the children. they are all pretty well now. Carolines' boy is a fine fellow, a month old. he is to be named Henry for his grandpa Eyring,[112] and Thomas['s] boy [Owen Thomas Romney, age 3 months] is a very bright little fellow. There has been a great deal of sickness lately, and we are having very windy weather this month after the lovely storms of a few weeks ago. I fear there will be but little fruit this season as there has been quite heavy frost since the blossoms came out. still I think it a sin to grumble and find fault when I read in the papers, the accounts of the terrible storms, tornadoes, etc. which passed over many of the states on the 9-10 of this month. what a terrible destruction of life & property. we see by the last paper that Br. [John] Pymm is dead—another of Fathers old friends. what changes in St. George as elsewhere, in the last few years. What has become of Brother Hunt and wife, Br. Cousins? Sr. Baker is dead I hear, and poor old Sr. Defreize is still alive.[113] poor old soul has been blind for years, and it seems as if death would prove a happy release to her. still she lives on. how strange and incomprehensible it all seems, when young mothers with life, hopes, and happiness apparently before them—sometime no doubt we will understand the *why's* and *wherefore's*.

Where do you live now. have you a home of your own yet, and what have you done with your home in Salt Lake and the old Mitchell place? Please give my love to the children and your wife if you have one, if so write and tell me particulars also love to all the folks.

Your loving sister

Catharine

In February 1904, Catharine and Miles traveled to the neighboring state of Sonora so that Miles could minister to members of the church in his capacity as a patriarch and as president of the high *priests quorum. They were accompanied by Hannah's son Gaskell and Catharine's seven-year-old Vernon, whose legs were paralyzed after the bout with polio and required Catharine's daily ministrations. They visited many family members and friends, who treated them royally, and stayed four or five days with their son Thomas, his wife Lydia, and their three children. Upon their return, Catharine gathered her children around her at bedtime to describe the experiences of their journey. Miles went to Hannah's home. About nine o'clock, he suffered a chest pain and asked that the family be called together. Before they could arrive, he passed away. The family sent for the bishopric to administer to him, hoping that he would be restored to life as had happened two years previously. But this time he was gone.[114] At the funeral, Anthony W. Ivins said that Miles P. Romney had lived the principle of plural marriage as perfectly as anyone Ivins had known.[115] After Miles died, Millie left the family farm, but Hannah, Catharine, and Annie continued to live there together for a few more years.*

18" Dec. 1904
Colonia Dublanes   Chihuahua   Mex
Mr & Mrs. Thomas P. Cottam

My Dear Brother & Sister   It was with pleasure that I received your most welcome letter of the 5" ult. The first line which I have had from any of you since shortly after Mile's death. when I think I wrote to you all together in answer to yours, and I have just been thinking for a week or two that I would do the same again, to give you Christmas greetings but as I have recieved your dear welcome letter I will answer it and you might let Geo. & Chas. read it and save writing the same things over, which I should have to do if I wrote seperately. I wish you all, Bros. Sisters, Nephews & Neices a Merry *Merry* Christmas & a Happy New Year. We are all well with the exception of colds. I have quite a bad one for a week past. Rather lonesome as there are only six of us on the farm today. and in fact I was the only one during Sunday School. Park [age 22] and Orin [Annie's son, age 20] started to Juarez very early this morning and the rest of the folks went the day before yesterday, to attend the Conference yesterday and today and S[unday].S[chool]. Convention tomorrow. Park is to have a part—Leo [Hannah's son, age 17] went after a load of wood Friday and has not got back yet. he is the only one of the boys working on the farm now and is quite a load for so young a boy, but he is doing well, tho he is not thro putting in wheat yet. last year was so very dry that crops & stock suffered terribly but we have had so much rain this fall that we hope to have better ones next year. Hannah went back [to St. Johns] three months ago to visit the girls [Isabell and Minnie, Hannah's daughters]. we have not heard from her for two or three weeks. she was still at Isabells [Romney Platt, age 41] and didn't know when she would get up to see Minnie [Romney Farr, age 36]. St. Johns is such a cold bleak place that I fear she has chosen a bad time of year for her visit. I don't know how Thomas [age 28] is as I have not heard from him for some weeks, but I expect to see him this week as I heard his name was down to take a part in the convention, so it is likely he has come up to conference. Mattie [Romney Brown, Carrie's daughter, age 34] has had a hard time this summer. she has had three children down with typhoid, and her oldest boy had his leg badly cut in a wire fence while on horseback.

Junius [age 26] was down two or three weeks ago to a board meeting (he is one of the counsellors to the Supt. of S.[unday] S[chool]. of the Stake) he and family were well then. He is teaching in the Academy again this winter and is still postmaster. Ann [Romney Clayson, Annie's daughter, age 25] is helping him in the office. he was Supt. of the store thro the summer and they wanted him to keep it but Br. [Guy C.] Wilson was determined to have him back in the school as they couldn't fill his place satisfactorily and he had promised to teach before they engaged him for the store.

Yes Caroline [age 30] has another son [Leland Eyring, age 1 month, died two days after this letter was written]. I was with her a few days while she was sick. Ed. [Eyring] was down this past week on business and she would have come with him but the baby had a cold and she was afraid to bring him out this cold weather.

Miles [Hannah's son, age 35] & George [Hannah's son, age 30] and families are well I believe. Miles is in the carpenter business and George is one of the faculty in the academy. Gaskell [Hannah's son, age 33] & family are getting along well. he is also in the carpenters business here and Park works for him and boards at home. they have plenty of work, but as you say, cash is very scarce.

We are getting along as well and even better than we could have expected. Miles left us with a year or two bread on hand. we have some good cows and some chickens so with careful management and economy we will, I think be able to get along nicely, but I assure you we miss our dear, wise, industrious husband, there is so much to look after, so much responsibility that we never realized. so much outdoor work, and so many things that have to go undone. How could it be otherwise, but we cannot complain, but trust in the Lord and do the best we can and we certainly have much to be thankful for. I feel very thankful for my children and trust that the Lord will give me wisdom to properly train those still under my care so that they may become good Latter Day Saints. We have four of the children going to the [Juarez] Academy this winter and the rest all go to school here. Vernon [age 8] & Frank [Annie's son, age 7] go in the afternoon and herd the cows in the forenoon. Vernon is quite handy on his crutches. they also help Leo about harrowing, leveling etc. Annie and I with the help of some of the children and a mexican to chop our wood etc. run our molasses mill this fall. we had pretty good luck, made between two & three hundred gallons. Ann has a nice little home in Juarez. Erastus [Annie's son, age 18] & Ella [Annie's daughter, age 16] board with her.

Sr. Emma Woodruff and Sr. Sara Jane Cannon one of Br. George Q Cannons widows were here last week in the interest of the Relief Society. they spent one night and part of a day with us. we had a very plesant visit. tho Sr. Woodruff was not very well, and still feels very badly at the loss of her son & wife. her visit brought vividly to mind the changes that have taken place in the last 18 years, when we were all together with our dear Parents. Yes I certainly do miss fathers letters as he always kept me posted about things at home.

Sr. Ivins was down and took dinner with us about two weeks ago. I asked her if she saw you when she was up at conference, but she said she didn't but saw Sr. [Ann Cannon] Woodbury. Please give my love to all your family to the boys and their families, as also to William [Thompson] and his family as well as to enquiring friends. How is Mary Lund getting along? Your loving sister

C. J. Romney

Please accept of my congratulations on your attainment to so important an office [member of the Utah Legislature]. I pray our Heavenly Father to assist you to do much good to your constituents and fill it with honor.

Catharine's son Thomas had married Lydia Ann Naegle, daughter of a well-to-do merchant in neighboring Sonora, in 1899, about a year after returning from his mission. By 1905 they had a small home in Colonia Morelos and three young children. Lydia had come to the marriage with some means, which they invested in the Morelos Development Company, along with Orson Brown and two other partners. Believing a certain area in Sonora to be rich in minerals, they bought and installed a processing plant, and Thomas built a small adobe house near the plant, where they lived with their three young children. The machinery did not function well, however, and the quality of the ore was so poor that the cost of processing it exceeded the value of the final product. Determining the venture a failure, they were planning to return to their home in Morelos when a great flood washed down the mountain, forcing them to evacuate it in the middle of the night. The water only reached floor level, and after a few days they were able to return to their home in Morelos. Even though they had heard rumors of the devastation caused by the flood in Colonia Oaxaca, where Lydia's mother lived, they were surprised to find that the town had been completely washed away, except for a few houses on high ground.[116]

4″ Dec. 1905
Colonia Dublan
Mr. & Mrs. Thos. C. Romney

My Dear Thos & Lydia   I wrote to Mattie [Romney Brown] last week while in Juarez, and as I have not posted it yet I think I will enclose this, as the boys have heard that the mine has stopped, and I don't know where a letter will find you but she will likely have a chance to forward it if you are still there. we heard Sat. that a telegram had come to Prest. [Anthony W.] Ivins that Oxoaca [Colonia Oaxaca, Sonora, Mexico] is laid waste and 30 families homeless. This seems terrible and if that is the fate of Oxoaca, what has been done to Morales is the question I ask myself. I [hope] that they are at least as favored in the fact of no lives being lost, as is the case there. The boys said Br. [Orson] Brown was in town the other day but he didnt come down   I should so like to have seen him and heard from you. but the man who has been working there from the States told Orin [Annie's son, age 21] that you were feeling dreadful. I feel to sympathize with you very much my dear son, but still my dear you have much to be thankful for if you have your wife and children spared to you and especially health and strength to labor for them, and after all my dear it may be a blessing in disguise that you have not turned out to be a millionair, for the precious lives which have been entrusted to your care, and the blessing of each others love and confidence, together with the blessings of the Gospel are worth more to you than mines of wealth. so do not despair. I do hope & pray that your home and property has not been destroyed but that you may be able to go home and be prospered and be comfortable. I await with great anxiety to hear from you all particulars. do write soon. I wonder so about the grist mill pumping plant etc. which you are interested in with Orson [Brown] and others. well my dears, I hope for the best, but whatever your losses, cheer up and start in with renewed determination to succeed at your trade even if mining is a failure.

I wish you all a merry christmas and a happy New Year. I came home last Thursday, leaving Gertrude [Stowell Romney, Junius's wife] still in bed but getting better [after having a baby]. Junius can walk around some now for which we are very thankful. The girls pretty well. Emmas[117] baby [Anthony Ivins Eyring, born October 30, 1905] weighs 12 lbs now. Gertrudes little babe [Catherine Kathleen Romney, born November 15, 1905] is very poor but we considered it a mercy it was alive at all.

Good bye and God bless you all.

Your loving mother

C. J. Romney

Annie went to Utah last Tuesday. I did'nt get here in time to see her.

Give my love to your ma, Lydia.

Aunt Annie sends love to you and Mattie.

In about 1907, Hannah, Catharine, and Annie sold the Romney farm to Hannah's son Gaskell and divided the proceeds. Hannah and Annie both had homes built in Dublan. Catharine had a home built in Juarez on the lot adjacent to the home of her son Junius and his family.[118] The wives remained friendly, but they did not live together again.

NOTES

1. Polygamy was tolerated but not legal in Mexico. D. Michael Quinn, "LDS Church Authority and New Plural Marriages, 1890-1904," *Dialogue: A Journal of Mormon Thought* 18 (1985):17. Mexico's minister of colonization encouraged the Mormons to settle there, expressing the view that very few of those persecuting the Mormons "confined themselves to one woman," and that if Mexico would legalize polygamy, it would become "one of the strongest nations on earth." Helaman Pratt, Diary, May 14, 1885, LDS Church Archives.

2. Hubert Herring, *A History of Latin America from the Beginnings to the Present* (New York: Alfred A. Knopf, 1968), 330-31.

3. Ibid., 340.

4. Thomas C. Romney, *The Mormon Colonies in Mexico* (Salt Lake City: Deseret Book, 1938), 56.

5. Thomas C. Romney, *A Divinity Shapes Our Ends as Seen in My Life Story* (Salt Lake City: Published by Author, 1953), 34; Thomas C. Romney, *Life Story of Miles Park Romney* (Independence Mo.: Zion's Printing and Publishing, 1948), 177.

6. Thomas C. Romney, *A Divinity Shapes Our Ends*, 34.

7. Miles had written Hannah when he was in Salt Lake City asking her to have Will meet them at San Simon with a team. Hannah H. Romney, "Autobiography of Hannah Hood Hill Romney," photocopy of typescript in author's possession, 13; Thomas C. Romney, *Life Story of Miles Park Romney*, 181.

8. Thomas C. Romney, *Life Story of Miles Park Romney*, 181.

9. Ibid., 181-82.

10. Ibid., 181.

11. Thomas C. Romney, *The Mormon Colonies in Mexico*, 56.

12. Ibid., 57.

13. Pratt, Diary, May 13, 1885.

14. Ibid., May 11-20, 1885.

15. Original letter in possession of Ella F. Bentley, Provo, Utah; photocopy in author's possession.

16. Erastus Snow to J.W.L (or Wm. L.) Allen [possibly Wilford Woodruff], April 20, 1886, typescript, Andrew Karl Larson Collection, Utah State Historical Society.

17. Thomas C. Romney, *Life Story of Miles Park Romney*, 182.

18. Letter in possession of Edward L. Kimball, Provo, Utah.

19. Pratt, Diary, February 15 and 27, 1886. General Pacheco had previously approved the town plot. He frequently expressed his willingness to help the colonists in any way that he could. Pratt, Diary, January 29, February 16, 1886. Under the laws of 1883 and 1884, Díaz was allowed to organize surveying companies, which would receive one-third of public lands they surveyed and low prices for more. Herring, *A History of Latin America*, 332. Part of the responsibility of the Campo Company, as grantee, was to settle colonists on the land. John Taylor and George Q. Cannon to Erastus Snow, May 10, 1886, quoting Erastus Snow to John Taylor and George Q. Cannon, April 20, 1886, photocopy of typescript, John Taylor Family Papers, Manuscripts Department, University of Utah Libraries.

20. Erastus Snow to J.W.L. Allen (or Wm. L. Allen), April 20, 1886, typescript, Andrew Karl Larson Collection, Utah State Historical Society; Thomas C. Romney, *Life Story of Miles Park Romney*, 184-85.

21. The details of Hannah's courageous trip to Mexico are found in Hannah H. Romney, "Autobiography," 11-16.

22. Ibid., 17.

23. Annie Romney to Eleanor Jarvis, 5 September 1886, in possession of Ella F. Bentley, Provo, Utah; Hannah H. Romney, "Autobiography," 17.

24. Thomas C. Romney, *Life Story of Miles Park Romney*, 191-93.

25. Hannah H. Romney, "Autobiography," 18.

26. George T. Cottam, Diary of George T. Cottam, October 2, 1886, photocopy, Special Collections, Southern Utah University, Cedar City, Utah.

27. With their first month's pay, they bought a dress for Catharine and a book for Caroline. Thomas C. Romney, *A Divinity Shapes Our Ends*, 34; Thomas C. Romney, *Life Story of Miles Park Romney*, 188.

28. Cottam, Diary, December 25, 1886, and January 1, 1887.

29. Woodruff had been in hiding upstairs in the Thomas Cottam home. Junius Romney, talk given at Garden Park Ward sacrament meeting, Salt Lake City, Utah, July 31, 1966, photocopy of typescript in author's possession, 1.

30. Cottam, Diary, January 7, 1887.

31. Thomas C. Romney, *A Divinity Shapes Our Ends*, 36-37.

32. Lula R. Clayson, "Catherine Jane Cottam Romney—A," photocopy of typescript in author's possession, 8.

33. Emma C. Thompson, daughter of Catharine's sister Emma, married John Squire on February 11, 1886.

34. Under the terms of the contract between the Mexican government and I. G. del Campo Company from whom the Mormons purchased the land for Colonia Juarez, a certain percentage of its inhabitants would be native Mexicans. Rail passage would be paid by the Mexican government. Letter from Erastus Snow to John Taylor and George Q. Cannon, 29 April 1887, photocopy of typescript, John Taylor Papers, Manuscripts Department, University of Utah Libraries. Helaman Pratt led a group of converts from Mexico City to the colonies. Life there was totally different from that to which they were accustomed, and almost all of them returned home dissatisfied and unhappy with the church. Rey Pratt, "History of the Mexican Mission," *Improvement Era*, August 22, 1911, 490; Henry Eyring, Journal of Henry Eyring, typescript, Special Collections, Brigham Young University, 64-65.

35. Henry Eyring, superintendent of the co-op store in St. George, was called to Mexico to establish a co-op store in Juarez. He brought with him his second wife, Dessie, who was Catharine's good friend, and three of the Eyring children. They arrived in the old camp Colonia Juarez on April 8, 1887. Eyring, Journal, 63-64. For more information on the Eyring family, see Appendix 1.

36. The pioneers obtained lye for making soap by pouring water on a barrel of cottonwood and willow ashes. The water drippings from the barrel were boiled with grease to make a soft soap. Zaidee Walker Miles, "Pioneer Ways and Pioneer Women," in Hazel Bradshaw, ed., *Under Dixie Sun: A History of Washington County by Those Who Loved Their Forebears*, comp. Daughters of the Utah Pioneers (Panguitch, Utah: Garfield County News, 1950), 95; E. J. Seegmiller, "Pioneer Ways in Early Days," in Bradshaw, *Under Dixie Sun*, 103.

37. Kane County, Utah, is adjacent to Washington County, the location of St. George.

38. Regarding the move to the new townsite, Henry Eyring remembered, "We moved there about May 1st. I immediately took up two lots and with

Bro R's aid fenced them and put up a log cabin. our log-house was at that time quite a respectable improvement, and the first floor laid in Juarez was in that cabin." Eyring, Journal, 64.

39. The two men had been called as missionaries to Mexico City. Erastus B. Snow would be accompanied by his second wife, Ann. Andrew Karl Larson, *Erastus Beman Snow* (Dugway, Utah: Pioneer Press, 1973), 166, 171.

40. Pioneer Day, July 24, is a celebration commemorating the arrival of the pioneers in the Salt Lake Valley on July 24, 1847.

41. Will Romney returned to Salt Lake City, where he became a typesetter and later co-owner of Century Printing Company. Thomas C. Romney, *Life Story of Miles Park Romney*, 328.

42. Bathsheba B. Smith, wife of Apostle George A. Smith, became the fourth general president of the Relief Society. Andrew Jenson, *Latter-day Saint Biographical Encyclopedia* (Salt Lake City: Jenson History Company, 1901-36), 1:699, 4:196.

43. Erastus Snow commissioned Miles P. Romney to build a two-story adobe home for him in Colonia Juarez. It cost $1,400 and, for a long time, was called "the big house." Erastus Snow wanted to encourage the colonists to build well in Mexico, according to the Manuscript History of the Juarez Ward, LDS Church Archives.

44. Miles's brother, Joseph Romney, lived in Cottonwood, ten or twelve miles south of Salt Lake City. Caroline Eyring Miner, *Miles Romney and Elizabeth Gaskell Romney and Family* (Salt Lake City: Publishers Press, 1978), 131-32. Catharine had stopped in Salt Lake City while en route to Mexico in January 1887.

45. The poem appeared in the *Woman's Exponent*, August 7, 1887.

46. Following the death of President John Taylor, Wilford Woodruff, on behalf of the Quorum of Twelve Apostles, sent an epistle to the members of the Church of Jesus Christ of Latter-day Saints, dated October 10, 1887, regarding, among other things, the authority of the Quorum of the Twelve Apostles to preside over the church following the death of the president. James R. Clark, *Messages of the First Presidency* (Salt Lake City: Bookcraft, 1965, 1970), 3:132-55; *Deseret News*, October 12, 1887.

47. Dessie Eyring, Henry Eyring's second wife, was sending greetings to his first wife.

48. Charles L. Walker of St. George recorded that in March and part of April 1888 he had been "obliged to hide up from the U.S. Deputies who are seeking me night and day to arrest me and drag me to prison for obeying the commands of God, My Eternal Father. They came to my house and threatened to break down the doors if the folk did not open them immediately. They then ransacked the entire house kicking the carpets and rugs about trying to discover as they imagined some secret passage to a cellar or hiding place. . . . Several of the Brethren have been arrested and their families subpoened as witnesses against them." Andrew Karl Larson and Katherine Miles Larson, eds., *The Diary of Charles L. Walker* (Logan, Utah: Utah State University Press, 1980), 687.

49. Erastus White Snow, son of Erastus and Minerva White Snow, died March 20, 1888.

50. Robert C. Lund was a partner in Woolley, Lund and Judd, Dixie's "most famous mercantile firm." Andrew Karl Larson, *I Was Called to Dixie, the Virgin River Basin: Unique Experiences in Mormon Pioneering* (Salt Lake City: Deseret News Press, 1961), 260.

51. Erastus Snow died in Salt Lake City, May 27, 1888. He had been preparing to return to Mexico to make his home in a two-story adobe house "of modern architure," built by Miles P. Romney. Manuscript History of the Juarez Ward, LDS Church Archives; Andrew Karl Larson, *Erastus Snow: The Life of a Missionary and Pioneer for the Early Mormon Church* (Salt Lake City: University of Utah Press, 1971), 702.

52. He is asking for the address of George Jarvis, his brother, who was on a mission to England.

53. Thomas P. Cottam was an expert plasterer. In 1886, he spent six months supervising the ornamental plaster work in the Manti Temple. He made his own plaster by hauling the rock to their property and boiling it. William Howard Thompson, ed., *Thomas Cottam 1820, and His Wives, Ann Howarth 1820, and Caroline Smith 1820* (St. George, Utah: Thomas Cottam Family Organization, 1987), 2:560.

54. Urie Macfarlane, teenage son of John M. Macfarlane, went to the mountains to the sawmill to get wood to build their house, which was to be constructed by Miles P. Romney. L. W. Macfarlane, *Yours Sincerely, John M. Macfarlane* (Salt Lake City: Published by Author, 1980), 235, 243, 247.

55. Amy Pratt Romney, "Ranching in Old Mexico," in Kate B. Carter, comp., *Heart Throbs of the West* (Salt Lake City: Daughters of the Utah Pioneers, 1939-49), 12:294-95; Thomas C. Romney, *Life Story of Miles Park Romney*, 250-65; Thomas C. Romney, *A Divinity Shapes Our Ends*, 44-48.

56. Thomas C. Romney, *Life Story of Miles Park Romney*, 205.

57. A prize possession of the Pratt family was a certificate signed by Porfirio Díaz that Helaman Pratt's cheese was the best made in Mexico. His daughter Amy wrote, "Father got the certificate and gold medals—Mother did the work." Amy Pratt Romney, "Ranching in Old Mexico," 294-95.

58. Victoria Josephine Jarvis, Eleanor's sister-in-law, married Edmond George Miles six years later on June 30, 1895. At the time of this letter she was twenty-three years old.

59. John M. Macfarlane taught school in the meetinghouse for a few months in the winter during his first couple of years in Colonia Juarez. He served as a school commissioner throughout the time he lived in Mexico. Macfarlane, *Yours Sincerely*, 249.

60. Amanda Cannon died on November 10, 1889, at age nineteen.

61. Miles A. Romney married Frances Turley on September 15, 1889.

62. Ann Smith Cottam, wife of John Cottam, Thomas Cottam's brother, died January 2, 1890, in Salt Lake City at age sixty.

63. Henry Eyring recorded that he bought a "small stock of merchandise" for the "contemplated Coop store at Juarez." A frame store having

been built, he opened business on January 1, 1889, "with a stock of goods of about $15,000.00." Eyring, *Journal*, 66.

64. Possibly she is referring to the expense incurred by the Cottams in outfitting Catharine's family and paying their fare to Mexico. Thomas C. Romney, *Life Story of Miles Park Romney*, 188-89.

65. George and Rachel Cottam's fourth child and oldest son, nine-year-old George, died on May 3, 1890. Each subsequent year, George noted in his diary the age that his son would have been if he had lived.

66. A cotton fabric with a satin finish.

67. A light dress fabric of wool or cotton and wool.

68. George F. Jarvis, Eleanor's husband, was arrested for polygamy. He was eventually convicted and fined $50. George F. Jarvis, "Life Sketch of George Fredrick Jarvis," photocopy of typescript, Utah State Historical Society, 6-8.

69. Ara O. Call and Annie Romney Call, *Life and Family of Orin Nelson Romney and Albertha F. Romney, 1884-1965*, (Provo, Utah: N.p., 1984), 33; Hannah H. Romney, "Autobiography," 20-21; Thomas C. Romney, *Life Story of Miles Park Romney*, 262; Thomas C. Romney, *A Divinity Shapes Our Ends*, 49.

70. This letter was copied from a typescript that Edyth J. Romney said she had typed but did not remember the source. No original was found.

71. Lizzie Macfarlane was already in Mexico. Tilly Macfarlane, another wife of John M. Macfarlane, arrived in Colonia Juarez on November 13, 1891. John M. Macfarlane had agreed to operate a store in Casas Grandes owned by H. L. Hall while Hall returned to Provo, Utah, for a year. Macfarlane, *Yours Sincerely*, 267, 254.

72. Hubert Adams Macfarlane was born January 20, 1891.

73. Charles S. Cottam, Catharine's brother, served as a missionary in Alabama from May 1891 to July 1893, leaving his wife, Beata, and two young children, Mary and Walter, in Salt Lake City. Lucile C. Fish, "I Remember Papa, Charles Smith Cottam," in Thompson *Thomas Cottam*, 2:740-42.

74. Over fifty years later, Catharine's son Thomas recalled the cornbread as being "minus the buttermilk and eggs so necessary to make it truly palatable." Thomas C. Romney, *A Divinity Shapes Our Ends*, 40.

75. Amelia Thompson married Benjamin Franklin Pendleton, Jr., on November 26, 1891.

76. John M. Macfarlane died June 4, 1892, in St. George. The two wives who were living in Mexico, Tilly and Lizzie, did indeed sell their goods at a great sacrifice and return to St. George. The children of John's first wife, Ann, who had remained in St. George, were mostly grown and able to care and provide for her. But Lizzie and Tilly had younger children to support. In fact, Lizzie's baby was not yet weaned. Tilly and Lizzie worked to support themselves and their children by doing such things as taking in boarders, nursing the sick, cooking for weddings, and doing washing and ironing. Eventually, all their children were able to go to school, except for Urie, who

always helped the others go to school out of his limited salary. Macfarlane, *Yours Sincerely*, 278, 287-89.

77. Mormons believe that through the power of the priesthood, they may be "sealed," that is, united as a family for eternity. This sealing ordinance is performed in the temple at the time of a temple wedding. Because the Saints living in Mexico did not have a temple in their country, couples would marry civilly, journeying to the temple to be sealed when they had the opportunity to do so.

78. Charles Cottam was released from his mission on July 18, 1893. Fish, "I Remember Papa," 742.

79. Mormons make a practice of compiling a "Book of Remembrance" in which they list the names of family members, together with their dates of birth and death and performance of church ordinances.

80. Annie was pregnant with her daughter Erma, born June 17, 1893, in Colonia Juarez, Mexico.

81. Miles A. Romney was assigned to missionary work in the Manchester area of England.

82. Emily ("Millie") Eyring, daughter of Henry Eyring, married William Snow, a son of Erastus Snow, in 1887. At a young age, she was left a widow with two small children, Theresa and Beatrice. In the late 1890s, she married Miles P. Romney and had her own home built on the Romney farm. Thomas C. Romney, *Life Story of Miles Park Romney*, 282, 283.

83. Caroline and Ed's wedding followed a relationship of several years. Not far into their courtship, Caroline's father learned that Ed had been smoking and forbade her to see him. For two years, they met at social gatherings. Finally, her father relented. Caroline Eyring Miner and Edward L. Kimball, *Camilla: A Biography of Camilla Eyring Kimball* (Salt Lake City: Deseret Book, 1980), 6.

84. The train went north through Salt Lake City then south, making it a longer trip to St. George than to Salt Lake City, even though St. George is closer to Mexico.

85. Edward C. Eyring married Caroline Romney, and Edward F. Turley married Ida E. Eyring in a double ceremony in the Salt Lake Temple, October 11, 1893. Ida Eyring Turley remembered, "We returned home safely. A double wedding reception was held at the home of Henry and Mary B. Eyring. It was the largest and most important social event that had been held in the Colonies. We entertained 80 people at dinner and all the adult population were invited to the dance in the evening." Ida E. Turley, Addendum to Journal of Henry Eyring, 72-73.

86. Kate B. Carter, "The Mormons in Mexico," in Kate B. Carter, comp., *Treasures of Pioneer History* (Salt Lake City: Daughters of the Utah Pioneers, 1952-57), 3:195.

87. Mormons pay a tenth of their increase to the church as tithing. At the end of the year they "settle" their tithing with the bishop by declaring whether or not they have paid a full 10 percent. Miles would have been acting in his capacity as counselor to Bishop George W. Sevey when he helped to settle tithing.

88. Catharine's son Thomas later recalled one of these rehearsals: "The Dramatic Company was practicing the play, 'Damon and Pythias' for presentation when a well-nigh tragedy occurred. George, a son of director Miles P. Romney, was taking the part of Pythias and Ern Turley, a man of large proportions, was the executioner. 'Pythias' lay prone upon the floor with his neck over the block while the executioner stood with a broad-axe in his hands ready to behead the prisoner. The unreality of Turley's position aroused the impatience of director Romney and in a thundering tone he shouted: 'Make it real! Make it real!' The wielder of the axe, being of an excitable nature, was in the act of bringing it down upon the head of George when fortunately someone nearby grabbed his arm, thus preventing a decapitation. Never again would Miles P. permit that the axe be used, but in its place was a wooden blade painted to represent the real thing." Thomas C. Romney, *Life Story of Miles Park Romney*, 212.

89. John Taylor was the third president of the Church of Jesus Christ of Latter-day Saints.

90. Josiah G. Hardy, a longtime friend of Thomas Cottam, died on January 12, 1894, at age eighty.

91. The Mormons celebrated Mexican Independence Day in much the same way they celebrated the Fourth of July. The firing of guns, sounding of church bells, and the music of the Juarez band brought Mexicans from neighboring towns for a parade in the morning and a program in the park in the afternoon, followed by a picnic dinner and a dance in the evening. Thomas C. Romney, *Life Story of Miles Park Romney*, 236-43.

92. Thomas C. Romney, *A Divinity Shapes Our Ends*, 59.

93. *Deseret News*, July 16, 1895, quoted in Thomas C. Romney, *A Divinity Shapes Our Ends*, 60.

94. Thomas C. Romney, *A Divinity Shapes Our Ends*, 64-92. His mission journals are located in the LDS Church Archives, a gift of Edyth J. Romney.

95. See *The Doctrine and Covenants of the Church of Jesus Christ of Latter-day Saints* (Salt Lake City: Church of Jesus Christ of Latter-day Saints, 1981), 215-16.

96. Harry Whipple died on June 10, 1896, at age twenty-seven.

97. At the time Miles married Millie, plural marriages were performed in Mexico with the permission of the First Presidency of the church. Quinn, "LDS Church Authority and New Plural Marriages," 78.

98. This letter was taken from a typescript which said 9" of July, rather than 4" of July. But, a "4" could easily be mistaken for a "9," the 4th of July is a name of a holiday, and the 9th of July does not fall on a Sunday during any of the years Thomas was on his mission. July 4, 1897, was a Sunday.

99. Read, "I have a good notion to tell you how I have got it fixed [even though] you *are* a boy."

100. Camilla Eyring later married Spencer W. Kimball, who became the twelfth president of the Church of Jesus Christ of Latter-day Saints.

101. Agnes Macdonald, wife of Alexander F. Macdonald, kept the post office and a small store in Colonia Garcia. She was born in Scotland and had lived in St. George. She was a friend of the Romneys, having worked with

Hannah on the Ladies Co-op. *Deseret Weekly*, March 12, 1898; Bradshaw, *Under Dixie Sun*, 309.

102. Vernon Romney became a prominent lawyer in Salt Lake City, a director of the State Savings and Loan Association, a leader in the national Republican party, and the father of eight children.

103. Charles Cottam's wife, Beata, died April 13, 1899.

104. Ann's husband, William Argent Clayson, died while he was serving his mission, leaving her with a baby daughter. Thomas C. Romney, *Life Story of Miles Park Romney*, 351.

105. Eleanor R. Farnsworth, "Miles P. Romney," typescript, Nelle S. Hatch Collection, BYU Archives, 2; Thomas C. Romney, *Life Story of Miles Park Romney*, 282, 283.

106. Ella Farnsworth Bentley, "A Glimpse into the Life of Annie Maria Woodbury Romney," photocopy of typescript in author's possession, 20.

107. Ibid., 18, 19.

108. Caroline Cottam Webb, the twenty-two-year-old daughter of George and Rachel Holt Cottam and wife of George W. Webb, died February 15, 1901. The month prior to her death, Caroline had a baby girl. The day after the baby was born, her little boy, George, died. Cottam, Diary, January and February, 1901.

109. Charles S. Cottam married Mary Gertrude Judd on June 25, 1903.

110. Emma Cottam Thompson died on April 24, 1901.

111. Mary Ann Cottam Miller, George Cottam's oldest child, was teaching school to support her two small boys and her husband while he was serving a mission to the eastern states. During the winter of 1900-1901, while she was teaching school at the Court House in St. George, two of her sisters, Rachel and Carrie, and Carrie's little boy died. Her grief over these deaths caused her not to want to return to school, but the next year she taught at Gunlock. During the first part of the year, relatives cared for her two boys. After Christmas, her mother cared for one of the boys, and Mary Ann took the other boy to school with her. Wilma Petty and Frank J. Petty, comps., *A History of George Thomas Cottam and Rachel Holt Cottam, Their Children and Their Ancestors* (Cedar City, Utah: Published by Authors, 1977), 18-19.

112. Henry Eyring became a world-famous chemist receiving many honors, including fifteen honorary doctorates and membership in the National Academy of Sciences, and eighteen prizes, including the National Medal of Science, the Priestly Medal, the Berzelius Medal in Gold awarded by the Swedish Academy, and Israel's Wolf Prize. Henry Eyring, *Reflections of a Scientist* / Henry Eyring, ed. Harden Romney Eyring (Salt Lake City: Deseret Book, 1983).

113. The two women mentioned were sister wives. Sr. Mary Ann DeFriez, having left her husband in England, married George Baker in St. George. The two wives did not get along, and Sr. DeFriez soon left. Grace Jarvis Fenn, "Reminiscences of Grandma 'Baker,' " in Margaret Jarvis Over-

son, comp., *George Jarvis and Joseph George DeFriez Genealogy* (N.p., 1954), 37.

114. Hannah H. Romney, "Autobiography," 22; Thomas C. Romney, *Life Story of Miles Park Romney*, 285-90; Thomas C. Romney, *A Divinity Shapes Our Ends*, 120-21.

115. Thomas C. Romney, *Life Story of Miles Park Romney*, 290.

116. Thomas C. Romney, *A Divinity Shapes Our Ends*, 119-27.

117. Emma Romney married Edward Christian Eyring on November 3, 1903.

118. Bentley, "A Glimpse into the Life of Annie Maria Woodbury Romney," 22; Frank Romney, interview by Jesse Embry, June 2, 1976, LDS Polygamy Oral History Project, Charles Redd Center for Western Studies, Brigham Young University, BYU Archives, 4; Junius Stowell Romney, "Autobiography of Junius Stowell Romney," 1971, Special Collections, Brigham Young University, 4.

Colonia Juarez. Prior to the Mormon exodus from Mexico in 1912, they "had about all [they] could wish for." (Courtesy of the Utah State Historical Society)

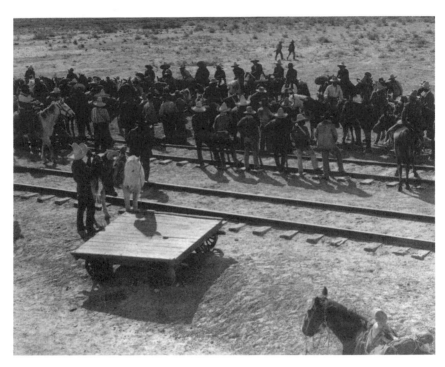

Mexican revolutionary army. (Courtesy of Brigham Young University Photoarchives)

Mormon colonists preparing to leave for the United States by train, July 1912. (Courtesy of the Church Archives, Church of Jesus Christ of Latter-day Saints)

Mormon refugees in El Paso, Texas, July 1912. (Courtesy of the Church Archives, Church of Jesus Christ of Latter-day Saints)

Catharine and her children: Lula, Junius, and Vernon. (Courtesy of the St. Johns Stake Family History Center)

PART FOUR

Return Home

During the first decade of the twentieth century, the Mormons in Mexico were favored with a prosperous and peaceful community life. By the autumn of 1911, all of Catharine's children except Lula and Vernon had married,[1] and Catharine enjoyed the association of her children and grandchildren.[2] In 1906, Catharine had accompanied her daughter Emma to Utah so that Emma could attend the temple.[3] There they had visited with Cottam relatives, who presented Catharine with a Bible that had been given to her grandmother one hundred years earlier.[4] Catharine encouraged her children in their studies at the Juarez Academy and took classes there herself.[5] Catharine's son Thomas recalled, "It now seemed that we had about all we could wish for. . . ."[6] In 1912, however, this peaceful scene was interrupted by the Revolution of 1910, which lasted more than a decade and devastated much of Mexico.[7]

The social and economic conditions in Mexico that precipitated the Revolution of 1910 had their roots in the colonial period, when Spanish kings had rewarded loyal subordinates with rights to large tracts of land. By the time Mexico gained its independence in 1821, most of the best land was owned by fewer than 5,000 hacendados.[8]

During the next half-century, the country knew little but turmoil. When Porfirio Díaz became president in 1876, neither people nor property was safe. The economy was in shambles—farms languishing, mines deteriorating. Under Díaz, order was restored, and the national economy grew. But Díaz's policies left the poor poorer as ever more land was transferred to large landholders. Each year peons became more in debt to their overlords. Díaz's police force quickly squelched all uprisings, but by 1910 the country was fully ripe for revolution.[9]

When Francisco Madero, Díaz's opponent for the election of 1910, gained support, Díaz had him thrown into prison, and Díaz loyalists declared Díaz president. After a brief time in prison, Madero went to Texas, declared himself president, and called for Díaz's resignation and honest elections. Madero began the revolution at Casas Grandes, where he was victorious.[10]

One incident which took place during the Madero Revolution that directly affected Catharine's life was the killing of Juan Sosa.[11] For weeks, Mormons at Colonia Juarez had complained that personal property was being stolen. Certain Mexicans were suspected, and, in fact, some of the property was found at the home of Juan Sosa. Four or five Mormon deputies went to Sosa's home to arrest him. While one of them was squeezing under the barbed wire fence, Sosa hit him on the head with the side of his shovel. The chief deputy ordered the men to fire, and Sosa was killed.

The deputies were arrested and imprisoned at Casas Grandes. Guy C. Wilson, accompanied by Thomas C. Romney, appealed to a General Creighton, Madero's subordinate, who ordered the release of the deputies. When this order was ignored, Wilson and Romney went directly to Madero. Madero asked that the deputies be brought before him for a hearing. Crowds of Mexicans were in the streets as the deputies were brought to Madero. Someone recognized them, and the crowd rushed at them, threatening their lives. Wilson immediately went to Madero, whose brother came to the scene, ordered the crowd to disperse, and told the prisoners to escape.

When Madero's forces left the region to attack Ciudad Juarez, threats against the deputies forced them into hiding. One of the deputies, John Telford, hid at Catharine's house for about six weeks. Afraid of a gun, Catharine slept with a large knife tucked under the head of her mattress. One night, some Mexicans who had threatened to shoot him in revenge came to the house. They waited outside the house all night but did not attack.

After leaving Casas Grandes, Madero attacked Ciudad Juarez (across the border from El Paso, Texas), where he was again victorious. He then marched south to Mexico City, gathering strength and taking cities with little or no opposition.[12] In Mexico City, he was hailed as a redeemer.[13] Once empowered, however, Madero proved weak and ineffective and was slow in reforming land policies. His former friends, led by Orozco and Salazar, became discontented and began a counterrevolution in the north of Mexico.[14]

During the Madero Revolution Mexicans had demanded needed materials from the Mormons. Now mobs of Mexican rebels confiscated Mormon property and threatened bodily harm.[15] In all, nine Mormons were assassinated.[16] Time and again, when the criminals were delivered to authorities, they were allowed to escape.

Hostile action was directed toward Americans in general. The rebels believed that the United States was harming their cause. In March 1912, the U.S. secretary of state advised all Americans to leave the country.[17] By August of that year, 42,000 had fled, the Mormons included.[18]

In accordance with advice from both church and U.S. government leaders, the Mormons had been determined to assume a position of neutrality. Junius Romney, as president of the Juarez Stake, had met with General Salazar, who repeatedly promised protection but could not or would not keep his promise. Nevertheless, the Mormons had remained neutral, despite increasing Mexican hostility, including a speech by Salazar announcing intent to drive Americans from Mexico.[19]

During the Madero Revolution, guns had been imported freely from the United States. In March 1912, however, the U.S. government had placed an embargo on the export of arms to Mexico,[20] and the Orozco forces had become desperate for guns. The final incidents precipitating the Mormons' exodus involved attempts by the Mexicans to obtain guns from the Mormons.[21]

On July 12, 1912, a rebel leader in Colonia Díaz demanded that the residents deliver all their arms and ammunitions to him by ten o'clock the next morning. Junius and his counselor, Hyrum S. Harris, immediately took this report to Salazar. Having been awakened to hear their story, the general lashed out against the officer who had demanded the guns. He said that no such demands were to be made on the colonists—"todavia no" (not yet). He then caught himself as though he had said something he was not supposed to. At that moment it occurred to Junius that the Mormons might have to leave Mexico.

Later that month, Salazar called for a meeting with Mormon leaders and told them that all guarantees were rescinded. When Junius protested that he had believed these guarantees to be valid, Salazar responded, "Those are mere words, and the wind blows words away."[22] Salazar announced that they had decided to take away all the colonists' arms and ammunition, and he demanded that they give them up. Otherwise, he said, "we will consider you

as our enemies and will declare war on you immediately."[23]
Salazar allowed Junius to go with a Mexican representative to meet
with church members at Colonia Dublan. Thousands of rebels surrounded the town. Feeling that it would be suicidal to fight the
rebels, they surrendered their old guns. From Dublan, Junius tele-
phoned to Juarez to arrange a meeting that evening. By two in the
morning, the men decided to make a show of delivering their guns.
They delivered their old guns, keeping a cache of new arms that
they had smuggled into the country. They sent the women and children to El Paso by train.[24]

By this time, Catharine was in failing health. Her daughter, Lula,
then eighteen, remembered:

> We didn't know we had to leave until early that morning and the
> wagon came to take us to Pearson, the nearest railway station, at ten.
> We left cake and chicken in the oven and started out with less than
> a dollar, my mother an invalid who was to know little but suffering
> till her death in 1918.
>
> On the way to the station we were stopped by a drunken Mexican
> who ordered us to get out and be searched. And while we waited for
> the train at Pearson I walked out by the side of the station house to
> see if the train was coming and a crowd of Mexican soldiers rode up
> and surrounded me and I was quite terrified, as the horses stamped
> around me. I suppose they only wanted to frighten me for they
> laughed and rode away.
>
> We rode all day squeezed into the train like cattle without a drop
> of water to drink until about 3 a.m. when we reached El Paso, Texas.
> We had food in a box under the bench but it was impossible to get it
> because of the crowd. I think I stood on one foot all the way as there
> wasn't room to put the other one down. On the seat right in front of
> me was Sr. J——, one of the most doleful creatures I ever saw. She
> grumbled every foot of the way, her pet peeve being lack of space,
> food, drink and especially the loss of her dear chickens. "I am sure I
> left them locked up," she said, "and those darned Mexicans will kill
> them all. I have taken such good care of them. Why, the first winter
> I was in Dublan, I knit hoods for every one of them." "Oh, was it that
> cold?" I asked in surprise. How she laughed. "Well you are dumb.
> You goose, I meant I knit hoods to get money to buy them." Of
> course, others laughed too, and I was embarassed, but it was well
> worth it, for I had never seen the grouch smile before. . . .
>
> Later that day 2 older girls behind me started to sing a Sunday
> School song, "Are you ever burdened with a load of care? Does the
> cross seem heavy you are called to bear? . . . When you look at others
> with their lands and gold, think that Christ has promised you his
> wealth untold. Count your many blessings, angels will attend, help

and comfort give you to your journey's end. Count your blessings, name them one by one. Count your many blessings; see what God has done." I looked up at my poor sick mother. The tears were streaming down her tired face, but she smiled at me when she saw me looking at her, and I tried to smile back. I think I grew up that day.[25]

Thomas's wife, Lydia, and their five children were traveling with them:

Luckily Lydia had a wee bit of money and paid for one bed for Mother and herself and little baby. A tiny inside room with no windows, but they could at least rest a little. Then Vernon, Lydia's four older kiddies and I lay on the floor, partly under the bed. The next night, money gone, some man from El Paso took us down to a dirty dump by the railroad track, 53 of us, and we sat on our rolls of bedding. Some slept sitting there, but mother almost died, so she and I walked outside and it was a bit cooler. The third night they put some of the refugees in another room and brought springs which they set on the floor for poor mother.[26]

Catharine, Lula, and Vernon moved frequently during the next several years. For a few weeks, they shared a three-room apartment in El Paso with Thomas, Junius, Park, and their families.[27] Then they visited for about a month with Ethel and Ida and their families in Douglas, Arizona. When they returned to El Paso and learned they could not go back to Mexico, they accepted the hospitality of relatives in St. George for a season. The next summer, they spent time with Junius's and Park's families in Los Angeles. In July, when Ethel's husband Mitchell Lillywhite died, Lula and Catharine went to Arizona to be with her. Vernon joined them later.

[June 22, 1913, postmark on postcard]
Box 703   Mesa City   Arizona
Mr. Vernon Romney

My Dear Son,   We got here all right yesterday. Dr. sent us up here to the farm in his car. Girls so glad to see us. Ethel is as well as can be expected. the trip was quite hard on her. How are you standing the hot Weather. Write often. they all wished you had come. With best love.

Mother

Forward all mail to Ed [Eyring] in care of Dr. [Will] Platt. Been raining very hard today.

"What a blessing was this mother in those days of sorrow," remembered Ethel.[28] *After about eleven months with her, Catharine became very sick and went to Salt Lake City for an operation. The doctors decided not to operate, however, considering it too risky. She became bloated and was in considerable pain. They did not expect her to live. Finally she asked Lula and Vernon to pray that, if she could not get well, God would take her quickly or at least ease the pain, but "his will be done." Then slowly she began to get better. Although she was never fully well and was able to get out and about only with a great deal of difficulty, she seemed to enjoy life. They rented a small apartment from cousin Carrie Smith for ten dollars a month. Vernon worked, and Lula attended school.[29]*

12" Nov 1914
725 W. 3rd N.

My Dear Son & Daughter   Thos. & Lydia & Children   I will take time to write a few lines this morning, so that it will be ready to send whenever Vernon gets time to write. We were so glad to get your last letter written to Vernon, and to know that you are getting along so well in your school work [at Brigham Young Academy, Provo, Utah], and enjoy it so much, and that you all like your new house so well, and especially that you have plently of butter and milk. they go a great way toward a living, especially where there are a number of children, and all of you fond of milk. We buy a pint a day, which does pretty well for our mush. but of course we miss it for cooking with. Park [age 32] and Junius [age 36] sent us four large sacks of potatoes which I think will pretty well do us for the winter, as we had already bought a bushel. so this is a great help to us. and

I think we could manage with our rent and living expenses. But as next month is the time our tithing & insurance will be due, and Vernon [age 18] needing a new outfit of clothing, shoes, etc. for winter he feels quite blue sometimes, and of course it is quite a heavy load for a boy of his age. But I feel that we have been greatly blessed, as a family, and me especially, since I am feeling so much better, and am able, with what Lula [age 20] can do, to keep things going in the home. I do so desire that Lula may be able to graduate, and hope & pray that I may be able to keep going, as it is quite hard for her to catch up with her back work. You know school started five weeks before she did. She likes her school very much.

I expect Camilla [Caroline and Ed's daughter, age 19] and Mary [Caroline and Ed's daughter, age 16] to come and spend the xmas [Christmas] holidays with us. we had nice letters from them the other day, and from all the girls quite lately. they want me to send their love to you folks, as all are so busy, with their own and public work. Caroline is Pres[iden]t of the religion class. and Emma working in the Primary. they seem to like Pima quite well. Ed [Eyring] had been gone down to Juarez a week when they wrote to look after his interests there. They say Beatrice [Snow, Millie's daughter] is to be here to get married the latter part of this month. Minnies girl, Laura [age 20] was here to see me one day. she is going to school [at Brigham Young Academy] in Provo. also Pearl [Miles A. and Frances's daughter, age 24] came to see me. Miles [A.] and part of his family are back in Mex. Good bye. Love to all.

Mother

20" Nov. 1914
725 W. 3rd N.

Dear Lydia   You will see by the date of the enclosed letter that it has been written for over a week. I left it for Lula to post, when I went up to spend a few days with Gertrude, and I guess she did'nt have a stamp, so will enclose it with this, in answer to your nice long letter, which came while I was gone. I found Junius had left the day before for Castle Valley to be gone two or three weeks, and when he comes back, will have to leave again, for California and expects to be gone two or three months. I was gone five days, had a nice visit with Gertrude & children, but felt that I ought to be at home so that Lula would have more time to study as she is having quite a time to catch up with her back work, these short days, when she has so much to do at home.

Caroline & Emmas address is Pima Arizona. Parks, Cornish, Cache Co. Utah. Ethels, Douglas Ariz, Box 165. Idas' Mesa Ariz.

I am so glad you all like your new home, that you are having such a nice time socially. And that Thos. is making such a success of his work. I feel that he will be able to be a great benefit to the young people there, thro the assistance of the Spirit of the Lord. I am also glad to know that the children are all doing so well, in school, and like it so much, and Pauline [Thomas and Lydia's daughter, age 9] getting along so well with her music. As to the deep snow and cold weather, it seems wonderful, and makes me almost shiver. the fall here has been very fine, but plenty cold enough to suit me.

The girls were all well when I heard last. Please give my love to your mother [Pauline Beck Naegle] when you write. excuse this scribbling as it is time for the postman and I want to get him to take it.

Best love to Thos. and all the children. That certainly must be a smart boy. Grandma would like to hear his music. I am so thankful to be so much better. Auntie [Hannah] is in Hichita [Hachita, New Mexico] with Eugene [Hannah's son] and Ethel [Eugene's wife]. I got a nice letter from her lately. Lovingly.

Mother

By the winter of 1915 Catharine was well enough to travel. She spent an extended Christmas season in Mesa, Arizona, visiting her daughters Ethel Lillywhite and Ida Alldredge and their families.

Nov. 16″ 1915
Mr. Vernon Romney

My Dear Son,   I am going to sit on the porch in the warm sunshine, to answer your last two letters, so you will excuse pencil, as it is inconvenient to use a pen & ink on my knee. Vonda [Ida's daughter, age 3] is by me holding her doll. baby [Leona, Ida's baby] asleep and, Ida, Br. Chas. W. & his Uncle gone to Phoenix to the fair. I expect to go to Sr. Coplans with the children to spend the day. if Leo [Alldredge, Ida's husband] has time to take us down, when he comes back for his next load of passengers. Lister, Daisy & Eleanor went there in the buggy yesterday, got back home about 8.p.m. and had a nice time Ethel says. started about 4-30.a.m. You didn't tell me about your gray suit.

Well, Vernon dear, you don't know how I appreciate your dear, newsy letters. also the enclosed money. as well as the stamps, altho Leo has very cheerfully taken my numerous letters, stamped & posted them, he said he wondered if you thot they were too poor to furnish me with stamps?

I am so sorry to hear that Gertrude [Junius's wife] and the children, have been having such a time of sickness. if I don't get time to answer Juniu[s]'s letter today, tell him I shall do so soon. Ida had quite a sick time last week with LaGrippe and billiousness. & Leo seemed to be threatened with appendicitas for several days, but took a course of medicine from Dr. Openshaw, and is feeling pretty well again. It is a very busy time with him during the fair. doesn't get home some nights till 11.30. They have raised his wages to $3.50 instead of $3.00 per day. and let him off at 4:30 p.m. on Sunday, as he is class leader in mutual [Young Men's Mutual Improvement Association]. I believe.

I am thankful to say, I am feeling fine, only that my eyes ar[e] still bad. Ethel says Lucina [Lillywhite, wife of Horace Lillywhite, who was a brother of Ethel's husband, Mitchell Lillywhite] is feeling some better again. I am so glad you keep well.

Earl has gone. I hope he will be successful. Now Vernon dear, I wish you would get you a nice warm night shirt and consider it my xmas present to you. so you will save me posting one to you, and you to me, thus serving a double purpose. We had such cold nights last week, after the rain storm, that I heard Leo proposing to Ida, that they get mother a hot water bottle for xmas: so I told them I would rather have it now, and get the extra months comfort. and it is certainly nice.

21″ Well dear this is Monday morning, and my letter not finished. Leo came just as I was writing, took us to Sr. Coplans, had a nice visit   the girls took full charge of the babies as they think lots of them. A young man who called there told me that he saw Belle [Isabell Romney Platt] and four of her girls at the fair the day before, and Sr. Lisens told me since that they and their husbands, were all at the dance here Fri. night, all but the Dr. [Will Platt, Isabell's husband] & Nellie [Platt Stevens, daughter of Will and Isabell Romney Platt] & her husband & Miles [Platt, son of Will and Isabell Romney Platt]. they came over in an auto I think. We have had a very busy time this last few days, conference and so much company. Lucina was down. to meeting. and grandma, Ethel & Mitchell [Ethel's son, age 3] & Lela Coplan to dinner yesterday. Br. [Apostle Anthony W.] Ivins was at Irenes to dinner with her father & others. Willie Smith staid here Friday night. he is principal of the St. Joseph school, and came to convention at Pheonix. is still single. wished me to give his love to Junius, please tell him. He took a Miss Inez Earl to the dance. so he may be contemplating matrimony. My cold is better. cough almost gone. but my eyes are quite sore. Am so thankful you keep well. Oceans of love from

Mother.

22" Nov. 1915
Mesa, Arizona

Dear Junius & Gertrude,   I see Leo has forgotten to take my letter to post, so will try to get Juniu[s]'s letter answered and enclose and get him to post when he goes at 2.p.m. We were so glad to get your most welcome letter of the 12" but certainly sorry to hear of yours and the childrens illness, and that Gertrude [Junius's wife] and the little girls were still sick. but from a later letter from Vernon, was thankful to learn that they were still on the improve, and I do hope & pray that ere this you are all entirely well again. and that the children will all escape that terrible disease. am so sorry it is raging again and of the death of those who have been taken off with it. Ida says it was here not long ago and proved fatal in nearly evry case, but the Drs. & officers were successful in soon stamping it out, so it did'nt spread far. Leo & Ida disclaim any but the best of feelings of love for all of you, and will write as soon as they can but this last week has been an extremely busy one, between the fair, Conventions & Conference all coming about the same time, and he has had to miss them all, except one or two evening sessions. The Conference has been most excellent, and the girls tell me the Conventions of the M.I.A. [Mutual Improvement Association] has been splendid, the best they ever went to. Br. Oscar Kirkham & Ann Cannon of the [Mutual Improvement Association] General Board have been here. And Br [Apostle Anthony W.] Ivins. H. S. Cummings & Seymour B. Young at conference. instructions were fine. Br. Ivins especially so. his sermon yesterday on the fulfillment of Prophecy, was most inspiring. also Prest. Udalls [David K. Udall, former bishop in St. Johns]. who was a visitor. he told me the evening before, when I met him that he regretted not being able to get down to see you when in the City and intend[ed] to write to you. sends kind regards. Br. Ivins seemed very much surprised to see me here. said he didn't know I had left the city. George Sevey [former bishop in Juarez] came to me in the meeting house yesterday and inquired about you   sent kind regards, also Sr. Belle Johnson, poor soul, she still grievs. about her boys. Josey is with her Father sixty miles beyond Tucson, has five children living. Minerva here on the ranch with her and Belle, with whom she leaves her four children and goes out nursing most of the time. So many people inquire about you folks and ask me to remember them to you, but I often forget to.

Yes I am thankful to say I am better. cough almost gone again, but my eyes are rather worse, quite sore in fact.

I am so glad you have had letters from Thos. & Park & that all are well, but so sorry about the poor crop. and hard time financially. but hope something will come your way so you can meet your obligations.

Ethel has sold one of her grey mares for $100.00. and Horace [Lillywhite] has paid $30.00 that he owed her, so it will, together pay the interest on the farm debt but the principal is still owing. due in Mch [March].

As you say the Lord has certainly blessed us. I do certainly appreciate the improvement in my health & opportunity of visiting my girls. Lula [age 21] seems to be getting along quite well with her school. she is a dear, good girl. I too appreciate the fact of our being out of Mexico. no desire to return. I would like to be kindly remembered to all of Gertrudes folks, when you see or write to any of them Gertrude.

I went on Sat. evening, with the girls to the open house to one of the convention sessions of the M.I.A. and witnessed an illustration of the way dances are, and should be conducted under their auspices. by Br. Kirkham   he gave them some fine dancing lessons. says they have established a rule of beginning their dances at 8 and dismissing at 11 and when the young people found out that they meant what they said and were prompt. they are becoming a success, tho. at first met with many objections   There was also a demonstration of the method being carried out of the manner of carrying out the "Home Evening"[30] given by Br. Reese & family. one of the Stake Presidency of the young men. I don't know when I have enjoyed any thing of a social nature so much; he is a rather short round faced, bald headed man, whose plesant, cheerful expression would drive away the blues. his wife a nice looking young woman with two sweet little children. look about the age, or possibly a little older than Vonda [age 3] & Leona [age 1] who acted, on the stage just as if they were at home. he had Willie Smith & Miss Earl, and a boy & girl about the size of Olive [Junius and Gertrude's daughter, age

14] & Junius [Junius and Gertrude's son, age 12]. added to his family. They had a family song. then explained that the next should be prayer. then the Father. asked Dorothy the little three or four year old girl to give a recitation, which she did, so cute, and followed by two or three others. he then asked Sr. Reese to sing and play on the piano.

Then the daughter sang, and the son (William) was asked to relate some of his missionary experience, which, tho unexpected by him was very interesting to the audience, his first labors in the Mex. mission. (Br. Ivins seemed quite pleased with it.) one of their friends dropped in, Prof. Hansen, Musical director, and Stake Pres. of Religion work. for the Stake, and they invited him to stay and called on him for music   he is certainly fine. Then the Father & Mother sang a beautiful duet. their old love song. which made them appear as real lovers, and. then Dorothy passed nuts and candy   the baby woke up and got out of her buggy and sauntered around so good natured and cute. With love and kiss to all the dear children and bushels of love to both of you from

Mother.

The Brs. Huber send kind regards to all of you, also grandma, and boys. & John & Susie Butler were here to dinner on Sat. they are doing well. at Lehi. she has raised over a hundred dollars worth of Turkeys. but will only sell part of them. going to keep the hens. she says John has raised about $300.00 of glonila[?] maize. plenty of good vegetables, etc. and gets $60.00 per month for being water master. She has put up 10 gallons of pickles. besides lots of fruit. won four or five prizes in the fair. they bot 75 dollars worth of bees, which have paid for themselves this the first year. She's certainly a "chip of the old block." Eh?

Excuse this long, rambling epistle. dont read it if you are too busy.

27" Dec. 1915
Mesa   Ariz.
Mr. Vernon Romney

My own dear boy   Christmas is over, and we will settle down to normal life again, we have had so many callers, children, and confusion of one kind, and another, that I have'nt had time, nor opportunity to write for several days, as I had planned to do and now I have about 14 letters to write to acknowledge xmas presents, I think I never recieved so many at any one time, and these mischievious children, Leo & Ida, who got them from the office, put them away till late xmas Eve, when we were ready to dress the tree. I had quite a time opening and examining the contents. and I expect you would like as the others did to join me in looking them over. so here goes. a beautiful xmas folder from Auntie [Hannah] and a pretty little one from Eugene [Hannah's son] & Ethel [Call Romney, Eugene's wife]. A nice letter and kerchief from Aunt Annie. A good letter and kerchief from M. A. [Mary Ann] Whittaker [Catharine's cousin], with beautiful lace of her own make around it.

From. Beckie & Carrie [Smith, Catharine's cousins] a pretty box containing a most beautiful white apron from Beckie and three bks. from Carrie   one of them of lovely drawn work by her own making I suppose. also a from Joseph a fine picture of himself, natural as life. he makes a very nice picture   I had sent my Brothers & cousins, Auntie [Hannah], Aunt Annie & Mille [Eyring Snow Romney] each a booklet, as well as my girls, Camilla [Caroline's daughter, age 21] & Mary [Caroline's daughter, age 17]. Camilla sent the girls and Leo and I together a box of xmas cake. but as we had our pudding, cake, etc. made, will likely not cut it till New Year, or for our birthday. am sure it will be good. next comes Aunt Rates [Rachel's] annual offering of work aprons. dark blue this time, two of them. the dear good soul, she is determined I shall not be without something to work in as long as I live, this makes seven in the last three years, and I certainly appreciate them. Next comes a parcel from my two eldest girls [Caroline and Emma]. a beautiful white crepe de chine waist, which they have made for me. and presents for each of the girls and children. white embroidered aprons of their one make for each of the girls. and Maggie Lillywhite, & Sr. Huber sent me kerchiefs. and Grandma a nice piece of lace. before she went to Benson. Then comes a pakage from Junius & Gertrude & children. which I certainly do prize. that beautiful picture of the dear children, a lovely warm skirt, and kerchief.

From Park & Vilate a very beautiful kerchief & xmas card.

From Ethel two pairs of nice, warm, cashmere stockings, which were very timely. Leo & Ida a hot water bottle & pretty little tatted silk tie. dark blue.

Our dear Lula sent me, what do you think—A fine leather satchel, very similar to one which I got from my baby boy. both of which I assure you I greatly prize, and shall try to live long enough to wear them both out. you remember how you both used to hate to see me carrying that old one. so you were both of one mind, we had quite a laugh over it, but it brot up a very tender remembrance, of a certain scene, of a dearly loved boy, of eight years of age, who came running down the street by the W.M. a number of years ago, holding out a little satchel which he had selected, and paid for, with his own money. I shall never carry one of which I shall feel more proud, nor more appreciative if they are really very much prettier, and expensive. There has been quite a controversy between the girls about the probable cost of these, as they are certainly very good ones. now I guess you will have to satisfy their curiosity when you write again. another thing I must not forget to mention, and which I certainly do prize is the beautiful card, and the tender message of love and appreciation which it bears and which is fully reciprocated as well as the good pure life you are leading. which is more to me than all the other presents you could give me. Who is the young lady of the tie. and the one who invited you to spend xmas. tell me all about how you spend the holidays, what you got etc.

Br. Huber says, tell you he thinks of you if he doesn't get time to write. All well with us, and hope you are well again. Did you find the list of Mex. losses?[31] Are you a member of and worker in the Farmers Ward? Oceans of love from

Mother.

Back in Salt Lake City, Catharine lived with Junius and his family. She wrote the following letter to her daughter Lula, who had finished school and accepted a teaching job in Hurricane, Utah, a small town near St. George.

Oct. 9, 1916[32]
Salt Lake City, Ut.
Miss Lula Romney

My own dear, sweet Girl;   It is such a long time since I heard from you or so it seems to me, and I was disappointed that I didn't get a letter yesterday or any word from the other girls as Caroline was having very sore eyes and I took her name to the temple to be prayed for. I have been at the temple the last two Tuesdays to be prayed for, because of my eyes. I went up with Sister Ehlyra whose little Ruth as you know has such bad eyes that the Drs. want to take one of them out. But her mother has such faith in the power of the Priesthood that she feels sure it can be healed in time.

Metia [Romney, wife of Hannah's son George] wanted to go with me. She has very poor health lately, sick headache etc.

I have had nine fine treatments by Mrs. Udall. Her office is in the Gymnasium. She offered to treat me when she was down here with Bro. & Sr. Pace at conference time. She assured me she would like me to come in every Tues, Wed, Thurs, or Sat. and she is so sweet and made me feel so welcome and so much at home. The gym has been decorated the last few days with autumn leaves, most artistically interspersed with skulls and other gruesome things.

I went to S[unday]. School and had a splendid class. Bro. Brown, Principle of the children's school, gave such a fine lesson on the first, second & third chapters of *Parent* and *Child*. Also today I listened to a sermon given by Apostle James E. Talmage. I am so glad I heard it. I took the street car at the corner to save walking so much. After the services at the tabernacle I went to Cousin James Smith's, just across the street from the temple square. They were so pleased to see me. We had a nice lunch and he played the piano for me, while I ate and Aunt Hettie [Smith, wife of James Smith] washed the dinner dishes and we all went to the tabernacle together in the afternoon.

Well, sweetheart, I answered your last letter and I forget when it was, so hardly know where to begin what else to write about. If you can get quite a lot of dried figs please do. Dr. Udall says they are fine for constipation. Ground up with a food grinder. Please get some for me and for yourself too. They raise so many good figs in St. George and I am sure in Hurricane also. Send mine up by parcel post and get plenty for yourself. But don't grind them all up for medicine. I prefer to eat them whole, just off the trees. A delicious medicine, I always enjoyed.

I am so thankful that I feel so much better than I have for a long time and if I feel as well in 3 or 4 weeks from now and if the weather is favorable, I may go to St. George for Thanksgiving; if not I may wait until nearer Christmas and watch for suitable weather, if the boys are able to let me have the money, but the farm has not produced well this year. Now when potatoes are such a good price, they have only enough for use and seed.

They have to pay so much for help at harvest time and are having a hard time to make the heavy payments they agreed to make, thinking the potatoes would bring in much more like they did last year. And Park will have to pay a lot for harvesting the beets. I sent the lamp up and they were surely glad to get it. Said it makes a good light.

Gertrude is so busy the last week or two. She left her sewing to make our garments. So now she has Olive's school dresses to make. The students are to have navy blue dresses again.

She bought Kathlene [Junius and Gertrude's daughter, age 10] a nice light blue cashmere dress and Margaret [Junius and Gertrude's daughter, age 7] a maroon one which they wore today. Junius was in El Paso when he wrote. He said he would be several weeks and perhaps months before he was back. He had gone down with Apostle George Albert Smith to the Irrigation Congress, and with others to the Dedication of the Hoover Dam, etc. Now he has to attend strictly to business [selling insurance], I suppose.

We are quite well again. Gertrude was quite sick for 2 or 3 days last week, couldn't go out at all last Sunday.

Thank you so much for the money you sent me last week. I didn't know you had sent it until I was thanking Vernon.

Love to my little girl,

Mother

In November 1916, Catharine went to St. George.[33] In February, she became very sick, and Caroline came from Arizona to care for her.[34] Sometimes she did not know what was going on around her and would call out for her youngest son, Vernon.[35] She finally became well enough that she could return to Salt Lake City. In September 1917, Junius drove her and Lula to Cache Valley in northern Utah. Catharine would visit with her son Park and his family in Cornish, and Lula would teach school in nearby Trenton.[36]

16" Sept. 1917

Dear Junius & Vernon   It is not quite time for mail man so, so will write a few lines in answer to your welcome letter Vernon, which came yesterday. the check which you sent me, certainly came in very handy as I will likely not use it for the original purpose, which I told you about, but to help her [Lula] get some warm winter under wear, as Vilate [Park's wife] tells me it will simply be out of the question for her to do without them, in this severe cold winter, especially coming from the south. I loaned it to Vilate yes, to buy some over ripe apples, three bushels, for 60 cts.   by putting them up this morning them up to apple sauce, she will get about 24 quts.

Now my dear Junius from your letter to Park this week which I heard him read, I larn, as also, I know also by their necessity for thier lack of winter clothing, etc. that you will not any of you be able to furnish me with traveling money, neither build my room at Pima this year,[37] and as I feel so well, and so full of faith that I shall not get down this winter that I feel sure I can safely stay north this winter. and I am almost sure that I could pay my board and stay at James [Smith, Catharine's cousin living in Salt Lake City], where

I could be in easy walking distance of all the meetings when weather is fine, and never have to stayp [step] outside if not. if you think favorably of my plan tell me and I will write to them. then I do want to see Thomas. and that would only be one mo. [month] later than I left last and if we then thot. it necessary could have company of some teachers from south to institutes. far as the south of Utah.

    fondest love to you all.

Mother

18" Sept 1917

Dear Vernon   No decent ink nor pen, so excuse pencil. I have got so homesick to see my baby, and suporter, or main one, at present, that I feel like the next best thing to do is to talk to you for a little while this morning. How are you in health & spirits? How is Gertrude's health? How are you getting on in your Ward duties? Do you take sufficient recreation? These, and many other things I think about, in the silent hours of the night when I can't go to sleep. Lula came home Friday after school. got a ride most of the way. and Park took her back Mon morning (he is very good to her) so it cost her nothing. she was very blue when she came. conditions worse than she expected. but Eddie [Clayson] spent a very plesant evening with us. on Sun. and I noticed she seemed in much more cheerful, and hopeful mood next morning.[38] her disposition seems to pine for some congenial compansionship of either sex of near her own age. besides her stomach trouble is very bad, and general health, not what I would like to see it. that too helps to make her low spirited, I hope another year will see change in her prospects, so she can if she has to make school teaching her life work, she will be in a condition to do it easier, and lay away something for a rainy day. I suppose Junius is in Arizona? what news from him? I noticed in a letter from him to Park of recent date, the [he] expecded to go. and glad to hear him say that he could depend on J. S. [Junius Stowell Romney, Junius's son, age 14] for help in beet harvesting. as they must cut down expenses. I think no one can realize that more than they do at this end. both Co. [company] and personal. as he has, as yet no warm undercloths. gloves for the cold outdoor work, nor over coat for Sunday wear. and of course their added expenses this year, to be met. Junius said he had never, since he commenced business in this country, been so hard up for cash to meet his obligations, personal and otherwise. I guess the car for one thing. Have you heard any more about our house? John Tilford [Telford] and family have gone back home [to Mexico], he to run the Jackson mill for the Taylors, who bought Br Jackson out. Poor Sr. Saville, in bed for nine months, she hopes to soon get well enough to join them, if only to lay her body down among friends. they found not a pane of glass left in either house. They would stay at Maggie Bentleys till their house was made habitable. she wrote to Vilate. We are all pretty well, excepting my eyes, no better. Best love to all of the folks. Remembrance to Earl.

Now dear, we were talking about your future. I know my son, that whatever profession you choose you can, with the blessing of the Lord, without whose help we can accomplish nothing worthwhile.) you will make a success. But I have been wondering if, just at this time of stress you would feel fully justified in withdrawing your support from the two Co's, in which you are personally interested. until they are at least on a safe footing? Could you however, to advantage to yourself, and the. In[surance]. Co., change your occupation, become an active agent. tho perhaps do better when spring opens. and more plesant weather prevails. you would still be a producer and not dependant on days wages. however I should not take any important step without making it a matter of prayer and also asking advice of your older brothers. "in counsel there is safety." Junius said to Park, it will require our united efforts, and we will yet own the farm, for the prospects were not so favorable. as you could wish, reverses make him more determined to succeed. I[t] reminds me of a story when I was a child. An old man, on his death bed, told his two sons to bring him a bundle of sticks, tightly bound and told them to break them, this they couldn't do, he then to loose them and break them one by one, of course this was easily accomplished! a good lesson in united effort. These thots, of course are only suggestions. I never claimed to have a head for business.

What did you think of what I suggested of my own plans for winter? If I find I really need to go South for part of the Winter, Ida [Romney Alldredge] said they had plenty of room, then as soon as you boys can afford to build me a room on Ed's [Eyring, husband of Caroline and Emma Romney Eyring] farm, I will be very glad to go.

Beatrice wants me to tell you to come up.

Derald [Park's son] went over to the Greeks to take a tool home this morning, and one of them gave him a nickle. he told his Father to take him to the store, and he could buy a great big sack of candy.

Well; love. I remain as ever your loving mother

C. J. Romney.

kind remembrance to Earl and any friends who may chance to inquire.

love to Junius when you write. no word from Pima [Caroline and Emma's home] for a long time.

Thank Olive [Junius's daughter, age 16] & J. S. [Junius S., Junius's son, age 14] for the newsy letter they are going to write.

The following was written on an undated scrap in the Vernon Romney Collection.

My Dear Boy. Mother knows how it hurts. but *Father* knows best. and our greatest trials often turn out to be our greatest blessings in the end.

21″ Sept. 1917

My dear Vernon,   I got your most welcome letter yesterday, just after sending one to you. I am in full accord with the plans agreed on by Junius and yourself.[39] so is Park. All join me in love. I shall go home on Oct 1″ Monday. if nothing unforsoon [unforeseen] happens.

You certainly misunderstood my meaning in regard to James & Ettie, I didn't expect to go on charity. but to pay board. and only house room free. don't think I have lost all *pride.*[40]

All well. only Vilate not feeling very well.

Perhaps if Junius can get the girls to find someone from there or Thatcher who I could g[o] back with. Please send me money for my ticket home. you can get it from bank on my acct and 50 cts. over.

lovingly

Mother

Catharine returned to Salt Lake City to the home of her son Junius. There she died on January 6, 1918.[41] Lula said that the following fragment was the last letter she received from her dear mother.

fashioned flounces with several rows of black velvet baby ribbon around the skirt, sleeves, black lace on the edge, it looked very pretty, it was made with polynaise. and tight fitting basque, another very pretty one with polynaise all puffed and tucked and quite a stylish looking one for the time when it was fashionable. I saw in my remembrance the rise and decline of these various fashions, and wore them myself. one young woman had a beautiful suit of plum colored velvet, somebodys wedding gown perhaps. and it reminded me of an evening, never to be forgotten by me. when I wore one of the same cut and color, and was dancing with your Father then. I was still miss Cottam, but being urged to change my name.

A brother Anderson was dressed as a fisherman, with his boots, sacks'[?] suit, fishing reel, and basket of fish on his arm. they were a foot or more in length, and appealed to my appetite. he danced very gracefully with all these evidences of his occupation. But the most interesting of all to me was the Scotch Sword dance. He danced alone on the stage, came out with two long swords. laid them crossing each other, he was dressed as a scotch. Hilander, bare legs to the knee, sandals laced up the leg as you have seen them in pictures, deep plaited kilt, cloak over one shoulder, a beautiful feather ornament, dangling from his waist, and scotch cap. and I never saw such graceful dancing in my life, never touching the swords, he was greatly encored. and had to return and repeat it. Then we went down to get the pie plates and Gertrude [Junius's wife] found a small table at which we seated ourselves, she called for cake, I for squash pie etc. all very nice, our companions (as the table was just big enough to seat four, was a Br & Sr Peterson whom Gertrude made me acquainted with. and home, found a tank of good warm water, took a bath and into bed. The last time I went to the Temple. Tuesday. got a splendid blessing, made a special mention of my eyes and they seem much clearer and better. Walked up with Metia [Romney, wife of Hannah's son George], ate a piece of bread & butter and tomato, then just in time to get in to recital, after went to the bureau. Got acquainted with a Sr. Horne who keeps, the upstairs chamber of pioneer relics, a very interesting place I should like you to visit when you come home. President [Brigham] Youngs table, the sugar bowl with spoon and contents just as he last used them, his coat. Old spinning wheel with yarn on the spindle, cards, with the wool still on them, and many things too numerous to more than glance at. Sr. Horne invited me to come into the rest room, where I laid down on the beautiful sofa and rested for along time till I went to take treatment. I, at her invitation shared her lunch. she is so nice, sister to Ella Thurber & Emily Payne.

Good bye. The Lord bless and strengthen me is my daily prayer. Lovingly

Mother

NOTES

1. Caroline married Edward Christian Eyring October 11, 1893; Thomas married Lydia Ann Naegle, December 12, 1899; Junius married Gertrude

Stowell October 10, 1900; Park married Mary Vilate Lee October 8, 1908; Emma married Edward Christian Eyring November 3, 1903; Ethel married Mitchell Woodruff Lillywhite August 25, 1911; and Ida married Leo Alldredge August 26, 1911. Thomas C. Romney, *Life Story of Miles Park Romney* (Independence, Mo.: Zion's Printing and Publishing, 1948), 371-74.

2. Thomas's daughter Pauline remembered that Catharine would send the children outside to look for pins that had been dropped by the women while sewing on the sunbaked patio. When the children found the pins and brought them to her, Catharine would gather the children in her arms and tell them how wonderful they were. Conversation with Pauline Romney Thomander, April 1986.

3. Lula Romney Clayson, "The Life of Catherine Jane Cottam Romney," photocopy in author's possession, 16; George T. Cottam, Diary of George T. Cottam, October 23, 1906, photocopy, Southern Utah University Special Collections, Cedar City, Utah.

4. The Bible is in the possession of Catharine's great-great-grandson, Alan Parkinson.

5. Clayson, "Life," 20.

6. Thomas C. Romney, *A Divinity Shapes Our Ends as Seen in My Life Story* (Salt Lake City: Published by Author, 1953), 147; see also F. LaMond Tullis, *Mormons in Mexico: The Dynamics of Faith and Culture* (Logan: Utah State University Press, 1987), 92-93.

7. Hubert Herring, *A History of Latin America from the Beginnings to the Present* (New York: Alfred A. Knopf, 1968), 339. Thomas C. Romney also attributes the Mormon exodus to the contrasting cultures of the Mormons and Mexicans and to Mexican envy of the Mormons' prosperity. Thomas C. Romney, *The Mormon Colonies in Mexico* (Salt Lake City: Deseret Book, 1938), 148.

8. Herring, *A History of Latin America*, 331-34.

9. Ibid., 325-38.

10. Thomas C. Romney, *The Mormon Colonies in Mexico*, 150.

11. Ibid., 162-66.

12. Ibid., 150-51.

13. Herring, *A History of Latin America*, 339.

14. Thomas C. Romney, *The Mormon Colonies in Mexico*, 150-51.

15. Ibid., 149-81.

16. Ibid., 169.

17. Joseph Romney, *The Exodus of the Mormon Colonists from Mexico* (Master's dissertation, Department of History, University of Utah, 1966), 6-8, citing Nelle Spilsbury Hatch, *Colonia Juarez: An Intimate Account of a Mormon Village* (Salt Lake City: Deseret Book, 1954), 164; *Papers Relating to the Foreign Relations of the United States, 1912* (Washington, D.C.: Government Printing Office, 1919), 720, 735; and *Deseret Evening News*, August 15, 1912.

18. *Deseret Evening News*, August 15, 1912, cited in Joseph Romney, *Exodus*, 6.

19. Joseph Romney, *Exodus*, 6-8.

20. Ibid., 7, citing *United States Statutes at Large*, vol. 37, part 2, 1732, 1733.

21. The following account is based on Junius Romney, talk given at the Rose Park Stake priesthood meeting, Salt Lake City, Utah, July 13, 1966, photocopy of typescript in author's possession; Junius Romney, talk given at the Garden Park Ward sacrament meeting, Salt Lake City, Utah, July 31, 1966, photocopy of typescript in author's possession; and Thomas C. Romney, *The Mormon Colonies in Mexico*, 172-81.

22. Thomas C. Romney, *The Mormon Colonies in Mexico*, 176.

23. Ibid., 178.

24. Ibid., 179-81.

25. The account is one of several versions of these incidents found in the personal writings of Lula Romney Clayson in the author's possession.

26. Clayson, personal writings.

27. Thomas C. Romney, *A Divinity Shapes Our Ends*, 157.

28. Ethel Romney Lillywhite Peterson, an untitled sketch of the life of Catharine Jane Cottam Romney stapled to Eleanor R. Farnsworth, "Miles Park Romney," typescripts in Miles P. Romney file, Nelle S. Hatch Collection, BYU Archives, 3.

29. Lula Romney Clayson, untitled autobiographical sketch, photocopy of typescript in author's possession, 4-13.

30. In 1915, the First Presidency instituted a "Home Evening" program in which they encouraged members of the church to meet with their children at least monthly to teach them the principles of the gospel in a pleasant and happy atmosphere. This program was reintroduced in the late 1960s and continues to be emphasized in the church. James R. Clark, *Messages of the First Presidency* (Salt Lake City: Bookcraft, 1965, 1970), 4:337-39.

31. Catharine's property left in Mexico included a house ($875.00), household furniture and supplies ($494.37), farm and garden implements ($10.00), stock investments ($250.00), city lot ($500.00), bearing fruit trees ($250.00), young fruit trees ($250.00), bushels of beans ($3.00), milch cows ($375.00), calves ($75.00), and twelve chickens ($6.00), all of which produced an annual income of $50.00. Items listed on a printed form, El Paso Texas, August 23, 1912, Vernon Romney Collection, BYU Archives.

32. This letter was taken from a handwritten copy made by Lula Romney Clayson. Punctuation and spelling are standardized. Lula also provided a handwritten copy of a letter of October 1, 1916, with slightly different wording and a few different details, from 1556 South 2nd East [Junius's home], Salt Lake City, Utah, which is omitted.

33. Cottam, Diary, November 25, 1916.

34. Ibid., February 6, 1917.

35. Caroline Romney Eyring to Vernon Romney, January 19, 1918, Vernon Romney Collection, BYU Archives.

36. Vernon to Thomas, September 1, 1917, and Vernon to Lula, September 13, 1917, Vernon Romney Collection, BYU Archives.

37. Catharine's sons were planning to build her a home on the Edward Eyring property in Pima, Arizona, so she could be near her daughters, Caroline and Emma. At the time of her death, she had been planning to move there in a few weeks. Thomas C. Romney, *A Divinity Shapes Our Ends*, 181.

38. Lula Romney married Edward Clayson on June 7, 1918.

39. They suggested that it might be best to go ahead and build a house for her in Pima. Vernon to Mrs. Catherine J. Romney, September 18, 1917, Vernon Romney Collection, BYU Archives.

40. In her letter of September 16, 1917, Catharine had suggested that she board with her cousin James Smith and his wife, Ettie (Henrietta), in Salt Lake City. Vernon had responded negatively, saying that they wouldn't need hired help and that if they had her stay with them it would be "more an act of charity than anything else." Vernon to Mrs. Catherine J. Romney, September 18, 1917, Vernon Romney Collection, BYU Archives.

41. She died from erysipelas. Thomas C. Romney, *A Divinity Shapes Our Ends*, 182.

Genealogy

CALKIN (CALKINS), MARIETTE ("Aunt Mariette"). An elderly schoolteacher who lived next door to the Miles P. Romney family in St. George, Utah. Her husband, Asa Calkin, was a lawyer in New York when he joined the church and moved to Utah. Eight of her nine children died in infancy.

COTTAM FAMILY. Thomas Cottam (1820-1896), Caroline Cottam (1820-1890), and their children:

Emma (1850-1901) married William Thompson
    Emma b. 1869
    Penelope ("Nelly") b. 1871
    William Alma b. 1874
    Mary Elizabeth b. 1877
    Joseph Smith b. 1880
    George Thomas b. 1883
    Ezra Cottam b. 1887
    Samuel b. 1891
George (1852-1934) married Rachel Holt
    Mary Ann b. 1875
    Rachel Parthenia b. 1877
    Caroline b. 1878
    George Thomas b. 1880
    Ada b. 1882
    James Franklin b. 1884
    Maggie b. 1886
    John Henry b. 1888
Catharine (1855-1918) married Miles P. Romney
    Caroline b. 1874
    Thomas Cottam b. 1876

Junius b. 1878
Claude b. 1880
Park b. 1882
Emma b. 1884
Ethel b. 1888
Ida b. 1891
Lula b. 1894
Vernon b. 1896
Thomas P. (1857-1926) married Emeline Jarvis
Emma Jarvis b. 1882
Thomas b. 1884
Heber b. 1886
Arthur b. 1888
Annie b. 1890
Moroni Jarvis b. 1892
Walter Pace b. 1894
Ivins b. 1896
Clarence b. 1899
Eva b. 1902
Charles S. (1861-1950) married (1) Beata Johnson
Mary b. 1885
Charles Walter b. 1888
Ruth b. 1894
Myrtle b. 1896
married (2) Mary Gertrude Judd
Clair Smith b. 1904
Minerva b. 1905
Lucile b. 1907
Leila b. 1907
Thelma b. 1910
Owen b. 1912
Naomi b. 1914
Gertrude b. 1917

CROSBY, JOSEPH AND MAUDE. Friends of the Romneys in St. George and St. Johns. Joe Crosby was a carpenter, who worked for Miles building houses at Nutrioso, Arizona. He was one of Miles's witnesses to make final proof on his claim at Kitchen Springs and was one of the defendants in the perjury case. He was acquitted at the perjury trial in 1885. Maude was an actress in the St. Johns dramatic productions.

DEFRIEZ, SISTER. Mary Ann Godfrey Defriez. Also known as M. A. Baker, as she married a Mr. Baker in St. George but did not

continue to live with him. Mother of Fanny Jarvis. Her son Eben-
ezer, who had joined the church in Australia, and his companion,
David K. Udall, were the missionaries who preached the gospel to
the DeFriez family in England. She wrote the words to the hymn,
"Master the Tempest Is Raging." She was acquainted with the Romneys in St. George, St. Johns, and Mexico.

EYRING FAMILY. Henry Eyring, his wife Mary Bonelli, and his
wife Deseret ("Dessie") Fawcett. As a young man, Henry Eyring emigrated from Germany to the United States, joined the church, and
married Mary Bonneli. Henry and his first wife, Mary, are referred to
in the letters as "Brother and Sister Eyring," probably because they
were both a generation older than Catharine. His second wife,
Dessie, was Catharine's age. The sequence of events in Dessie's life
parallels that of Catharine's in several respects. Born in 1852 in Salt
Lake City, she moved with her family to Dixie in 1861. When she
was nineteen, she married Henry Eyring, twenty-two years her se-
nior. Two years following their marriage, he was called on a mission
to Switzerland and Germany. In 1887, he responded to Erastus
Snow's request to help establish the Mormon colonies in Mexico.
Brother Eyring, Dessie, and three of the Eyring children arrived in
Colonia Juarez in April 1887, a couple of months after Catharine
and her children arrived there. He served as president of the Mexico
Mission in Mexico City from 1887 to 1889 and established the Juarez Co-op. In 1890, he returned to Utah to get Mary Eyring and the
rest of the children. Henry and Mary's son, Edward C. Eyring, married Caroline Romney and Emma Romney. Henry and Mary's
daughter, Emily ("Millie") Eyring Snow, widow of Erastus Snow's
son, William, married Miles P. Romney.

IVINS, ANTHONY W. Catharine's lifelong friend, who moved to St.
George with his parents as a child. At her funeral he told of joining
Catharine and their other childhood friends in her father's shop and
listening to her father tell stories. He was the first stake president in
Colonia Juarez. When he was called as an apostle in 1907, Junius
Romney succeeded him.

JARVIS FAMILY. George and Ann Pryor Jarvis, converts to the
church from England, were among the first to pioneer in St. George,
Utah. George Jarvis, speaking at Caroline Cottam's funeral, recalled
that he had known of her in England.

George and Ann's oldest son George married Eleanor Woodbury,
who was a sister of Annie Romney and a friend of Catharine to
whom some of the letters in this collection were addressed. George
and Eleanor's children were:

Eleanor ("Ella" or "Ellie") b. 1874
George b. 1876
Orin b. 1878
Clarence b. 1880
Annie Catherine b. 1882
Frank b. 1886
John b. 1888
Rosa b. 1891

George and Ann's daughter Emeline married Catharine's brother Thomas P. Cottam. Other Jarvis children mentioned in the letters include Sam and his wife Fanny, who lived in St. Johns, Arizona, and Mexico; Margaret and her husband Charles, who rented a house in Snowflake to Miles P. Romney for Catharine and Annie when they were hiding from the federal marshals; Heber, who also lived in the St. Johns area; and Josephine, who visited Arizona with her parents.

PLATT FAMILY. Henry John Platt, a saddle maker, and his wife Almeda Jane were friends of the Romneys from St. George who moved to Arizona. Their son Henry married Angie Lang, and their son Will married Isabell Romney. Will Platt worked for Miles as a carpenter in Nutrioso, Arizona. He later became a doctor, and he and Isabell settled in St. Johns.

PRATT FAMILY. Dora Wilcken Pratt, a plural wife of Helaman Pratt, and her five children rode the train to Mexico with Catharine and her children. Helaman Pratt, son of Apostle Parley P. Pratt, was one of the first missionaries to Mexico. He figured prominently in the missionary and colonization work in Mexico. He owned Cliff Ranch in the Sierra Madre Mountains in Mexico, where the Pratts (Dora and her children) and Romneys both lived for several years.

ROMNEY FAMILY. Miles P. Romney (1843-1904) and his wives, Hannah (1842-1929), Carrie (1846-1879), Catharine (1855-1918), Annie (1858-1930), and Millie (1870-1947), and their children:

Hannah Hood Hill, married May 10, 1862

Isabell	1863-1919
Elizabeth	1866-1867
Mary Ann ("Minnie")	1868-1951
Miles A.	1869-1939
Gaskell	1871-1955
George	1874-1935
Ernest	1877-1951
Maggie	1880-1902

Eugene	1883-1946
Leo	1887-1939

Caroline Lambourne, married March 23, 1867, divorced

Will	1868-1931
Martha ("Mattie")	1870-1943

Catharine Jane Cottam, married September 15, 1873

Caroline	1874-1954
Thomas	1876-1962
Junius	1878-1971
Claude	1880-1887
Park	1882-1943
Emma	1884-1957
Ethel	1888-1970
Ida	1891-1943
Lula	1894-
Vernon	1896-1964

Annie Marie Woodbury, married August 1, 1877

Ann	1879-1953
Alice	1881-1923
Orin	1884-1965
Erastus	1886-1920
Eleanor ("Ella")	1888-1956
Ivie	1890-1975
Erma	1893-1981
Frank	1897-1983

Emily ("Millie") Eyring Snow, married February 1897
Millie, widow of William Snow, had two children,
Theresa and Beatrice Snow.

Miles P.'s parents, Miles and Elizabeth Gaskell Romney, who emigrated from England, were also pioneers in St. George. Miles Romney was a leading architect who directed construction of the St. George Temple and Tabernacle. They were the parents of eight other children, two of whom are mentioned in the letters. Their daughter Mary Romney Lund acted in theatrical productions in St. George. Mary's husband, Robert Lund, was a partner in the mercantile firm, Woolley, Lund & Judd, whose business provided much-needed capital for the growth of southern Utah. A son, George, was a prominent financier in Salt Lake City.

SNOW FAMILY. Erastus Snow was a prominent church authority instrumental in establishing the Mormon settlements in St.

George, Utah; St. Johns, Arizona; and the Mormon colonies in Mexico. A member of the leading councils of the church from the time of Joseph Smith, he was appointed to the Council of Twelve Apostles in 1849. Always in the forefront of exploration and colonization, he was one of the first two to enter the Salt Lake Valley in 1847. His wives included Artimesia Beman, Minerva White, Elizabeth Rebecca Ashby, and Julia Josephine Spencer. Hannah corresponded with Minerva, with whom she was friendly from their days working in the Ladies' Co-op and the Relief Society in St. George. Minerva and Elizabeth both visited with Hannah in Mexico. Artimesia's son Erastus B. Snow and his wife Ann went to Mexico City as missionaries. Miles P. Romney's wife Millie was a widow of Erastus Snow's son William.

TENNEY FAMILY. Nathan Tenney, his son Ammon, and their families. Nathan Tenney was killed in a shoot-out in St. Johns, Arizona, on June 24, 1882. Ammon Tenney was an early explorer and missionary in Arizona. He negotiated the purchase of land for the Mormon settlement in St. Johns. In 1884, he was convicted of polygamy and spent time in the federal prison in Detroit, Michigan. His second wife, Eliza Udall Tenney, sister of Bishop David K. Udall, was with her sister-in-law, Ida Hunt Udall, and Catharine and Annie Romney when they went to Snowflake to hide from the federal marshals who sought them as witnesses against their husbands for polygamy. The Tenneys also lived in Mexico.

UDALL FAMILY. David K. and Ella Udall left prosperous circumstances to move to St. Johns, Arizona, in 1880, when he was called there to act as bishop. Catharine refers to them as "Bp. Udall" and "Sr. Udall." His second wife, Ida Frances Hunt, Catharine's friend, moved with her family to Snowflake in 1879 and clerked for Bishop Udall in the St. Johns Co-op before marrying him in 1882. She left St. Johns during the polygamy raids, going first to Snowflake and later to Nephi, Utah. She was the first president of the Young Ladies' Mutual Improvement Association in the Eastern Arizona Stake. The family suffered much as the result of spurious charges of perjury brought against David in connection with Miles's attempt to perfect his claim to a parcel of land. He was convicted by the court but shortly thereafter was pardoned by President Grover Cleveland.

WOODBURY FAMILY. Orin and Ann Cannon Woodbury moved to St. George, Utah, in 1861, the first year of its settlement. Their children of interest in these letters include Annie, wife of Miles P. Romney; Eleanor, wife of George Jarvis and recipient of several of Catharine's letters; and George, who married Rowena ("Roz") Romney, Miles's niece, and died as a young man. Ann C. Woodbury spent many years promoting the silk industry in the St. George area and served as president of the St. George Stake Relief Society. Ann was a sister of Apostle George Q. Cannon, who became a member of the First Presidency, and a sister-in-law of President John Taylor.

Excerpts from the *Orion Era*

The *Orion Era* was a newspaper produced by the Romney family in St. Johns, Arizona, in 1883-84. Catharine's son Thomas said that she wrote a weekly column for the paper, and the following articles, which appeared in the *Orion Era* over the name "Gertrude," are the only two in the extant issues that appear to have been written by a woman.

WASH DAY[1]

This is a day proverbial for discomforts. A day that men dread-flee from as they would from the "plague," they prefer a cold dinner and not come home till supper time. (I need not say that this part of the programme suits the wife uncommonly well.)

The unhappy visiter, who is so unfortunate as to drop in on "wash day," will scarcely meet with a semblance of hospitality, and if she persuades herself that she is welcome, her hostess is likely wishing she had stayed at home till another time.

Under the most auspicious circumstances, it is a day of hurry and bustle, even the little ones do not get their accustomed care; and woe be to all who come in the way, if John has gone off without cutting any wood, which is too often the case; but if he has cut the two armsfull which he really believes will do the washing, and perhaps part of the ironing, she feels somewhat mollified and almost indulges in a laugh at the innocence of men in regard to such matters, and then she thinks, "Poor John, he has to work *so* hard I wont complain, for I guess he thinks he has done well;" and she heroically goes to work to chop what is lacking; after which she has considerable water to carry, and sundry odd jobs that really cannot wait, until she gets a late start at a large washing.

At last she is ready, and rubs away furiously, until she gets the fine clothes nearly rubbed out of the first suds, when baby cries and refuses to be good with Susie's attentions, nothing will do but ma, so she attends to his wants, and puts him to sleep in his crib; and is just congratulating herself on getting back to her work so soon, when little Johnny comes in crying lustily; he has cut his finger, and by the time he is pacified and his wound dressed, her suds is cold.

But everything has an end, and washing is not an exception, if it is a long time coming, and she looks with pardonable pride at her lines full of clean white clothes, and feels somewhat repaid for her time and trouble. But her work is not done if her washing is, and when she turns into the house her heart almost dies within her, it is a chaos to which she must restore order. The kitchen floor must be scrubbed, for tomorrow is ironing day, and there will be no time then; then the sweeping and dusting must be done, and the children washed and combed, as they have been neglected all day. Next she must clean herself up, as she dislikes to have John see her looking untidy.

Now it is almost dark, and supper must be hastily prepared, as John will soon be home, tired and hungry, for he had only a cold dinner, (his wife, mind you, hasn't taken time to eat any except an odd bite or two while wait[ing] on the children. But she [doesn't] think of that.)

Now, John, this is a critical moment, much depends on you whether the domestic atmosphere is pleasant or otherwise; just come in with a smile and a kind word, and you will be almost certain to meet with kindness and smiles in return. Walk out and chop the night's wood and bring it in, and carry her a pail of water, without even waiting for a hint, and it will dispel every cloud from the domestic horizon, and she will declare in her heart that there never was such a man; you will reach the acme of perfection in her eyes.

Just try it, all you husbands; it wont cost you much, and see how much you will gain, (I mean of course all who are thus situated.)

But if on the other hand you come home in a churlish, disagreeable, fault-finding humor, you may expect the vials of her wrath to be poured upon your devoted head, for your wife has born about all that woman's nature can be expected to bear for one day.

Don't tell her you can't see why she is so late with supper, when you want to go over and chat with Brown awhile, and when she reminds you it is "wash day," declare that you could do a washing in half the time.

Don't select the evening of wash day for telling her of the many trials you have to encounter in battling with the outside world, any other time she would sympathise with you, but remember there *is* a limit to a womans patience, and make some allowances.

Gertrude.

MAKE HOME BEAUTIFUL[2]

"Make home beautiful, make home pleasant." How many times have our hearts thrilled with delight on listening to the beautiful, old-fashioned song containing these words, and yet how limited is our understanding of the full and complete meaning of these two short sentences. How few of us take this for our text, and live up to it as closely as we might. I believe there is (in all of us) some room for improvement, and we might find it to our advantage to bestow a little serious thought even upon those subjects, which may appear to some of minor importance, the observance of which would contribute to the happiness of ourselves and families.

The making of home a pleasant and desirable place is, in my opinion, a very important part of "Womans mission."

Home is her kingdom. If there is any place on earth where she may expect to find comfort and happiness, it is at home, consequently, not only her own happiness, but that of her husband and children, depends in a great measure on the condition of that home.

Woman, as a rule, is endowed with a certain amount of tastes, and ingenuity which it is her duty (and should be her pleasure) to use in beautifying and adorning herself and surroundings; not carrying it to excess, to the neglect of other and more important duties, but by expending what few leisure hours she may have in such a way that she may reap a rich harvest of satisfaction.

No matter how poor a people may be, many opportunities are within their reach, if they have the will and ambition to grasp them.

Some appear to think that something good to eat is all that is necessary. This is very essential, but how much more tempting, if well arranged on a nice white tablecloth, with clean knives, and polished glasses!

A clean, well scrubbed floor and white-washed or papered walls, are conducive to comfort, but we need not stop here, and feel that we have all that we want.

Do we ever think how much more attractive is a room with pictures, flowers and ornaments, than is an empty shell, (be it ever so costly,) with bare walls and nothing but the necessary, or indispensible articles of furniture?

I don't believe there are many men but would notice and appreciate the difference, and depend upon it, it has a bearing on the tastes and feelings of children.

We can be comfortable, without being wealthy.

How many men there are who are well to do, and are good providers, who have cheerless, comfortless homes.

There are numberless little knick-knacks which women can make with very little expense, which imparts an air of refinement and culture, even to a log cabin, and when a husband sees his wife trying to cheerfully make the best of her poor circumstances, it will be likely (if he is a true man) to stimulate him to greater exertion, in striving to add to home comfort and convenience.

Gertrude.

NOTES

1. *Orion Era*, November 10, 1883, Special Collections, University of Arizona Library, Tuscon.

2. Ibid., September 29, 1883.

BIBLIOGRAPHY

Arrington, Leonard J. *Brigham Young: American Moses.* Urbana: University of Illinois Press, 1986.

———. *Great Basin Kingdom: An Economic History of the Latter-day Saints, 1830-1900.* Cambridge, Mass.: Harvard University Press, 1958.

Arrington, Leonard J., and Davis Bitton. *The Mormon Experience: A History of the Latter-day Saints.* New York: Random House, 1980.

Bentley, Ella Farnsworth. "A Glimpse into the Life of Annie Maria Woodbury Romney." Photocopy of typescript in author's possession.

Bentley, Joseph T. *Life and Letters of Joseph C. Bentley: A Biography.* Provo, Utah: Published by Author, 1977.

Black, Susan Easton. *Membership of the Church of Jesus Christ of Latter-day Saints 1830-1848.* Provo, Utah: Religious Studies Center, Department of Church History and Doctrine, Brigham Young University, 1989.

Bleak, James G. "Annals of the Southern Utah Mission." LDS Church Archives, Salt Lake City, Utah.

Bradshaw, Hazel, ed. *Under Dixie Sun: A History of Washington County by Those Who Loved Their Forebears.* Compiled by Daughters of the Utah Pioneers, Washington County Chapter. Panguitch, Utah: Garfield County News, 1950.

Brooks, Juanita. Juanita Brooks Collection. Utah State Historical Society, Salt Lake City, Utah.

Call, Ara O., and Annie Romney Call. *Life and Family of Orin Nelson Romney and Albertha F. Romney, 1884-1965.* Provo, Utah: N.p., 1984.

Carter, Kate B. "The Mormons in Mexico." In *Treasures of Pioneer History,* vol. 3, compiled by Kate B. Carter. Salt Lake City: Daughters of the Utah Pioneers, 1952-57.

Carter, Kate B., comp. *Heart Throbs of the West.* 12 vols. Salt Lake City: Daughters of the Utah Pioneers, 1939-51.

———. *Our Pioneer Heritage.* 20 vols. Salt Lake City: Daughters of the Utah Pioneers, 1958-77.

————. *Treasures of Pioneer History.* 6 vols. Salt Lake City: Daughters of the Utah Pioneers, 1952-57.

Clark, James R. *Messages of the First Presidency.* 4 vols. Salt Lake City: Bookcraft, 1965, 1970.

Clayson, Lula Romney. "Catherine Jane Cottam Romney—A." Photocopy of undated manuscript in author's possession.

————. "Catherine Jane Cottam Romney—B." Photocopy of undated manuscript in author's possession.

————. Family and personal histories (photocopies) and correspondence in author's possession.

————. "History of My Life." Photocopy of undated manuscript and typescript in author's possession.

————. "Life History of Catherine Jane Cottam Romney." Photocopy of undated manuscript in author's possession.

————. "The Life of Catherine Jane Cottam Romney." Photocopy of undated typescript in author's possession.

————. "Part of My Life History: Childhood and Youth." Photocopy of undated manuscript in author's possession.

————. "Stories by Aunt Lula." Audiocassette recorded by Heber and Genevieve Moulton, Bountiful, Utah.

————. Untitled autobiographical sketch. Photocopy of undated manuscript in author's possession.

Clayton, Roberta. Roberta Clayton Collection. Brigham Young University Archives, Provo, Utah.

Cottam, Charles S. "Brief History of Thomas Cottam." Photocopy of undated typescript, Cottam Family Collection, Brigham Young University Archives, Provo, Utah.

Cottam, George T. Diary of George T. Cottam, 1875-1928. Photocopy, Special Collections, Southern Utah University, Ceder City, Utah.

Cottam, Thomas. "A Short Family History of Thomas Cottam and His Wives and Children, Wrote Chiefly from Memory, St. George, Washington County, Utah Territory USA, March 30, 1893." Typescript, Juanita Brooks Collection, Utah State Historical Society, Salt Lake City, Utah.

————. Thomas Cottam's Record Book, June 18, 1877, St. George, Utah. Photocopy from William Howard Thompson, St. George, Utah, in author's possession.

————. Thomas Cottam's Record Book, St. George, January 1, 1881. Photocopy from William Howard Thompson, St. George, Utah, in author's possession.

Cottam Family Collection. Brigham Young University Archives, Provo, Utah.

Cottam Family Organization. "History of George Thomas and Rachel Holt Cottam, Their Children and Their Ancestors." In possession of Ronald Riding, Provo, Utah.

The Doctrine and Covenants of the Church of Jesus Christ of Latter-day Saints. Salt Lake City: Church of Jesus Christ of Latter-day Saints, 1981.

Edmunds, Jasmine Romney. Conversation with author, July 1990.

Evans, Beatrice Cannon, and Janath Russell Cannon, eds. *Cannon Family Historical Treasury.* Salt Lake City: George Cannon Family Association, 1967.

Eyring, Henry. Journal of Henry Eyring. Typescript, Special Collections, Brigham Young University, Provo, Utah.

Eyring, Henry. *Reflections of a Scientist / Henry Eyring.* Edited and with a foreword by Harden Romney Eyring. Salt Lake City: Deseret Book, 1983.

Family Group Sheet Collection. Family History Library of the Church of Jesus Christ of Latter-day Saints, Salt Lake City, Utah.

Farnsworth, Eleanor R. "Miles P. Romney." Typescript, Nelle S. Hatch Collection, Brigham Young University Archives, Provo, Utah.

Fenn, Grace Jarvis. "Reminiscences of Grandma 'Baker.' " In *George Jarvis and Joseph George DeFriez Genealogy,* compiled by Margaret Jarvis Overson. N.p., 1954.

Fish, Joseph. "History of the Eastern Arizona Stake of Zion and of the Establishment of the Snowflake Stake, 1879-1893." Typescript, George S. Tanner Collection, Brigham Young University Archives, Provo, Utah, and Special Collections, University of Utah Libraries, Salt Lake City, Utah.

Fish, Lucile C. "I Remember Papa, Charles Smith Cottam." In *Thomas Cottam 1820, and His Wives, Ann Howarth 1820, Caroline Smith 1820,* vol. 2, edited by William Howard Thompson. St. George, Utah: Thomas Cottam Family Organization, 1984.

Flake, Omer D. *William J. Flake: Pioneer—Colonizer.* N.p., n.d.

Gardner, Robert, Jr. "History of Robert Gardner, Jr.: Written by Himself at St. George, Utah, 1884 Jan. 7." Typescript, Brigham Young University Library, Provo, Utah.

Gates, Susa Young. *History of the Young Ladies' Mutual Improvement Association of the Church of Jesus Christ of Latter-day Saints from November 1869 to June 1910.* Salt Lake City: Deseret News, 1911.

Gibbons, Helen Bay. *Saint and Savage.* Salt Lake City: Deseret Book, 1965.

Hafen, A. K. *Devoted Empire Builders: Pioneers of St. George.* St. George, Utah: N.p., 1969.

——— . *Dixie Folklore and Pioneer Memoirs.* St. George, Utah: N.p., 1961.

Hatch, Nelle Spilsbury. *Colonia Juarez: An Intimate Account of a Mormon Village.* Salt Lake City: Deseret Book, 1954.

——— . Nelle Spilsbury Hatch Collection. Brigham Young University Archives, Provo, Utah.

Herring, Hubert. *A History of Latin America from the Beginnings to the Present.* New York: Alfred A. Knopf, 1968.

Jarvis, Eleanor C. Diary of Eleanor C. W. Jarvis. Photocopy of typescript, Utah State Historical Society, Salt Lake City, Utah.

Jarvis, George F. "Life Sketch of George Frederick Jarvis." Photocopy of typescript, Utah State Historical Society, Salt Lake City, Utah.

Jenson, Andrew. *Latter-day Saint Biographical Encyclopedia.* 4 vols. Salt Lake City: Jenson History Company, 1901-36.

"Journal History of the Church of Jesus Christ of Latter-day Saints," 1900–present. LDS Church Archives, Salt Lake City, Utah.

Kline, Mary Jo. *Guide to Documentary Editing.* Baltimore: Johns Hopkins University Press, 1988.

Krenkel, John H., ed. *The Life and Times of Joseph Fish, Mormon Pioneer.* Danville, Ill.: Interstate Printers and Publishers, 1970.

Larson, Andrew Karl. Andrew Karl Larson Collection. Utah State Historical Society, Salt Lake City, Utah.

———. *Erastus Beman Snow.* Dugway, Utah: Pioneer Press, 1973.

———. *Erastus Snow: The Life of a Missionary and Pioneer for the Early Mormon Church.* Salt Lake City: University of Utah Press, 1971.

———. *I Was Called to Dixie, the Virgin River Basin: Unique Experiences in Mormon Pioneering.* Salt Lake City: Deseret News Press, 1961.

———. *The Red Hills of November.* Salt Lake City: Deseret News Press, 1957.

Larson, Andrew Karl, and Katherine Miles Larson, eds. *The Diary of Charles L. Walker.* Logan, Utah: Utah State University Press, 1980.

Levine, Albert J. *From Indian Trails to Jet Trails: Snowflake's Centennial History.* Snowflake, Ariz.: Snowflake Historical Society, 1977.

McClintock, James H. *Mormon Settlement in Arizona: A Record of Peaceful Conquest of the Desert.* Phoenix: Manufacturing Stationers, 1921. Reissued with a foreword by Charles S. Peterson, Tuscon: University of Arizona Press, 1985.

Macfarlane, L. W. *Yours Sincerely, John M. Macfarlane.* Salt Lake City: Published by Author, 1980.

Manuscript History of the Juarez Ward. LDS Church Archives, Salt Lake City, Utah.

Manuscript History of the St. Johns Ward. LDS Church Archives, Salt Lake City, Utah.

Miles, Zaidee Walker. "The First Christmas in St. George—1861." Andrew Karl Larson Collection, Utah State Historical Society, Salt Lake City, Utah.

———. "The Ladies' Co-op." Andrew Karl Larson Collection, Utah State Historical Society, Salt Lake City, Utah.

———. "Pioneer Ways and Pioneer Women." In *Under Dixie Sun: A History of Washington County by Those Who Loved Their Forebears,* edited by Hazel Bradshaw and compiled by Daughters of the Utah Pioneers, Washington County Chapter. Panguitch, Utah: Garfield County News, 1950.

Miller, Albert E., and Mary Ann Cottam Miller. "A Historical Story of the Building of Washington County, the Part Accomplished by the Tradesmen and the Buildings Erected." In *Under Dixie Sun: A History of Wash-*

ington County by Those Who Loved Their Forebears, edited by Hazel Bradshaw and compiled by Daughters of the Utah Pioneers, Washington County Chapter. Panguitch, Utah: Garfield County News, 1950.

————. *The Immortal Pioneers, Founders of the City of St. George, Utah*. St. George, Utah: N.p., 1946.

Miller, Mary Ann C. "Biography of George Thomas Cottam." In *Thomas Cottam 1820, and His Wives, Ann Howarth 1820, Caroline Smith 1820*, vol. 2, edited by William Howard Thompson. St. George, Utah: Thomas Cottam Family Organization, 1987.

Miner, Caroline Eyring. *The Life Story of Edward Christian Eyring (1868-1957)*. Salt Lake City: Publishers Press, 1966.

————. *Miles Romney and Elizabeth Gaskell Romney and Family*. Salt Lake City: Publishers Press, 1978.

Miner, Caroline Eyring, and Edward L. Kimball. *Camilla: A Biography of Camilla Eyring Kimball*. Salt Lake City: Deseret Book, 1980.

Overson, Margaret Jarvis, comp. *George Jarvis and Joseph George DeFriez Genealogy*. N.p., 1954.

Peterson, Charles S. *Take Up Your Mission: Mormon Colonizing along the Little Colorado River, 1870-1900*. Tucson: University of Arizona Press, 1973.

Peterson, Ethel Romney Lillywhite. An untitled sketch of the life of Catharine Jane Cottam Romney. Typescript stapled to "Miles Park Romney" by Eleanor R. Farnsworth, Nelle S. Hatch Collection, Brigham Young University Archives, Provo, Utah.

Petty, Wilma, and Frank J. Petty, comps. *A History of George Thomas Cottam and Rachel Holt Cottam, Their Children and Their Ancestors*. Cedar City, Utah: Published by Authors, 1977.

Pickett, Agnes. "A Brief Story of the Life of Emma Cottam." In *Thomas Cottam 1820, and His Wives, Ann Howarth 1820, Caroline Smith 1820*, vol. 2, edited by William Howard Thompson. St. George, Utah: Thomas Cottam Family Organization, 1987.

Pratt, Helaman. Diary, 1877-1886. LDS Church Archives, Salt Lake City, Utah.

Pratt, Rey. "History of the Mexican Mission." *Improvement Era*, August 22, 1911, 486-98.

Quinn, D. Michael. "LDS Church Authority and New Plural Marriages." *Dialogue: A Journal of Mormon Thought* 18 (1985):9-105.

Record of the St. Johns Ward. LDS Church Archives, Salt Lake City, Utah.

Romney, Amy Pratt. "Ranching in Old Mexico." In *Heart Throbs of the West*, vol. 12, compiled by Kate B. Carter. Salt Lake City: Daughters of the Utah Pioneers, 1939-51.

Romney, Annie M. Letters. Originals in the possession of Ella F. Bentley, Provo, Utah.

Romney, Catharine J. Catharine Jane Cottam Romney Collection. LDS Church Archives, Salt Lake City, Utah. (Contains letters written by Catharine J. Romney, Thomas Cottam, Charles Cottam, Miles P. Romney, and notes by Thomas C. Romney. Other letters are in the Vernon Romney Collection, Brigham Young University Archives, Provo, Utah, and in the possession of Lula Clayson, Maurine Boyd, Genevieve Moulton, Howard Thompson, and Jennifer Hansen.)

Romney, Frank. Interview by Jessie Embry, June 2, 1976. LDS Polygamy Oral History Project, Charles Redd Center for Western Studies, Brigham Young University, Brigham Young University Archives, Provo, Utah.

Romney, Gaskell, "Memories of My Father." In *Life Story of Miles Park Romney* by Thomas C. Romney. Independence, Mo.: Zion's Printing and Publishing, 1948.

Romney, Hannah H. "Autobiography of Hannah Hood Hill Romney." Photocopy of typescript in author's possession. A slightly edited version is published in "Three Pioneer Women Speak: Hannah Hood Hill Romney," in *Our Pioneer Heritage*, vol. 5, compiled by Kate B. Carter. Salt Lake City: Daughters of the Utah Pioneers, 1958-77.

Romney, Joseph. *The Exodus of the Mormon Colonies from Mexico*. Master's dissertation, Department of History, University of Utah, 1966.

Romney, Junius. "Impressions of My Father and Mother." In *Life Story of Miles Park Romney* by Thomas C. Romney. Independence, Mo.: Zion's Printing and Publishing, 1948.

———. Talk given at the Garden Park Ward sacrament meeting, Salt Lake City, Utah, July 31, 1966. Photocopy of typescript in author's possession.

———. Talk given at the Rose Park Stake priesthood meeting, Salt Lake City, Utah, July 13, 1966. Photocopy of typescript in author's possession.

Romney, Junius Stowell. "Autobiography of Junius Stowell Romney," 1971. Special Collections, Brigham Young University, Provo, Utah.

Romney, Miles P. Letters. Catharine Romney Collection, LDS Church Archives, Salt Lake City, Utah. Letter dated December 27, 1885, in possession of Edward Kimball, Provo, Utah; photocopy in author's possession.

Romney, Thomas C. *A Divinity Shapes Our Ends as Seen in My Life Story*. Salt Lake City: Published by Author, 1953.

———. *Life Story of Miles Park Romney*. Independence, Mo.: Zion's Printing and Publishing, 1948.

———. *The Mormon Colonies in Mexico*. Salt Lake City: Deseret Book, 1938.

Romney, Vernon. Vernon Romney Collection. Brigham Young University Archives, Provo, Utah.

St. George United Order Record Book, 1870-1903. LDS Church Archives, Salt Lake City, Utah.

St. Johns Ward Relief Society Minutes. LDS Church Archives, Salt Lake City, Utah.

Seegmiller, E. J. "Pioneer Ways in Early Days." In *Under Dixie Sun: A History of Washington County by Those Who Loved Their Forebears*, edited by Hazel Bradshaw and compiled by Daughters of the Utah Pioneers, Washington County Chapter. Panguitch, Utah: Garfield County News, 1950.

Smith, Jesse N. *Journal of Jesse N. Smith*. Salt Lake City: Deseret News, 1953.

Smith, Lot. Lot Smith Collection. Brigham Young University Archives, Provo, Utah.

Staheli, Mary Esther Gardner. *Descendants of Pine Valley Pioneers*. St. George, Utah: Art Press, 1980.

Stratton, Clifford J., and Marsha Romney Stratton. "Catherine's Faith: Vignette's from the Life of Catherine Jane Cottam Romney." *Ensign*, September 1981, 52-54.

Tanner, George S. George S. Tanner Collection. Brigham Young University Archives, Provo, Utah, and Special Collections, University of Utah Libraries, Salt Lake City, Utah.

Taylor, John. John Taylor Family Papers. Manuscripts Department, University of Utah Libraries, Salt Lake City, Utah.

Taylor, Samuel W., and Raymond W. Taylor, eds. *The John Taylor Papers*. Vol. 2, *The President*. Redwood City, Calif.: Taylor Trust, 1985.

Thomander, Pauline Romney. Conversation with author, April 1986.

Thompson, William Howard. "Emma Cottam: Pioneer, Wife and Mother." In *Thomas Cottam 1820, and His Wives, Ann Howarth 1820, Caroline Smith 1820*, vol. 2, edited by William Howard Thompson. St. George, Utah: Thomas Cottam Family Organization, 1987.

Thompson, William Howard, ed. *Thomas Cottam 1820, and His Wives, Ann Howarth 1820, Caroline Smith 1820*. 2 vols. St. George, Utah: Thomas Cottam Family Organization, 1987.

"To the Board of Directors of the St. George Library Association." Andrew Karl Larson Collection, Utah State Historical Society, Salt Lake City, Utah.

Tullis, F. LaMond. *Mormons in Mexico: The Dynamics of Faith and Culture*. Logan: Utah State University Press, 1987.

Udall, David K. David K. Udall Papers. LDS Church Archives, Salt Lake City, Utah. (Includes correspondence and Journal of the L D Saints Arrested and Tried.)

———. David K. Udall Papers, 1879-80. George S. Tanner Collection, Brigham Young University Archives, Provo, Utah, and Special Collections, University of Utah Libraries, Salt Lake City, Utah.

Udall, David K., and Pearl Udall Nelson. *Arizona Pioneer Mormon: David King Udall, His Story and His Family*. Tucson, Ariz.: Arizona Silhouettes, 1959.

Udall, Ida Frances Hunt. Autobiography and Diary, 1873-1905. Photocopy, LDS Church Archives, Salt Lake City, Utah.

United States Federal Census, Salt Lake County and Utah County, 1860-1880.

Woodbury, Ann Cannon. "Reminiscences of Ann Cannon Woodbury," edited by Angus M. Cannon. In *Cannon Family Historical Treasury*, edited by Beatrice Cannon Evans and Janath Russell Cannon. Salt Lake City: George Cannon Family Association, 1967.

Woodbury, John Taylor. *Vermilion Cliffs: Reminiscences of Utah's Dixie.* N.p., 1933.

Woodruff, Wilford. *Wilford Woodruff's Journal. 1833-1898.* Edited by Scott G. Kenney, Midvale Utah: Signature Books, 1985.

NEWSPAPERS AND MAGAZINES

Apache Chief, St. Johns, Arizona, 1884.

Deseret News, Salt Lake City, Utah, 1850-present.

Dialogue: A Journal of Mormon Thought, Logan, Utah.

Ensign of the Church of Jesus Christ of Latter-day Saints, 1971-present.

Improvement Era, Salt Lake City, Utah, 1897-1970.

Juvenile Instructor, Salt Lake City, Utah, 1866-1970 (changed to *The Instructor,* 1930).

Millenial Star, Manchester, Liverpool, and London, England, 1840-1970.

Orion Era, St. Johns, Arizona, 1883-85.

Woman's Exponent, Salt Lake City, Utah, 1872-1914.

U.S. COURT CASE

United States v. Tenney, 2 Ariz. 29, 8 Pac. 295, 1885.

INDEX

Some spellings are inconsistent in the historical record.